Simon of Samaria and the Simonians

Simon of Samaria and the Simonians

Contours of an Early Christian Movement

M. David Litwa

LONDON • NEW YORK • OXFORD • NEW DELHI • SYDNEY

T&T CLARK

Bloomsbury Publishing Plc, 50 Bedford Square, London, WC1B 3DP, UK
Bloomsbury Publishing Inc, 1359 Broadway, New York, NY 10018, USA
Bloomsbury Publishing Ireland, 29 Earlsfort Terrace, Dublin 2, D02 AY28, Ireland

BLOOMSBURY, T&T CLARK and the T&T Clark logo are trademarks of
Bloomsbury Publishing Plc

First published in Great Britain 2024
Paperback edition published in 2025

Copyright © M. David Litwa, 2024

M. David Litwa has asserted his right under the Copyright, Designs and
Patents Act, 1988, to be identified as Author of this work.

For legal purposes the Acknowledgments on p. ix constitute an extension
of this copyright page.

All rights reserved. No part of this publication may be: i) reproduced or transmitted in any form, electronic or mechanical, including photocopying, recording or by means of any information storage or retrieval system without prior permission in writing from the publishers; or ii) used or reproduced in any way for the training, development or operation of artificial intelligence (AI) technologies, including generative AI technologies. The rights holders expressly reserve this publication from the text and data mining exception as per Article 4(3) of the Digital Single Market Directive (EU) 2019/790.

Bloomsbury Publishing Plc does not have any control over, or responsibility for, any third-party websites referred to or in this book. All internet addresses given in this book were correct at the time of going to press. The author and publisher regret any inconvenience caused if addresses have changed or sites have ceased to exist, but can accept no responsibility for any such changes.

A catalogue record for this book is available from the British Library.

A catalog record for this book is available from the Library of Congress.

ISBN: HB: 978-0-5677-1295-0
PB: 978-0-5677-1299-8
ePDF: 978-0-5677-1296-7
eBook: 978-0-5677-1-298-1

Typeset by Deanta Global Publishing Services, Chennai, India

For product safety related questions contact productsafety@bloomsbury.com.

To find out more about our authors and books visit www.bloomsbury.com and
sign up for our newsletters.

For Lord Sobek

Contents

List of Figures	viii
Acknowledgments	ix
Note on Translations	x
List of Abbreviations	xi
Introduction	1
1 *The Great Declaration*	12
2 *The Concept of Our Great Power*	28
3 The Acts of the Apostles	39
Interlude: Simon as Cipher	55
4 Justin Martyr	60
5 Irenaeus	73
6 Tertullian	88
7 The Refutator	95
8 Origen of Alexandria	107
9 Eusebius of Caesarea	117
10 Epiphanius, Pseudo-Tertullian, and Filaster	127
11 The *Acts of Peter*	142
12 The Pseudo-Clementine *Homilies*	153
Conclusion	167
Appendix 1: Reconstruction of *The Great Declaration*	175
Appendix 2: Translation of *The Concept of Our Great Power*	182
Bibliography	187
Index	209

Figures

4.1	Coin of Flavia Neapolis during the reign of Antoninus Pius showing a Roman temple to Zeus on Mt Gerizim accessed by stairway	61
4.2	Inscription to Semo Sancus (CIL VI. §567) preserved in the Galleria Lapidaria of the Vatican Museum, first compartment (Dii gallery)	66
4.3	Statue of Kore found in a cistern in the ancient stadium of Sebaste	69
6.1	Christ the Good Shepherd, catacomb of San Callisto in Rome	92
10.1	The Varvakeion Athena, preserved in the National Archaeological Museum of Athens	134

Acknowledgments

I kindly wish to thank my colleagues and friends for reading and commenting on select chapters of this work: David Runia (Chapter 1), Jared Secord (Chapters 4–5), Jeremiah Coogan (Chapters 8–9), and the anonymous reviewers (Chapters 1–2). I thank members of my broader intellectual community online for helpful comments over the years.

I am especially grateful to my family for tolerating a writer as a husband and father—and for your continued love.

Translations

All translations in this volume, unless otherwise noted, are my own, including the works in the appendices.

Abbreviations

Note: Abbreviations of biblical and other works are taken from *The SBL Handbook of Style for Biblical Studies and Related Disciplines*, ed. Billie Jean Collins et al., 2d ed. (Atlanta: SBL Press, 2014). Other abbreviations are as follows:

ANRW	*Aufstieg und Niedergang der Römischen Welt*
Bibl.	Pseudo-Apollodorus, *Library of Mythology*
CIL	*Corpus Inscriptionum Latinarum*
DGWE	*Dictionary of Gnosis and Western Esotericism*, ed. Hanegraaff
Hom.	Pseudo-Clementine *Homilies*
Or.	*Orations* of Maximus of Tyre, ed. Trapp
PG	*Patrologia Graeca*, ed. Migne
Ref.	*Refutation of All Heresies*, ed. Litwa
Vita phil.	Diogenes, *Lives of Eminent Philosophers*

Introduction

With Simon of Samaria, we enter the maelstrom, a Charybdis of confused and cacophonous incriminations, slanderous stories, and inimical innuendo. It seems that the man Simon existed—as much as any other figure in recorded history—but he has long since been swallowed in the abyss of myth and countermyth. Accordingly, this book is chiefly about Simonians, the people who carried on the teachings related to Simon in support of a distinctly "Simonian" version of Christianity between the second and fourth centuries CE.[1]

Anti-Simon(ian) stories and reports begin to appear in the early to mid-second century CE. In the echo chamber of heresiological discourse, Simonian belief and practice is presented in increasingly wild ways. Since Simon became known as the head of the gnostic hydra and "the father of all heresies," a welter of stereotypical traits (sexual license, radical dualism, self-deification, and so on) were gradually attributed to him and to his heirs. This means that every report about Simon and on Simonian Christianity is riddled with slander, fictions, and clichés.

Trapped in the maze of these reports, readers' minds are so baited by presuppositions and hostile frameworks that it is hard to picture Simon as anything but a villain. He has been hounded and scapegoated so many times, readers can hardly form a positive ethical judgment of him.[2] Even among scholars, he is called a "sorcerer" and, with apparent tongue in cheek, "the bad Samaritan."[3] In heresiology, he is the antihero to Peter, anti-Christian, antichrist, opposite of everything good, noble, and worthy. He is symbolized, according to the *Acts of Peter* by a dancing, enslaved, Ethiopian woman—the lowest member of the ancient social hierarchy topped by the free, noble male.

It would seem that nothing remains of the Simonians beyond the roaring waves of rumors, rants, and hostile reports. As one scholar opines, the only surviving accounts of Simon's life and teachings have been written by his "opponents and critics."[4] As perduring as this judgment has been in scholarship, I hold it to be incorrect.

---

[1] This book expands and revises my treatment of Simonians in *Desiring Divinity: Self-deification in Ancient Jewish and Christian Mythmaking* (Oxford: Oxford University Press, 2016), 91–118; and *Found Christianities: Remaking the World of the Second Century CE* (London: T&T Clark, 2022), 45–60.

[2] James Phelan, *Experiencing Fiction: Judgments, Progressions, and the Rhetorical Theory of Narrative* (Columbus: Ohio State University Press, 2007), 10.

[3] For "sorcerer," see Mark Edwards, "Simon Magus," in *The Oxford Dictionary of the Christian Church*, ed. Andrew Louth, 4th ed. (Oxford: Oxford University Press, 2022). https://www.oxfordreference.com/view/10.1093/acref/9780199642465.001.0001/acref-9780199642465-e-6651 (accessed April 7, 2023). Edwards has also named his major treatment of Simon, "Simon Magus, the Bad Samaritan," in *Portraits: Biographical Representations in the Greek and Latin Literature of the Roman Empire*, ed. Mark Edwards and Simon Swain (Oxford: Clarendon, 1997), 69–91.

[4] Stephen Haar, *Simon Magus: The First Gnostic?* BZNW 119 (Berlin: Walter de Gruyter, 2003), 1.

There is a red thread allowing us to break through the labyrinth of heresiology, since an independent account of Simonian thought survives. Although it was studied heavily in the 1960s and 1970s, it has in recent times been neglected. I refer to the document called *The Great Declaration* (*Apophasis Megalē*) (henceforth, the *Declaration*). This fragmentary work was cited by the Refutator (the anonymous author of the *Refutation of All Heresies*) in the early third century CE. The date, meaning, and reconstruction of the *Declaration* are all contested. Accordingly, my initial chapter historically situates the text. The second studies an apocalypse from Nag Hammadi (*The Concept of Our Great Power*) which, I believe, employs Simonian terms and traditions. Both texts can be used to serve as a check against heresiological stories and reports (Chapters 3–10), not to mention the—equally hostile—novelistic portraits of Simon (Chapters 11–12) in the *Acts of Peter* and the Pseudo-Clementines.

Surprising as it seems, this has never been done in a full-length study on Simon—namely, starting with a Simonian source. Beginning with such a source—rather than an attack upon Simon—allows us to hear a different tune running below the cacophony of heresiological indictments. That being said, heresiology cannot be avoided, since it makes up the lion's share of data. Our task, then, is to read heresiology critically and carefully, so as not to perpetuate its frameworks, schemas, and assumptions. For too long, the friends, foes, and even fair-minded scholars of Simon(ians) have needlessly assented to the heresiologists when other ways of conceptualizing and framing the data are available.

Breaking the Spell

A good example of (tacitly) reinscribing heresiological discourse is the near ubiquitous perpetuation of the epithet invented by them. I refer to the title "Simon *Magus*." To quote Anita Mason, the "somber magnificence" of this title has been degraded until no one any longer knows whether it meant "a fire-priest of the ancient mysteries or a street-corner charlatan."[5] To the heresiologists, however, "magus" was not a compliment. It meant "quack," "deceiver," and "charlatan"; it was associated with greed and various kinds of vice. Accordingly, I question whether it is helpful to label Simon with this ossified heresiological tag.[6]

Admittedly, there have been attempts to redeem the title "magus." Stephen Haar, for instance, argues that Simon was not a magus in the pejorative sense, but an "adept in the traditions of the [Persian] Magoi."[7] His proposal is open-minded and thoroughly

---

[5] Anita Mason, *The Illusionist* (Abacus: Sphere Books, 1983), 6.
[6] Kurt Rudolph recognized that "Magus" is a conscious misrepresentation, but used it anyway (*Gnosis: The Nature & History of Gnosticism*, trans. Robert McLachlan Wilson [Edinburgh: T&T Clark, 1984], 294, 298). See further Florent Heintz, *Simon "Le magician": Actes 8, 5-25 et l'accusation de magie contre les prophètes thaumaturges dans l'antiquité* (Paris: Gabalda, 1997), 45; Ayse Tuzlak, "The Magician and the Heretic," in *Magic and Ritual in the Ancient World*, ed. Paul Mirecki and Marvin Meyer (Leiden: Brill, 2002), 416–26; Kimberly B. Stratton, "The Rhetoric of 'Magic' in Early Christian Discourse: Gender, Power and the Construction of 'Heresy,'" in *Mapping Gender in Ancient Religious Discourses*, ed. Todd Penner and Caroline Vander Stichele (Leiden: Brill, 2007), 89–114.
[7] Haar, *Simon Magus*, 307.

argued, but the evidence is wanting. The first surviving writer to claim that Simon engaged in the art of a magus (*mageuōn*) was the author of Acts (8:9). Justin Martyr first hitched "Simon" to "Magus," and in later heresiology it becomes a kind of surname.[8] Although it is true that "magus" could be used positively in the first century CE (witness Matt 2:1), this is not how Justin and his heirs used the term.[9] Nor is there anything truly positive in the use of *mageuōn* by the author of Acts. These writers were not trying to say that Simon was involved in the ancient Persian tradition of priestly incantation, sacrifice, astrological divination, and so on. To the contrary—they aimed to disqualify and socially degrade Simon by associating him with magical trickery.[10] Celsus, the critic of Christianity, said that Jesus was a magus, but scholars—let alone believers—would not tolerate the title "Jesus magus." And for some reason—though later Simonians identified Simon with Christ—the title "Simon Christ" has never caught on.

Humor aside, we need to be more careful about our language. If we modern readers hypothesize that Simon was a Persian(-style) magus, then we need more evidence beside the occasional positive use of "magus" in the Greco-Roman world. We need evidence of Simon's actual (Persian or Persian-inspired) practice along with his own act of self-identification as a Persian priest—and this we do not have. In fact, until we come to novelistic sources, Simon does not look anything like a magus, whether Persian or otherwise. He does not do any of the non-normative activities attributed to magicians (inscribing curse tablets, uttering spells, using foreign-sounding words, performing nightly rituals, putting pins in dolls)—or anything of the kind.[11] It is high time, therefore, to stop automatically naming Simon "magus."

Simonians and Samaritans

I will be content to call Simon by the name of the region to which he has the closest ties: "Simon of Samaria." The name appears in Irenaeus (*Simon Samarites*).[12] Perhaps when heresiologists located Simon in Samaria, they aimed to marginalize him and associate him with deviant religion (since they viewed Samaritanism as an aberrant form of Judaism).[13] Yet in Simon's day, there was more than one religion in Samaria. In

---

[8] Justin Martyr, *Dial.* 120.6; Irenaeus, *Haer.* 1.23.1; *Ref.* 6.9.1.
[9] For Justin's negative use of μάγος, see, e.g., *Dial.* 69.7.
[10] On the use of term "magus," see Albert De Jonge, *Traditions of the Magi: Zoroastrianism in Greek and Latin Literature* (Leiden: Brill, 1997); Fritz Graf, *Magic in the Ancient World*, trans. Franklin Philip (Cambridge, MA: Harvard University Press, 1997), 20–117; Matthew W. Dickie, *Magic and Magicians in the Greco-Roman World* (London: Routledge, 2001), 162–250; Haar, *Simon Magus*, 33–70; Leonard Costantini, "Dynamics of Laughter: The Costumes of Menippus and Mithrobarzanes in Lucian's *Necyomantia*," *American Journal of Philology* 140, no. 1 (2019): 101–22.
[11] Joseph E. Sanzo, "Early Christianity," in *Guide to the Study of Ancient Magic*, ed. David Frankfurter (Leiden: Brill, 2019), 198–239 at 204–5.
[12] Irenaeus, *Haer.* 1.23.1; cf. Justin, *1 Apol.* 26.2.
[13] See further Reinhard Pummer, *Early Christian Authors on Samaritans and Samaritanism: Texts, Translations and Commentary*, TSAJ 92 (Tübingen: Mohr Siebeck, 2002); Gary N. Knoppers, *Jews and Samaritans: The Origins and History of Their Early Relations* (Oxford: Oxford University Press, 2013).

this study, Samaria designates nothing beyond a region of central Palestine, the place where Simon lived and worked.

It is, of course, possible to translate *Simon Samarites* by "Simon the Samaritan." In my view, however, this would be hazardous, since only a late and fictional source (the Pseudo-Clementine *Homilies*) suggests that Simon held any special regard for the sacred mountain of the Samaritans, namely, Mount Gerizim.[14] Epiphanius, who directly attacked the Samaritans, never connected them with Simon.[15] In early sources, Simon is never said to have engaged in Samaritan cultic practices or holidays. He may well have read the Torah as a sacred book, but not the Samaritan version specifically. He and his followers did not reject the authority of the Hebrew prophets.[16] Of course, there were Samaritans in the province of Samaria. But the urban center of Samaria at the time, namely, the city of Sebaste, was predominately Gentile.[17] Samaria as a whole during Simon's time was ethnically and religiously diverse. We simply cannot assume, then, that Simon was a Samaritan.

Simon is often said to be from the town of Gitta (variously spelled), which was identified as a village in Samaria only in the early third century.[18] Modern experts have identified it with el-Jatt in west Samaria.[19] Recently, however, the town has been located further south in Idumea and identified with Gath, city of Goliath (1 Sam 17:4).[20] None of the heresiologists made this connection, but it would surely be fitting that the great enemy of Peter came from the same city as the juggernaut opponent of King David. Where exactly Simon was born is, unfortunately, not clear. Suffice it to say, one can no longer claim that Simon was a Samaritan because he was from a Samarian village.[21]

A History of Research

Simon is a figure that appears numerous times in early Christian literature, including in a book that made it into the New Testament (Acts). Accordingly, studies on Simon—as opposed to Simonians—have been rife. I cannot hope to review every relevant study

---

[14] Ps.-Clementine, *Hom.* 2.2. In the *Ante Nicene Fathers* translation of the *Recognitions* 2.7, it is said that "by nation" Simon is a "Samaritan" (*Samaraeus*), but a better translation of the Latin is "Samarian." (Alexander Roberts and James Donaldson, ed., *Ante-Nicene Fathers*, vol. 8 [Peabody: Hendrickson, 1995], 98.) For the Latin text, see Bernard Rehm and Georg Strecker, ed., *Die Pseudoklementinen II. Rekognitionen in Rufins Übersetzung*, 2nd ed. (Berlin: Akademie, 1994), 55.

[15] Epiphanius, *Pan.* 9.

[16] Pummer, *Early Christian Authors*, 3.

[17] Josephus, *Ant.* 15.292–6; Strabo, *Geog.* 16.2.34; for Sebaste's temple to Caesar, Josephus, *J.W.* 1.403; *Ant.* 15.297–8. See further Bruce W. Hall, *Samaritan Religion from John Hyrcanus to Baba Rabba* (Sydney: Mandelbaum Trust, 1987), 270–2.

[18] *Ref.* 6.7.1.

[19] Jürgen Zangenberg, "Δύναμις τοῦ θεοῦ. Das religionsgeschichtliche Profil des Simon Magus," in *Religionsgeschichte des neuen Testaments: Festschrift für Klaus Berger*, ed. Axel von Dobbeler, Kurt Erlemann and Roman Heiligenthal (Tübingen: A. Francke, 2000), 519–40 at 525. In the *Barrington Atlas of the Greek and Roman World*, ed. Richard J. A. Talbert (Princeton: Princeton University Press, 2000), "Geth" is located not far southeast of Caesarea (69, B5).

[20] Clemens Scholten, "Zum Herkunftsort des Simon Magus," *VC* 69 (2015): 534–41.

[21] *Pace* Gerd Theissen, "Simon Magus—die Entwicklung seines Bildes vom Charismatiker zum gnostischen Erlöser," in *Religionsgeschichte des neuen Testaments*, 417–18.

since the advent of critical scholarship. It suffices for me to engage with the major scholarly treatments of the past fifty years.[22]

In 1974, Karlmann Beyschlag opposed the thesis that Simon was a "gnostic" in a sense informed by the heresiologists. The image of Simon as (first) "gnostic" appeared at least a century after the historical Simon.[23] No clear data in Acts indicates that its author was familiar with Simon as a gnostic. Simon, if he identified with an entity called "the Great Power," was, according to Beyschlag, only a magician who identified himself with "the divine supreme power."[24] There were decades of historical progression lying between Simon the "divine man" as depicted in Acts 8 and Simon the "highest Power" as he appears in heresiology. In the meantime, Simonian emanationism (divine Thought leaping from Mind) developed as a result of a collapsing and mashing together of a more elaborate Valentinian theology. None of the later Simonian material gets us back to the first century and to Simon's own self-conception.

The year after Beyschlag's book appeared, Gerd Lüdemann independently published what sounded like a rebuttal. According to Lüdemann, Simon was the source or inspiration for a distinctive gnostic (or "proto-gnostic") system. His immediate followers, who were primarily Gentile, called him "the Great Power" and worshiped him as the avatar of Zeus honored on Mt. Gerizim.[25] A hundred years later, Simon's disciples were still worshiping Simon as Zeus—this time as Trusty Zeus—on Tiber Island in Rome. They identified Helen with Athena and the biblical Wisdom who fell into this world and who became a symbol of the fallen soul.[26] Simonian salvation came via self-knowledge.[27] Neither Simon nor Simonians were originally Christians.

In some sense, these two monographs have never been surpassed. Scholars still debate whether Simon was (primarily) a gnostic vilified as a magus or a magus made into a gnostic. In my view, both theories are incorrect, and I have written this book to explain why. At present, however, it suffices to say that scholarship in the past forty years has gradually tended to agree with Beyschlag over Lüdemann on most points. Lüdemann's position that Simon was already worshiped as Zeus and had a (proto-) gnostic system involves too many leaps in logic.[28] Historically speaking, it is vital not to blend later attacks on Simonians with Simon's own thought and profile.

At the same time, Beyschlag's position has major weaknesses—many of which were exposed in an eighty-page review by Kurt Rudolph.[29] Here I can only be brief. The idea

---

[22] For earlier sources, see Haar, *Simon Magus*, 10–32.
[23] Karlmann Beyschlag, *Simon Magus und die christliche Gnosis*, WUNT 16 (Tübingen: Mohr Siebeck, 1974), 77–8.
[24] Beyschlag, *Simon Magus*, 102–3.
[25] Lüdemann, *Untersuchungen zur simonianischen Gnosis* (Göttingen: Vandenhoeck & Ruprecht, 1975), 40–54.
[26] Lüdemann, *Untersuchungen*, 101–2.
[27] Lüdemann, *Untersuchungen*, 80–1.
[28] Roland Bergmeier, "Die Gestalt des Simon Magus in Act 8 und in der simonianischen Gnosis—Aporien einer Gesamtdeutung," *ZNW* 77 (1986): 267–75.
[29] Rudolph, "Simon: Magus oder Gnosticus? Zum Stand der Debatte," *Theologische Rundschau* 42, no. 4 (1977): 279–359. See also Wayne Meeks, "Simon Magus in Recent Research," *Religious Studies Review* 3 (1977): 137–42. Another review of the literature was offered by Robert McL. Wilson, "Simon and Gnostic Origins," in *Les Actes des Apôtres: Traditions, redaction, théologie*, ed. J. Kremer (Leuven: Leuven University Press, 1979), 485–91.

that Simonian thought is a reduced and blended version of Valentinian theology has never been accepted among scholars since it too involves many intuitive leaps of logic. Furthermore, Beyschlag's preference for one stream of the heresiological tradition—reconstructed from Epiphanius, Pseudo-Tertullian, and Filaster—is suspect. It is Irenaeus who had access to the earliest thoroughgoing anti-Simonian source, the *Syntagma* of Justin Martyr. All later heresy reports are in some way dependent on Irenaeus, whose anti-Simonian reading of Acts 8:9-24 set the course for all later interpretations of it. Beyschlag and Lüdemann are equally open to the criticism of allowing heresiology (and Acts counts, in my view, as a heresiological narrative) to become the fundamental data for studying Simon(ians). Both rejected the *Declaration* as a source, and only lightly touched upon other potentially Simonian traditions from Nag Hammadi.

A 1985 study by Jarl Fossum sought to contextualize Simon in the history of Samaritan religion. According to Fossum, the figure of the prophet like Moses was a known entity among Samaritans of the first century CE, and Simon (among others) tried to fulfill that role.[30] He both bore the divine name in his lifetime and was thought to ascend, like Moses, to heaven. According to Fossum, Simon was a gnostic, and Simonian Gnosticism was essentially a heterodox form of Samaritanism.

I have already questioned the view that Simon was a Samaritan. Perhaps he was at some point—there is simply no reliable evidence. Nevertheless, Fossum built his entire argument on the assumption that Simon and his earliest followers were Samaritans. He dubiously used Samaritan sources stretching from the fourth century CE to the Middle Ages in order to reconstruct first century CE Samaritan thought. For instance, Moses is bearer of the divine name in the fourth-century Samaritan text *Memar Marqah*, but this text was edited into the medieval period and is not a reliable witness to first-century Samaritan belief.[31] There is no first-century evidence that Samaritans expected a prophet like Moses who would ascend to heaven and bear the divine name. Even in late Samaritan sources, Moses is never called "the Great Power" like Simon (Acts 8:10). "Power" or "the Great Power" in late Samaritan sources refers to the Samaritan deity (Yahweh). More accurately, as Fossum points out, "great power" is an *attribute* of Yahweh.[32] It does not consistently refer to a being subordinate to Yahweh, such as the deified Moses or a prophet like him. Finally, the singular appeal to Samaritan sources to explain "the Great Power" is unnecessary, since Beyschlag and Lüdemann had already demonstrated that the title was regularly used outside of these sources.[33] It was never distinctly Samaritan in the first place.

Fossum's methods well exemplify what Samuel Sandmel called "parallelomania."[34] To construct Simon as the prophet like Moses, Fossum stirred a cauldron of magical texts, novels, Nag Hammadi lore, Samaritan doxologies, fragments of patristic treatises,

---

[30] Jarl Fossum, *The Name of God and the Angel of the Lord: Samaritan and Jewish Concepts of Intermediation and the Origin of Gnosticism*, WUNT 36 (Tübingen: Mohr Siebeck, 1985), 112–29; 162–91.
[31] Beyschlag, *Simon Magus*, 94.
[32] Fossum, *Name of God*, 175.
[33] E.g., Hegesippus in Eusebius, *Hist. eccl.* 2.23.13; *Life of Adam and Eve* 28.2; *Ref.* 7.36.1 (spoken of Melchizedek; cf. Epiphanius, *Pan.* 55.1.1).
[34] Samuel Sandmel, "Parallelomania," *JBL* 81 (1962): 1–13.

Jewish pseudepigrapha, and so on. The elements of this motley brew all floated in what seems like a void outside of space and time. The fact that Fossum began with late and novelistic sources (the *Acts of Peter* and the Pseudo-Clementines) shows both a deficiency in historical method and a failure to engage with scholarship on Simon (both Beyschlag and Lüdemann had independently and cogently rejected these novels as reliable sources). Moreover—and despite his citations of far-flung material from the Rabbis and medieval Samaritan chronicles—Fossum almost entirely ignored the *Declaration*.[35]

In 1997, Mark Edwards traced the transformations of Simon in the early church. Although he showed a healthy skepticism of Acts and the heresiologists, he (like all scholars) selectively accepted portions of their testimony. Simonianism was "an aberrant religion in Samaria which was strong enough to obstruct the infant mission of the Church."[36] Helen was Simon's "bride," not his spiritual daughter; she was also a "harlot."[37] Thus far the heresiologists. Sometimes Edwards even went beyond them, such as in the claim that Simon in Acts had a "lust for power."[38] The *Acts of Peter* and the Pseudo-Clementines are "apostolic fictions."[39] The *Declaration* is "forged," philosophical (apparently unlike Simon himself), and Valentinian.[40] These judgments are brief and unevidenced. In the end, we really do not know what Edwards believes about Simon, due to all the hedging: "It is probable that he lived, possible that he preached strange gods, conceivable that he even claimed to be one; but all these acts and thoughts may be laid at the door of different Simons, or of none."[41]

A pair of chapters sums up the views of Simon among two leading German scholars at the turn of the millennium.[42] Both Gerd Theissen and Jürgen Zangenberg denied that the historical Simon was deified.[43] Rather, he was viewed as a (or the) representative of God, a divine epiphany. Both scholars also rejected the view that Simon was a (pre-) gnostic. Theissen conceived of Simon and his followers as Samaritans—though he thought only "pagan" Samaritans (later) deified Simon.[44] By contrast, Zangenberg—an expert in Samaritanism—fit Simon into a Gentile milieu, citing evidence for Gentiles in Samaria, and in particular Sebaste. He pointed out that "the (Great) Power" and "the Standing One" are not specifically Samaritan terms.[45] According to Theissen,

---

[35] The survey of T. Adamik (treating Simon in heresiological sources and in the *Acts of Peter*) does not break new ground and is too brief to be included in this survey ("The Image of Simon Magus in the Christian Tradition," in *The Apocryphal Acts of Peter: Magic, Miracles and Gnosticism*, ed. Jan Bremmer [Leuven: Peeters, 1998], 52–64.).
[36] Edwards, "Bad Samaritan," 75.
[37] Edwards, "Bad Samaritan," 75–6.
[38] Edwards, "Bad Samaritan," 71.
[39] Edwards, "Bad Samaritan," 85.
[40] Edwards, "Bad Samaritan," 82.
[41] Edwards, "Bad Samaritan," 77–8. Edwards adds (88) that Simon "at most ... courted a reputation in Samaria by his miracles" and that he "peddle[d] angelology."
[42] Theissen, "Simon Magus," 407–32; Zangenberg, "Δύναμις τοῦ θεοῦ," 519–40.
[43] Theissen, "Simon Magus," 418; Zangenberg, "Δύναμις τοῦ θεοῦ," 532.
[44] Theissen, "Simon Magus," 419, 431.
[45] Zangenberg, "Δύναμις τοῦ θεοῦ," 524. Cf. Hans G. Kippenberg, *Garizim und Synagoge: Traditionsgeschichtliche Untersuchungen zur Samaritanischen Religion der aramäischen Periode* (Berlin: de Gruyter, 1971), 346–8.

Simonians became "gnostic" only after being attacked in the Jewish War (66–73 CE); only some of them became Christians.[46]

The next monograph to be written on Simon was by Stephen Haar (2003). Haar has already been introduced as trying to depict Simon as a Persian-style priest.[47] Yet there is nothing particularly Persian about Simon. The idea that he practiced the ancient traditions of the magi led Haar to speculate unnecessarily about Simonian incest (since Persian magi reputedly had sex with their mothers).[48] According to Haar, the historical Simon was a "charismatic figure" who "exercised considerable ability, authority, and influence." His expertise in divine things was "self-proclaimed." Simon identified himself with the "Standing One" and allowed people to call him the primal God. He would not have rejected the adjective "gnostic" in the sense of knower.[49] Haar, however, characterizes Simon as a "pre-Gnostic," which apparently means that Simon's ideas led to "Gnosticism" as defined by the Messina convention in 1966.[50] The whole issue is somewhat confused, however, since Haar himself recommends jettisoning the modern construct of "Gnosticism."[51]

A more convincing treatment of Simon and "magic" is presented by Florent Heintz. Heintz proposed a critical model for studying accusations of magic in ancient texts and then applied the results to Simon in Acts 8. As Heintz observed, it is often the case that people in ancient literature are accused of being a magus, either directly or by innuendo, using the standard techniques of invective. In many cases, however, the accused did not self-identify as a "magus," and never performed works similar to those of a magus. The magus accusation was a way for hostile writers to socially degrade figures who considered themselves to be wonderworking prophets, freedom fighters, and sages.

According to Heintz, the historical Simon was probably a Samaritan prophet who proclaimed the coming of the "restorer," a prophet like Moses. Simon genuinely converted to Christianity, but was denied a leadership position, which caused a schism. The story of Simon in Acts 8 was molded to exalt Jerusalem-based Christian leaders (Philip and Peter) at Simon's expense.[52]

The most recent engagements with Simon have been chapter-length surveys. The Simon of Birger Pearson was a Samaritan wonder worker and prophet who had "nothing to do with Christianity."[53] He "claimed a divine role for himself ('the Great Power of

---

[46] Theissen, "Simon Magus," 430–1.
[47] Haar, *Simon Magus*, 134–58.
[48] Haar, *Simon Magus*, 287–91, 305. Simonians are only accused of promiscuous intercourse (*Ref.* 6.19.5), not incest specifically (cf. Clement, *Strom.* 3.2.11.1).
[49] Haar, *Simon Magus*, 307.
[50] Haar, *Simon Magus*, 298–9. See Ugo Bianchi, ed., *Le origini dello Gnosticismo: Colloquio di Messina 13–18 Aprile 1966* (Leiden: Brill, 1967).
[51] Haar, *Simon Magus*, 302.
[52] Heintz, *Simon "Le magicien"*, 143–8. Heintz's views resemble those of Klaus Berger, "Propaganda und Gegenpropaganda im frühen Christentum: Simon Magus als Gestalt des samaritanischen Christentums," in *Religious Propaganda and Missionary Competition in the New Testament World: Essays Honoring Dieter Georgi*, ed. Lukas Bormann, Kelly del Tredici, and Angela Standhartinger (Leiden: Brill, 1994), 313–17 at 316–17. See the review of Heintz in Alexandre Faivre and Cécile Faivre, "Rhétorique, histoire et débats théologiques: A propos d'un ouvrage sur Simon 'le magicien,'" *Revue des Sciences Religieuses* 73, no. 3 (1999): 293–313.
[53] Birger A. Pearson, *Ancient Gnosticism: Traditions and Literature* (Minneapolis: Fortress, 2007), 26.

God')."⁵⁴ During the reign of Claudius, Simon was active in Rome and worshiped there by Samaritans.⁵⁵ He had an "essential Gnostic myth" inspired by Middle-Platonism, Jewish-Samaritan biblical traditions, and allegories of Greek mythology.⁵⁶ The idea that Simon appeared as Father, Son, and Spirit is "undoubtedly false" apparently because it is Christian.⁵⁷ The *Declaration* contains "all sorts of learned and quasi-learned information," but it is not by Simon, "the Samaritan magus."⁵⁸

April D. DeConick deserves the credit of taking the *Declaration* seriously. She returns to the older view that Simon himself wrote it, adding the suggestion that it was "meant for a more advanced audience."⁵⁹ Nonetheless, her reading of the *Declaration*—in contrast to earlier scholarship—gnosticizes it, such that it is about the human spirit freeing itself from the "dominion of the rebellious angels"—who, incidentally, never appear in the *Declaration*.⁶⁰

DeConick frames Simon as a "gnostic," founder of "a Gnostic religion."⁶¹ She builds her understanding of Simon on the Pseudo-Clementines, claiming that Simon was a former Dosithean who married Helen and with her "set up a priesthood to officiate their worship as the Father God and Mother God."⁶² Following Epiphanius, she claims that Simonian initiation "involved the memorization and pronouncement of all the names of the angels-turned-monsters." Simonian initiates engaged in "sacred sexual practices within a consecrated space they called the Holy of Holies. They considered their ritual sexual intercourse to reenact the blessed union of the Father God and the Mother God."⁶³

As far as I can tell, these statements are derived from DeConick's own unargued extrapolations from our most unreliable heresiological data (Epiphanius, the Pseudo-Clementines, and the Refutator, mostly). Sometimes going beyond the heresiologists, DeConick sometimes adjusts the data, claiming that Simon disparaged the Mosaic law, and that he declared the death penalty for any of his followers who obeyed it.⁶⁴ These remarks are at loggerheads with the fact that, in the *Declaration*, "Simon" cites Torah numerous times and organizes his thoughts around a reading of Genesis 1–3.

---

54 Pearson, *Ancient Gnosticism*, 27.
55 Pearson, *Ancient Gnosticism*, 27.
56 Pearson, *Ancient Gnosticism*, 29–30.
57 Pearson, *Ancient Gnosticism*, 30.
58 Pearson, *Ancient Gnosticism*, 32–3. The survey of Ingrid Hjelm ("Simon Magus in Patristic and Samaritan Sources: The Growth of a Tradition," in *Die Samaritaner und die Bibel / Samaritans and the Bible: Historische und literarische Wechselwirkungen zwischen biblischen und samaritanischen Traditionen*, ed. Jörg Frey, Ursula Schattner-Rieser, and Konrad Schmid [Berlin: de Gruyter, 2012], 263–84) does not constitute a novel interpretation of Simon. The speculative theory that Simon was a Greek grammarian who corrected the LXX in the time of Cleopatra II (175–115 CE)—and who even translated the LXX Pentateuch—is not worthy of refutation (Paul Carbonaro, "Simone le magicien et la Bible grecque," *RB* 121–123 [2014]: 414–26 at 423–4).
59 April D. DeConick, *The Gnostic New Age: How a Countercultural Spirituality Revolutionized Religion from Antiquity to Today* (New York: Columbia University Press, 2016), 102.
60 DeConick, *Gnostic New Age*, 102.
61 DeConick, *Gnostic New Age*, 100.
62 DeConick, *Gnostic New Age*, 101–2.
63 DeConick, *Gnostic New Age*, 103.
64 DeConick, *Gnostic New Age*, 103, 150.

Duncan MacRae studied Simon in light of anti-imperial rhetoric and (orthodox) Christian self-definition.[65] His data comes from Justin Martyr, Irenaeus, Tertullian, and the *Acts of Peter*. Justin linked Simon with idolatry by inventing the tradition that Simonians worshiped Simon in the form of a Roman state god (Semo Sancus). Irenaeus accused Simonians of idolatry, saying that they worshiped Simon and Helen in the form of two other state deities: Jupiter and Minerva. Tertullian used Simon to criticize Roman deifications: Romans failed to distinguish between the divine and the dead. In the *Acts of Peter*, Simon becomes a self-seeking recipient of idolatry and his failed flight over Rome parodies rituals of Roman apotheosis. According to MacRae, the real Simon is lost to history. What we have are hybrid depictions of Simon as a "heretic" implicated in Roman practices of "idolatry" and apotheosis.

Jan Bremmer's chronological treatment of the sources (beginning with Acts, Justin, and Irenaeus) is mostly descriptive. He spends most of his time on the most unreliable sources for Simon, namely, the *Acts of Peter* and the Pseudo-Clementines. He provides a detailed literary and philological analysis. At the same time, he does not move beyond the paradigm of Simon as "a kind of learned magician" who combined "magic with intellectual pursuits" like "various gurus of the second and third centuries CE."[66] It is evident that Bremmer is more interested in Simon as a character in fiction, though he vaguely describes the historical Simon as a wandering Judean "religious entrepreneur . . . an intellectual with some kind of message."[67]

The Way Forward

What is striking about Simon(ian) scholarship is its diversity: there are common tendencies, but no two scholars say exactly the same thing about Simon. This diversity is partly due to the fact that scholars pick and choose which sources they focus on, and these choices are determined chiefly, it seems, by their own interests. A study that focuses only on Acts will present a different Simon from one that concentrates on Justin and Irenaeus. An article that treats Epiphanius, Filaster, and Pseudo-Tertullian will present a Simon dissimilar to how he appears in the *Refutation*. Simon in the *Acts of Peter* looks significantly different than he does in the Pseudo-Clementines. It is surprising, on this score, how seldom data from Tertullian, Origen, and Eusebius is brought into the conversation. Simonian ideas in Nag Hammadi texts are generally neglected. It is high time for a new comprehensive study of Simon which covers the sources from the early second to the late fourth century CE.[68]

---

[65] Duncan E. Macrae, "Simon the God: Imagining the Other in Second-century Christianity," in *Geneses: A Comparative Study of the Historiographies of the Rise of Christianity, Rabbinic Judaism, and Islam*, ed. John Tolan (Abingdon: Routledge, 2019), 64–86.

[66] Jan N. Bremmer, "Simon Magus: The Invention and Reception of a Magician in a Christian Context," *Religion in the Roman Empire* 5 (2019): 246–70 at 262.

[67] Bremmer, "Simon Magus," 248, 251.

[68] Although I aim to be comprehensive, I cannot be exhaustive. Some of the sources for Simon overlaps in content and do not require a separate discussion. For instance, the Simon of the *Didascalia Apostolorum* and the *Apostolic Constitutions* is almost entirely constructed out of Acts, the *Acts*

The great diversity in Simonian studies has another cause. The data is at once underdetermined (ambiguous) and overdetermined (by heresiological frameworks). In effect, then, new methods applied to Simon(ian) scholarship are hindered by the fact that heresiological frameworks have yet to be transcended.[69] The whole question of whether Simon was (the first) "gnostic," for instance, plays on a field created by the heresiologists. We can redescribe Simon as a religious entrepreneur who worked wonders. The redescription is helpful, in my view, but a skeptic might still say that it just flips the valence of "magus" as it was conceived by Simon's enemies. Where we can make real progress, I propose, is by taking the focus off of Simon and putting it onto Simonians. This refocusing of the subject matter, combined with the careful application and study of an actual Simonian source (the *Declaration*), has the potential to redirect the conversation and to create new insight.

---

of *Peter* and (in the case of the *Apostolic Constitutions*), the Pseudo-Clementines. I have therefore judged a separate chapter on these texts unnecessary.

[69] Karen L. King, "Social and Theological Effects of Heresiological Discourse," in *Heresy and Identity in Late Antiquity*, ed. Eduard Iricinschi and Holger M. Zellentin (Tübingen: Mohr Siebeck, 2008), 28–49.

1

The Great Declaration

Introduction

A single document has a claim to being a distinctly Simonian source preserved in its original language, namely, the set of excerpts from *The Great Declaration*.[1] This title is attested by the Refutator (the author of the *Refutation*).[2] Yet the actual name of the work could well have been the *Declaration of the Great Power*.[3] What remains of the *Declaration* is translated in Appendix 1. The report in which it is embedded I will call "the 'Simon' report."[4]

The *Declaration* has been understudied in recent years, due in part to the view that it is late and derivative.[5] Some modern treatments of Simon and Simonians fail to mention the *Declaration* at all.[6] Even if scholars take it into account, they tend to

---

[1] *Ref.* 6.11.1. This chapter revises and expands material found in M. David Litwa, *Desiring Divinity*, 92–7 and Litwa, "Gnostic Self-deification: The Case of Simon of Samaria," *Gnosis* 1 (2016): 157–76 at 168–70.

[2] M. David Litwa, ed., *Refutation of All Heresies*, WGRW 40 (Atlanta: SBL Press, 2016), xxvii–liii; 361–87; Emanuele Castelli, "Saggio introduttivo: L'*Elenchos*, ovvero una 'biblioteca' contro le eresie," in *'Ippolito.' Confutazione di tutte le eresie*, ed. Aldo Magris (Brescia: Morcelliana, 2012), 21–56.

[3] *Ref.* 5.9.5.

[4] Only one other heresiologist touched on the *Declaration*, namely, Theodoret, *Fab.* 1.3. Theodoret evidently did not have the *Declaration* itself, but only the excerpts in *Ref.*

[5] E.g., Ernst Haenchen, "Simon Magus in der Apostelgeschichte," in *Gnosis und Neues Testament: Studien aus Religionswissenschaft und Theologie*, ed. Karl-Wolfgang Tröger (Berlin: Gütersloh, 1973), 267–80 at 269; H.-M. Schenke, "Hauptprobleme der Gnosis: Gesichtpunkte zu einer neuen Darstellung des Gesamtphänomens," in *Der Same Seths: Hans-Martin Schenkes Kleine Schriften zu Gnosis, Koptologie und Neuem Testament*, ed. Gesine Schenke Robinson, Gesa Schenke, and Uwe-Karsten Plisch (Leiden: Brill, 2012), 160–73 at 168; Barbara Aland, "Gnosis und Philosophie," in *Was ist Gnosis? Studien zum frühen Christentum, zu Marcion und zur kaiserzeitlichen Philosophie* (Tübingen: Mohr Siebeck, 2009), 45–90 at 84; Hans Friedrich Weiss, *Frühes Christentum und Gnosis: Eine rezeptionsgeschichtliche Studie* (Tübingen: Mohr Siebeck, 2008), 124.

[6] E.g., Werner Foerster, *Gnosis: A Selection of Gnostic Texts*, ed. R. McL. Wilson, 2 vols. (Oxford: Clarendon, 1972), 127–32; Christoph Markschies, *Gnosis: An Introduction*, trans. John Bowden (London: T&T Clark, 2003), 73–7; Markschies, "Genesis 1 and the Beginnings of Gnosticism," *ZAC* 26, no. 1 (2022): 25–44 at 33–6; Bremmer, "Simon Magus," 246–70.

subordinate it to heresiological reports (coming from Justin, Irenaeus, and so on).[7] This is problematic, in my view, given that the *Declaration* is, as I will argue, a better source for understanding the earlier forms of Simonian thought.[8]

The Refutator's Method

Since the *Declaration* is embedded in the *Refutation*, it is necessary to examine the Refutator's sources and method. Josef Frickel, believed that the Refutator did not have the actual *Declaration*, but a paraphrase of it.[9] His views are based on the theory that the Refutator mechanically copied out his sources. This theory has recently been refuted.[10] Only a brief response to Frickel is now required: the frequent use of "he says" in the "Simon" report is most likely the work of the Refutator.[11] Its use is not systematic (indicating, as Frickel argued, distinct paragraph divisions). It is, as it usually functions in ancient literature, a device used to signal reported speech.[12]

Explicit quotes from the *Declaration* seem apparent only in *Refutation* 6.9.4 and 6.18.2-7. Overall, the Refutator seems to have paraphrased the other selections from the *Declaration*, which is why the content sometimes seems choppy and incomplete. The Refutator may only have preserved a fraction of the *Declaration*, and he did not necessarily excerpt the text in order. The Refutator also sprinkled in several sardonic comments and interjections.[13]

When the Refutator paraphrased his material, he was at least consistent. This point can be seen by comparing his two reports on "Simon." The epitome of "Simon" in *Refutation* 10.12.1-4 is more or less an overview of the same material in *Refutation* 6.9-17. Below, I sample these texts, indicating the linguistic overlaps in **bold**.

---

[7] E.g., Rudolph, *Gnosis*, 294-8; Simone Pétrement, *A Separate God: The Christian Origins of Gnosticism* (New York: Harper & Row, 1990), 233-46; Pearson, *Ancient Gnosticism*, 23-32.
[8] Histories of research on the *Declaration* can be found in Edwin Yamauchi, *Pre-Christian Gnosticism: A Survey of the Proposed Evidence* (London: Tyndale Press, 1973), 62-5; Haar, *Simon Magus*, 97-9.
[9] Josef Frickel, *Die "Apophasis Megale" in Hippolyts Refutatio (VI 9-18): Eine Paraphrase zur Apophasis Simons* (Rome: Pontifical Institute of Oriental Studies, 1968). See further on this question Barbara Aland, "Die Apophasis Megale und die simonianische Gnosis," in *Was ist Gnosis*, 91-102; Jaap Mansfeld, *Heresiography in Context: Hippolytus's Elenchus as a Source for Greek Philosophy* (Leiden: Brill, 1992), 322.
[10] Sebastian Hanstein, *Studien zur Redaktionellen Gestaltung des Sonderguts in der Schrift, "Widerlegung aller Häresien" unter besonderer Berücksichtigung der Darstellung der sog. Peraten* (Rheinischen Friedrich-Wilhelms-Universität Bonn, 2020), 169-95.
[11] Catherine Osborne, *Rethinking Early Greek Philosophy: Hippolytus of Rome and the Presocratics* (London: Duckworth, 1987), 214-27.
[12] Pace Frickel, *"Apophasis"*, 203.
[13] E.g., *Ref.* 6.14.1 ("Simon deifies himself").

Ref. 10.12.1	*Ref.* 6.9.5
There is an infinite power, the root of the universe. This infinite power, he says, is fire. According to him the fire is not simple, as most people say the four elements are simple and suppose that this fire is simple too. Rather, the nature of the fire is twofold, and of its twofold nature he calls one part hidden and the other manifest. The hidden elements are hidden in the manifest elements of the fire, and the manifest elements of the fire have come to be by virtue of the hidden elements.[14]	There is an infinite power, the root of the universe, he says. This infinite power is fire. According to Simon the fire is not simple, as most people say the four elements are simple and suppose that this fire is simple too. In fact, the nature of the fire is twofold, and of its twofold nature, he calls one part hidden and the other manifest. The hidden elements are hidden in the manifest elements of the fire, and the manifest elements of the fire have come to be by virtue of the hidden elements.[15]

The overlap is almost exact. This is important because, as Frickel argued, these summaries are probably independent.[16] The linguistic overlap indicates, though does not guarantee, that the Refutator was basically faithful to report the key points of his Simonian source. At the very least, he did not invent information. He felt no need to do so, since he believed that the words of his opponents refuted them.[17]

---

[14] ἀπέραντόν εἶναι δύναμιν, ταύτην ῥίζωμα τῶν ὅλων εἶναι. ἔστι δέ φησιν ἡ ἀπέραντος δύναμις, τὸ πῦρ, κατ' αὐτὸν οὐδὲν ἁπλοῦν, καθάπερ οἱ πολλοὶ ἁπλᾶ λέγοντες εἶναι τὰ [δὲ] τέσσαρα στοιχεῖα καὶ τὸ πῦρ ἁπλοῦν εἶναι νενομίκασιν, ἀλλ' εἶναι τοῦ πυρὸς τὴν φύσιν διπλῆν· καὶ τῆς διπλῆς ταύτης καλεῖ τὸ μέν τι κρυπτόν, τὸ δέ φανερόν· κεκρύφθαι δὲ τὰ κρυπτὰ ἐν τοῖς φανεροῖς τοῦ πυρός, καὶ τὰ φανερὰ τοῦ πυρὸς ὑπὸ τῶν κρυπτῶν γεγονέναι.

[15] τὴν ἀπέραντον δύναμιν, ἥν ῥίζα εἶναι τῶν ὅλων φησίν. ἔστι δὲ ἡ ἀπέραντος δύναμις, τὸ πῦρ, κατὰ τὸν Σίμωνα οὐδὲν ἁπλοῦν, καθάπερ οἱ πολλοὶ ἁπλᾶ λέγοντες εἶναι τὰ τέσσαρα στοιχεῖα καὶ τὸ πῦρ ἁπλοῦν εἶναι νενομίκασιν, ἀλλὰ γὰρ εἶναι [τὴν] τοῦ πυρὸς διπλῆν τινα τὴν φύσιν· καὶ τῆς διπλῆς ταύτης καλεῖ τὸ μέν τι κρυπτόν, τὸ δέ τι φανερόν.

[16] Frickel, *"Apophasis"*, 73–4; Frickel, "Hippolyt von Rom: Refutation, Buch X," in *Überlieferungsgeschichtliche Untersuchungen*, ed. Franz Paschke (Berlin: Akademie, 1981), 217–44.

[17] *Ref.* 5.28.1; 9.16.2. Salles-Dabadie credited the Refutator with accuracy since the Refutator also copied out the mistakes and corruptions of his sources (*Recherches sur Simon le Mage: L'Apophasis megalè'* [Paris: Gabalda, 1969], 42).

Scope, Genre, and Authorship

The excerpts run from *Refutation* 6.9.3 to 6.18.7. They must be distinguished both from the Refutator's opening story (6.7.2–6.9.2) and from his closing comments on Simon, Helen, and Simon's death which derive from Irenaeus and other sources (6.19.1–6.20.4).

From the excerpts we have, we can determine that the heart of the *Declaration* (from *Ref.* 6.12–17) is an allegorical reading of Genesis 1–3, a type of treatise later called a *hexaemeron*.[18] A *hexaemeron*, most simply defined, is a work commenting on the six (or seven) days of creation, incorporating contemporaneous scientific and medical lore to create a picture of the divine and human worlds. In this *hexaemeron*, the various creations in Genesis 1 signify paired powers: heaven and earth represent Mind and Thought, sun and moon are Voice and Name, while air and water symbolize Reasoning and Conception.[19] These Powers are summed up in the Seventh Power, a name for Wisdom who appears in the Hebrew scriptures (e.g., Prov 8).

The Refutator, who attacked Simon's disciples, occasionally introduced his excerpts with an opening, "they say" (*Ref.* 6.15.3, 6.17.2). The "they," in my view, does not necessarily indicate group authorship of the *Declaration*. It rather represents the Refutator's struggle against a global category of Simonians, all of whom putatively asserted the material in the *Declaration*.

The Refutator more often introduced his excerpts with "Simon says," or the like. "Simon," however, never introduces himself in what survives. There was apparently some textual clue—perhaps a subtitle or epigraph of some sort—that generated the Refutator's unwavering conviction that Simon himself spoke the *Declaration*. This is not the sort of data the Refutator would invent, in my view. After all, the Refutator would not have intuited that the *Declaration* was Simonian based on his knowledge of previous heresiology. The content is significantly distinct. Presumably, then, there was a now lost contextual clue connecting the *Declaration* to Simon.

Some scholars have proposed that Simon wrote the original form of the *Declaration*.[20] Others have argued that its philosophical sophistication indicates a later author and date.[21] The latter argument is flawed, however, since Simon could well have been philosophically inclined and the eclectic philosophy of the work (bits of Plato, Aristotle, Empedocles, and others) all predate Simon. The only conclusive way to exclude Simon's authorship is to show that the *Declaration* came after his lifetime.

---

[18] I owe this insight to Tuomas Rasimus (personal communication). The *Declaration* may be the first known instance of a *hexaemeron* in Christian literature. See further Christoph Markschies, *Christian Theology and its Institutions in the Early Roman Empire: Prolegomena to a History of Early Christian Theology* (Waco: Baylor University Press, 2015), 256–8.
[19] *Ref.* 6.13.1.
[20] Frickel, "*Apophasis*", 203; Salles-Dabadie, *Recherches*, 71–9, 127–44.
[21] Ernst Haenchen, "Gab es eine vorchristliche Gnosis?" *ZTK* 49 (1952): 316–49 at 336–7, 349; Haar, *Simon Magus*, 274.

Date

The author of the *Declaration*, whom we can call the Declarator, alluded to the gospel of Matthew (3:10, 12) or a form of Luke (3:9, 17),[22] both of which were likely not written prior to 80 CE. It is arbitrary to exclude New Testament citations as later additions. The quotations are well integrated into the text. Accordingly, the *Declaration* cannot have been written prior to about 85.

The upper dating limit is provided by the Naassene Preacher. This Preacher was a versatile and cosmopolitan Christian theologian whose daring discourse was excerpted in the *Refutation* 5.6-11.[23] The Preacher quoted from a variety of sources, one of them being the *Declaration*, as can be seen in the following sample. (In what follows, words in **bold** indicate word-for-word parallels and underlined words or phrases indicate conceptual ones.)

The Declaration (*Ref.* 6.9.4)	The Naassene Discourse (*Ref.* 5.9.5)
This is the <u>letter</u> of **Declaration**, of Voice, and of Name from the Thought of **the Great** and Infinite **Power. Thus it will be sealed, hidden, veiled, lying in the dwelling where the root of the universe is established.**[24]	Moreover **this**, he claims, is the <u>speech</u> of God, which, he says, is the <u>speech</u> of **Declaration** of **the Great Power. Thus it will be sealed, hidden, and veiled, lying in the dwelling where the root of the universe is established.**[25]

The first sentence of the Naassene quote is a paraphrase with citation markers ("he says") of what we find in the *Declaration*. The second sentence is a direct quotation, agreeing verbatim with a fourteen-word chain of the *Declaration* (counting Greek words).

At least one scholar has argued that the Refutator inserted these lines of the *Declaration* into the Naassene report.[26] Yet in book 5, the Refutator had not arrived at his exposition of the *Declaration*, and turning to a different source conflicts with his usual method—proceeding from one document before turning to the next. I grant that the Refutator often blended his reports by adding elements and phrases employed from memory. Yet this sort of conflation is different from quoting verbatim a fourteen-word chain. The Refutator had no compelling reason to quote the *Declaration* as the capstone

---

[22] *Ref.* 6.9.10.
[23] *Ref.* 5.6.3–5.11.1. See M. David Litwa, *The Naassenes: Exploring an Early Christian Identity* (London: Routledge, 2023).
[24] τοῦτο τὸ γράμμα Ἀποφάσεως φωνῆς καὶ ὀνόματος ἐξ ἐπινοίας τῆς μεγάλης δυνάμεως τῆς ἀπεράντου. διὸ ἔσται ἐσφραγισμένον κεκρυμμένον κεκαλυμμένον, κείμενον ἐν τῷ οἰκητηρίῳ, οὗ ἡ ῥίζα τῶν ὅλων τεθεμελίωται.
[25] τοῦτο ἐστὶ τὸ ῥῆμα τοῦ θεοῦ ὅ ἐστι ῥῆμα Ἀποφάσεως τῆς μεγάλης δυνάμεως. διὸ ἔσται ἐσφραγισμένον καὶ κεκρυμμένον καὶ κεκαλυμμένον, κείμενον ἐν τῷ οἰκητηρίῳ οὗ ἡ ῥίζα τῶν ὅλων τεθεμελίωται.
[26] José Montserrat Torrents, *Los Gnósticos: Introducciones, tradución y notas* (Madrid: Gredos, 1983], II, note ad loc. I owe this reference to Maria Grazia Lancellotti, *The Naassenes: A Gnostic Identity among Judaism, Christianity, Classical and Ancient Near Eastern Traditions* (Münster: Ugarit-Verlag, 2000), 313, n.352.

of the Preacher's commentary on a hymn to Attis.[27] The Preacher himself, however, was inclined to cite other sources (such as the *Gospel according to the Egyptians*) to support his thought. The Preacher also made use of the *Declaration* later in his discourse when he allegorized the rivers in paradise.[28]

It is worth noting, moreover, that the Preacher extended his quotation from the *Declaration*. He qualified the "root of the universe" as "the root of aeons, powers, and thoughts; the root of gods, angels, and spirits sent forth; the root of things that are and of things that are not, of things born and unborn, of things incomprehensible and comprehensible, the root of years, months, days, hours—an indivisible point from which the smallest being begins and grows by degrees."[29]

Conceivably, this expansion could have been the imaginative addendum of the Preacher, but I am inclined to think that it continues to quote the *Declaration* since, (1) it interrupts the Preacher's discourse, and (2) because the "indivisible point" (*stigmē ameristos*) is a distinctively Simonian phrase used in another location of the *Declaration*.[30] For the Preacher's ability to quote from various places of a source without attribution, we can compare his already documented use of the *Gospel of Thomas*.[31] It is reasonable, then, to conclude that the Preacher had a copy of the *Declaration*—just like the Refutator—but that the Preacher provided a fuller quote of his material when he cited it.

When did the Naassene Preacher write? Dating him is a challenge, but signs point to a period late in the second century CE. Mainly this is because the Preacher combined elements of Ophite theology (God as Human and Child of the Human[32]) with a Valentinian theory of tripartite humanity.[33] Only someone later in the second century could have interwoven these originally independent strands. The tripartite theory of humanity was fully developed, it seems, by the time Heracleon wrote his *Commentary on John* about 175 CE.[34] Thus we should probably assign the Naassene discourse a date sometime between 180 and 210 CE. The *Declaration*, accordingly, can be dated from about 85 to 200 CE.

---

[27] See further Frickel, *"Apophasis"*, 169–98; Frickel, *Hellenistische Erlösung in christlicher Deutung. Die gnostische Naassenerschrift: Quellenkritische Studien, Strukturanalyse, Schichtenscheidung, Rekonstruktion der Anthropos-Lehrschrift* (Leiden: Brill, 1984), 78–82.

[28] *Ref.* 5.9.15–17, based on material now reflected in *Ref.* 6.15.1–6.16.3.

[29] *Ref.* 5.9.5. In fact, the quote from the *Declaration* could well extend to *Ref.* 5.9.6, ending with the quote from Ps 18:4 LXX.

[30] *Ref.* 6.14.6.

[31] Steven R. Johnson, "Hippolytus's *Refutatio* and the *Gospel of Thomas*," *JECS* 18, no. 2 (2010): 305–26.

[32] *Ref.* 5.6.4–6.

[33] *Ref.* 5.6.7. Bernard Pouderon's attempt to show that the *Declaration* depends on Valentinian theology fails to convince. The fact that in *Ref.*'s report on Valentinus, the creator and the soulish level is identified with fire does not mean that it influenced the Declarator's view that the superior, transcendent deity is a kind of spiritual fire. The two deities (the creator and transcendent God), as Pouderon recognized, are not the same ("La notice d'Hippolyte sur Simon: cosmologie, anthropolgie et embryologie," in *Les Pères de l'église face à la science médicale de leur temps*, ed. Véronique Boudon-Millot and Bernard Pouderon [Paris: Beauchesne, 2005], 49–72 at 53–5).

[34] Heracleon in Origen, *Comm. Jo.* 10.210–15; cf. Clement of Alexandria, *Exc.* 56.

No Knowledge of John

There are indications, however, that the *Declaration* appeared earlier than 200 CE. First of all, its author seems not to have known the gospel according to John. The notion that Simon, along with all humans, was born from the mixing of "bloodlines" may be considered an allusion to John 1:13.[35] Yet since the phrase "from bloodlines" is fairly common in ancient Greek, one cannot establish a secure connection.[36]

The author of the *Declaration*, moreover, used "Logos" to refer to scripture and to Moses.[37] For an author to identify Moses with the Logos would be surprising if he or she had knowledge of John 1:1 ("In the beginning was the Logos"). The lack of engagement with John may point to an early date, since by the mid-second century, it seems, John was a commonly recognized authority among early Christian writers, and those who knew the other gospels (such as Matthew and Luke) often employed John as well.[38]

The Absence of Helen

There is another piece of evidence signaling an early date for the *Declaration*, namely, its failure to mention Helen. Anyone who knows the Simonian reports from Justin and Irenaeus knows how central Helen was to later Simonian theology.[39] Helen represented Simon's primal Thought (*Ennoia*). She was the incarnation of the creatrix who made the angels but was later abused by them and forced into human bodies.

The absence of Helen from the *Declaration* is striking because its author was clearly familiar with a figure called Thought (*Epinoia*), offspring of Mind.[40] The Declarator called *Epinoia* "the Seventh Power," represented by the seventh day of creation. She is also identified with the Spirit hovering over the waters in Genesis 1:2. Humans are made in the image of *Epinoia*.[41] She is clearly a central figure, but she is not identified with Helen, who, in what survives, is never so much as named.

In his addendum to the *Declaration*, of course, the Refutator was eager to add Helen, but here he filled in material from Irenaeus.[42] We have reason to believe, moreover, that the Helen tradition was introduced by Justin, Irenaeus, and the Refutator in order to defame Simon—since Helen was vilified as a (former) sex worker.

Simon Not Identified with the Great Power

The third indication of the *Declaration*'s early date is its failure to identify Simon with the Great Power. Simon as the Great Power—interpreted as the highest Power—

---

[35] *Ref.* 6.9.2; 6.9.5.
[36] ἐξ αἱμάτων is found, e.g., in Euripides, *Ion* 693; Ps 15:4 LXX; 50:16 LXX; *Historia Alexandri Magni* Recension E, 74.8; Porphyry, *Cave of Nymphs*, 14.
[37] *Ref.* 6.13.1; 6.14.7; 6.15.4.
[38] See further Charles E. Hill, *The Johannine Corpus in the Early Church* (Oxford: Oxford University Press, 2004), esp. 224, 230–5.
[39] See further Jarl Fossum, "The Simonian Sophia Myth," *Studi e Materiali di Storia delle Religioni* 53 (1987): 185–97; Virginia Burrus, "The Heretical Woman as Symbol in Alexander, Athanasius, Epiphanius, and Jerome," *HTR* 84, no. 3 (1991): 229–48.
[40] *Ref.* 6.18.2–6.
[41] *Ref.* 6.14.3–6.
[42] *Ref.* 6.19.1–4. See further Osborne, *Rethinking*, 68–86.

became a stable part of the heresiological tradition by the late second century CE. Not once, however, does the author of the *Declaration* call Simon the Great Power. Instead, he creates a narrative world in which all people can become one with a being called the "Infinite Power" when they are fully conformed to God's Image.[43] Simon is never singled out as the one who becomes the Infinite Power, let alone the Great Power. Indeed, when one reads the *Declaration*—apart from the framework and presuppositions of the Refutator—there is nothing special about Simon at all. If we believe the Refutator, Simon merely spoke the *Declaration* as some sort of prophet.

Of course this theory can be reversed. But we have to ask what is more likely: that the Declarator completely masked two staple elements of later Simonian theology—Simon as the Great Power and Helen as Thought—or that he was not yet familiar with them. In my view, once the proclaimer (Simon) became the proclaimed (the Great Power), there was no turning back.[44] Simon as Great Power and Helen as Thought became the foundations of later Simonian theology and an author—Simonian or otherwise—was not at liberty to ignore them.

In sum, these three pieces of evidence (no knowledge of John, the absence of Helen, and failure to identify Simon with the Great Power) support a date of the *Declaration* prior to 150 CE. The reports of Justin (about 150 CE) and Irenaeus (about 180 CE) would then represent later stages of Simonian thought when Helen was a major figure and when "the Great Power" title was said to have been claimed by Simon himself. Since the Declarator knew the gospel of Matthew or a form of Luke, then we can propose a date range between 85 and 150 CE.

Knowledge of Medicine

Can we be still more precise? I think we can, if we focus on the Declarator's knowledge of medicine. The Declarator's allegorical interpretation of Eden reveals a detailed knowledge of embryology. He knew that in the womb, breath (*pneuma*) passed from mother to child through the umbilical cord.[45] This point was already known in the Hippocratic tradition.[46] Yet this tradition seems to have asserted that the embryo could breathe through its mouth and nose[47]—a point which the Declarator denies: "for the fetus . . . neither receives food through the mouth nor breathes it through the nostrils . . . [T]he fetus is entirely bundled in what is called the amniotic membrane (*chitōni amniōi*) and is nourished through the umbilical cord (*di' omphalou*)."[48]

As it turns out, the medical writer Soranus (flourished 100–130 CE) made the same two points in the same order. To quote his *Gynaecology*: "The majority say that, in

---

[43] Schmithals, *The Office of Apostle in the Early Church*, trans. John E. Steely (Nashville: Abingdon, 1969), 162–3.
[44] Schmithals, *Office of Apostle*, 160–1.
[45] *Ref.* 6.14.9–11.
[46] Hippocrates, *Nature of the Child* XII.6; XIII.3. Commentary by Iain M. Lonie, *The Hippocratic Treatises on Generation, On the Nature of the Child, Diseases IV*, Ars Medica 7 (Berlin: de Gruyter, 1981), 146–56. For general discussion, see Owsei Temkin, *Hippocrates in a World of Pagans and Christians* (Baltimore: Johns Hopkins University Press, 1991), 109–48.
[47] Hippocrates, *Nature of the Child* XVII.3.
[48] *Ref.* 6.14.11. See further Marie-Hélène Congourdeau, "L'embryologie dans le Corpus hippocratique," in *Sur la manière don't l'embryon reçoit l'âme*, ed. Luc Brisson (Paris: J. Vrin, 2012), 19–30, esp. 25.

addition, the embryo possesses another membrane called the amniotic (*chitōna . . . amneion*) . . . Besides, they say, it [fluid] could not be drawn in through the mouth, since respiration takes place through the umbilical cord (*dia tou omphalou*)."⁴⁹

The linguistic parallels are close. Perhaps this is not surprising, since this teaching, as Soranus notes, was known to "the majority" of medical writers in the early second century CE. There is, however, a lengthier parallel between the Declarator and Soranus, one worth quoting in full. (Here again, words in **bold** indicate word-for-word parallels while <u>underlined</u> words or phrases signal conceptual ones.) Here Soranus and "Simon" discuss the structures of the uterus.

Soranus (*Gynaecology* 1.19)	*The Declaration* (*Ref.* 6.14.8-10)
Now from the fleshier parts and from parts along the upper uterus there extends from above a thin organ which naturally merges into the midsection of embryos, the **epigastrium**, the region of the **umbilical cord**. And when this organ grows into the embryo it is called the **umbilical cord**. It is divided into four vessels: **two venal and two arterial**. Through these the material of **blood** and **breath** is conveyed to nourish embryos. . . .	For on each side of the umbilical cord two arteries are extended, which serve as channels of **breath**, and **two veins**, which serve as channels of **blood**. Now he says that when the **umbilical cord** flows from Eden (the placenta), it is organically joined with the fetus at the **epigastrium** (which all commonly call the "**umbilical cord**"). Secondly, the two veins (coursing along what are called the "gates of the **liver**") nourish the fetus as conveyers of blood brought from Eden (the placenta).
Most think that the veins go into the **liver** and the arteries into the heart. Herophilus, however, . . . thinks that the arteries feed into a main artery stretched out <u>along the vertebrae</u>. But before the two arteries feed into the **main artery**, they extend obliquely on each side of the **bladder**.⁵⁰	At the same time, the arteries (which we said were channels of breath) that surround the **bladder** on both sides along the broad bone join the **great artery** (the one <u>along the spine</u> called the "aorta").⁵¹

⁴⁹ Soranus, *Gynecology* 1.19 (Burguière).

⁵⁰ ἀπὸ μέντοι τῶν σαρκωδεστέρων καὶ τῶν κατὰ τὸν πυθμένα μερῶν ἄνωθεν ἀπομηκύνεταί τι σῶμα λεπτόν, ἐμφύεται δὲ κατὰ [τὸ] μέσον τὸ τῶν ἐμβρύων ἐπιγάστριον, ἔνθα τόπος ὀμφαλοῦ. Καὶ αὐτὸ δὲ τὸ ἐμβρύῳ ἐμφυόμενον [ὡς] σῶμα καλοῦμεν ὀμφαλόν. Συγκέκριται δ' ἐκ δ' τὸν ἀριθμὸν ἀγγείων, δύο φλεβωδῶν καὶ δύο ἀρτηριῶν δι' ὧν εἰς θρέψιν ὕλη αἱματική καὶ πνευματική παρακομίζεται τοῖς ἐμβρύοις. . . . οἱ δὲ πολλοὶ τὰς φλέβας μὲν εἰς τὸ ἧπαρ οἴονται, τὰς ἀρτηρίας δὲ εἰς τὴν καρδίαν. Ἡρόφιλος δὲ τὰς φλέβας μὲν εἰς τὴν κοίλην φλέβα <τὰς> ἀρτηρίας δὲ εἰς τὴν παχεῖαν ἀρτηρίαν τὴν παρατείνουσαν τοῖς σπονδύλοις, πρὸ δὲ τῆς εἰς αὐτὴν ἐμφύσεως παρὰ τὴν κύστιν αὐτὰς πλαγιοφορεῖσθαι παρ' ἑκατέρας πλευράς (Soranus, *Gynaecology* 1.19 [Burguière]).

⁵¹ ἑκατέρωθεν γὰρ τοῦ ὀμφαλοῦ δύο εἰσὶν ἀρτηρίαι παρατεταμέναι, ὀχετοὶ πνεύματος, καὶ δύο φλ(έβ)ες, ὀχετοὶ αἵματος. ἐπειδὰν δέ, φησίν, ἀπὸ τοῦ Ἐδὲμ χορίου ἐκπορευόμενος ὁ ὀμφαλὸς ἐμφύη τῷ γεν<ν>(ω)μένῳ κατὰ τὸ ἐπιγάστριον—ὃ κοινῶς πάντες προσαγορεύουσιν ὀμφαλόν—αἱ δὲ δύο φλέβες, δι' ὧν ῥεῖ καὶ φέρεται ἀπὸ τοῦ Ἐδὲμ τοῦ χορίου τὸ αἷμα, κατὰ τὰς καλουμένας πύλας τοῦ ἥπατος—αἵτινες τὸ γεννώμενον τρέφουσιν—αἱ δὲ ἀρτηρίαι—ἃς ἔφημεν ὀχετοὺς εἶναι πνεύματος,

It was apparently common knowledge in the early imperial period that the umbilical cord was made up of four vessels: two veins and two arteries that circulated blood and breath, respectively.[52] This data appears, for instance, in *On the Names of the Parts of the Body* §232, a reference work produced by Rufus of Ephesus (*floruit* 100 CE).[53] It is mentioned several times by Galen as well.[54]

Nevertheless, the order of the discussion and their overlapping technical terms indicate that the Declarator either used Soranus or his source, perhaps the *Midwifery* of Herophilus (or an epitome of it).[55] Soranus became a well-known writer in the early to mid-second century CE. If the author of the *Declaration* knew Soranus specifically, then he was probably writing after 120 CE. I would therefore propose a date range for the *Declaration* between 120 and 150 CE.[56]

This range makes it impossible for Simon to be the author of the *Declaration*. Even if one rejects dependence on Soranus, the gospel quotations still indicate a date after 85 CE. We do not know when Simon was born, but if he was a contemporary of Jesus and Paul, he would likely be dead by 85. (In the *Acts of Peter*, Simon dies after his encounter with Peter in Rome, which was presumably in the early 60s CE.) One can, then, attribute the *Declaration* to an early second-century Simonian who, it seems, wrote in Simon's own voice, or at least attributed the work to Simon.

Provenance

We gather from the *Suda* that Soranus studied in Alexandria but lived and worked in Rome during the reigns of Trajan and Hadrian.[57] We do not know when he wrote his *Gynaecology*, but it was presumably in the early second century CE. The Simonian author would have had immediate access to this material in Alexandria or Rome. The Refutator knew the *Declaration* by about 220, but the Naassene Preacher had

ἑκατέρωθεν περιλαβοῦσαι τὴν κύστιν κατὰ τὸ πλατὺ ὀστοῦν—πρὸς τὴν μεγάλην συνάπτωσιν ἀρτηρίαν—τὴν κατὰ ῥάχιν καλουμένην ἀορτήν—, καὶ οὕτως διὰ τῶν παραθύρων ἐπὶ τὴν καρδίαν ὁδεῦσαν τὸ πνεῦμα.

[52] For earlier theories, see Aristotle, *Gen. an.* 2.4, 740a24–37; 2.7, 745b22–746a28.
[53] Ἐκ δὲ τοῦ χορίου ἐκπεφύκει ὁ ὀμφαλός, δύο φλέβες καὶ δύο ἀρτηρίαι. (I owe this reference to Dawn LaValle Norman, personal communication.)
[54] Galen, *In Hippoc. alim.* 4.5 (Kühn 15.387–8): ἔστι γὰρ ἐν αὐτῷ ἀγγεῖα τέτταρα, δύο μὲν ἀρτηρίαι, δύο δὲ φλέβες ... καὶ διὰ τούτων ... ἕλκει τὸ ἔμβρυον αἷμα καὶ πνεῦμα ("There is in it [the placenta] four vessels, two arteries and two veins ... and through these ... the embryo ... draws blood and breath"); Galen, *Use of Parts* 15.4–5 (Kühn 4.224–40); Galen, *On the Dissection of the Uterus* 5.1; 10.14; Galen, *On the Formation of the Fetus* 2.3–4; 3.4. Diethard Nickel, ed., *De foetuum formatione*, Corpus Medicorum Graecorum V 3,3 (Berlin: Akademie, 2001), 60, 64. Pouderon isolates several differences between the embryology of the Declarator and Galen ("La notice d'Hippolyte sur Simon," 65–6).
[55] Heinrich von Staden, *Herophilus: The Art of Medicine in Early Alexandria* (Cambridge: Cambridge University Press, 1989), 218–19, 298.
[56] The author of the *Declaration*, if he used Soranus, was not the only Christian author to do so. Tertullian, a generation later, paraphrased Soranus's *On the Soul* in his work of the same title. See J. H. Waszink, ed., *Quinti Septimi Florentis Tertulliani: De Anima*, VCSup 100 (Leiden: Brill: 2010), 23–30.
[57] *Suda* Σ 851–2 (Adler 4.407). See further Ann Ellis Hanson and Monica H. Green, "Soranus of Ephesus: *Methodicorum princeps*," in *ANRW* II.37.1 (Berlin: de Gruyter, 1996), 969–1073; Vivian Nutton, *Ancient Medicine*, 2nd ed. (London: Routledge, 2013), 199–206.

the *Declaration* even earlier (180–210 CE). The Preacher was probably writing in Alexandria, as I have argued elsewhere.⁵⁸

Furthermore, the *Declaration* seems to present a metaphysics that was associated with the first-century BCE Platonist Eudorus of Alexandria.⁵⁹ According to this metaphysics, an unknown and unknowable first principle emanates two opposing principles called Monad and (the indefinite) Dyad. Eudorus seems to have been the first to place a transcendent One as first principle above the Monad-Dyad pair. The monad he called "ordered, determined, knowable, male," whereas the dyad he called "disordered, undetermined, unknowable, female."⁶⁰

We can compare this teaching with the *Declaration*:

> There are two offshoots of all the aeons, having neither beginning nor end. They are from a single root, which is a Power: invisible and incomprehensible Silence. One of these appears above—a great power, Mind of the universe, pervading all things, and male. The other is below: Thought, who is magnificent, female, and generates all things.⁶¹

Although the terminology is different, the structure is similar:

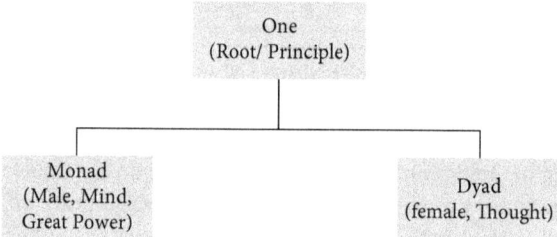

The Monad-Dyad pair—coded as male-female, heaven-earth—is Pythagorean lore that predates Eudorus.⁶² Nonetheless, the structure of the transcendent One *above* the

---

⁵⁸ Litwa, *The Naassenes* 6–7.

⁵⁹ For Eudorus, see further John Dillon, *The Middle Platonists: 80 BC to AD 220*, 2nd ed. (Ithaca: Cornell University Press, 1996), 127–8; Irmgard Männlein-Robert, "Eudoros von Alexandrien," in *Die Philosophie der Antike Band 5/1. Philosophie der Kaiserzeit und der Spätantike*, ed. Christoph Riedweg, Christoph Horn and Dietmar Wyrwa (Basel: Schwabe, 2018), 555–62.

⁶⁰ Eudorus in Simplicius, *In Aristotelis physicorum libros commentaria*, ed. Hermann Diels (Berlin: Reimer, 1892), 9, 181.20–30.

⁶¹ *Ref.* 6.18.2–6: δύο εἰσὶ παραφυάδες τῶν ὅλων αἰώνων, μήτε ἀρχὴν μήτε πέρας ἔχουσαι, ἀπὸ μιᾶς ῥίζης, ἥτις ἐστὶ δύναμις Σιγὴ ἀόρατος, ἀκατάληπτος. ὧν ἡ μία φαίνεται ἄνωθεν, ἥτις ἐστὶ μεγάλη δύναμις, Νοῦς τῶν ὅλων, διέπων τὰ πάντα, ἄρσην· ἡ δὲ ἑτέρα κάτωθεν, Ἐπίνοια, μεγάλη, θήλεια, γεννῶσα τὰ πάντ(α).

⁶² See, for instance, the Pythagorean ὑπομνήματα reported by Alexander in Diogenes Laertius, *Vita phil.* 8.25, which does not place a transcendent ἀρχή above the monad and dyad. Cf. also the report on Xenocrates in Aetius, *Placita* 1.7 §21: "the Monad and the Dyad are gods, the former as male having the rank of Father and ruling in heaven, which he also calls Zan and odd and Intellect, who for him is the first god, the latter as female having the role of Mother of the gods (μητρὸς θεῶν δίκην), presiding over the region under the heaven, who for him is the soul of the universe" (ἥτις ἐστι αὐτῷ ψυχὴ τοῦ παντός) (trans. Jaap Mansfeld and David Runia, *Aëtiana V: An Edition of the Reconstructed Text of the Placita with a Commentary and a Collection of Related Texts. Part 4: English Translation, Bibliography, Indices* [Leiden: Brill, 2020], 2077). See further John Dillon, "Xenocrates'

Monad-Dyad is Eudoran, and this is the pattern that appears in the *Declaration* (with Silence as the power *above* Mind and Thought).[63]

By the time one comes to Numenius in the mid-second century CE, the philosophical language has changed. The indefinite Dyad is identified with matter, and it is an independent entity no longer said to come from the Monad.[64] Accordingly, the author of the *Declaration* probably depended on a distinctly Eudoran tradition prior to the formulations of Numenius (about 150 CE). The specific dependence on Eudorus might suggest an Alexandrian provenance, as does the dependence on Soranus and/or Herophilus—two doctors who lived in Alexandria.[65]

Additional evidence for an Alexandrian provenance is Clement's familiarity with the Simonians. "The Simonians," he said, "aim to be exactly conformed (*exomoiousthai*) to the Standing One, whom they worship."[66] Significantly, Clement did not identify Simon with the Standing One—despite the heresiological tradition. This point conforms to what we find in the *Declaration*, where "Simon" never calls himself the Standing One.

Second, Clement uses a word (*exomoiousthai*) that is close to the *Declaration*'s term (*exeikonizō*) to describe Simonians' exact conformation to God.[67] This word is used nine times in the *Declaration*, and in each case it refers to assimilation to God, a God who is called "the One Who Stood, Stands, and Will Stand." One cannot say whether Clement was familiar with the *Declaration* specifically, but he seems to have been familiar with one of its traditions (Simonians exactly conform to the Standing One) in Alexandria about 200 CE.[68]

It is also worth noting that Celsus, in the 160s–170s CE, was familiar with Simonians and "Helenians" (followers of Helen).[69] Many scholars agree that Celsus wrote in Egypt or at least sojourned there for a considerable time.[70] I have argued for Celsus's

---

Metaphysics: Fr. 15 (Heinze) R3-examined," *Ancient Philosophy* 5 (1986): 47–52; Leonid Zhmud, "Pythagorean Number Doctrine in the Academy," in *On Pythagoreanism*, ed. Gabriele Cornelli, Richard McKirahan, and Constantinos Macris (Berlin: de Gruyter, 2013), 323–44.

[63] See further Charles H. Kahn, *Pythagoras and the Pythagoreans: A Brief History* (Indianapolis: Hackett, 2001), 97–9; Michael Trapp, "Neopythagoreans," in *Greek and Roman Philosophy 100BC–200AD, Volume II*, ed. Robert W. Sharples and Richard Sorabji (London: Institute of Classical Studies, 2007), 347–64 at 351–5; Mauro Bonazzi, "Eudorus of Alexandria and the 'Pythagorean' Pseudepigrapha," in *On Pythagoreanism*, 385–404; Joel Kalvesmaki, *The Theology of Arithmetic: Number Symbolism in Platonism and Early Christianity* (Washington, DC: Center for Hellenic Studies, 2013), 18–25.

[64] Numenius, frag. 52 (des Places 95).

[65] Salles-Dabadie also proposed an Alexandrian provenance for the *Declaration*, based on his comparison with Philo and Hermetic literature (*Recherche*, 106).

[66] Clement, *Strom.* 2.11.52.2. It is striking that Roelof van den Broek could claim, on the basis of this text that, "What we certainly know is that the Simonians called Simon 'the Standing One' (*ho hestōs*), as is testified *int. al.* by the non-Gnostic writer, Clement of Alexandria, *Stromateis*, II,52,2" ("Simon Magus," in *DGWE*, ed. Hanegraaff, 1069–73 at 1072). In my view, this is a misreading of the passage.

[67] *Ref.* 6.9.10; 6.10.2; 6.12.3; 6.12.4; 6.14.6; 6.16.5; 6.16.6; 6.17.2; 6.18.1.

[68] If the Coptic *Apoc. Pet.* (NHC VII,3) is Alexandrian, it is also significant that it mentions, as most scholars think, Simonians in 74.28–34. See Michel Desjardins and James Brashler, "Apocalypse of Peter," in *The Coptic Gnostic Library: A Complete Edition of the Nag Hammadi Codices*, 5 vols. (Leiden: Brill, 2000), 4.201–48.

[69] Origen, *Cels.* 5.62.

[70] See, e.g., Horatio Lona, *Die 'Wahre Lehre' des Kelsos übersetzt und erklärt* (Freiburg: Herder, 2005), 56.

Alexandrian provenance elsewhere and will not repeat those arguments here.[71] In later tradition (the Pseudo-Clementines), Simon himself was educated in Egypt—though we cannot verify the accuracy of this report.[72]

It may also be relevant that the Declarator quotes from the book of Wisdom, widely credited with an Alexandrian provenance. Wisdom, according to "Simon" is spirit (*pneuma*), "an image (*eikōn*) from an incorruptible form, alone (*monē*) ordering (*kosmousa*) everything (*panta*)."[73] According to the book of Wisdom, Wisdom is a spirit (*pneuma*), the image (*eikōn*) of God's goodness (Wisd 7:22, 26). This Wisdom, "although one (*mia*), . . . beneficently administers all things (*ta panta*)" (7:27; 8:1).

Preliminary Results

To sum up: the Declarator was probably a devotee of Simon who produced a Simonian writing in Egypt between 120 and 150 CE. My dating is based on (1) the absence of John's gospel, (2) the missing Helen, (3) the lack of identification of Simon with the Great Power, and (4) resemblances to Eudoran Middle Platonism prior to Numenian modifications. If I am right about the dating, the *Declaration* represents a stage of Simonian thought prior to what we find in Acts 8:10, where Simon himself is deified by "all" Samarians as "the Great Power" (Chapter 3). The relatively early date of the *Declaration*, which likely appeared before Justin's *1 Apology*, emphasizes its importance as a source for the earliest recoverable Simonian thought. The *Declaration* is not a traditional heresiological report. It is, rather, a fairly detailed, if selective and paraphrased, account of an early second-century Simonian's thought. Thus the *Declaration* should take priority when it comes to reconstructing the earliest recoverable Simonian theology.

Theology

This theology is not helpfully deemed "gnostic" in a global or typological sense.[74] The Declarator began by identifying God as an infinite, intellectual fire, a cosmic energy which also dwells in humans. The fire has a hidden (noetic) and manifest (material) aspect. Material reality emerges from the manifest aspect. The essence of God is hidden, and this is why the ultimate deity is called Silence.[75] God is the transcendent One,

---

[71] M. David Litwa, *Early Christianity in Alexandria* (Cambridge: Cambridge University Press, 2024).
[72] Ps.-Clem, *Hom.* 2.22.
[73] *Ref.* 6.14.4–5.
[74] The *Declaration* "does not inquire into the problem which is so decisive for all later Gnosticism, as to how matter could have developed and how the eternal power could have been mixed with it." It "knows nothing at all of a genuine dualism" and lacks "any redeemer figure" (Schmithals, *Office of Apostle*, 160). Cf. Salles-Dabadie, *Recherches*, 41–76, 141–4.
[75] *Ref.* 6.18.2.

signified by a single solitary point.[76] God is also "the Standing One" (*ho Hestōs*), a divine name found in Philo of Alexandria.[77]

A brief comparison with Philo is suggestive. In describing the creation of the world, Philo wrote that God made incorporeal beings which include heaven, earth, air, abyss, water, spirit, and light (archetype of the sun).[78] These entities are comparable to the mental (or verbal) entities represented by heaven, earth, air, water, sun, and moon in the *Declaration*. For his part, Philo understood Heaven and Earth to refer to Mind (*Nous*) and Perception (*Aisthēsis*).[79] Like the author of the *Declaration*, Philo was fascinated by Neo-Pythagorean mathematics, and made much of the number seven.[80] Although Philo did not personify seven, he did call her a "power."[81] He said that other philosophers likened seven to Athena born from the head of Zeus.[82] Pythagoreans specifically made seven "Director of the universe."[83] By means of the number seven, all things on earth are brought to completion.[84]

According to the *Declaration*, God made Heaven and Earth (Gen 1:1) which the author took to represent Mind (*Nous*) and Thought (*Epinoia*).[85] Mind is "the Great Power."[86] Thus "the Great Power" is subordinate to an unknown high God. From Mind and Thought come four paired powers (Voice-Name; Reasoning-Conception), making a total of six, as indicated by the six days of creation. The seventh day symbolizes the Seventh Power who is in turn identified with the Spirit hovering over the waters (Gen 1:2) as well as Wisdom (Prov 8:23).[87] Wisdom is the mother of this cosmos and she "generates all things."[88] She is never said to fall, make angels, or to become incarnate in a human body.

Wisdom is the Image of God according to which humans are made. Humans become God's likeness by bearing Wisdom's fruit (Gen 1:26). The Human mind is a manifestation of Wisdom in the two latter phases of her existence. Wisdom "stood" in her identity with the primal God, "stands" in the unredeemed human intellect, and

---

[76] *Ref.* 6.14.6; 5.9.5
[77] Runia, "Witness or Participant? Philo and the Neoplatonic Tradition," in *The Neoplatonic Tradition: Jewish, Christian and Islamic Themes*, ed. A. J. Vanderjagt and D. Pätzold (Cologne: Dinter, 1991), 36–56 at 47–51. In his n. 41, Runia cites the more important passages with their biblical lemmata: *Cher.* 18–19 (Gen 18:22); *Post.* 19–30 (Gen 18:22; Deut 5:31); *Gig.* 48–9 (Num 14:44; Deut 5:31); *Conf.* 30–2 (Deut 5:31; Exod 7:15); *Somn.* 1.241 (Gen 31:13; Exod 17:6); *Somn.* 2.221–30 (Exod 17:6; 24:10; Gen 18:22; Deut 5:31; 5:5); *Deo* (Gen 18:22). See also D. Winston and J. Dillon, *Two Treatises of Philo of Alexandria: A Commentary on De Gigantibus and Quod Deus Sit Immutabilis* (Chico: Scholars Press, 1983), 261–3.
[78] Philo, *Opif.* 29.
[79] Philo, *Leg. All.* 1.1.
[80] See, e.g., Philo, *Opif.* 89–127.
[81] Philo, *Opif.* 101.
[82] Cf. Plutarch, *Is. Os.* 10 (*Mor.* 354e).
[83] Philo, *Opif.* 100.
[84] Philo, *Opif.* 101–2. See further David T. Runia, *On the Creation of the Cosmos according to Moses: Introduction, Translation, and Commentary* PACS 1 (Leiden: Brill, 2001), 273–7.
[85] *Ref.* 6.13.1.
[86] *Ref.* 6.18.3.
[87] Cf. Philo, *Leg. All.* 1.15–18.
[88] *Ref.* 6.18.3.

"will stand" as the redeemed human mind made into God's likeness.[89] Human minds can be understood as micro instantiations of Wisdom, the divine Image.

The material world is designed for human intellects to mature and bear fruit. In the end, however, flesh will pass away like withered grass.[90] The human mind came from God, but if it does not conform to God, it will be destroyed with the (material) world (1 Cor 11:32).[91] If, however, the mind obtains God-likeness, it "will be in substance, in potential, in magnitude, in finished perfection one and the same as the Unborn and Infinite Power."[92] Salvation, in short, means deification and deification, in this system, amounts to identification with the infinite God.

The Declarator's Profile

Everything we know about the Declarator must be inferred from the *Declaration* itself. The following reconstruction is hypothetical but, I think, reasonable. He—or possibly she—was an early second-century Alexandrian theologian, as indicated by (1) knowledge of traditions from Philo, Eudorus and Soranus (and/or Herophilus), (2) use of the Wisdom of Solomon,[93] and (3) a possible reception by Clement of Alexandria.[94] In terms of education, the author was well trained in the allegorical exegesis of the Bible. Such an education could have occurred anywhere, but a major intellectual center like Alexandria fits well and accords with Philonic and later Christian emphases in this city. The author obtained an impressive Hellenic education, as indicated by knowledge of Greek poetry and the latest trends in Greek medicine and philosophy. He or she cited and allegorized Homeric poetry,[95] and quoted Empedocles.[96] The author was also familiar with Heraclitus's God called "ever-living fire"—a theology adapted by the Stoics (God as fiery breath).[97]

Despite this rich display of Hellenic learning, however, the author was primarily a biblical exegete. Isaiah was a favorite text, and the Pentateuch seems to have been particularly authoritative.[98] God as fire was inspired by Deuteronomy 4:24, 9:3 ("the Lord is a consuming fire"). Heaven and Earth are treated as living entities on the basis of Isaiah 1:2 ("Hear, Heaven, and Listen, Earth"). The author also quoted or alluded to gospel and Pauline literature (for instance, Matt 3:10 or Luke 3:9; 1 Cor 7:9; 11:32) in

---

[89] *Ref.* 6.13.1; 6.17.1–2.
[90] *Ref.* 6.10.2.
[91] *Ref.* 6.14.6.
[92] *Ref.* 6.12.3. According to Philo, God is infinite, and infinite are his powers (ἀπερίγραφος γὰρ ὁ θεὸς, ἀπερίγραφοι δὲ καὶ αἱ δυνάμεις αὐτοῦ) (*Sac.* 59).
[93] *Ref.* 6.14.4–5.
[94] Clement, *Strom.* 2.11.52.1–4.
[95] The *Odyssey* 10.304–6. See further Hugo Rahner, *Greek Myths and Christian Mystery*, trans. E. O. James (London: Burnes & Oates, 1963), 210–11.
[96] *Ref.* 6.11.1.
[97] Heraclitus in Clement, *Strom.* 5.14.103.6. For Stoic influences, see Salles-Dabadie, *Recherche*, 78–82. It is not clear that God as fire is the creator, even if fire "is the treasury of all existing things" (*Ref.* 6.9.8).
[98] The five senses are symbolized by the five books of Moses (*Ref.* 6.15.1–6.16.4).

creative and integrated ways.[99] We are not at liberty to remove these citations based on assumptions about what the original text must have looked like.

Was the Declarator a Christian? First of all, a Christian identity does not negate a (previous) Judean or Samarian identity. Suffice it to say, however, the Declarator's citations from the gospels and Paul indicates a Christian identity. Admittedly, the author never mentions Jesus, at least in the surviving excerpts. Still, failure to mention the Galilean does not deprive one of a Christian identity, especially at a time when Christianity was being invented. Ernst Haenchen denied that the *Declaration* was Christian, in part because it did not speak of sin and guilt.[100] The argument is wrongheaded, since it presumes a form of Christianity that only became normative later. The Refutator assumed that the Declarator was a Christian—otherwise he would not have bothered to excerpt him in his catalogue of Christian "heresies."

The Declarator's theology was informed by Judean scriptural traditions. Even if the Jews themselves were decimated in Alexandria in 117 CE, their traditions of theology and allegorical exegesis perdured and were exploited by later Christians. One of these Christians—a contemporary of Valentinus, Basilides, and Carpocrates—was a Simonian philosopher and biblical exegete who wrote the *Declaration*. It is possible that the wellsprings of the Declarator's theology go back to Simon, but the connections, unfortunately, are no longer clear. All we have is the early second-century *Declaration*, which, as the earliest Simonian source we have, can now be used to check the data of Acts and the heresiological reports.

---

[99] *Ref.* 6.9.10; 6.14.6; 6.17.4; 6.16.5.
[100] Haenchen, "Gab es," 336.

2

The Concept of Our Great Power

Introduction

Before we come to Acts and the heresy reports, it is important to take a brief detour into the Nag Hammadi codices. As argued in the previous chapter, the *Declaration* is the only text, in my view, that can be called a Simonian primary source. Nevertheless there is a second text —generally neglected—that touches on Simonian terms and traditions. I refer to the text preserved in Nag Hammadi codex VI,4 traditionally called *The Concept of Our Great Power*. It is perhaps better translated *The Understanding of Our Great Power*. I will henceforth call it *Great Power*. It was apparently thought to contain the speech of a divine being called Great Power as revealed by an unnamed narrator. Those unfamiliar with the text will find it translated in Appendix 2.

Scholarship on *Great Power* has not been plentiful, in part because the text has gaps and, due to difficulties in the Coptic, is sometimes hard to grasp.[1] Most scholars agree that the work was composed in Greek and translated into Coptic sometime in the third or fourth century CE. Some scholars consider it a fusion of two or more texts. Yet even if it was sewn together from separate sources, it can now been read as a relatively coherent, if rough-hewn work. Sometimes the Great Power speaks in the first person. In the majority of cases, however, the narrator uses the third person to refer to "our Great Power." The text, if not an apocalypse, can be classified as apocalyptic discourse.[2] In what follows, I will argue that *Great Power* has several important Simonian features that should be taken into account.

Outline

For ready access to the text, I present the following outline:

I. Introduction (36.1-27): Salvation for those who Know the Great Power
    a. Foreshadowing: "Know the One who Came" (36.28–37.5)

---

[1] To date, only two monographs have been published on *Great Pow*, namely Pierre Cherix, *Le concept de notre grande puissance* (Göttingen: Vandenhoeck & Ruprecht, 1982); and Francis E. Williams, *Mental Perception: A Commentary on NHC VI,4, The Concept of Our Great Power*, Nag Hammadi and Manichean Studies 51 (Leiden: Brill, 2001).

[2] Williams, *Mental Perception*, xxxiv–xxxv.

II. A Rewriting of Genesis 1
   a. The Original Abyss (37.6-12)
      i. Lord of the Abyss (37.12-23).
      ii. The Spirit (37.23-29)
      iii. The Rest of Creation (37.29–38.5)
      iv. The Birth of the Human Soul (38.5-12)

III. A Rewriting of Genesis 6
   a. The Fleshly Age and the Flood (38.13–39.15)
      i. Intervening Exhortation (43.3-11)

IV. The Animate Age (39.16–33)
   a. Exhortation (39.33–40.9)
   b. The Mother of Flame (40.9–23)
   c. The Story of Christ's Triumph (40.24–42.23)
   d. The Mission after Christ's Death (42.22–43.2)
   e. Flashback: Christ in the First Age (43.11–29)
   f. The Rulers Strike Back (43.29–44.10)
   g. The Ruler of the West (44.10–31)
   h. The Counterfeit and the Antichrist (44.31–45.24)

V. The Final Conflagration (45.24–47.8)

VI. Description of Final Salvation (47.9–48.15)

Simonian Features

The most obvious Simonian feature of the work is the use of "the Great Power" title to refer to God (compare also its reference to the "Power exalted over all powers").[3] The title is not distinctly Simonian, but the Simonians, it seems, tried to "trademark" it. They worshiped "the Great Power" as the Mind of the Universe and Father of Thought. The Great Power is, as in the *Declaration*, not identified with Simon. In heresiological literature, Simon is of course the focus of Simonian thought, but that is not the case in the *Declaration* or the *Great Power*.

Francis E. Williams sketched several other important similarities shared by *Great Power* and the *Declaration*.[4] The Great Power is "infinite" in the *Declaration* and "immeasurable" in *Great Power*.[5] In both texts, the Great Power inscribes information,[6] dwells in the human soul,[7] and consists of an intellectual fire.[8] Salvation, in both works, means assimilation to the Great Power—or rather its Image.[9] (We know from Clement

---

[3] *Great Pow.* 47.11–12.
[4] Williams, *Mental Perception*, l–liv.
[5] *Ref.* 6.9.4–5; 6.12.2–3; 6.13.1; 6.14.2–4; *Great Pow.* 47.12.
[6] *Ref.* 6.18.2; *Great Pow.* 36.15; 37.15.
[7] *Ref.* 6.9.4–5; *Great Pow.* 38.6–9.
[8] *Ref.* 6.9.3–6; *Great Pow.* 37.29–31.
[9] *Ref.* 6.9.6; 6.12.3; 6.14.5–6; *Great Pow.* 36.8–10.

that Simonians tried to assimilate to the Standing One.¹⁰) In both the *Great Power* and the *Declaration*, Salvation is described as "standing."¹¹ In addition, unassimilated (or material) persons are, in the end, annihilated by destructive (not divine) fire.¹² I can add three other similarities: both the *Declaration* and *Great Power* interpret Genesis 1, both make use of an oracular style, and both seem fascinated by numbers.¹³

There are also major differences between the texts. The Great Power in the *Declaration* is identified with the subordinate figure of Mind. Such subordination is not clear in *Great Power*. *Great Power* is, furthermore, an apocalyptic discourse which tells a story of Noah, Jesus, and antichrist.¹⁴ It mentions Wisdom, but not the Seventh Power or the Standing One. It speaks of a lower creator and never mentions Moses. It never openly quotes from the Prophets or the New Testament—though gospel and Pauline texts were evidently known.¹⁵ It is not a *hexaemeron*, and shows no interest in medical lore. The *Declaration*, in turn, offers scant attention to salvation history and eschatology. A conflagration is briefly mentioned, but there is no timeline of future events. The *Declaration* calls Moses "Logos," whereas the *Great Power* offers that title to Jesus.¹⁶ Jesus is a character in *Great Power*, though he is (as in the *Declaration*) never named.

It seems evident, then, that the *Declaration* and *Great Power* were written by different persons with considerably different interests and identities. At the same time, these persons tapped into a common fund of traditions and terminology. In my view, the author of *Great Power* knew Simonian terms and traditions, even though he or she was not Simonian *per se*. In what follows, I will say something about whether *Great Power* reflects knowledge of a Simonian group.

Provenance

Where was *Great Power* written? Even if one imagines several stages of composition, nearly every indication points to Egypt as the place of writing and transmission. The text mentions a demon called "Sasabek," which is apparently adapted from the Egyptian

---

10 Clement, *Strom.* 2.11.52.1–4.
11 *Ref.* 6.17.1; *Great Pow.* 43.8–11.
12 *Ref.* 6.16.6; *Great Pow.* 47.6–7.
13 *Great Pow.* 43.21–2; 46.27–8. Cf. Philo, *Praem.* 65. Josef Montserrat-Torrents thought that *Great Pow.* depended on the *Declaration* ("El Pensamiento de Nuestro Gran Poder [VI 36,1-48.15]," in *Textos gnósticos: Biblioteca de Nag Hammadi. III Apocalipsis y otros escritos* [Madrid: Trotta, 2000], 113–28 at 116), but there is insufficient evidence.
14 Sergey Minov, "Noah and the Flood in Gnosticism," in *Noah and His Book(s)*, ed. Michael E. Stone (Atlanta: SBL Press, 2009), 215–36; David Brakke, "The Seed of Seth at the Flood: Biblical Interpretation and Gnostic Theological Reflection," in *Reading in Christian Communities: Essays on Interpretation in the Early Church*, ed. Charles Bobertz and David Brakke (Notre Dame: University of Notre Dame Press, 2002), 41–62.
15 See esp. the retelling of Jesus's earthly ministry in *Great Pow.* 40.24–41.13. The reference to the rulers who kill Jesus is reminiscent of 1 Cor 2:8.
16 *Great Pow.* 44.3.

alligator deity Sobek (often associated with aggression).[17] The author refers to primeval waters "without beginning," waters which provide the earth's foundation.[18] Perhaps this is a nod to the primal abyss of Genesis 1:2. Yet one can also point to the primeval—and eternal—waters of Nun out of which the first mound of earth arises in Egyptian lore.[19] The use of the locution "ruler of the west" to refer to an imperial ruler indicates that the author was somewhere east of Rome. At the same time, Palestine ("the place where the Logos first appeared") is said to be east of the author's location.[20] A location east of Rome and west of Palestine could be Asia Minor, Greece, or Egypt. But there is no independent evidence for Asia Minor or Greece. In addition, in both the Hermetic Poimandres and *Great Power*, the element of fire is said to emerge from water.[21] Hermetic literature arose and was apparently best known in Egypt. Finally, the period of purgatorial detention for souls—1,468 years—is close to the approximately 1,460-year cycle of Sothis (when lunar and solar years coincide).[22]

All these hints, albeit subtle, indicate that an Egyptian provenance is our best hypothesis for *Great Power*. The text was also discovered in Upper Egypt (Nag Hammadi), where it evidently had a prehistory in both Greek and Coptic. An Egyptian origin also explains how the text could absorb Simonian notions and terms, since Egypt is the probable provenance of the *Declaration*.

Date

Williams thought that *Great Power* referred to events in Palestine during the Jewish War (66–73 CE).[23] After Christ's defeat of the rulers,

> cities shuddered. Mountains collapsed. The ruler comes up with the rulers of the western lands as far as the east, namely the place where the Logos first appeared. Then the earth shook and the city trembled. Then the birds ate and were gorged on the corpses. The earth mourned along with the inhabited world. They became a wasteland. (43.29–44.10)

---

[17] *Great Pow.* 41.29. see further Marco Zecchi, *Sobek of Shedet: The Crocodile God in the Fayyum in the Dynastic Period* (Perugia: Tau, 2010).

[18] *Great Pow.* 37.8.

[19] Geraldine Pinch, *Egyptian Mythology: A Very Short Introduction* (Oxford: Oxford University Press, 2004), 46; J. P. Allen, *Genesis in Egypt: The Philosophy of Ancient Egyptian Creation Accounts* (New Haven: Egyptological Seminar, 1988); Mpay Kemboly, *The Question of Evil in Ancient Egypt* (London: Golden House, 2010), 37–66.

[20] *Great Pow.* 44.3.

[21] *Great Pow.* 38.4–5; CH 1.5 (πῦρ ἄκρατον ἐξεπήδησεν ἐκ τῆς ὑγρᾶς φύσεως); cf. CH 3.2 (πυρὶ τῶν ὅλων διορισθέντων καὶ ἀνακρεμασθέντων).

[22] Williams, *Mental Perception* 179 ("the period over which the beginning of the lunar year, and the beginning of the year, which was dated from the rising of Sirius, returned to a calendar date on which they coincided"), citing Carsten Colpe, "Heidnische, jüdische und christliche Überlieferung in den Schriften aus Nag Hammadi I," *JAC* 15 (1972): 5–18 at 14. See also Colpe, *Einleitung in die Schriften aus Nag Hammadi* (Münster: Aschendorff, 2011), 81, n.6.

[23] Williams, *Mental Perception*, lxii.

Williams's hypothesis is plausible, since Christians often wanted to connect the death of Jesus at the hands of (Judean and superhuman) "rulers" to the wasting of Judea from 68 to 73 CE.[24] Williams believed that the initial version of *Great Power* was written in the second century CE. He asserted, however, that an updating occurred at the hands of Christian scribe sometime after 363 CE.[25] He made this deduction because he took the following to refer to Emperor Julian (reigned 361–363):

> Then the ruler of the west arose. And from the east he will perform a work. He will teach people in his wickedness. He wishes to destroy every teaching of the message of true wisdom. He loves the lying wisdom. For he engaged what is ancient. He wished to introduce evil, though he clothed himself in dignity. He could not, since great was the defilement of his clothes. Then he raged; he appeared; he wanted to go up and cross over to that place. Then the season comes. He complied and changes the edicts. (*Great Power* 44.13-31)

I do not see any clear reference to Julian in this passage. In fact, I think it better reflects a ruler closer in time to the events of 70 CE—namely Trajan or Hadrian. Both emperors came from west (Rome) to the east. Both brought destruction upon Jewish—and likely Samari(t)an—communities in Egypt (Trajan in 117 CE) and Palestine (Hadrian in 135 CE).[26] Julian did nothing against Judeans or Samaritans. He apparently wanted these peoples, with their distinctive religious traditions, to thrive in opposition to Christianity. Both Trajan and Hadrian were traditionalists, supporting the ancient Roman values and gods. Hadrian, at least, had a reputation for Hellenic wisdom. His "defilement" may refer to his pederastic relationship with Antinous. Trajan was at one time east of Palestine (in the Parthian war) and grew angry when Jews rebelled in Cyrene, Egypt, and perhaps in Palestine. The "edicts" could refer to Mosaic decrees about circumcision, since Hadrian prohibited circumcision at some point before or after the Bar Kokhba revolt (132–135 CE). Likely we cannot reconstruct the exact scenario that lies behind the vague description quoted above, but we need not leap from the events in 70 to the 360s CE.

There is another interpretation advocating a late date for *Great Power*. In 1979, Frederik Wisse proposed that the text referred to Anomoeans, namely Arian Christians who argued that the Father and Son were essentially unlike each other.[27] Yet—as most translators have realized—the Coptic term *nianhomoion* simply refers to "disparate" or "unlike things"—and thus improper—for the audience. In context, these "disparate things" correlate with evil lusts, desires, and "heresies." Marvin Meyer translates: "Avoid evil lusts and desires and whatever deviates from who you are."[28]

---

[24] E.g., Eusebius, *Hist. eccl.* 3.5–8.
[25] Williams, *Mental Perception*, lxiv.
[26] According to Eusebius (*Theophany* 4.23), "these two mountains [Gerizim and Jerusalem] were destroyed and besieged in the days of Titus and Vespasian and in the days of Hadrian" (*Eusebius Werke. Dritter Band, Zweiter Teil. Die Theophanie. Die griechischen Bruchstücke und Übersetzung der syrischen Überlieferung*, ed. Hugo Gressman and Adolf Lamniski, 2nd ed. [Berlin: Akademie, 1992], 201).
[27] *Great Pow.* 40.7.
[28] *Great Pow.* 40.5–8 in Marvin Meyer, ed., *The Nag Hammadi Scriptures: The International Edition* (New York: HarperOne, 2007), 397.

According to the theory of Josef Montserrat Torrents, the author of *Great Power* "moved in the circle of Valentinian teaching."[29] Although he may be correct, there is little evidence for distinctly Valentinian ideas in *Great Power*. It refers to a fleshly and soulish age, but not to fleshly, soulish, and spiritual people. Its author presents a basically positive view of the creator, but not the Valentinian view in which the creator progresses in knowledge. Wisdom also appears in *Great Power*, but not the specifically fallen Wisdom (Achamoth) in Valentinian lore.

There is apparent mention of the saved entering "the age of the bridal chamber," but the reading here is disputed, since the manuscript reads "the age of judgment" (*paiōn ᵉmphap*). Hans-Martin Schenke was convinced that *hap* here was a form of the Coptic word *hop*, meaning "feast," "marriage feast" or "bridal chamber."[30] If we choose "bridal chamber," then the Valentinian echo is hard to deny. The debate over how to translate this word will continue. Suffice it to say, little in the treatise shows clear knowledge of "classical Valentinianism" as it was known in the works of second-century Valentinians like Ptolemy, Heracleon, Theodotus, and Marcus.[31] Themes like eternal rest and the final conflagration are too common to be distinctly Valentinian.

Another indication of date is the use of "evil heresies."[32] Such language might seem to reflect a time after "heresy" (*hairesis*) became a solely pejorative term in Christian polemic (i.e., after Justin Martyr).[33] If that was the case, however, the author would not have needed to add the adjective "evil" (*hoou*) to "heresies." We are still, accordingly, at a time when a *hairesis* could refer more neutrally to a "choice," "school," or "sect" (as in Josephus). Marvin Meyer even translates "heresies" by "dispositions."[34]

An early-second-century date for *Great Power* is also supported by two of the same silences seen in the *Declaration*: (1) Simon is not yet identified with the Great Power, and (2) Wisdom is not associated with Helen. After Justin Martyr (about 150 CE); these two points become core elements in Simonian tradition.

Great Power's allusions to biblical texts provide a chronological starting point. An allusion to Ephesians 2:15 is plausible. Here Jesus is said to have "disabled" or "destroyed" (*katargēsas*) "the law of commandments" (*ton nomon tōn entolōn*). In *Great Power*, we learn that Jesus's "word destroyed (*bōl ebol*) the law of the age" (*pnomos ᵉmaiōn*).[35] The "law" in the latter case may refer to the law of birth and death.[36] Even so, the language of Christ destroying the law is probably an echo of Ephesians (roughly 65–120 CE).

The author of *Great Power* was familiar with a Synoptic gospel, though it is difficult to tell which one. We learn that the infant Jesus drank breast milk, that (as an adult) he spoke in parables, and proclaimed the age to come.[37] Knowledge of Jesus's infancy

---

[29] Montserrat Torrents, "El Pensamiento," 118.
[30] Schenke, "Das Verständnis unserer grossen Kraft, (NHC VI,4)," in *Nag Hammadi Deutsch*, ed. Hans-Martin Schenke, Hans-Gebhard Bethge and Ursula Ulrike Kaiser, 2 vols. (Berlin: de Gruyter, 2001), 2.483–93 at 492, n.15.
[31] *Pace* Montserrat Torrents, "El Pensamiento," 116.
[32] *Great Pow.* 40.8.
[33] Alain Le Boulluec, *La notion d'hérésie dans la littérature grecque II-II siècles*, 2 vols. (Paris: Augustinian Studies, 1985), esp. 1.36–7, 39, 48–91.
[34] Meyer, *Nag Hammadi Scriptures*, 397.
[35] *Great Pow.* 42.6.
[36] Williams, *Mental Perception*, 123.
[37] *Great Pow.* 40.29–32.

might suggest a gospel which included his birth from Mary, thus a version of Matthew or Luke.

There is also probably some knowledge of 2 Thessalonians and the book of Revelation. Revelation 13 speaks of a "second beast" who convinces the world to worship the "first beast," usually taken to be an antichrist figure. The second beast performs "great signs" (*sēmeia megala*) to lead astray (*planaō*) earth's population (13:12-13). In *Great Power*, a counterfeit (*antimeimon*) is distinguished from an antichrist figure.[38] This counterfeit performed "great signs" (*hen noč ᵉnsēmeion*). He set up a throne for Antichrist, who becomes "god of the world." At this point, people go astray (*ᵉrplana*).[39] The linguistic and conceptual overlap is significant. The declaration about the enthroned and deified antichrist is similar to 2 Thessalonians 2:4, where the antichrist figure sits in the temple of God and manifests himself as a god.[40]

Finally, there is possible knowledge of 1 Peter 3:18-20, which says that Christ, when "made alive in spirit" went and preached in spirit to "the spirits in prison." It is contested who these spirits are, but one could take them to refer to evil spirits called "rulers"—one of them being the ruler of Hades. Perhaps this is how the author of *Great Power* read 1 Peter. If so, it would not be coincidence that the authors of *Great Power* and of 1 Peter both spoke of Noah as well as Christ preaching "in the days of Noah."[41]

Knowledge of these biblical texts suggests that *Great Power* was written sometime after 100 CE. There is nothing else in *Great Power* that would firmly suggest a date after 150 CE. All indications, in fact, indicate a date prior to 150 CE (use of "heresies" to mean "opinions" or "sects," Simon not identified with the Great Power, Helen not identified with Wisdom). Of course, the text was later translated into Coptic and probably modified in small ways in the course of transmission; yet we need not imagine a scribe interpolating an anti-Arian label or a paragraph to refer to a fourth-century emperor. If the author of *Great Power* knew the later policies of Hadrian, I would suggest a date between 135 and 150 CE.

Of course, one could argue that the writer removed "offensive" elements from his text. This is the argument of Williams, who writes, "the scurrilous-sounding tale of Simon and his paramour Helen may well be a Catholic parody of it. It would not be surprising if some later Simonian thinkers wished to modify the tale, removing the scandal which it had occasioned."[42] This hypothesis should be queried. Was it really offensive to later Simonians that Simon's companion—not necessarily his "paramour"—was identified with Wisdom and that Simon was the Great Power? One could view such elements as offensive to *heresiologists*. But these notions became central doctrines in Simonian thought, teachings which most Simonians, at least in Rome, came to uphold. In my view, they were not "offensive," and thus would not have been omitted.

---

[38] *Great Pow.* 45.2.
[39] *Great Pow.* 45.7-16.
[40] αὐτὸν εἰς τὸν ναὸν τοῦ θεοῦ καθίσαι ἀποδεικνύντα ἑαυτὸν ὅτι ἐστὶν θεός. It is something of a curiosity that H.-M. Schenke identified Simon of Samaria as the antichrist figure in *Great Pow.* because he thought 47.27-8 referred to a failed flight to heaven ("Die Bedeutung der Texte von Nag Hammadi für die moderne Gnosisforschung," in *Gnosis und Neues Testament: Studien aus Religionswissenschaft und Theologie*, ed. K.-W. Tröger (Berlin: de Gruyter, 1973), 13–76 at 52.
[41] Cf. Clement of Alexandria, *Strom.* 6.6.44.5–6.6.46.5.
[42] Williams, *Mental Perception*, lv.

Apocalyptic Discourse

Since the author of *Great Power* was not a Simonian *per se*, there is no surprise that elements of the text do not appear Simonian. Simonians, for instance, are not known to have written apocalypses. At the same time, Simonians were probably conversant with them. In the *Declaration*, humans assimilated to God are depicted as fruits set in a storehouse. Unassimilated humans, in turn, are "chaff thrown into the fire."[43] This is a classic apocalyptic image based on a saying of John the Baptizer (Matt 3:10; Luke 3:9). Irenaeus claimed that Simon promised to dissolve the world and to free his followers from the tyranny of the world-making angels.[44] Simonians, like many Christians, believed that the world was coming to a (violent and fiery) end.[45] Accordingly, even though the *Great Power* includes significantly more end-time speculation, it is not beyond the pale of Simonian thought.

We need not, however, go too far by claiming that the *Great Power* presents a distinctly Simonian eschatology. For instance, an antichrist figure appears in *Great Power*, though there is nothing distinctly Simonian about him.

Theology and Christology

The author of *Great Power* believed in a single and unattainable God, called the Great Power, the Power over other powers. The Great Power is a personal being who loves those whom s/he saves.[46] Possibly the Great Power is androgynous because s/he is referred to with both feminine and masculine pronouns.[47]

The Great Power arranged for there to be a creator, an administrator of the fleshly creation. He is called the "father of flesh" and is associated with fear and light. Beyond his lower status and association with fear, there is nothing strongly negative about him. His thoughts are pure. He fulfills a positive function in the universe and disappears when the cosmos is burned away.

As for Christ, the author of *Great Power* emphasizes that he spoke—not just to Israel—but to the world. Christ was a true human being who drank the breast milk of his mother. He was also a divine being insofar as he was the Logos (John 1:1). Christ easily dominated the rulers and reversed the law of death. He was also active in the time of Noah, and Noah may even have been a previous incarnation of Christ.

The pattern of salvation in Christ best conforms to the *Christus victor* model. Christ triumphs over demonic rulers as in 1 Corinthians 2:8, although his cross is never mentioned. What receives attention is Christ's trip to Hades. There he confounds the master of Hades, who cannot grasp him (1 Pet 3:16; 4:6). It is not said that Christ

---

[43] *Ref.* 6.9.10.
[44] Irenaeus, *Haer.* 1.23.3.
[45] *Apoc Pet.* 5; 2 Pet 3:7–13. See further Beyschlag, *Simon Magus*, 207–10.
[46] *Great Pow.* 47.20–6.
[47] *Great Pow.* 36.16.

preaches to the dead in Hades. He simply conquers death and demons and then ascends in triumph to heaven.

All of this material has parallels in other Christian literature. None of it need be considered (distinctly) Simonian.

Ethics

Against Williams, I do not see any convincing evidence that the author of *Great Power* prohibited sex. The author urged his readers to avoid evil lusts and desires, but this was standard Christian admonition found in the mouths of non-celibate writers.[48] Williams understood the mysterious "Mother of the flame" in *Great Power* to be "a demonic temptress, the authoress of sexual passion"—but this is unnecessary.[49] She might well be an angel in charge of unspecified fires. The author of the *Declaration* believed that an internal flame within humans turned into semen (among men) and milk (among women). But he did not excoriate sex or breastfeeding. Semen and milk represent elements necessary for spiritual growth.[50]

In other literature, Simonians are never depicted as rejecting sex and marriage. In fact, heresiologists portray them as licentious. The author of *Great Power* confessed that, "We too acted (*an*^{e}*rprassa*) according to the birth of the flesh of creation set down by the law-giving ruler. Yet we have come to be in the unchanging age."[51] It is not clear that living in the unchanging age means that the implied readers are to cease living according to their fleshly origin.[52] Both fleshly and future types of life overlapped in a situation of "now and not yet."

A Simonian Group?

Even if *Great Power* was composed—as seems likely—by an individual, that person wanted to project some kind of communal consciousness. He or she referred to "*our* Great Power," and made use of the first-person plural, as in "*We* have come to be in the unchangeable age."[53] The author of this text at least imagined speaking to a larger group.

Unfortunately, we do not have any solid information about this group or whether it empirically existed in antiquity. If it did, it may have sponsored a ritual meal, as indicated by the "true food" and "water of life."[54] It seems reasonable that it was located in Egypt, where *Great Power* was arguably composed. It was probably not the same group of people addressed in the *Declaration*. Both texts, however, independently

---

[48] *Great Pow.* 40.6–7.
[49] Williams, *Mental Perception*, 99.
[50] *Ref.* 6.17.5–7.
[51] *Great Pow.* 48.9–13.
[52] *Pace* Williams, *Mental Perception*, 200.
[53] *Great Pow.* 48.12–13.
[54] *Great Pow.* 40.4–5.

attest that groups with access to Simonian traditions lived in Egypt and were active there in the second century CE.

It is likely that Justin, who knew Simonians in Samaria and Rome, was unaware of Simonian group(s) and their writings in Egypt. Neither he nor any other heresiologist made mention of them prior to the Refutator, who paraphrased the *Declaration*. Modern scholars should, however, be aware of regional variations among Simonians. Simonians in Egypt, presumably, had a different theology than their counterparts in Samaria and Rome, at least in the early second century. They did not view Simon as the Great Power, nor did they understand Helen as Wisdom.

They may, however, have affirmed transmigration. The author of *Great Power* thought that Christ spoke "in" Noah in prediluvian times. He wrote that Jesus, "lived the first age, traveling within it until it perished. He preached 120 years."[55] Possibly Christ was thought to be incarnate in Noah. If so, one can move from part to whole: the transmigration of one soul leaves open that of others. Transmigration was a live option for Christians living in Egypt. It was supported by Basilideans and Carpocratians.[56] It would not surprise if the belief flourished among Egyptian Simonians.[57]

Unfortunately, we do not know much else about Simonians or Simonian traditions in Egypt. By the third century CE, Origen was convinced that Simonians were few.[58] He later claimed, with a polemical edge, that Simonians no longer existed.[59] Apparently Origen never met a Simonian in Egypt. It should be noted, however, that Origen's notion of Simonianism was influenced primarily by the heresiological tradition and the book of Acts. He expected Simonians to identify Simon with the Great Power, but that is not what we find in the *Declaration* or *Great Power*. Thus if Origen had come to know these texts, or persons who read them, he probably would not have recognized them as Simonian.

Results

What can we say about Simonian Christianity as it is known from *Great Power* and the *Declaration*? Whoever wrote these texts worshiped the Great Power and saw the human soul as in some sense its image, as mediated (in the *Declaration*) by a Wisdom figure (the Seventh Power). The Simonians reflected by these works were Christians, as can

---

[55] *Great Pow.* 43.17–19.
[56] Winrich Alfried Löhr, *Basilides und seine Schule: Eine Studie zur Theologie- und Kirchengeschichte des zweiten Jahrhunderts*, WUNT 83 (Tübingen: Mohr Siebeck, 1996), 212–18; M. David Litwa, *Carpocrates, Marcellina, and Epiphanes: Three Early Christian Teachers of Alexandria and Rome* (London: Routledge, 2022), 119–33.
[57] Sami Yli-Karjanmaa argues for a doctrine of transmigration shared by Philo and Clement of Alexandria: *Reincarnation in Philo of Alexandria*, Studia Philonica Monographs 7 (Atlanta: SBL Press, 2015); "Clement of Alexandria's Position on the Doctrine of Reincarnation and some comparisons with Philo," in *Studia Patristica CX: Papers presented at the Eighteenth International Conference on Patristic Studies held in Oxford 2019*, ed. Markus Vinzent (Leuven: Peeters, 2021), 75–90.
[58] Origen, *Cels.* 1.57.
[59] Origen, *Cels.* 6.11.

be seen from their use of Pauline and gospel literature. The author of the *Declaration* was apparently not familiar with John, but the writer of *Great Power* probably was. In *Great Power* 43.33, for instance, the rulers rage against Christ called "life," which seems to allude to John 14:6 ("I am the life"). The idea that the spirit has "life in itself" echoes John 5:26 (the Son "has life in himself").[60] The Simonian traditions represented by *Great Power* and the *Declaration* interpreted Genesis in Platonic fashion. Their view of salvation was conditioned by Platonic categories. Salvation meant rest and eternal stability, conforming to the image of the Great Power, who is said to stand—that is, to subsist—in the most ontologically rich sense.

The author of *Great Power* was aware of the spread of Christianity to "many" in various places. He viewed the first Christian missionaries as "publishing" (or possibly "abandoning") Christ's message "according to their desire."[61] Evidently this is a criticism of competing Christian movements, who did not have truth and salvation like the upholders of Simonian tradition. The language suggests that the author was in an area where diverse Christian movements competed for recognition, with none of them prevailing. Such a situation would fit Egypt in the early second century CE.

In short, the teachings contained in *Great Power* and the *Declaration* are different, but they are in some ways compatible. When brought together, they represent other, broadly Gentile, variants of early-second-century Christianity in Egypt and existed in competition with other Christian movements at the time. The author of *Great Power* was not a Simonian. At the same time, he or she knew of Simonian traditions—and perhaps persons—around 135 CE. These traditions were compelling and attractive enough to be plucked, adapted, and woven into an apocalyptic discourse in part spoken by the Great Power herself.

---

[60] *Great Pow.* 37.28–9.
[61] *Great Pow.* 43.1. The Coptic reads ⲕⲱ ⲉϩⲣⲁï which could mean "publish" or "abandon".

3

The Acts of the Apostles

Introduction: The Date of Acts

Acts is generally considered to be the earliest account regarding Simon of Samaria.[1] The previous chapters, however, cast doubt upon this judgment. Scholarship dates Acts anywhere between the 60s and the 150s CE.[2] If it was written between 125 and 150 CE, then it may not in fact be our earliest source. This issue is important, so it merits investigation.

Recently Karl L. Armstrong has (re-)asserted an early dating of Acts (62–63 CE). Some of his arguments are invalid, such as the appeal to a putative consensus that "the majority of scholars view Acts (in varying degrees) as a historical document."[3] A historical document can be mixed with a host of fictional elements demanded by the creation of a narrative.[4] If it is true of modern history, it is all the more true of ancient *historia*.[5] Armstrong's argument is beside the point, however, since even if there were a consensus that everything in Acts was historical, it would not determine when it was composed.

In essence, Armstrong restates the patristic position: "Luke is the author of Luke (and Acts) and was in some capacity a companion of the Apostle Paul."[6] He leans heavily on source criticism, but his imagined sources are speculative and unproven. They include "memory" and "oral traditions."[7] The proof of such traditions is the use

---

[1] Beyschlag, *Simon Magus*, 7; Lüdemann, *Untersuchungen*, 39; Haar, *Simon Magus*, 71.
[2] Joseph Fitzmyer, *The Acts of the Apostles: A New Translation with Introduction and Commentary* AB 31 (New York: Doubleday, 1998), 53–4; Richard Pervo, "Acts in the Suburbs of the Apologists," in *Contemporary Studies in Acts*, ed. Thomas E. Phillips (Macon: Mercer University Press, 2009), 29–46.
[3] Karl L. Armstrong, *Dating Acts in its Jewish and Greco-Roman Contexts* (London: Bloomsbury, 2021), 72.
[4] Hayden White, "The Question of Narrative in Contemporary Historical Theory," *History and Theory* 23, no. 1 (1984): 1–33.
[5] T. P. Wiseman, "Lying Historians: Seven Types of Mendacity," in *Lies and Fiction in the Ancient World*, ed. Christopher Gill and T. P. Wiseman (Exeter: University of Exeter Press, 1993), 122–46; A. J. Woodman, *Rhetoric in Classical Historiography: Four Studies* (London: Croom Helm, 1988); T. P. Wiseman, *Clio's Cosmetics: Three Studies in Greco-Roman Literature* (Totowa: Rowman and Littlefield, 1979); Michael Grant, *Greek and Roman Historians: Information and Misinformation* (London: Routledge, 1995), 61–99; M. David Litwa, *How the Gospels Became History: Jesus and Mediterranean Myths* (New Haven: Yale University Press, 2019), 22–45.
[6] Armstrong, *Dating Acts*, 72.
[7] Armstrong, *Dating Acts*, 73.

of "we" in several passages of Acts.[8] Armstrong believes that the "simplest" explanation is that the author of these passages was a companion of Paul (though this would not necessarily be "Luke").

This "simple" solution is in reality simplistic given what we know of ancient historiographical conventions. Authors who wanted to appear as eyewitnesses could use the first person to increase the reality effect of their discourse.[9] Thus it is no surprise that the author of Acts sporadically used "we" and depicted himself as an eyewitness in the preface to Luke (1:1-4). These rhetorical stances do not reliably indicate date. The author never claimed to have used notes or an itinerary or a diary (from Antioch or elsewhere).[10] Theories about such sources are speculative and lead to false problems such as how "Luke" saved his notes as he swam ashore from the shipwreck described in Acts 27:44.[11]

The point where the author of Acts chose to end his narrative is also not an indication of the text's date. A historian can end a work anywhere she pleases, regardless of modern sensibilities about what counts as complete or relevant. Armstrong's attempt to follow "the simple solution observed by the ancient writers—that Luke wrote only what he was aware of" is once again simplistic.[12]

It is also inaccurate. As Armstrong himself points out, John Chrysostom knew that the author of Acts focused on what was of "immediate importance" (*ta katepeigonta*) to his rhetorical and literary goals.[13] The fire in Rome and the destruction of the Jewish temple were evidently not of immediate importance for these goals. Even though the author likely knew these events (Luke 13:35; 19:43-44), he created a kind of cliff-hanger with Paul under house arrest at Rome. If he were to report everything, he would, Chrysostom observed, "make the reader dull and jaded (*nōthei poiei kai eklelumenon*)."[14]

Yet Armstrong urges: "No credible historian, whether ancient or modern, much less the 'first Christian historian,' could invent such an ending [to Acts] if these events [the fire in Rome, Paul's trial under Nero, the destruction of Jerusalem] had already passed."[15] If the author was writing in the second century, however, his omission of Paul's death makes sense, since 2 Timothy (4:6) and 1 Clement (5:7) cover it. Tacitus and Suetonius treated mother-killing Nero.[16] Josephus related the temple's destruction (he was an eyewitness).[17] The fact that "Western" variants of Acts do not substantively

---

[8] Acts 16:10-17; 20:5-15; 21:1-18; 27:1-28:16.
[9] M. David Litwa, "Literary Eyewitnesses: The Appeal to an Eyewitness in John and Contemporaneous Literature," *NTS* 64, no. 3 (2018): 343-61.
[10] Armstrong, *Dating Acts*, 56.
[11] Armstrong, *Dating Acts*, 67.
[12] Armstrong, *Dating Acts*, 99.
[13] John Chrysostom, *Homilies on Acts* 1.1 in *PG* 60.15, line 34. An English translation is cited by Armstrong, *Dating Acts*, 107-8.
[14] Chrysostom, *Hom. Acts* 55.2 in *PG* 60.382, line 40.
[15] Armstrong, *Dating Acts*, 153-5 (this quotation on 155).
[16] Tacitus, *The Annals*, trans. John Jackson. LCL 312 (Cambridge, MA: Cambridge University Press, 1937); Suetonius, *Lives of the Caesars*, ed. J. C. Rolfe. 2 vols. LCL (Cambridge, MA: Harvard University Press, 1913-14).
[17] Josephus, *J.W.* 6-7.

change its ending shows that ancient Christians did not share Armstrong's assumptions about what Acts, written after 64 CE, should have included.

In sum, Armstrong operates under a fallacy: because an author did not mention key events that happened later in the narrative time of writing, one can use the narrative time of writing to determine its composition in historical time. This argument is rather like saying that a historian of the American Civil War writing in 1965, because she did not mention any of the key events regarding Lincoln's death and Sherman's burning of Atlanta, must have written prior to 1864. Despite Armstrong's rhetorical pleas to represent the only "rational" and "consistent" position, his argument fails to persuade.[18]

One can, however, agree with Armstrong—who repeats Richard Pervo—that the dating of Acts to the late first century (80–95 CE) is little more than a political compromise.[19] It makes sense that Acts would, with Luke, be dated after the destruction of the temple referred to in Luke 13:35 ("your house is abandoned") and 19:43-44 (the Roman fortifications and siege of Jerusalem).[20] Yet nothing demands that the upper limit be set between 80 and 95 CE, apart from the inference that the author was Paul's traveling companion. That inference, however, is unsound, since the author of Acts never said he knew Paul personally. The use of the first-person plural and the deployment of supposedly vivid historical details can be explained by the techniques of narrative fiction and the possible use of sources closer in time to Paul.

What, then, is the evidence of a later (post 95 CE) dating? First of all, the author (or editor) of Luke-Acts seems to have used Josephus, and in particular the latter books of the *Antiquities*, which date to about 93 CE. Indications of dependence are rife, though I will note only three. First, Acts presents Gamaliel mentioning Theudas and Judas the Galilean as rebels in the same—non-chronological—order as Josephus, along with the same connection between Judas and "the census" (Acts 5:36-37).[21] Second, the author of Acts combined the sicarii, mentioned as urban assassins by Josephus, with "the Egyptian" (Acts 21:38). These sicarii—historically unrelated to "the Egyptian"— are both mentioned in the same context with the same names by Josephus.[22] By melding two distinct but juxtaposed reports in Josephus, evidently, the author of Acts mistakenly presented the Egyptian as *leader* of the sicarii.[23] Finally, the author of Acts borrowed details from Josephus about the death of "Herod" Agrippa I (Acts 12:20-23).[24] In this passage, the king publicly appears in Caesarea wearing royal garb. In response to people proclaiming his divinity, the king acquiesces to the praise and

---

[18] Armstrong, *Dating Acts*, 170–1, 156, 185.
[19] Armstrong, *Dating Acts*, 3, citing Pervo, "Acts in the Suburbs," 31.
[20] Milton Moreland, "Jerusalem Destroyed: The Setting of Acts," in *Engaging Early Christian History: Reading Acts in the Second Century*, ed. Rubén R. Dupertuis and Todd Penner (Durham: Acumen, 2013), 17–44.
[21] Josephus, *Ant.* 20.97–102. See further Richard Pervo, *Dating Acts between the Evangelists and the Apologists* (Sonoma: Polebridge, 2006), 152–60; Steve Mason, *Josephus and the New Testament*, 2nd ed. (Peabody: Hendrickson, 2003), 251–96; Steve Mason, "Was Josephus a Source for Luke-Acts?" in *On Using Sources in Graeco-Roman, Jewish and Early Christian Literature in honor of Joseph Verheyden*, ed. John S. Kloppenborg, Geert Roskam and Stefan Schorn (Leuven: Peeters, 2022), 199–246.
[22] Josephus, *J.W.* 2.254–61; *Ant.* 20.164–71.
[23] See further Pervo, *Dating Acts*, 161–6.
[24] Josephus, *Ant.* 19.343–50.

meets a sudden demise.[25] All these events are, in combination, reported nowhere else but in Josephus. An appeal to unknown and speculative sources (like oral tradition) cannot trump what we know from surviving accounts. Accordingly, Acts is best dated sometime after 93 CE.

Another indication of date is the author's use of a Pauline letter collection. The story of Paul's escape from Antioch (Acts 9:25) borrows language from 2 Corinthians 11:33.[26] 2 Corinthians provides the reason why Paul had to escape from Antioch, a reason apparently assumed in Acts. From the same chapter in 2 Corinthians (11:25), evidently, the author of Acts presented data that Paul was stoned (Acts 14:19-20) and shipwrecked (27:44). Acts probably takes its portrait of Paul the persecutor from Galatians 1:13, borrowing the distinctive verb *portheō* (Acts 9:21) and the distinctive collocation "being a zealot" (*zēlōtēs hyparchōn* in Gal 1:14; Acts 22:3). Key phrases also appear from Ephesians, such as "preaching peace" (in Eph 2:17 and Acts 10:36) and "with all humility" (in Eph 4:2 and Acts 20:19).[27] From Romans there is also thematic and verbal overlap that God is not a "receiver of faces" (*prosōpolēmptēs*, Acts 10:34 from Rom 2:11), as well as the distinctive phrase "boiling in spirit" (*tōi pneumati zeō*, Rom 12:11; Acts 18:25).[28] Acts's extensive borrowings from 1 Thessalonians have been documented elsewhere.[29] If the author of Acts knew 1 Thessalonians, 2 Corinthians, Galatians, Ephesians, and Romans, he was probably using a Pauline letter collection, a collection that—at its earliest—appeared at the end of the first century CE.[30] Probably the collection that Acts employed was later, however, since canonical 2 Corinthians is not attested before 120 CE.[31]

The author of Acts reported that Jesus's devotees were first called Christians (*Christianoi*) in Antioch (Acts 11:26). The name *Christianoi* is not attested prior to Ignatius, who was from Antioch.[32] The earliest dating of Ignatius's letters is about 110 CE. Yet recent and revised datings put them in the 130s or 140s.[33] According to Andrew Gregory, there is no secure evidence to prove the use of Acts until Irenaeus

---

[25] See further Richard Pervo, *Dating Acts*, 170–8.
[26] Note the use of διὰ τοῦ τείχους and the verb χαλάω.
[27] εὐαγγελίζω εἰρήνην; μετὰ πάσης ταπεινοφροσύνης.
[28] Pervo collects about ninety uses of Pauline letters by the author of Acts in *Dating Acts*, 139–40.
[29] Lars Aejmelaeus, *Die Rezeption der Paulusbriefe in der Miletrede (Apg. 20:18-35)* (Helsinki: Suomalainen Tiedeakatemia, 1987); Steve Walton, *Leadership and Lifestyle: The Portrait of Paul in the Miletus Speech and 1 Thessalonians*, SNTSMS 108 (Cambridge: Cambridge University Press, 2004), esp. 157–85. I agree with Aejmelaeus against Walton that the author of Acts used 1 Thessalonians directly.
[30] Pervo, *Dating Acts*, 343; Harry Y. Gamble, *Books and Readers: A History of Early Christian Texts* (New Haven: Yale University Press, 1995), 82–143; Ian J. Elmer, "The Pauline Letters as Community Documents," in *Collecting Early Christian Letters*, ed. Bronwen Neil and Pauline Allen (Cambridge: Cambridge University Press, 2015), 37–53.
[31] Pervo, *Dating Acts*, 62. 2 Cor was apparently unknown to 1 Clem.
[32] Ignatius, *Eph.* 11:2; *Magn.* 2:4; *Rom.* 3:2.
[33] T. D. Barnes, "The Date of Ignatius," *ExpTim* 120 (2008): 119–30; Allen Brent, "Ignatius of Antioch in Second Century Asia Minor," in *Intertextuality in the Second Century*, ed. D. J. Bingham and C. N. Jefford (Leiden: Brill, 2016), 62–86; Jonathan Lookadoo, "The Date and Authenticity of the Ignatian Letters: An Outline of Recent Discussions," *Currents in Biblical Research* 19, no. 1 (2020): 88–114.

about 180 CE.³⁴ A later dating is also supported by arguments which contextualize Luke-Acts as a response to Marcion who flourished in the 130s and 140s.³⁵

The evidence as a whole inclines me to date Acts between 120 and 150 CE. This would make Acts contemporary with the writing of the *Declaration*. As I have pointed out, however, the author of Acts seems familiar with traditions that postdate the *Declaration* (Simon identified as the Great Power). Below I will address the question whether the author knew the *Declaration* itself. For now, I turn to an exposition of Acts 8:9-24.

Simon's Debut

Acts 8 begins with followers of "the Way" (the Jesus movement) scattering from Jerusalem, spreading the gospel as they go. One of these followers was the "deacon" Philip (Acts 6:5), who evangelized an unnamed city of Samaria and worked wonders there. In the midst of this Samarian mission, Simon appears.

> A certain man by the name of Simon was in the city beforehand working as a magus and amazing the nation of Samaria. He claimed to be somebody great. Everyone from small to great fawned on him, claiming, "He is the so-called Great Power of God." They fawned on him because he had for a long time amazed them with the deeds of a magus. So when they believed in Philip who preached the gospel of the kingdom of God and the name of Jesus Christ, and men and women were being baptized, Simon also believed and was baptized. He clung closely to Philip. While observing the signs and great miracles, he was amazed.
>
> When the apostles in Jerusalem heard that Samaria had received the message of God, they sent to them Peter and John. These men descended and prayed over them that they receive holy Spirit, for it had not yet fallen on any of them. They were only baptized in the name of the lord Jesus. At that time, they laid their hands on them and they received holy Spirit.
>
> When Simon saw that the Spirit was given by the application of the apostles' hands, he offered them money, saying, "Give me also this authority so that whoever receives my hands laid upon them receives holy Spirit." But Peter said to him, "To hell with you and your money, since you supposed you could acquire the gift of God through cash! There is no lot or share for you in this service, for your heart is not straight before God. Repent therefore from this vice and supplicate the lord—if

---

[34] Gregory, *The Reception of Luke and Acts in the Period before Irenaeus: Looking for Luke in the Second Century*, WUNT II/169 (Tübingen: Mohr Siebeck, 2003), 299–351.

[35] John T. Townsend, "The Date of Luke-Acts," in *Luke-Acts: New Perspectives from the Society of Biblical Literature Seminar*, ed. Charles H. Talbert (New York: Crossroad, 1984), 47–62; Joseph B. Tyson, *Marcion and Luke-Acts: A Defining Struggle* (Columbia: University of South Carolina Press, 2006), 50–120; William O. Walker, "The Portrayal of Aquila and Priscilla in Acts: The Question of Sources," NTS 54 (2008): 479–95; Matthias Klinghardt, *The Oldest Gospel and the Formation of the Canonical Gospels*, 2 vols. (Leuven: Peeters, 2021).

he will forgive the supposition of your heart. For I see you in the bile of bitterness and in the chain of injustice." Simon answered: "Supplicate the lord for me that nothing happen to me as you said!" (Acts 8:9-24)

"The City"

If "the city" in which Simon worked designates any specific settlement, it was not Flavia Neapolis—which had not yet been built—but Sebaste, the city in central Palestine reconstructed by Herod the Great in honor of Augustus (27 BCE). Sebaste was a Hellenic city, with a temple to the divine emperor on its Acropolis and cults to several Greco-Roman deities (notably, Kore or Persephone). The Samaritan presence in the city was not large.[36] "The nation of Samaria" mentioned by the author of Acts would thus refer to inhabitants of the province of Samaria, which included, not just Samaritans, but a range of peoples.[37] It would make sense for Simon to earn his keep in a large and religiously diverse place like Sebaste.[38]

Simon's Titles

Simon is said to call himself "somebody great" (Acts 8:9). This was probably not Simon's actual way of self-identifying. It was, instead, a way for the author of Acts to depict him as a boaster.[39] In Acts, claiming "to be somebody (great)" is negative. It was the vaunt of Theudas, the revolutionary of Acts 5:36, a man said to be a false prophet who "came to nothing." Importantly, Simon never said he was the Great Power, though he never rejected the title either. Yet that was enough for the author of Acts to raise suspicions. Note that when "Herod" did not reject deifying praise, he was immediately "eaten by worms and died" (Acts 12:22-23).

Modern discussions of Simon mostly focus on his attributed title: "the so-called Great Power of God" (*hē dunamis tou theou hē kaloumenē megalē*) (Acts 8:10). The phrases "of God" and ("so-)called" have often been viewed as later additions.[40] (We see

---

[36] Reinhard Pummer, *Samaritans in Flavius Josephus* (Tübingen: Mohr Siebeck, 2009), 45.
[37] P. W. van der Horst, "Samaritans and Hellenism," in *Hellenism-Judaism-Christianity: Essays on Their Interaction* (Kampen: Kok Pharos, 1994), 48–58.
[38] Jürgen Zangenberg, *Frühes Christentum in Samarien: Topographische und traditionsgeschichtliche Studien zu den Samarientexten im Johannesevangelium* (Tübingen: Francke, 1998), 47–56; Zangenberg, "Δύναμις τοῦ θεοῦ," 520–5; Martina Böhm, *Samarien und die Samaritai bei Lukas: Eine Studie zum religionshistorischen und traditionsgeschichtlichen Hintergrund der lukanischen Samarientexte und zu deren topographischer Verhaftung*, WUNT II/111 (Tübingen: Mohr Siebeck, 1999), 37–101, 288.
[39] Heintz, *Simon "le Magicien"*, 116–18.
[40] E.g., Ernst Haenchen, *The Acts of the Apostles: A Commentary* (Oxford: Blackwell, 1971), 303, 307; Hans Conzelmann, *A Commentary on the Acts of the Apostles*, trans. James Limburg et al., Hermeneia (Philadelphia: Fortress, 1987), 63; Beyschlag, *Simon Magus*, 99–105; Lüdemann, *Untersuchungen*, 39–42, 47; Pétrement, *Separate God*, 241; Richard Pervo, *Acts: A Commentary*, Hermeneia (Minneapolis: Fortress, 2009), 209.

"of God" added in Luke 22:69, which adapts Mark 14:62.)[41] The use of "(so-)called" (*kaloumenē*) adds a note of skepticism and hints that "the Great Power" was a known quantity by the time the author of Acts wrote. Apparently the claim of the Samarians was that Simon was simply "the Great Power" (*hē dunamis megalē*).

Some scholars assert that this claim corresponded to the Simon's declaration: "I am the Great Power."[42] But the inference is unsound. Acts tells us that Simon claimed to be "somebody great" (8:9), not the Great Power. Only the Samarians called Simon the Great Power, not Simon himself.[43]

The Great Power title evidently refers to a divine being, otherwise unspecified. Recall that in the *Declaration*, the Great Power is not the highest deity; it referred to a being called "Mind," who fathered Thought (*Epinoia*).[44] The varied usage of "(the) Great Power" in other sources indicates that it could refer to God Most High or to a subordinate power.[45] Nothing in Acts clinches one interpretation or the other. The Samarians could have viewed Simon as a lower power or as the high God. Later interpreters chose which view made best sense to them.[46]

Simon's Deification

According to Acts, the Samarians deified Simon due to his wondrous works. The Simon of Acts does not, however, deify himself.[47] Celsus, the first to compose a book-length critique of Christianity, insisted that self-deifiers were plentiful in Palestine.[48] Magical practitioners (as attested in the *Greek Magical Papyri*) also sometimes claimed a divine

---

[41] See further Conzelmann, *Acts of the Apostles*, 63; Beyschlag, *Simon Magus*, 99–105; Lüdemann, *Untersuchungen*, 39–42, 47; Lüdemann, *Acts of the Apostles*, 116–17; Pétrement, *Separate God*, 241; Pervo, *Acts*, 209.

[42] Foerster, "Die 'ersten Gnostiker' Simon und Menander," in *Le origini dello Gnosticismo: Colloquio di Messina, 13-18 Aprile 1966*, ed. Ugo Bianchi (Leiden: Brill, 1970), 193–4; Lüdemann, *Untersuchungen*, 40; Conzelmann, *Acts of the Apostles*, 63.

[43] Pace Theissen, "Simon Magus," 413 (*seine Selbstapotheose*); cf. Craig Keener, *Acts: An Exegetical Commentary*, 4 vols. (Grand Rapids: Baker Academic, 2013), 3.1511 ("Simon is clearly wrong to claim the title").

[44] *Ref.* 6.18.3.

[45] Hegesippus called God "the Great Power" (τῆς μεγάλης δυνάμεως) according to Eusebius, *Hist. eccl.* 2.23.13. Nevertheless, in *PGM* 4.1275–80, "the great power" (τὴν μεγίστην δύναμιν) is subordinate to a higher God (ὑπὸ κυρίου θεοῦ τεταγμένην). Cf. *PGM* 4.640. In a Lydian inscription, Mēn is the "great power of the immortal God" (μεγάλη δύναμις τοῦ ἀθανάτου θεοῦ) (printed with comments in G. H. R. Horsley, *New Documents Illustrating Early Christianity* [North Ryde: Macquarie University, 1983], 31–2). More sources are cited in Beyschlag, *Simon Magus*, 106–20. In other sources, the Great Power also appears as a subordinate being or manifestation of the high God (2 Macc 3.38–9; Philo, *Mos.* 1.111; *Fug.* 97; *Abr.* 183; *Leg.* 3.73). Cf. *Allog.* (NHC XI,3) 50.23, 57.39. See further Lüdemann, *Untersuchungen*, 46–9.

[46] Rudolph, "Simon: Magus oder Gnosticus?" 320–8.

[47] Pace Lüdemann, *Early Christianity according to the Traditions in Acts: A Commentary*, trans. John Bowden (London: SCM Press, 1989), 96; DeConick, *Gnostic New Age*, 101; Foerster, "Die ersten Gnostiker Simon und Menander," 190–6 at 194; Jarl Fossum, "Samaritan Sects and Movements," in *The Samaritans*, ed. Alan D. Crown (Tübingen: Mohr Siebeck, 1989), 293–389 at 364–5.

[48] Origen, *Cels.* 7.9.

identity or temporary immortalization.⁴⁹ Accordingly, some scholars who accept that Simon was a "magus" have inferred that he claimed divinity.

This judgment is hasty, however, since we do not know if the historical Simon self-described as a magus or whether his performance as magus is a construction of Acts. It is, at any rate, methodologically dubious to use parallels from later polemical literature in order to fill in gaps from different texts. Even if we credit Celsus, what he polemically wrote about self-deifying prophets in Palestine in the reign of Marcus Aurelius tells us nothing certain about what Simon said about himself in Samaria 140 years earlier.⁵⁰ Supposed religio-historical parallels ought not to control the interpretation of Acts. It is essential first to understand the context and tendencies of the text itself.

The author of Acts was in the habit of portraying Gentiles as deifiers of anyone who produced a miracle. We see this in the episode of Paul and Barnabas at Lystra (Acts 14:8-28). The apostolic team performed a healing. All of the sudden the whole town is shown garlanding an ox for sacrifice to the duo as incarnations of Zeus as Hermes. The implied reader is meant, it seems, to have a chuckle at these polytheistic dupes.

The author of Acts did not assume that the Samarians in Acts 8 were good monotheists. They were, after all, just as ready to deify Simon as any Gentile group. Evidently the author—probably with good reason—assumed that a Samarian city like Sebaste was predominately Gentile.

"Magus"?

In Acts, Simon as "the Great Power" is associated with the works of a magus (Acts 8:9). Whether or not Simon was or called himself a magus cannot be known.⁵¹ What we do know is that ancient authors regularly accused their opponents of practicing magic. Simon "doing the works of a magus" (*mageuōn*) is not an objective description, but an attempt to create a (narrative) reality.⁵²

To be sure, a "magus," unlike the term *goēs* ("sorcerer" or "charlatan") is a polyvalent term. It can refer to a Persian priest, an independent provider of purifications and initiations, or simply a quack.⁵³ It is true that, in the first century CE, doing the work of

---

49 Morton Smith, *Jesus the Magician* (New York: Harper & Row, 1978), 96–104; M. David Litwa, *Becoming Divine: An Introduction to Deification in Western Culture* (Eugene: Cascade, 2013), 70, 73–4.

50 *Pace* Foerster, who quotes Origen *Cels.* 7.9 and comments that these "prophets betray a self-consciousness similar to that of Simon" (*Gnosis: A Selection* 1.28).

51 *Pace* Harold Remus who claimed, on the basis of Acts 8:9, that Simon applied the term "magician" to himself ("Magic, Method, Madness," *MTSR* 11 [1999]: 258–98 at 270).

52 J. Z. Smith, "Trading Places," in *Ancient Magic and Ritual Power*, ed. Marvin Meyer and Paul Mirecki, Religions in the Greco-Roman World 129 (Leiden: Brill, 1995), 13–27; Heintz, *Simon "le Magicien"*, 36–54, 102–42; David Frankfurter, "Ancient Magic in a New Key: Refining an Exotic Discipline in the History of Religions," in *Guide to the Study of Ancient Magic*, ed. David Frankfurter (Leiden: Brill, 2019), 3–20; Radcliffe Edmonds, *Drawing Down the Moon: Magic in the Ancient Greco-Roman World* (Princeton: Princeton University Press, 2019), 1–54, 379–418.

53 For the ancient magus, see Graf, *Magic*, 20–117; Dickie, *Magic and Magicians*, 162–250; Haar, *Simon Magus*, 33–70; Costantini, "Dynamics," 101–22.

a magus (healing, purifying, raising the dead) could be respectable among some circles in certain circumstances.[54]

Nonetheless, the context and usage of the author of Acts indicates that Simon doing such work was not viewed positively.[55] Simon performing as a magus puts him in the same league as Elymas the blinded magus (Acts 13:6, 8) and contrasts him with the apostolic wonderworker Philip. Simon might have astounded people, just as Philip did, but the wonders of Simon were inferior to those of Philip, such that Simon himself was amazed by what Philip could perform.[56] The author of Acts contrasted Simon with Philip; Philip manifested the "true" power of God, Simon according to Acts was not, in fact, so great.[57]

Historically speaking, it is probably inaccurate to describe Simon as a magus or magician. After all, there is no evidence in Acts that Simon performed any "magical" deeds. He is not portrayed as drowning cats by night or whispering formulas under a full moon. He never uses a book of spells, shows off stones which absorb astral energies, wears a talisman filled with fingernails or feathers, employs barbarous names, or calls upon the tribe of daimones. If the author of Acts had such data about Simon, we can be sure he would have used it to fill out his portrait of Simon "performing as a magus" (Acts 8:9).

These observations are important since some readers of Acts uncritically accept that Simon was a magician. After all, nearly everybody—though significantly *not the author of Acts*—calls him "Simon magus." (The old adage works here: if you repeat something long enough, one is bound to believe it.) Some scholars go further and invent data to make Simon fit a "magus" profile. For instance, J. D. M. Derrett claimed that Simon practiced "spirit-possession" and spoke "in trance with the deity's/demon's voice."[58] He also described Simon as a "peripatetic practitioner of the occult."[59] Such data does not derive from Acts. The sources of such eisegesis are often patristic reports, where Simon does come to be called "magus."[60]

---

[54] Apuleius, *Met.* 2.12; Philo, *Somn.* 1.53; *Prob.* 74.; *Sib. Or.* 3.227. For a magus raising the dead, see Lucian, *Men.* 6; *Fug.* 8; Chariton, *Chaer.* 5.9.4; Diogenes Laertius, *Vita phil.* 8.1.3; 9.11.61; Dio Chrysostom, *Or.* 36.38–48.

[55] Zangenberg, "Δύναμις τοῦ θεοῦ," 526–9; Marco Frenschkowski, *Magie im antiken Christentum: Eine Studie zur Alten Kirche und ihrem Umfeld* (Stuttgart: Anton Hiersemann, 2016), 212–18; Melissa Aubin, "Beobachtungen zur Magie im Neuen Testament," *Zeitschrift für Neues Testament* 7 (2001): 16–24.

[56] Haar, *Simon Magus*, 176.

[57] See further Hans-Josef Klauck, *Magic and Paganism in Early Christianity: The World of the Acts of the Apostles*, trans. Brian McNeil (Fortress: Minneapolis, 2003), 18–19; Todd Penner, *In Praise of Christian Origins: Stephen and the Hellenists in Lukan Apologetic Historiography*, Emory Studies in Early Christianity (London: T&T Clark, 2004), 196–208.

[58] Derrett, "Simon Magus (Acts 8 9–24)," *ZNW* 73 (1982): 52–68 at 53.

[59] Derrett, "Simon Magus," 53. Derrett's thesis that Simon intended to purchase from Peter something like a pagan priesthood is also unconvincing (61–2, 68).

[60] Heintz, *Simon "le Magicien"*, 4–26.

Was Simon Converted?

In the opinion of April DeConick, "Simon's conversion is bogus. It is a Christian attempt at propaganda."[61] In this judgment, she followed her teacher, Jarl Fossum, who called Simon's conversion "unthinkable."[62] By contrast, Stephen Haar observed: "The skepticism voiced by various commentators over the genuineness of Simon's conversion cannot claim to be occasioned by anything in the text."[63] Other scholars concur.[64] Let's examine the evidence.

In Acts, Simon submits to baptism, a baptism which is later qualified as "in the name of the Lord Jesus" (Acts 8:16). On the surface, no question mark is thrown against the validity of Simon's baptism and the reality it represents (the forgiveness of sins).[65] The author simply wrote that Simon "believed" (*episteusen*) (Acts 8:13). The object of Simon's belief is unspecified, but one can infer from the context that it was the contents of Philip's message (Acts 8:12). According to Acts, then, Simon had a legitimate baptism.

Yet was the historical Simon baptized? Lüdemann understood Simon's baptism as a way for the author of Acts to subordinate Simon to Philip. It was an act of power over Simon, thus probably the author's invention.[66] In my view, however, seeing baptism as an act of dominance is questionable. What happened to the historical Simon is out of reach. If we limit ourselves to Simon's character in the story, however, *he* at least would probably not have accepted the idea that being baptized made him subordinate to Philip. Baptism for Simon was a way to receive Spirit and power and to become a Christian leader.

There is another point to consider. To the author of Acts, it seems, Simon's baptism was something of an embarrassment. It would have been easier for him to dismiss Simon as a non-Christian contender of the apostles. Nevertheless, he had to pass on what likely came to him as tradition—that Simon was a genuinely baptized believer. As a believer, Simon had at least the potential for gaining legitimate spiritual power. It is true, of course, that the heresiological tradition almost unanimously rejected the authenticity of Simon's faith and baptism, but we need not follow it.[67]

Though the author of Acts could not outright deny that Simon was a Christian, he had subtle ways of planting suspicions about his character. In Acts 8:14, the pillar apostles Peter and John descend from Jerusalem to supervise and legitimate

---

[61] DeConick, *Gnostic New Age*, 104.
[62] Fossum, *Name of God*, 164; cf. Pearson, *Ancient Gnosticism*, 30; Gilles Quispel, *Gnosis als Weltreligion* (Zürich: Origo, 1951), 53; Hans Jonas, *The Gnostic Religion: The Message of the Alien God and the Beginnings of Christianity* (Boston: Beacon, 1958), 103.
[63] Haar, *Simon Magus*, 180.
[64] E.g., Rick Strelan, *Strange Acts: Studies in the Cultural World of the Acts of the Apostles*, BZNW 126 (Berlin: de Gruyter, 2004), 212; Patrick Fabien, "La conversion de Simon le magicien [Ac 8,4–25]," *Bib.* 91 (2010): 210–40 at 218–28.
[65] Later authors would claim that, though Simon was baptized, his heart was not enlightened by Spirit (Cyril, *Catechetical Lectures*, prologue 2; cf. 3.7; 6.14).
[66] Lüdemann, *The Acts of the Apostles: What Really Happened in the Earliest Days of the Church* (Amherst: Prometheus, 2005), 117, 120.
[67] In the *Apostolic Constitutions* 6.7.2 (Metzger), Simon not only believed and was baptized, but persevered in fasting and prayer (προσκαρτεροῦντος τῇ νηστείᾳ καὶ τῇ προσευχῇ).

the Samarian mission. There is reasonable theory that the author of Acts invented this episode (Acts 8:14-25). It seems sensible that he had a tradition about Philip evangelizing Samaria. He then somewhat hurriedly replaced Philip with Peter, prince of the apostles, who was more qualified to initiate the Gentile mission (Acts 10)—as well as to put Simon in his place. Philip re-emerges later in Acts 8:26, picking up smoothly after he disappeared in 8:14.[68]

The insertion of the chief apostles is not without cost to the narrative. It puts a mysterious and significant delay between the believing Samarians' baptism and their reception of the Spirit.[69] This is because the Spirit only comes (in this story) when the apostles lay their hands on the converts.[70] One might assume that Simon too received the Spirit through the apostles—though this is never said.[71] There may even be indication that Simon never received Spirit. After all, if Simon could not convey it, he may never have had it. We are never told that Peter and John laid their hands on Simon.

Simon saw the Spirit transferred and offered to pay money for this power (Acts 8:17-19). It is sometimes assumed that Simon, once he obtained Spirit, was going to charge other people to receive it through him.[72] (In fact, this is exactly what Epiphanius later claimed in the fourth century CE.) Simon would thus fit the typology of the greedy magician. In Acts, however, Simon only offers to give *away* money, not to receive it. The author of Acts never said how Simon would have used his new authority.

That being said, the author of Acts does make it difficult to sympathize with Simon. Observe the swift and biting nature of Peter's response: "To hell with you and your money!" (8:20).[73] The stinging rebuke seems overblown and perhaps even hypocritical. This same apostle oversaw the deaths of two Christians who failed to pay the church what they claimed (5:1-11).[74] Perhaps (as Irenaeus said) Simon misunderstood spiritual realities because of his "magical" mentality. But this again assumes that Simon was a magician.

---

[68] See further C. R. Matthews, "The Acts of Peter and Luke's Intertextual Heritage," *Semeia* 80 (1997): 207–22 at 214–19.
[69] Elsewhere in Acts there is no delay between baptism and receiving the Spirit (Acts 2:23; 10:44–8).
[70] In other cases (e.g., Acts 9:17–18), an apostle is not necessary, and the reception of the Spirit precedes baptism (e.g., Acts 10:44–8).
[71] C. K. Barrett, "Light on the Holy Spirit from Simon Magus," in *Les Actes des Apôtres: Traditions, redaction, théologie*, ed. J. Kremer (Leuven: Leuven University Press, 1979), 281–95 at 291). Cf. Klauck, *Magic and Paganism*, 20. Kaspar Dalgaard is too hasty in his claim that Simon did not receive Spirit ("Peter and Simon in the Acts of Peter; Between Magic and Miracles," in *Studies on Magic and Divination in the Biblical World*, ed. Helen R. Jacobus, et al. (Piscataway: Gorgias Press, 2019), 169–80 at 171.
[72] G. H. Twelftree, "Jesus and Magic in Luke-Acts," in *Jesus and Paul: Global Perspectives in Honor of James D. G. Dunn. A Festschrift for his 70th Birthday*, ed. B. J. Oropeza, D. K. Roberson, D. C. Mohrmann (London: T&T Clark, 2009), 46–58 at 49; D. Marguerat, "Magic and Miracle in the Acts of the Apostles," in *Magic in the Biblical World: From the Rod of Aaron to the Ring of Solomon*, ed. T. Klutz (London: Bloomsbury, 2003), 100–24 at 119; Klauck, *Magic and Paganism*, 20–1.
[73] Τὸ ἀργύριόν σου σὺν σοὶ εἴη εἰς ἀπώλειαν. By his condemnation, Fabien points out, it is Peter who comically resembles a magician ("Conversion," 229–30).
[74] Barrett has shown how sensitive the author of Luke-Acts was about money, and how quick he was to disassociate Christian prophets from profit ("Light," 287–92; cf. Heintz, *Simon "Le magicien"*, 122–7).

Even if Simon did wish to monetize his authority, it would be no sure sign that his faith was feigned.[75] After all, "the worker is worthy of his wages" (Luke 10:7). Perhaps Simon's mistake was an honest one. Readers can well observe that the immediate connection of laying on hands and the reception of Spirit seems to work by the operation itself in Acts 8:17.[76] Here the Spirit does not blow where it wills (John 3:8). It arrives when the apostles apply their hands.

It is unfortunate that some scholars repeat the heresiological claim that Peter cursed Simon.[77] As Patrick Fabien points out, Peter speaks in the optative mood.[78] He states a potential reality, not a fact. Simon's destruction is not willed by Peter, who orders Simon to pray. Harsh as it is, the reprimand is designed to inspire repentance, and it apparently succeeded.

Peter's rebuke could well have ended at this point. Nevertheless, the author of Acts adds a remark not demanded so much by the narrative as by the will to undercut Simon's authority. The apostle pronounces: "You do not have a lot or share in this message!" (Acts 8:21). This is probably not an attempt to exclude Simon from "the Christian community," but only from the apostolic tribe.[79]

At the same time, Peter's exclusionary tactic seems like overkill. Why cannot Simon, after the proper training, become a teacher and vessel of Spirit like Paul did later in the story? Paul had an even worse record prior to his conversion. At the beginning of Acts 8, the curtain opens on Paul (aka Saul) the ruthless persecutor of the church and an accomplice in Stephen's murder (Acts 8:1, 3). In spite of his past, Paul became a fully authorized Christian leader, dispenser of Spirit, and the chief protagonist in the latter half of Acts (13-28). All this was granted to Paul by the Jerusalem apostles—who, incidentally, expected Paul to make donations to their church (Gal 2:10).[80]

Simon's offer to pay money is, by contrast, a venial sin Still, he is officiously excluded from apostolic privilege, and not authorized to be a missionary.[81] Peter offers a clairvoyant rationale: Simon's "heart is not straight before God" (Acts 8:21). These words are carefully crafted. They echo Psalm 77:37 (LXX), a verse which speaks of the refractory attitude of ancient Israelites. These sinners of old beheld divine miracles and rebelled, since "their heart was not straight" with God.

---

[75] Susan Garrett's view that Simon's offer of money is "quintessentially satanic" and indicative of "diabolical greed" is excessive (*The Demise of the Devil: Magic and the Demonic in Luke's Writings* [Minneapolis: Fortress, 1989], 72). For further critique of Garrett, see Heintz, *Simon "le magicien"*, 15–22.

[76] The author of Acts tried to distinguish "true religion" and "magic" (Garrett, *Demise*, 76-8), but as J. D. G. Dunn points out, the "Christian practice of laying on hands or exorcism may look very much the same [as magic], and indeed have a very similar effect (cf. [Acts] 8.9–11 with 8.6, 8 and 13)" (*The Acts of the Apostles*, [Valley Forge: Trinity Press, 1996], 109). The hand imposition "had all the characteristics of a magic technique" (Bruce Malina and John Pilch, *Social-Science Commentary on the Book of Acts* [Minneapolis: Fortress, 2008], 64).

[77] E.g., Garrett, *Demise*, 70; Strelan, *Strange Acts*, 212–15; Goran Vidović, "Good Doggy, Bad Dog: Rivalry between Peter and Simon Magus in Early Christian Apocryphal Literature," *Philotheos* 16 (2016): 58–72 at 61.

[78] Fabien, "Conversion," 233 (εἴη εἰς ἀπώλειαν).

[79] *Pace* Dalgaard, "Peter and Simon," 171.

[80] Pétrement, *Separate God*, 243.

[81] See further Haar, *Simon Magus*, 183; Fabien, "Conversion," 231–2.

Would Simon—who beheld such miracles—share their fate? Peter commands him to repent and pray (8:22). "For I see," the apostle adds, "you in the bile of bitterness and in the chain of injustice" (v.23). The words are harsh, though admittedly less mordant than Jesus's rebuke of Peter: "Get behind me, Satan!" (Mark 8:33; Matt 16:23). Haar argues that Peter's censure of Simon, "is neither a sentence of condemnation nor excommunication, but a rebuke ... given in pious duty to a 'neighbor.'"[82] Haar is to be commended for not replicating patristic polemic about Simon being excommunicated and cursed. At the same time, he is aware that bile and bitterness are characteristic of the idolater in Deuteronomy 29:17 (LXX).[83] The allusion to the idolater in this passage and to the rebel in Psalm 77 subtly cast aspersions on Simon's character.

Still, Simon is not unrepentant. He does not angrily stamp away, conniving to begin a competing movement. Instead, he wails for prayer (8:24). The apostles are Simon's mediators before God; Simon is in complete—even groveling—submission to them.[84] Codex Bezae even says that at the end of this episode, Simon wept without ceasing.[85] In this way, Simon resembles Simon Peter who "wept bitterly" after he had denied Jesus three times (Luke 22:62).

Results

In sum, we have an ambiguous portrait of Simon. On the surface, the author of Acts portrays a repentant, apparently believing Simon, stiffly rebuked for his apostolic pretensions, and humbled—even humiliated—before the pillar apostles. On the level of allusion and inference, however, the legitimacy of Simon's faith and Christian identity is queried. First, Simon is never explicitly said to receive Spirit. Intertextual echoes of ancient rebellion and idolatry reverberate behind the story. Although Simon wails, the reader does not know if his heart becomes right. And though Simon begs, Peter and the apostles (somewhat unkindly) do not pray for him or lay their hands upon him. In the end, fans and critics of Simon can (and do) draw very different conclusions from this tale.[86]

---

[82] Haar, *First Gnostic*, 185, comparing Matt 18:15; Lev 19:17.
[83] "Let there not grow among you a root sprouting with bitter gall" (μή τίς ἐστιν ἐν ὑμῖν ῥίζα ἄνω φύουσα ἐν χολῇ καὶ πικρίᾳ). Cf. Lam 3:15, 19; Isa 58.6 (σύνδεσμον ἀδικίας). See further Heintz, *Simon "Le magicien"*, 127–30. Garrett takes the language to imply "that Simon, though he has supposedly entered into the Christian community, is still an idolater, subject to punishment because [he is] still trapped (along with all idolaters) under the authority of Satan" (*Demise*, 71).
[84] Heintz, *Simon "Le magicien"*, 141–2.
[85] See further Joseph Rius-Camps and Jenny Read-Heimerdinger, *The Message of Acts in Codex Bezae: A Comparison with the Alexandrian Tradition*, 3 vols., Library of New Testament Studies 302 (New York: T&T Clark, 2006), 2.139, 146–7.
[86] See further Fabien, "Conversion," 238–9.

Social History

What was the author of Acts trying to accomplish in his own time by telling this story (or rather stories) about Simon? Why bother with Simon at all, who is nothing but a minor character in a narrative charting the triumphant march of the gospel toward Rome?

My hypothesis is that Simon could not be ignored. He could not be ignored because the author of Acts knew of Simonians in the region of Samaria. In order to undermine their claims to Christian identity, he invented a tale about Simon being a former magician as well as Peter's rebuke of Simon. The author assumed that Simon founded the Simonians. He could thus undermine the Simonians by neutralizing Simon. The fact that Simon is not completely damned, however, might indicate that the author still held out hope for Simonians.[87]

According to this hypothesis, a Simonian Christian movement existed in Samaria when the author of Acts wrote between 120 and 150 CE. The Simonian movement was a problem for this author because it complicated his neat picture of early Christian beginnings from Jerusalem. He could not deny that Simonianism was a form of Christianity. To the contrary, he portrayed their founder as a baptized believer. The problem was, according to Acts, that Simonian Christianity was without apostolic approval and the inspiration of the Spirit.

The author assumed that Simonian Christianity in Samaria was initiated by a wonderworking figure called Simon. But the author tried to depict Simon as a self-promoting quack. According to Acts, there was nothing apostolic about Simon and therefore his group lacked credentials. The only true Christianity was the author's Petrine (or Jerusalemite) brand. But if and when this brand actually arrived in Samaria is a matter of dispute. Recall that the author portrays "all" Samarians lauding Simon (Acts 8:10). The fact that "all" Samarians initially follow Simon may hint at the extent of Simonian Christianity in Samaria.

The author of Acts probably assumed that Simonian Christians came from Gentile populations. He seems to have known little about Samaritan Yahwism in Palestine. Gerizim is never mentioned, nor the Samaritan Pentateuch, nor the Samaritan view of the prophets. According to Acts, Simonians were likely not former Samaritans; they were portrayed as gullible deifiers who became Christians independently of Peter and Paul.

Did Simonians in early-second-century Samaria venerate Simon as "the Great Power" or is this a fiction of the author of Acts? One cannot entirely rule out invention here, but the use of "the *so-called* Great Power" indicates that the author was using a title known to Simonians and others. We can confirm that the title had a Simonian flavor from its use in the *Declaration*. In the *Declaration*, however, the title is never applied to Simon but to *all* Christians conformed to God's image.

From where, then, did the author of Acts learn of "the Great Power" title? It was a designation that could refer to a variety of divinities in the Greco-Roman world.[88]

---

[87] Theissen, "Simon Magus," 414 (citing earlier sources).
[88] See n. 45 above.

But the author of Acts probably did not pluck it from the general culture to speak of Simon specifically. My conjecture is that he had some kind of Simonian source. Prior to Irenaeus, the only surviving and distinctly Simonian source to mention "the Great Power" is the *Declaration*.[89]

This observation does not prove that the author of Acts knew the *Declaration*. Yet there is another point to consider. As Lüdemann observed, there is subtle evidence that the author knew Simonian terminology referring to Simon's primal "Thought" (Acts 8:22).[90] Lüdemann failed to note, however, that the word for "Thought" used in Acts is distinctive to the *Declaration*. That is to say, the author of Acts referred to the "supposition" (*epinoia*) of Simon's heart (Acts 8:22), which is, incidentally, the only time this word is used—not just in Acts, but in the entire New Testament. In the heresiological reports, Simon's Thought almost exclusively appears as *Ennoia*.[91] Only in the *Declaration* does she appear as *Epinoia*, and *only* as *Epinoia*.[92]

This observation is suggestive, but it is still no smoking gun for dependence. One must be content to hypothesize that the author of Acts knew some of the distinctive terms of early Simonianism also represented in the *Declaration*. He then placed some of its terminology in the mouth of first-century Samarian followers of Simon (Acts 8:9-10). Interestingly, although the author of the *Declaration* believed that *every* person could be a divine manifestation, the author of Acts portrayed divinity as ascribed to Simon alone. In doing so, he either adjusted Simonian theology to emphasize the (negatively colored) deification of Simon or he knew Simonian traditions in Samaria or Rome that did in fact identify Simon with the Great Power.

Conclusion

To sum up, why did the author of Acts pause to confront Simon in Samaria? At the very least, I believe, he felt threatened by real Simonians in Palestine. All was not right with Christianity in this region, and the author could not ignore a place so close to Jerusalem, source of the apostolic mission (Acts 1:8).

What, then, can we conclude about early-second-century Simonians in Samaria? Quite in spite of himself, the author of Acts hinted that there was another form of Christianity in Samaria whose roots could not be traced back to Jerusalem. Instead, Simonians in Samaria traced their form of Christianity back to Simon. Apparently Simonians in Samaria venerated Simon not as a magus, but as a divine manifestation (the Great Power). The strategy of the author of Acts was not to deny Simon's (and the Simonians') Christian identity, but to deprive this founder of any legitimate authority and power to convey Spirit. In this way, Simonian Christianity could be dismissed

---

[89] *Ref.* 6.13.1; 6.18.3.
[90] Lüdemann, "The Acts of the Apostles and the Beginnings of Simonian Gnosis," *NTS* 33 (1987): 420-6 at 424. See further Lüdemann, "Die Apostelgeschichte und die Anfänge der simonianischen Gnosis," in *Studien zur Gnosis*, ed. Gerd Lüdemann (Frankfurt am Main: Peter Lang, 1999), 7-20 at 18-20.
[91] E.g., Justin *1 Apol.* 26.3.
[92] *Ref.* 6.9.4; 6.12.2; 6.18.3-4, 7. Cf. *Thunder* (NHC VI,2) 14.10.

as aberrant, illegitimate, and destined to be replaced by the author's own "apostolic" brand.

If this really was the author's expectation, however, it was mistaken. In other reports beginning about the mid-second century, Simon the Great Power would successfully spread his form of Christianity spatially and temporally. Eusebius, who rewrote the story in Acts, claimed that Simonians were still baptizing in his day (the early fourth century CE). But Simonian Christians lived not only in Eusebius's immediate vicinity (Palestine). The *Declaration* and *Great Power* hint at their presence in Egypt around the same time. As we shall see in the upcoming Interlude, Simon was imagined as a veritable globetrotter who visited Corinth and perhaps Asia Minor as well. To top it off, Justin Martyr shows that a sizable contingent of Simonians had, by the mid-second century, made it to Rome. Simonian Christianity was a movement, in short, that went from Samaria to the ends of the earth (Acts 1:8).

Interlude

Simon as Cipher

Introduction

Before treating Simonians in Rome, we must deal with the imagined Simon of Asia Minor (modern Turkey) and Greece. My discussion can be brief, since—though the battle against Simon(ians) stretched across the entire Mediterranean—there is no reliable evidence of Simonians or distinctly Simonian teachers between Rome and Palestine. There are only passing mentions of Simon with little attempt to develop his character or any distinctive elements of his teaching.

The Epistle of the Apostles

Probably in the 140s CE, Simon is named in the *Epistle of the Apostles* (*Epistula Apostolorum*), a gospel writing attributed to the eleven chief disciples of Jesus. It was probably composed in Asia Minor, but Egypt and Syria are also candidates.[1] This *Epistle* (probably not originally a letter) was first composed in Greek. At present, however, it must be pieced together from fragments found in other languages (Ethiopic, Coptic, and Latin).

In its opening paragraph, the *Epistle of the Apostles* refers to Simon along with Cerinthus as two faceless enemies contemporary with the apostles. We hear nothing about their biographies or their backgrounds. The chronology also seems incorrect. Historically speaking, Simon and Cerinthus were not contemporaries. Simon flourished in the mid-first century CE, whereas Cerinthus worked toward the turn of the second. Simon was in Samaria, Cerinthus in Asia Minor. There is no evidence that they ever met or influenced each other. The implied reader of the *Epistle* presumably only knows that they are villains. Simon and Cerinthus are said to kill people with their

---

[1] Detlef G. Müller, "Die Epistula Apostolorum," in *Antike christliche Apokryphen in deutscher Übersetzung I. Band Evangelien und Verwandtes. Teilband 2*, ed. Christoph Markschies and Jens Schröter (Tübingen: Mohr Siebeck, 2012), 1062–92; Charles E. Hill, "The *Epistula Apostolorum*: An Asian Tract from the Time of Polycarp," *JECS* 7, no. 1 (1999): 1–53; Francis Watson, *An Apostolic Gospel: The 'Epistula Apostolorum' in Literary Context* (Cambridge: Cambridge University Press, 2020), 1–11. In what follows, I use Watson's edition.

"venom." How they do so is never told. We only know that they traveled "around the world" putatively perverting "the words and the work, that is Jesus Christ."[2]

If Simon perverted Jesus (or Jesus's words and work, or both), then presumably he had a christological doctrine. Apparently, then, the Simon of the *Epistle* was imagined as a competing Christian teacher. Readers are strongly warned to disassociate from him, which might suggest he had his own church network. If there were Simonians in Asia Minor, however, their presence is not corroborated by any other source.[3]

It is sometimes said that the *Epistle of the Apostles* fights "docetism."[4] Ironically, it is not Christ but Simon who is in danger of appearing docetic. He twice flashes on the screen of the text, but we do not actually know who he is or where he comes from. There is no attempt to connect him with the Simon of Samaria in Acts. What Simon taught, despite the length of the *Epistle*, cannot safely be construed through a process of mirror reading. Even if one chooses to reverse engineer Simon's teachings, it would only produce a hybrid doctrine supposedly shared by Simon and Cerinthus, a hybridized anti-gospel which may go back to neither.[5]

3 Corinthians

Intriguingly, details from Simon's teachings are supplied in another falsely attributed writing, namely, *3 Corinthians*.[6] This document typically refers to an exchange of epistles attributed to Paul and five Corinthian Christian leaders. In the third or fourth century CE, it seems, *3 Corinthians* was woven into the *Acts of Paul*. Prior to that time, it circulated independently and was, until modern times, accepted as canonical in many churches of Syria and Armenia. Since *3 Corinthians* makes use of the Pastoral Epistles (1-2 Timothy and Titus), it is probably late second century CE at the earliest.[7]

According to *3 Corinthians*, Simon came to Corinth—not with Cerinthus—but with another partner in crime, Cleobius. (About this same time as *3 Corinthians* was written, Hegesippus juxtaposed Simon and Cleobius in his *Memoirs*.[8]) Reportedly,

---

[2] *Ep. Apost.* 1.1–3; 7.1–2. For venom, cf. 35.6.
[3] The author of *Ep. Apost.* Only speaks in vague terms of people "who believe in my name but follow evil and teach vain teaching" (37.4, trans. Francis Watson); cf. 50.8.
[4] Müller, "Epistula Apostolorum," in *Antike christliche Apokryphen* I/2.1063 (*strikt antidoketisch*).
[5] For differences in their profile and teaching, see Litwa, *Found Christianities*, 33–60.
[6] For a translation, see J. K. Elliott, *The Apocryphal New Testament: A Collection of Apocryphal Christian Literature in an English Translation* (Oxford: Clarendon, 1993), 379–82. See also Richard Pervo, *The Acts of Paul: A New Translation with Introduction and Commentary* (Cambridge: James Clarke & Co., 2014), 253–64; Gerard Luttikhuizen, "The Apocryphal Correspondence with the Corinthians and the Acts of Paul," in *The Apocryphal Acts of Paul*, ed. Jan Bremmer (Kampen: Kok Pharos, 1996), 75–91, esp. 75–9.
[7] See further A. F. J. Klijn, "The Apocryphal Correspondence Between Paul and the Corinthians," *VC* 17 (1963): 2–23; Benjamin L. White, *Remembering Paul: Ancient and Modern Contests over the Image of the Apostle* (Oxford: Oxford University Press, 2014), 108–34; Steve Johnston, "La Correspondance apocryphe entre Paul et les Corinthiens: Problèmes relies à l'identification des adversaires," in *Colloque international. "L'évangile selon Thomas et les textes de Nag Hammadi." Québec, 29-31 mai 2003*, ed. Louis Painchaud and Paul-Hubert Poirier. Bibliothèque Copte de Nag Hammadi: Études 8 (Québec: Presses de l'Université Laval, 2007), 187–230.
[8] Hegesippus in Eusebius, *Hist. eccl.* 4.22.5.

these two traveling teachers taught a form of Christianity with six features: (1) the prophets are not to be used, (2) the almighty (or creator) is not God, (3) there is no resurrection of the flesh, (4) humans were not created by God, (5) Jesus did not come in flesh (he was not born of Mary), and (6) the world was made by angels.

All six features are given without explanation, nuance, or context. They negate key features of what may have been a creed boiled down from the letters of Ignatius, who passed through Asia Minor. The creed may well have sounded something like this: "I believe in God almighty, maker of heaven and earth, and in Jesus Christ, proclaimed by the prophets, truly born of Mary according to the flesh, who was raised in flesh along with all who believe in him."

In the introduction to *3 Corinthians*—as it is found in the *Acts of Paul*—we find overlapping and slightly more precise teachings: that Simon (1) denies the resurrection of the flesh but posits a resurrection of the spirit, (2) says that the human body is not God's creation, (3) that God did not create the world, (4) that God does not know the world, (5) that Jesus was not crucified except in appearance, and (6) that Jesus was not born of Mary or in the line of David.[9]

According to these reports, Simon becomes a negative demiurgist: a person who denies that the creator (or the Judean lord) is the true God. This data is suspect because we hear nothing of Simon's negative demiurgy either in the *Declaration* or in the book of Acts. In fact, the *Declaration* represents positive demiurgy: it distinguishes the creator from God, but portrays the creator as Wisdom (*Epinoia*). That Wisdom is the true and *benevolent* creatrix is a stable element in Simonian lore.

According to Irenaeus, the angels who served Wisdom did the work of creation. Creation through angels is also found in *3 Corinthians*. But in *3 Corinthians*, these angels are not depicted as evil, and they are unrelated to Wisdom (who is never mentioned). The reports are, accordingly, not in sync. Therefore, there is not sufficient evidence to say that Simon or Simonians believed in a single, evil creator.[10]

If Simon(ians) were not negative demiurgists, then they likely had no problem with human flesh. The flesh may fall like a flower (as we read in the *Declaration*), but it is not evil.[11] In the later heresy reports on Simon, we never hear of a lower creator who makes the world and human bodies. The world and human bodies were, presumably, the good creation of Wisdom—even if she used angels as her instruments.

Outside of *3 Corinthians*, Simonians are never said to have denied Jesus's incarnation. Since they had no problem with the flesh, they would have had no need to deny Jesus's virgin birth, his Davidic descent, or his bodily suffering on the cross—assuming they cared about such things. They also never denied a general resurrection of the flesh. A resurrection of the spirit, or of a pneumatic body, seems to have been a Pauline idea (1 Cor 15:49-51), and one later developed by the intellectual heirs of Valentinus.[12]

[9] Cf. *Didascalia* 23 (Stewart-Sykes).
[10] On negative demiurgy see M. David Litwa, *The Evil Creator: Origins of an Early Christian Idea* (Oxford: Oxford University Press, 2021).
[11] Ref. 6.10.2.
[12] See Troels Engberg-Pedersen, *Cosmology and Self in the Apostle Paul: The Material Spirit* (Oxford: Oxford University Press, 2010); M. David Litwa, *We Are Being Transformed: Deification in Paul's Soteriology* (Berlin: de Gruyter, 2012), 119–71. For Valentinians on resurrection, see esp. *Treat. Res.* (NHC I,3).

As for the rejection of the prophets, this data is repeated by later heresiologists (see Chapters 5, 7, 10). Yet it, too, is doubtful. Heresiologists accused both the Samaritans and the Sadducees of rejecting the prophets, but Simonians were probably not former Samaritans, and they definitely were not Sadducees. As we can see from the *Declaration*, a Simonian author had no problem appealing to Isaiah and Daniel as authorities.[13] Tertullian will later claim that Simonians called up the souls of the prophets (Chapter 6).

In sum, even if one or two teachings in *3 Corinthians* seem vaguely Simonian, we have no compelling reason to believe that its author had any reliable information on Simon or Simonian thought. The doctrines s/he imposed on Simon do not match the *Declaration* or later heresy reports. All this author knew, it seems, was that Simon was a "heretic" in Paul's time. S/he therefore used Simon as a cipher to attack second-century enemies (which probably included Marcionites, Sethians, and Valentinians). Evidently, the doctrines of these enemies were conglomerated and attributed to Simon—who became a forerunner of a catch-all (anti-)creed.[14]

The author of *3 Corinthians* probably put Simon in Corinth not because he had actually been there, but because Corinth was associated with those who denied the resurrection and with factionalism (1 Cor 1, 15). Corinth as a place of factionalism and disruption was also reinforced in the letter of 1 Clement. In short, we are dealing with an *imagined* Corinth and an *imagined* Simon who went there.[15] If indeed Simon went "around the world" (according to the *Epistle of the Apostles*), then surely he made it to Greece and Asia Minor. Nonetheless, there is no corroborating evidence of Simon or Simonians in either territory.

Conclusion

If we only had the *Epistle of the Apostles* and *3 Corinthians*, we would have to conclude that Simon, if he ever existed, was a mere cipher—a made-up globalized "heretic," symbol of them all. The Simon of these documents has no distinctive or stable teaching of his own. His doctrines reflect the notions opposed by Ignatius and Polycarp (church leader of Asia Minor) in the mid-second century. None of them resemble anything similar to the *Declaration*, and none of them are connected to an actual Simonian group.

Accordingly, this whole discussion of *3 Corinthians* and *The Epistle of the Apostles* can serve only as an interlude. It is not really about Simon or the Simonians. It is about the negative image of Simon fostered in the minds of two second-century Christian writers. Both of them probably lived in Asia Minor and were influenced by the traditions of Ignatius and Polycarp. They had no historically informed idea of who

---

[13] E.g., *Ref.* 6.9.8; 6.10.1.
[14] Vahan Hovhanessian, *Third Corinthians: Reclaiming Paul for Christian Orthodoxy* (Frankfurt am Main: Peter Lang, 2000), 126–31.
[15] Historically, if Paul had a problem with any "enemy" in Corinth, it was the Alexandrian Apollos, not Simon of Samaria.

Simon was. Indeed, they never even appealed to the information in Acts 8. The author of the *Epistle of the Apostles* presented Simon as little more than a rhetorical bogeyman. In *3 Corinthians*, Simon's teachings were prefilled from an early creed, duly negated. To make any progress at all in this history, what we need are better sources, sources that are linked to actual Simonian movements as they appeared in Samaria and Rome.

Enter Justin Martyr.

4

Justin Martyr

Introduction

Despite anticipating his own martyrdom, Justin did not call himself "Martyr" (his ecclesial and honorific epithet).[1] Historically, we could just as well refer to "Justin of Samaria," for he was a Gentile born in Flavia Neapolis at the foot of Mt. Gerizim. Justin directly called himself a Samarian, but he was not a Samaritan.[2] In fact, there is little evidence of any Samaritan presence in Neapolis during Justin's day. Until he became a young man, it seems, Justin lived as a Hellene among Hellenes.[3]

In Justin's day, a towering temple to Zeus Most High stood on the northern spur of Mt. Gerizim. Worshipers climbed a massive staircase—155 steps or more—to arrive at the temple after passing through a monumental gateway below. Flavia Neapolis had all the trappings of a Greek city: a theater, amphitheater, and a racecourse. The inhabitants were from multiple ethnicities, many of them retired soldiers. The people of the city were proud of their deities and of their civic structures, so proud that they minted coins depicting all manner of gods and emperors paired with their magnificent temple to Zeus.[4] (See figure 4.1.)

By his own testimony, Justin shopped a number of Greco-Roman philosophies. He inscribed his experience in a semi-fictionalized tale polished by hindsight. Justin ignored the Cynics, whom he condemned for their indifference. Nevertheless, he approximated their contumely.[5] He first attached himself to a Stoic, though he left when he realized his teacher lacked theological interests. He attended the lessons of an Aristotelian tutor, but abandoned him when it came time to pay tuition. Finding a Pythagorean, Justin was dismissed when his teacher discovered Justin's lack of liberal arts education (knowledge of math, music, astronomy, and so on). Justin could not

---

[1] Justin, *2 Apol.* 3.1; cf. Tatian, *Oration against the Greeks* 19.1.
[2] Justin, *Dial.* 41.3; 120.6. Hall, *Samaritan Religion*, 267–8.
[3] Recent introductions to Justin include Jörg Ulrich, "Justin Martyr," in *In Defence of Christianity: Early Christian Apologists*, ed. Jakob Engberg, et al. (Frankfurt am Main: Peter Lang, 2014), 51–66; Jared Secord, *Christian Intellectuals and the Roman Empire: From Justin Martyr to Origin* (University Park: Pennsylvania State University Press, 2020), 46–76.
[4] Zangenberg, *Frühes Christentum*, 35–47; Yitzhak Magen, *Flavia Neapolis Shechem in the Roman Period*, 2 vols. (Jerusalem: Israel Antiquities Authority, 2009), esp. 1.233–86. See also M. Rosenberg, ed., *City Coins of Palestine (The Rosenberger Israel Collection)* (Jerusalem: Rosenberg, 1977), 6 (§§8–9); Arthur Segal, *Temples and Sanctuaries in the Roman East: Religious Architecture in Syria, Iudaea/Palaestina and Provincia Arabia* (Oxford: Oxbow, 2013), 255–8.
[5] E.g., Justin, *2 Apol.* 3.6–7.

Figure 4.1 Coin of Flavia Neapolis during the reign of Antoninus Pius showing a Roman temple to Zeus on Mt Gerizim accessed by stairway. Currently housed in the Ashmolean Museum, Oxford. Roman Provincial Coins IV.3 no. 10934. URI: https://rpc.ashmus.ox.ac.uk/coins/4/10934.

bear the time it would take to learn these subjects, so he took the fast track with a local Platonist. This Platonist taught him about the intelligible world, the realm of Forms, and the goal of seeing God. Justin's soul grew wings and soared through the upper air. Even so, a single conversation with a mysterious old man by the sea was enough to dislodge Justin from Platonism as well. Like a typical novice, Justin found himself cornered by the old man's Socratic refutations. By Justin's own report, the mysterious sage set his heart on fire for the Hebrew prophets. In due course, Justin adopted the philosophy of the Christians.[6]

All told, it a rather unlikely story, and somewhat hackneyed to boot. The script was well known in antiquity: a young man attends the lectures of every philosopher he can find; all instructors fall short of his expectations. After wallowing in depression, the lad by chance finds just the right sage, becomes devoted to his system of thought, and—till his dying day—clings steadfast to certitude.[7] Lucian the satirist parodied such fashionable narratives of self-fashioning.[8] We need not tarry with Justin's tale since its point is clear enough: Christianity was the true philosophy, older and purer than any other.

---

[6] Justin, *Dial.* 2–7. See further J. C. M. van Winden, *An Early Christian Philosopher: Justin Martyr's Dialogue with Trypho Chapters One to Nine: Introduction, Text, and Commentary* (Leiden: Brill, 1971), 49–120.

[7] Porphyry, *Vita Plot.* 3; Pseudo-Clementine *Hom.* 1–2.

[8] Lucian, *Men.* 4–6; *Vit. auct.* (entire). See further Miguel Herrero de Jáuregui, "Ancient Conversion between Philosophy and Religion: Conversion and Its Literature," in *Anthropology in the New Testament and its Ancient Context. Papers from the EABS Meeting in Piliscsaba/Budapest*, ed. Michael Labahn and Outi Lehtipuu (Leuven: Peeters, 2010), 135–50; Sergi Grau, "Conversion to Philosophy in Diogenes Laertius: Forms and Functions," in *Religious and Philosophical Conversion in Ancient Mediterranean Traditions* (Leiden: Brill, 2022), 219–37.

Putatively, Justin taught Christian philosophy in an apartment above the baths of Myrtinus in Rome.[9] He went round the streets wearing a *pallium*, a thick robe which was the distinctive garb of philosophers.[10] He gathered a handful of disciples whom he seems to have trained, judging by his interests, in a christological reading of Jewish scripture. Fulfilled prophecy was very important to Justin since it allowed him to say that his Christian philosophy enjoyed both divine and ancient support.[11]

Justin and the Simonians

It was Justin's Christian enemies, he tells us, who lacked such support. Even as Justin adjured the emperors that his small sect be spared from persecution, he recommended a crackdown for his Christian opponents. One group of these opponents were mostly made up of Justin's own countrymen, Simonians from Samaria. Justin expressed serious concern about these Simonians in each of his surviving works.[12] He did not say explicitly that there were Simonians in Rome, but such can be inferred from his report about the veneration of Simon's statue (see below).[13]

Like the author of Acts, Justin attacked Simonians by assaulting their presumed founder, Simon. The opening volley began with Justin's *Syntagma against All Heresies*, composed about 145 CE.[14] Here Justin attacked a series of enemies, some of whom he later named: Simon, Menander, Marcion, Basilideans, Saturninians, and so on.[15] Since

---

[9] H. Gregory Snyder, "Above the Baths of Myrtinus: Justin Martyr's 'School' in the City of Rome," *HTR* 100, no. 3 (2007): 335–62.
[10] Justin, *Dial.* 1.2.
[11] See further M. J. Edwards, "On the Platonic Schooling of Justin Martyr," *JTS* 42 (1991): 17–34; Rebecca Lyman, "The Politics of Passing: Justin Martyr's Conversion as a Problem of 'Hellenization,'" in *Conversion in Late Antiquity and the Early Middle Ages: Seeing and Believing*, ed. K. Mills and A. Grafton (Rochester: University of Rochester Press, 2003), 34–54; Runar M. Thorsteinsson, "By Philosophy Alone: Reassessing Justin's Christianity and His Turn from Platonism," *Early Christianity* 3 (2012): 492–517; Jörg Ulrich, "What Do We Know about Justin's 'School' in Rome?" *ZAC* 16 (2012): 62–74; Tobias Georges, "Justin's School in Rome—Reflections on Early Christian 'Schools,'" *ZAC* 16 (2012): 75–87.
[12] Justin *1 Apol.* 26.1–3; 59.1, 4; *Dial.* 120.6; *2 Apol.* 15.1.
[13] Alastair H. B. Logan proposed that Justin Martyr "probably got his information about Simon being worshiped as a god in Rome, statue and all, from Simonians there" ("Magi and Visionaries in Gnosticism," in *Portraits of Spiritual Authority: Religious Power in Early Christianity, Byzantium and the Christian Orient*, ed. Jan Willem Drijvers and John W. Watt [Leiden: Brill, 1999], 27–44 at 32–3), citing *1 Apol.* 26.1–3; 56.2–4; *2 Apol.* 15.1; *Dial.* 120.6. See further Edwards, "Bad Samaritan," 69–91. Pieter W. van der Horst argues that "Justin does not say that Simon was worshipped by Samaritans-in-Rome" ("Samaritans at Rome?" in *Japhet in the Tents of Shem: Studies on Jewish Hellenism in Antiquity* [Leuven: Peeters, 2002], 251–60 at 259). But the question is whether there were *Simonians* (who might also have been from Samaria) in Rome.
[14] For Justin's *Syntagma*, which I hold to be both written and promoted by Justin himself, see Geoffrey S. Smith, *Guilt by Association: Heresy Catalogues in Early Christianity* (Oxford: Oxford University Press, 2014), 21–142; with Matthijs den Dulk, "Justin Martyr and the Authorship of the Earliest Anti-Heretical Treatise," *VC* 72 (2018): 471–83.
[15] Justin, *1 Apol.* 35.6.

the *Syntagma* is lost, however, we can only surmise what Justin wrote from his more abbreviated report in the *1 Apology* (about 150–54 CE).[16]

In this *Apology*, Justin claimed that evil demons "brought about the infamous and impious deeds alleged" against Christians—in particular, indiscriminate orgies and feasts of human flesh.[17] Demons did so in part by inspiring other sorts of Christians to appear. He explained:

> After the ascent of Christ into heaven, the demons were putting forward people claiming to be gods. These people were not only free from your prosecution but even judged worthy of honors. A certain Simon of Samaria from a village named for the Gittites in the time of Claudius Caesar and by an art activated by demons performed magical wonders in your royal city of Rome. He was considered a god and honored by you as a god with a statue. The statue was raised between the two bridges on the Tiber. It bears this inscription in Latin: "to Simon Sacred God."
>
> Nearly all the Samarians and a few also from other nations confess that this man is the primal God. Still today they worship him along with a certain Helen who voyaged round with him at that time. Prior to this, she stood on the roof of a brothel in Tyre of Phoenicia. They say that she was the first Thought (*Ennoia*) generated by him. (*1 Apol.* 26.1-3)

Justin largely repeated these traditions about Simon in his *1 Apology* 56.2-4. In his *Dialogue with Trypho* 120.6, he reminisced that in his *Apology*, "I said how they [Samarians] were misled, obeying their countryman Simon magus, whom they say is god above all rule, authority, and power." (Here for the first time, incidentally, Simon is called by what became his standard epithet.) The passage alludes to Ephesians 1:21, where it is said that God raised up Christ, seated him at God's right hand in heaven, "above all rule, authority, and power." The Simonian depiction of Simon, according to this passage, evidently filled the role of Christ.

Justin and Acts

The author of Acts reported that Simon, prior to his conversion, stunned the nation of Samarians such that "all" (*pantes*) Samarians declared Simon the Great Power (of God) (Acts 8:9-10). Justin used similar language: "virtually all (*pantes*) Samarians" worship Simon, along with some from other nations. It is possible that Justin and the author of Acts independently arrived at the same polemical exaggeration. Nevertheless, scholars have reasonably argued that Justin knew Acts, and I am persuaded.[18] After all,

---

[16] For further background, see P. Lorraine Buck, "Justin Martyr's *Apologies*: Their Number, Destination, and Form," *JTS* 54 (2003): 45–59.

[17] Justin, *1 Apol.* 23.3.

[18] *1 Apol.* 26.3. Haenchen, *Acts of the Apostles*, 8; Matthijs den Dulk, *Between Jews and Heretics: Refiguring Justin Martyr's Dialogue with Trypho* (London: Routledge, 2018), 145–54. Contrast Andrew Gregory, "Among the Apologists? Reading Acts with Justin Martyr," in *Engaging Early*

Acts speaks of Jesus's ascent (Acts 1) prior to introducing Simon (Acts 8). The larger storyline of Simon's debut in Rome, moreover, mimics the pattern Simon's activity in Acts: Simon works wonders; the Samarians are stunned, the magician is deified.

Whether or not Justin knew Acts, he heightened the anti-Simonian polemic. According to Acts, "all" Samarians deified Simon by calling him "the Great Power (of God)." According to Justin, Simon deified *himself* by proclaiming that he was the "primal God."[19] Two knives are twisted here: first that Simon was a *self*-deifier (a point not found in Acts) and second that he identified—not with a subordinate deity—but with the high God often called "Father" by Christians.

Justin venerated Jesus, not as the "primal God," but as a second-tier deity called "Logos." Justin believed his deified Jesus would be far more acceptable than the deified Simon. Throughout its history, Rome had long assimilated foreign deities and deified figures who were subordinate to the Roman high God, Jupiter Optimus Maximus. But that a no-name quack from some backwater village in the corner of the empire was worshiped as the high God would have been laughable.[20]

Justin escalated the polemic in another way. In Acts, Simon performed the deeds of a magus with no sign of Satan (Acts 8:9, 11). Justin's Simon, however, performed miracles under demonic inspiration. For Justin, these magical wonders may have included the invocation of demonic "dream senders" and "attendants" as they were called by the "magi" of his day.[21] In short, Simon as magical performer was not just a wonderworking quack; he was, so Justin, an agent inspired by demons.

This was not just a rhetorical game. This was the age in which Roman officials harbored deep suspicions about Christians, executing them simply because they would not renounce the name of "Christian." Justin made Simon appear arrogant and ridiculous by his self-deifying claims, if not utterly mad.[22] The point was not simply to make Simon and his crew appear foolish, but to make them appear as genuine threats to Roman order. If Simon as the high God offended Jupiter, then Simonians committed sacrilege and were subject to punishment by Jupiter's deputy on earth: the emperor.[23]

Christian History: Reading Acts in the Second Century, ed. Rubén R. Dupertuis and Todd Penner [Durham: Acumen, 2013], 169–86, Gregory, *The Reception of Luke and Acts in the Period before Irenaeus: Looking for Luke in the Second Century*, WUNT II/169 (Tübingen: Mohr Siebeck, 2003), 317–21.

[19] Justin, *Dial.* 120.6, cf. Eph 1:21. Πρῶτος ("first") probably indicates rank or degree. Haar, comparing Philo (*Migr.* 181; *Abr.* 115) and Rev 1:17; 2:8; 22:13, notes that πρῶτος is "not used as a comparative but stresses preeminence with allusions to pre-existence as well as the primal creation of all things" (*First Gnostic*, 245).

[20] As Clemens Scholten points out, Justin did not locate Simon's village in Samaria specifically ("Herkunftsort," 534–41).

[21] Justin, *1 Apol.* 18.3. See further Anna Scibilia, "Supernatural Assistance in the Greek Magical Papyri: The Figure of the Parhedros," in *The Metamorphoses of Magic*, ed. Jan N. Bremmer and Jan R. Veenstra (Leuven: Petters, 2003), 71–86.

[22] Pseudo-Apollodorus, *Bibl.* 1.9.7; Maximus of Tyre, *Or.* 29.4; 35.2. See further Wayne Meeks, "The Divine Agent and his Counterfeit in Philo and the Fourth Gospel," in *Aspects of Religious Propaganda in Judaism and Early Christianity* (Notre Dame: University of Notre Dame Press, 1976), 43–67 at 43.

[23] J. R. Fears, "Jupiter and Roman Imperial Ideology," in *ANRW* I.17.1, ed. Wolfgang Haase (Berlin: de Gruyter, 1981): 3–141.

Christians of all sorts had a reputation for orgies under cover of night and cannibalism.[24] It was thus highly provocative for Justin to insinuate that Simonians engaged in such activities. As he put it: "If indeed they perform those infamous and fantastical deeds, turning over the lamp, pell-mell copulation, and devouring human flesh, we do not know. But that they are not hunted and murdered by you, despite their teachings, we know well."[25] Clement of Alexandria made a more direct charge, that some Simonians were called "Entychitae" (Meet-uppers) because they had sex with whomever they met (presumably in the dark).[26] What we have here is scapegoating: redirecting global slander against Christians to a specific Christian group. It is hard to avoid the conclusion that Justin believed the Romans *should* hunt down and murder Simonians. The request for state persecution of "heretics" is an eerie premonition of what was to come two centuries later.

"Simon's" Statue

The Romans, however, did not view Simon as a threat or a magus. Reportedly, Simon so impressed the sacred senate and people of Rome with his miracles that they honored him with a statue. Justin understood the statue as a divine honor: Simon "was honored . . . as are the other gods."[27] The statue could be found, Justin reported, on Tiber Island with the inscription SIMONI DEO SANCTO: "To Simon, Sacred God."[28]

In 1574, "Simon's" statue base was discovered. To everyone's surprise, it read SEMONI SANCO DEO FIDIO SACRUM ("Dedicated to Trusty God Semo Sancus").[29] Semo Sancus was a Sabine deity who, at first glance, has nothing to do with Simon.[30]

---

[24] S. Benko, "Pagan Criticism of Christianity During the First Two Centuries," in *ANRW* 2.23.2, ed. Wolfgang Haase (Berlin: de Gruyter, 1980), 1055–118; Burton L. Visotzky, "Overturning the Lamp," *Journal of Jewish Studies* 38, no. 1 (1987): 72–80; Mark Edwards, "Some Early Christian Immoralities," *Ancient Society* 23 (1992): 71–82; C. De Vos, "Popular Graeco-Roman Responses to Christianity," in *The Early Christian World*, ed. P. F. Esler (London: Routledge, 2000), 869–89; Williams, *Rethinking*, 163–88; Jennifer Knust, *Abandoned to Lust: The Politics of Sexual Slander in Early Christian Discourse* (New York: Columbia University Press, 2006), 143–63; Bart Wagemakers, "Incest, Infanticide and Cannibalism: Anti-Christian Imputations in the Roman Empire," *Greece & Rome* 57, no. 2 (2010): 337–54.

[25] Justin, *1 Apol.* 26.7.

[26] Clement, *Strom.* 7.17.108.2.

[27] Justin, *1 Apol.* 56.2.

[28] Justin, *1 Apol.* 26.2.

[29] The full inscription reads: SEMONI SANCO FIDIO SACRUM SEX(TUS) POMPEIUS SP(URII) F(ILIUS) COL(LINA) MUSSIANUS QUINQUENNALIS DECUR(IAE) BIDENTALIS DONUM DEDIT ("Sextus Pompeius Mussianus son of Spurius, of the Collina tribe, five-year chief officer of the bidental society, gave this gift to Semo Sancus trusty god"). The inscription can be found in *CIL VI. Inscriptiones urbis Romae Latinae*, Eugenius Bormann and Guilemus Henzen, vol. 6, part 1 (Berlin: Georg Reimerus, 1876), §567, p. 108. Sextus Mussianus is also referred to in *CIL* XIV, 2839. Beyschlag noted that the statue was erected in the second century (*Simon Magus* 11, n.11), not the time of Claudius. See further Carl Erbes, "Petrus nicht in Rom sondern in Jerusalem gestorben," *Zeitschrift für Kirchengeschichte* 22 (1901): 1–47, esp. 12; Jacques Poucet, "'Semo Sancus Dius Fidius.' Une première mise au point," in *Recherches de philologie et de linguistique*, ed. M. Hofinger (Leuven: Leuven University Library, 1972), 53–68.

[30] Ovid, *Fasti* 6.213–18; Varro, *De Lingua Latina* 5.66; Augustine, *Civ.* 18.19.

Figure 4.2 Inscription to Semo Sancus (CIL VI. §567) preserved in the Galleria Lapidaria of the Vatican Museum, first compartment (Dii gallery).

Some have accused Justin of deliberate falsification.[31] Yet perhaps he was just confused or misinformed.[32] He may have observed Simonians gathered on Tiber Island in front of the statue and assumed that they worshiped it. Either Justin never checked the reported content of the inscription or he himself misread it, reading *sancto* instead of *sanco*. (In two other inscriptions, however, Semo Sancus is also referred to as *sanctus*.)[33]

Alternatively, the mistake was not Justin's; he merely reported the *Simonian* view of the statue. According to this theory, the Simonians identified Semo with Simon based on their general cultural knowledge and theology. Dionysius of Halicarnassus, for instance, identified *Dius Fidius* with *Zeus Pistios* (the Trusty Zeus), protector of

---

[31] Heintz, *Simon "Le magician"*, 121.
[32] Rudolph, "Simon: Magus oder Gnosticus," 325; cf. Beyschlag, *Simon Magus*, 11, n.11.
[33] *CIL* 6.1, §568 (found on the Quirinal hill): SANCO SANCTO SEMON(I) DEO FIDIO SACRUM DECURIA SACERDOTUM BIDENTALIUM RECIPERATIS VECTIGALIBUS ("To holy Sancus Semo, trusty god, this gift is offered from the society of bidental priests when revenues were recovered"). It is dated 201-300 CE. Another inscription reads SEMONI SANCO SANCTO DEO FIDIO SACRUM. DECURIA SACERDOT(UM) BIDENTALIUM (*CIL* 6.4.2, 30.994). Poucet ("Semo Sancus," 64) says that the latter inscription was found in 1880 on the Quirinal hill; and that it was the base of a marble statue resembling the archaic Apollo. It is dated to the late second or early third century CE and is now housed in the *Galleria Lapidaria* in the Vatican Museum.

oaths.³⁴ Since Simon was identified with Zeus, according to Irenaeus, Simonians in Rome made the identification between Simon and Semo. The names sounded similar due to itacism (the similar pronunciation of "i" and "e" sounds).³⁵ By interpreting Semo as Simon, Simonians could boast that the Romans had honored their founder with a statue—just like other philosophers, emperors, and heroes. By virtue of having a statue, Simon was literally enrolled in the Roman state pantheon. How much more integrated into the Roman civic cult could this group of Christians be?³⁶

The theory is ingenious, but not without problems. For Simon's identification with Zeus, one must depend on Irenaeus (about thirty years after Justin). Even if Irenaeus depended on Justin, he never said that Simonians identified Simon with Zeus *Pistios* specifically. Justin believed that Simonians identified Simon with the "primal God." To a Roman audience, at least, this primal God was Jupiter Optimus Maximus, a particular form of Zeus worshiped on the Capitoline hill in Rome, not the Trusty Zeus on Tiber Island. It may be that Dionysius of Halicarnassus was idiosyncratic: Semo was not strictly identified with the Trusty Zeus, but was one of his subordinates. It should also be kept in mind that there was more than one statue of Semo Sancus in Rome (Semo's official temple was on the Quirinal hill.) Neither Simonians nor Justin identified *other* statues of Semo with Simon, presumably. Thus the chain of inferences that Semo = Trusty Zeus = Zeus the primal God = Simon is unstable, to say the least.

Due to these problems, all that we can safely infer from Justin is that there was a mid-second-century tradition of Simon arriving in Rome to work wonders during the reign of Claudius (41–54 CE). The tradition may have been based on nothing more than the statue on Tiber Island itself, interpreted as Simon. Apparently this tradition was avowed by Simonians themselves. Justin had little to gain, in my view, by supplying evidence of Simon as a Roman state god (he was not bemused, but threatened).³⁷ The tradition was later adopted by various patristic writers (Irenaeus, Tertullian, Cyril of Jerusalem, Eusebius, Theodoret, and Augustine) along with the *Acts of Peter*.

Helen

According to Justin, the Primal God was the high God, the one whom Christians called "Father."³⁸ In the lofty language of Middle Platonism, the primal God was eternal, unspeakable, self-perfect, supreme in divinity and goodness.³⁹ A primal God would seem to imply a secondary one, and she is introduced as Thought (structurally parallel with the Logos in Justin's theology). To the Greeks, Logos was gendered as male while

---

³⁴ Dionysius of Halicarnassus, *Ant. rom.* 4.58.4. See further Arthur Bernard Cook, *Zeus: A Study in Ancient Religion*, vol. II, part 1 (Cambridge: Cambridge University Press, 1925), 724–6, n.5.
³⁵ Edwards, "Bad Samaritan," 74. Lüdemann, *Untersuchungen*, 49–56.
³⁶ See further Alain Le Boulluec, *The Notion of Heresy in Greek Literature in the Second and Third Centuries*, ed. David Lincicum and Nicholas Moore, trans. A. K. M. Adam et al. (Oxford: Oxford University Press, 2022), 78; Edwards "Bad Samaritan," 74; Den Dulk, *Between Jews*, 32, n.31.
³⁷ Pace Macrae, "Simon the God," 68.
³⁸ Justin, *1 Apol.* 60.5.
³⁹ Alcinous, *Handbook* 10.3.

Ennoia was female. Justin laughed at the idea that the image of God's Thought could assume female form.[40] Yet this is what many Greek and Romans believed: that Athena (the Roman Minerva) emerged from her Father's head as the embodiment of his wisdom.

We have already met "Thought" (*Epinoia*) in *The Great Declaration* (Chapter 1). According to this document, Mind—not identified with Simon—becomes Father when it generates *Epinoia*.[41] *Epinoia* in the *Declaration* is never identified with Helen, however. *Epinoia* is called the Seventh Power, and humans are made in her image.[42]

Exactly how and when *Ennoia* became identified with Helen of Tyre we do not know, but evidently some time prior to 150 CE. Justin claimed that the demons, who knew that God conceived and created the world through Logos, referred to Athena as the "first *Ennoia*," which is how Simonians referred to Helen.[43] To Simonians, apparently, Helen functioned as Athena in Greek lore—or rather, Athena symbolized the truth about Helen.

Some scholars have thought that Helen—of Troy not of Tyre—was already a goddess worshiped in Samaria.[44] They do so on the basis of a statue found in a cistern in the stadium at Sebaste. The statue represents a woman carrying a torch in one hand with a pomegranate and ears of grain in the other. Also in the cistern was an inscription which reads, "One god, master of everything, the great, invincible Kore."[45] The identification of the statue with "Kore" is generally granted. (Inscriptions and graffiti referring to Kore were also found in this stadium.) The identification of Kore with Helen is based on the discovery—in another location—of a plaque with the helmets of the Dioscuri (Helen's brothers) carved into limestone.[46]

Nevertheless, the identification of this "Kore" statue with Helen is dubious. There is no strong evidence that the caps of the Dioscuri are connected to the statue in the cistern. Helen of Troy did at one point carry a torch, but the torch is not a stable element in her iconography. Helen also has no strong associations with pomegranates and grain. The statue is labeled "Kore," which would most readily designate Persephone, daughter of Demeter. Kore appears on at least two surviving coins, one of which shows her in a pose like what we find in the statue. In iconography, moreover, Kore is often

---

[40] Justin, *1 Apol.* 64.5.
[41] *Ref.* 6.18.5.
[42] *Ref.* 6.14.5–6; 6.17.1.
[43] Cf. Justin, *1 Apol.* 64.5 (τὴν πρώτην ἔννοιαν) with 26.3. (τὴν ὑπ' αὐτοῦ ἔννοιαν πρώτην). Plato, called Athena Zeus's "mind and thought" (*Crat.* 407b, νοῦν τε καὶ διάνοιαν). Cornutus called her Zeus's σύνεσις (*Greek Theology* §20 in Boys-Stones 92–3); J. W. Crowfoot, *The Buildings at Samaria (Samaria-Sebaste I)* (London: Palestine Exploration Fund, 1942), 46–8, 62–7. See also G. H. R. Horsley, *New Documents Illustrating Early Christianity: A Review of the Greek Inscriptions and Papyri Published in 1976* (Sydney: Macquarie University, 1981), 105–7, no. 68 ("The Great Goddess of Samaria"). Heraclitus named her "wisdom in perfection" (*Homeric Problems*, ed. Donald A. Russell and David Konstan [Atlanta: SBL Press, 2005], 20, 37). Origen called Athena φρόνησις (*Cels.* 8.67), as did Porphyry, *Cave of Nymphs* 32 (φρόνησις).
[44] L.-H. Vincent, "Le culte de Helene à Samarie," *RB* 45, no. 2 (1936): 221–32; Bettany Hughes, *Helen of Troy: Goddess, Princess, Whore* (London: Pimlico, 2005), 282; Theissen, "Simon Magus," 425.
[45] εἷς θεός ὁ πάντων δεσπότης μεγάλη κόρη ἡ ἀνείκητος.
[46] Jodi Magness, "The Cults of Isis and Kore at Samaria-Sebaste in the Hellenistic and Roman Periods," *HTR* 94, no. 2 (2001): 157–77, esp. 160–1.

Figure 4.3 Statue of Kore found in a cistern in the ancient stadium of Sebaste.

depicted carrying a torch.[47] (She was queen of the underworld, traditionally associated with darkness.) She is also associated with pomegranates (eating a pomegranate seed forced her to remain in the underworld). She is also a fertility goddess. When she rises from the earth, the grain grows.

To be sure, Helen of Troy was a goddess, and she was worshiped in two cult sites, namely in Sparta and in Rhodes. At the same time, she was far from being a singular, invincible "master of everything." Such a designation would better fit the queen of the netherworld, especially if she had been identified with Isis.[48] Finally, it is impossible—even if Samarians identified this statue of Kore with Helen—that she influenced early second-century Simonians. The statue is dated, after all, to the late second century CE.[49]

Let us turn from Helen of Troy to Helen of Tyre. We do not know who Helen of Tyre really was. Justin was the first to pair Simon with Helen and to speak of them as travelling companions. Here it is easy to think of prior archetypes, namely Ahab

---

[47] See, e.g., "Persephone," in *LIMC* VIII.2 *Thespiades-Zodiacus et Supplementum Abila-Thersites* (Zurich: Artemis, 1997), 640–53, images 10–11, 21–2, 25, 35, 45, 70–1, 74.
[48] Apuleius, *Met.* 11.2. D. Flusser, "The Great Goddess of Samaria," *Israel Exploration Journal* 25, no. 1 (1975) 13–20 at 16.
[49] Flusser, "Great Goddess," 13.

of Israel and his Phoenician wife Jezebel (1 Kgs 16, 19, 21).[50] Is Helen of Tyre simply a historicized update of the primordial "wicked woman" from the Phoenician coast?

Justin wrote that Helen "stood on the roof" of a brothel in Tyre. It seems this was a rather crude way to refer to a sex worker in antiquity. "Roofer" (*stegitis*) was a known term for a female sex worker. According to Konstantinos Kapparis, a "brothel could be called 'roof' [(s)tegos] because of its shabby construction, something like a warehouse or workshop." If so, "it would only refer to a particular type of shabby brothel, and thus *stegitis* would have referred to a low-class prostitute. Alternatively, a brothel could be a larger building with multiple floors. In this case *stegos* could be an upper room or balcony from which prostitutes solicited men below; thus *stegitis* would not indicate a cheap or low prostitute."[51] I suspect that Justin, if he was specific, aimed to refer to Helen as a cheap sex worker in order to smear her reputation.

What can we say about Helen historically? Possibly Simon did have a companion named Helen. She need not have been a sex worker, since such a story could have emerged from the myth later attached to her (Chapter 5). Even if Helen was a sex worker, however, this would not have been by choice. As a formerly enslaved woman, she would have been placed in a brothel by her owners. Although Justin moralized, the Simon who encountered Helen is in this instance little different than Jesus who associated with sex workers and sinners. Simon's redemption of Helen could be interpreted as an act of lust. Yet it could also be read as a deed of compassion. Simon modeled a documentable Christian practice of freeing slaves from degrading labor.[52] The fact that Simon traveled round with Helen is little different from Jesus journeying with Mary Magdalene, from whom he drove out seven demons (Luke 8:2).

The historical Helen is probably lost to history; the best we can do is try to recover what Helen meant to second-century Simonians. Her character, as we shall see when we come to Irenaeus, was influenced by an allegorical reading of Helen of Troy. At present, it suffices to say that—whether mythic or historical or a bit of both—the Simonian Helen deserves to be taken seriously. Celsus, probably writing from Alexandria in the 160s or 170s CE, refers to Helen as a teacher among the Simonians. She was so honored that some Simonians were called "Helenians."[53]

Results

What, in sum, can Justin tell us about Simonians in the eternal city? Admittedly, everything Justin wrote stings with the barbs of invective. Yet even in a polemic, half-truths must be told.

---

[50] Tuomas Rasimus, "Jezebel in Jewish and Christian Tradition," in *Women and Knowledge in Early Christianity*, ed. Ulla Tervahauta, et al. (Leiden: Brill, 2017), 109–32.
[51] Konstantinos K. Kapparis, "The Terminology of Prostitution in the Ancient Greek World," in *Greek Prostitution in the Ancient Mediterranean* (800 BCE–200 CE), ed. Allison Glazebrook and Madeleine Mary Henry (Madison: University of Wisconsin Press, 2011), 222–55 at 242.
[52] J. Albert Harrill, *The Manumission of Slaves in Early Christianity* (Tübingen: Mohr Siebeck, 1995).
[53] Origen, *Cels.* 5.62.

Reading him, one gathers the impression that Simonian Christianity flourished in Rome, even if it did not include "virtually all" Samarians there. Simonians thrived in Rome at least long enough to make Justin sweat under his pallium. Simonians were considered—and evidently considered *themselves* to be—Christians, otherwise Justin would not attack them. He openly remarked that Simonians were called Christians and that they met together to enjoy a meal.[54] He seems also to imply that Simonians "confess the crucified Jesus as their Lord and Christ."[55] Despite being Christians, Simonians went unprosecuted—probably because unnoticed—by the Roman state.

Most Roman Simonians, it appears, came from the region of Samaria. But the movement, like most other early Christian sects, was open to people from other nations as well. How did Simonians from Samaria arrive in Rome? Perhaps they came in the early 130s to escape the mayhem of the Bar Kokhba war. Justin wrote that between 132 and 135 CE, Bar Kokhba singled out Christians for capital punishment.[56] These Christians could have included Simonians.

The idea that the historical Simon deified *himself* as the primal God is Justin's polemical inference and should be rejected as false testimony.[57] At the same time, Roman Simonians did, it seems, venerate Simon to the extent that he was honored as the father and founder of their fellowship. Granting that Roman Simonians viewed Simon as a manifestation of the divine, they had moved beyond Simonians in Alexandria, who viewed Simon as something like an inspired prophet and philosopher. If Simonians in Rome identified Simon with Mind as depicted in the *Declaration*, then Simon was not the high God, but a subordinate Power like the Logos. Justin believed that because Simon was father of *Ennoia*, he was considered to be the high God (analogous to Zeus). The *Declaration* clarifies that Mind and Thought in the Simonian system were subordinate to a higher entity.[58]

How did Simon move from inspired prophet to a divine figure? We might pose a similar question to Justin: how did Jesus, the preacher from Galilee, become the divine Logos? Historically speaking, the deification of Palestinian founder-heroes like Jesus and Simon was a complex process. There were many reasons for Christians to view a Jew from Galilee as a (subordinate) god, and not every Christian came to this conclusion.[59]

I suspect that for Simonians, there were good reasons for Simon, the proclaimer of divine truths, to become the proclaimed. Unfortunately, most of these reasons are now obscure to us due to Justin's exceedingly thin description of Simonian theology. One can speculate, however, that many of the same reasons for Jesus's deification applied to Simon: both Jesus and Simon were thought to have worked wonders, to have expressed

---

[54] Justin, *1 Apol.* 26.6; 35.6.
[55] Justin, *1 Apol.* 35.2.
[56] Justin, *1 Apol.* 30.6.
[57] This point was seen clearly by Pétrement, *Separate God*, 233–46.
[58] *Ref.* 6.18.3–5.
[59] M. David Litwa, *Iesus Deus: The Early Christian Depiction of Jesus as a Mediterranean God* (Minneapolis: Fortress, 2014); Larry Hurtado, *How on Earth did Jesus Become a God? Historical Questions about Earliest Devotion to Jesus* (Grand Rapids: Eerdmans, 2005); Michael F. Bird, *Jesus Among the Gods: Early Christology in the Greco-Roman World* (Waco: Baylor University Press, 2022).

divine wisdom, to have lived an immortal life after death, and so on. The Simon of Simonian Christians came to function as Christ, who ascended above every authority, rule, and power.

The exact Simonian view of Semo's statue is impossible to recover. I suspect that Simonians saw their Simon in Semo. Yet Justin's report is so muddled it does not inspire much confidence. For all we know, Tiber Island, with its statue, may have been nothing more than a meeting place for Simonians in Justin's time. It seems reasonably clear, however, that Simonians believed that their founder had preceded them at Rome and had received honor there.

Neither the Romans nor the Simonians viewed each other as a threat. Simonians were one of many groups in Rome who worshiped foreign gods and deified heroes. Despite this fact, they seem to have been rather well integrated into Roman society. Some may have considered their founder part of the Roman state pantheon. Perhaps they also participated in Roman rites and state holidays. Justin insinuated that they ate meat sacrificed to other gods, which would indicate some level of participation in Roman civic cults.[60] Justin had no evidence that Simonians practiced anything criminal, however. If he did, he would have reported more than insinuations.

If any Roman official actually read the *1 Apology*, Justin's argument against the Simonians would likely have seemed like a battle of frogs against mice. The statue on Tiber Island was never any real concern to Romans, who viewed Semo as a trusty god long before he was identified with Simon. If Roman officials had taken the time to verify Justin's reading of the statue base, they would likely have scorned Justin's error. There was never any need to tear down this local Jupiter of adjurations, despite Justin's pleas.

---

[60] Justin, *Dial.* 35.1.

5

Irenaeus

Introduction

Irenaeus was born somewhere in Asia Minor, likely the city of Smyrna (modern Izmir). As a young man, he encountered Polycarp, the same man whose theology may have influenced 3 *Corinthians*.[1] Possibly Irenaeus traveled with Polycarp to Rome in the early 150s. He probably spent a number of years in the imperial capital. By the 170s, however, Irenaeus was working as a presbyter in the city of Lugdunum (modern Lyon, France). In response to the New Prophecy movement, he brought letters of imprisoned martyrs to Rome (177 CE).[2] When he returned to Lyon, he was voted to replace its leader, Pothinus, who had since perished (178 CE).

As Irenaeus picked up the pieces of his Christian community, he launched an attack on a certain Christian group integrated into church networks in Rome and Gaul—the Valentinians. His work against them, written between 180 and 189 CE, was called *Refutation and Overthrow of Knowledge Falsely So-called* (more commonly known as *Against Heresies*). The work only survives complete in a fourth-century Latin translation, though pieces of the original Greek appear in ancient quotations.[3]

To vilify the Valentinians, Irenaeus tried to trace them to a better known and acknowledged enemy—the Simonians—who had already been attacked by Justin. Most scholars believe that *Against Heresies* Book 1.23-27 incorporates parts of Justin's *Syntagma*, written about 145 CE.[4] Between 145 and 180 CE, the *Syntagma* was probably updated at least once by an unknown editor.[5] Irenaeus then made his own additions and modifications, but he agreed with Justin in making Simon of Samaria his first and

---

[1] Irenaeus, *Haer.* 3.3.4; Eusebius, *Hist. eccl.* 5.20.5-7.
[2] Eusebius, *Hist. eccl.* 5.4.1.
[3] See further Paul Foster and Sara Parvis, ed., *Irenaeus: Life, Scripture, and Legacy* (Minneapolis: Fortress, 2012); John Behr, *Irenaeus of Lyon: Identifying Christianity* (Oxford: Oxford University Press, 2013); Päivi Vähäkangas, "'That Ill-formed Little Fox': Valentinians as the Enemy in Irenaeus's *Against Heresies*," in *The Faces of the Other: Religious Rivalry and Ethnic Encounters in the Later Roman World,* ed. Maijastina Kahlos. (Turnhout: Brepols, 2011), 83-104.
[4] Lüdemann, *Untersuchungen,* 100.
[5] Smith, *Guilt by Association,* 21-142. Giuliano Chiapparini's dating of Irenaeus, *Haer.* 1 to the 160s is not convincing ("Irenaeus and the Gnostic Valentinus: Orthodoxy and Heresy in the Church of Rome around the Middle of the Second Century," *ZAC* 18, no. 1 [2013]: 95-119). Even if the dating accepted, it only applies to the so-called Grand Notice (*Haer.* 1.1-11).

foremost foe. Irenaeus not only traced the Valentinians back to Simon; he made Simon the intellectual and spiritual wellspring of all the Christian groups he opposed.[6]

Unfortunately we do not know how much of Irenaeus's notice on Simon goes back to Justin, how much of it was influenced by later editors of the *Syntagma*, and how much of it is stems from Irenaeus. Irenaeus was from Asia Minor, so we would expect some of the doctrines attributed to Simon in *3 Corinthians* to show up in Irenaeus's report (and we are not disappointed). The *Syntagma*, on the other hand, was a product of Rome. One suspects, then, that Irenaeus combined his general knowledge of Simon he learned in Asia with the specific knowledge of Roman Simonians he learned from Justin. If so, Irenaeus's report is already a blend of different traditions, which should be kept in mind.

I translate it as follows:

> Simon the Samarian, that famous magus about whom Luke the disciple and follower of the apostles says: "Moreover, a man by the name of Simon who was in the city beforehand practicing magic and leading astray the Samarian people, said he was someone great. Small and great attentively listened to him, remarking, 'This one is the power of God which is called Great.' They were regarding him because for a long time he had deluded them by his magic arts." (Acts 8:9-11)

> Now this Simon, who feigned faith, supposed that even the apostles performed their healings by magic and not by the power of God and that through the imposition of hands those who believed in God through Christ Jesus preached by them were filled with holy Spirit. He suspected even this to have occurred through some greater knowledge of magic.

> He offered money to the apostles so that he also would receive this power for any whom he wanted holy Spirit to be supplied. He heard from Peter, "Your money be with you in ruin since you supposed you could possess the gift of God with money! There is no part or lot for you in this word, for your heart is not straight before God, for I see you in the bile of bitterness and in the chain of injustice." (Acts 8:20-23)

> Still more Simon did not believe in God and, full of desire, aimed to battle the apostles so as to appear glorious. He investigated the complete science of magic still more to drive many people into stupor. For he lived in the time of Claudius Caesar, by whom he was said to be honored with a statue on account of his magic. So this Simon was glorified by many as a god.

> He taught that he himself was the one who appeared among the Jews as the son of God, while in Samaria he descended as Father, and among the other nations came as holy Spirit. He taught that he was the highest Power, that is, the Father who is above all things and he allowed himself to be called whatever people might call

---

[6] Irenaeus, *Haer.* 1.23.2; 3, pref. See further Benjamin L. White, "How to Read a Book: Irenaeus and the Pastoral Epistles Reconsidered," *VC* 65 (2011): 125–49 at 144.

him. So Simon the Samarian, from whom all heresies were founded, has the stuff of this sort of sect.

When he bought a certain Helen, a prostitute from the city of Tyre in Phoenicia, he led her around, calling her the first Thought of his Mind, Mother of all, through whom in the beginning he conceived with his Mind to make angels and archangels. For she is the *Ennoia* leaping forth from him, knowing what her Father wills, who stepped down to the lower regions and gave birth to angels and powers, by which he said this world was made.

After she gave birth to them, she was restrained by them on account of spite, since they did not want to be thought the offspring of anyone. Simon himself was totally unknown to them, but his *Ennoia* was restrained by those powers and angels whom she brought forth. She suffered every disgrace from them so that she could not run above to her Father to the point that she was imprisoned in a human body.

Throughout the ages, she transmigrated as from container to container in different female bodies. She was in that famous Helen for whom the Trojan war was fought. This was why, when Stesichorus pilloried her in his verses, his eyes were blinded. Yet when he repented and wrote his *Palinodes*, in which he hymned her, his eyes were opened. She transmigrated from one body to another and out of it, always bearing disgrace. In most recent times, she served as a prostitute in a brothel. She is the lost sheep.

For this reason, Simon himself came to take her up first, free her from chains, then offer salvation to people by his own knowledge. For since the angels mismanaged the world, as each one coveted rule, he came to make things right and descended. He was transfigured and assimilated to the rulers, authorities, and angels, so as to appear as a human among humans, though he was not human. He also appeared to suffer in Judea, though he did not suffer. He said that the prophets spoke their prophecies inspired by the angelic creators of the world.

Accordingly, those who believe in him and Helen need not fret about the powers anymore. Still today, they do what they want as free persons. This is because people are saved by his grace, not by righteous works. For righteous works are not natural, but from convention, as the angels who made the world legislated. In this way, the angels reduced humans to slavery through the commandments. For this reason, Simon promised that the world would be destroyed and those under the rule of the world creators would be liberated.

Well then, their mystic priests live lustfully and perform magic acts, as each one can. They engage in exorcisms and incantations. They rigorously apply themselves to love charms and spells too, and what are called attendants, dream senders, and whatever other prestidigitations they have. They also have a statue of Simon made in the shape of Zeus and of Helen in the shape of Athena, and they worship them.

They also have their name from Simon, the founder of their most impious doctrine. They are called Simonians. It took its starting points from gnosis falsely-so-called (1 Tim 6:20), as one can learn from their own assertions.[7]

Data from Acts and Justin

Unlike Justin, Irenaeus explicitly quoted and summarized the book of Acts.[8] Interestingly, he supplied a brief resume for its author, who came to be thought of as a companion of Paul (not the apostles more generally). The need for such an introduction indicates that Acts was not, even by 180 CE, widely known and considered authoritative (it was not used in *3 Corinthians*, for instance).[9] Although Irenaeus surely considered Acts decisive, he did not introduce it as scripture.

His departures from Acts reveal the knife edge of his polemic. Acts says that the people of Samaria were "amazed" (*exestakenai*) by Simon's magic arts, just as Simon was amazed by Philip (Acts 8:11, 13). Irenaeus, taking the verb in a different sense, claimed that Simon drove them insane (*dementasset*).

Our heresiologist was selective in his quotations from Acts. He omitted Acts 8:12-13 where Simon believes and is baptized. The omission was not by accident. Irenaeus wanted to emphasize that Simon "feigned faith."[10] Thus mentioning his actual faith and baptism would have been counterproductive. Indeed, Irenaeus seems to have invented Simon's *disbelief*. After the clash in Judea, Simon supposedly renounced faith in God "still more." The remark is not only in tension with Acts, but with Irenaeus himself. If Simon "feigned faith" in the first place, he could not disbelieve to any greater degree. According to Irenaeus, Simon never was a Christian because he never relinquished his magical mentality. He believed that the apostles were simply greater magicians, sending Spirit upon people much like magicians would launch daimonic attendants.

Irenaeus eliminated anything that might redeem Simon's character in Acts and highlighted the pejorative parts. The Simon of Acts was neither greedy nor combative. He wailed for apostolic prayer after Peter's rebuke (Acts 8:24). Irenaeus omitted Simon's plea while highlighting Peter's outburst. Simon with his crooked heart in the bile of bitterness and chained to injustice was a Simon who could be dismissed as unchristian.

According to Irenaeus, Simon's greed for glory led him to contract a kind of holy war. This war would be won on Simon's terms—by knowledge of a greater magic. Accordingly, the Samarian threw himself into studying the complete science of magic so as, presumably, to perform greater wonders. Whence Irenaeus generated this picture of Simon as an aggressive anti-apostle is unknown, but it fits what we have already seen in *3 Corinthians* and the *Epistle of the Apostles*.

Justin, though uncited, is the source for other parts of Irenaeus's portrait. Simon succeeded in attaining fame. He was honored with a statue in the time of Claudius—a

---

[7] Irenaeus, *Haer.* 1.23.1–4.
[8] Acts 8:9–11 (quote); 18–19 (paraphrase); 20–23 (quote).
[9] Irenaeus, *Haer.* 1.23.1; cf. 3.1.1.
[10] Irenaeus, *Haer.* 1.23.1.

manifestly divine honor. Justin said much about this statue in his *First Apology*. For whatever reason, Irenaeus was more terse. He did not say that the statue was set up in Rome; he never claimed that Simonians worshipped it, and he did not quote its inscription. Perhaps there was already some embarrassment about the shakiness of Justin's claims; or perhaps Irenaeus wanted to avoid the idea that Simonians flourished in Rome.

Simonian Theology

Irenaeus provides the thickest description of Simonian theology in any heresiological source thus far. Reportedly, Simon first appeared among the Jews as God's son, then as Father in Samaria. This is a fascinating remark. It begins to make sense if we assume, with Justin, that Simon, for Simonians, was a manifestation of the ultimate deity—the God above all. In this light, it would be fairer to say that God or the highest Power became manifest as Son in Judea and as Father in Samaria.

It is unlikely that Irenaeus (or Justin) invented such doctrines. After all, this teaching—no matter how bizarre it seems to us—supports the Christian identity of Simonians (here I suspect that Roman Simonians are in mind). For the first time, we learn how Jesus was important for these Simonians. He was a revelation of God, but he was trumped by the revelation of the "Father" in Samaria. One can sense signs of Simonian one-upmanship, a kind of supercessionist impulse that makes Simonians better than their competitors (who only worshiped the Judean manifestation of God, or Jesus).

The radicality of the reputed claim has, in my view, yet to sink in. For the Simonians, it seems, Simon *was* Jesus. That is to say, the being who appeared in Samaria as Father *was the same one* who appeared in Judea as Son. Logically, then, everything written about Jesus in the gospels applied to Simon. Simon and Jesus were the same underlying being revealing two different levels of divine reality.

According to Simonians, the son of God was crucified. Nevertheless Jesus did not, reportedly, experience pain.[11] The charge resembles what we find in *3 Corinthians*, that Jesus was only crucified in appearance. This is in fact a common charge. Irenaeus wrote of his opponents that they uphold a Christ without suffering. Some of these opponents said that Jesus suffered from his human constitution (*ek tēs oikonomias*), not as a divine being.[12] Any Christian Platonist would try to make such a distinction. By the Platonic rule that God does not change, it was impossible for a divinity to undergo pain.[13] Even early catholics urged something similar: the man Jesus died, but the divine Logos dwelled, unsuffering, within him.[14]

---

[11] Beyschlag, *Simon Magus*, 188–93.
[12] Irenaeus, *Haer.* 3.11.3.
[13] Plato, *Resp.* 2.379a–380d.
[14] Origen, *Hom. Gen.* 8.9: *patitur ergo Christus, sed in carne . . . Verbum vero 'in incorruptione' permansit* ("Thus Christ suffered, but in flesh . . . The Word, however, remained in incorruption"); cf. Clement of Alexandria, *Paed.* 1.5.23.2; *Acts of John*, 101–2; *Ep. Pet. Phil* (NHC VIII,2) 139.15–22; *1 Apoc. Jas.* (NHC V,3) 31.15–22. Some early Christian sources say that it was Simon of Cyrene who

The report is reminiscent of something said in the *Declaration*, that one is born and able to suffer when in potentiality, but when formed according to God's likeness," one becomes "passionless" or without suffering.[15] Jesus, if anyone, had attained likeness and even identity with God. As such, he was without suffering. Even after his death, according to the *Great Power*, the "mode of his flesh" could not be seized.[16]

Irenaeus understood Jesus's painlessness polemically: the Simonian Jesus was not truly human. To be sure, the Simonian Jesus probably did fall short of Irenaeus's definition of humanity. Yet one can pose the same query about early catholic versions of Jesus: if he did not truly suffer in his divine nature, was he actually human? It is possible that Simonians distinguished the suffering humanity of Jesus from his unsuffering divinity while still arguing that the human and divine in him were unified. We know from the *Great Power* that Jesus's humanity was not in question. He drank "in truth from the milk of his mother."[17]

After Jesus died and was resurrected, presumably, the highest Power did not dwell in heaven for long. It became incarnate in Simon himself. Now, historically, Simon was a contemporary of Jesus. Evidently the assumption was that, after Jesus departed earth, God wrapped himself in the flesh of the Samarian sage. Thus the (higher) revelation of God in Samaria could follow on the heels of the (lower) revelation in Judea.[18]

The revelation of God as "Father" accentuates its intensity and clarity. One might say that the highest Power partially revealed himself to Judeans, but to Samarians, he came in full force. Jesus was truly divine, but Simon was a higher and purer manifestation of God. In this way, "Simon the Great Power"—an ambiguous title in Acts—became Simon the "highest Power," and "Father of all."

The highest Power had a third manifestation, as Spirit among the nations.[19] This claim is distinctive. Assuming it accurately reflects (Roman) Simonian views, we do not know when the highest Power appeared as Spirit, whether before the other two manifestations or afterward. Perhaps it was both. Presumably Simon as Spirit fulfilled the function of the holy Spirit in other Christian groups. He was ever present, empowering his community in whatever land they found themselves—Samaria, Egypt, Italy, and beyond. The theology implicitly recognizes and undergirds the multiethnic character of the Simonians (something known from Justin). Simonian truth was for all nations, and all had access to it through Spirit. In this way, the Simonians talked back, it seems, to the author of Acts: far from Simon not bestowing Spirit, he *was* Spirit.

The Simonian doctrine of Spirit seems different from what we find in the *Declaration*. In the *Declaration*, the Spirit over the waters (Gen 1:2) is identified with the Seventh Power, the Wisdom figure.[20] At the same time, the Seventh Power seems consubstantial

---

was crucified, while Christ stood by laughing (Basilides in Irenaeus, *Haer.* 1.24.4; *Disc. Seth* [NHC VII,2] 55.30–56.19; *Apoc. Pet.* [NHC VII,3] 81.3–21).

[15] *Ref.* 6.18.1.
[16] *Great Pow.* 42.1–2.
[17] *Great Pow.* 40.29–30.
[18] Cyril of Jerusalem (*Catechetical Lectures* 6.14) claimed that Simon revealed himself as Father on Mt. Sinai. The tradition is uncorroborated. I suspect it is Cyril's error, but if true, it would suggest that Simonians had no problem with the giving of the Law on Mt. Sinai.
[19] Irenaeus, *Haer.* 1.23.1.
[20] *Ref.* 6.14.4.

with the Infinite (or highest) Power. They both share the same epithet "Infinite" and manifest the same sort of Power.[21]

The Simonians, as reported by Irenaeus, were trinitarian modalists. Modalists believe that the persons of the Trinity all referred back to the same entity. Father, Son, and Spirit were not, that is, ultimate and stable "persons," distinct from eternity past. They were, rather, modes of the same being appearing at different times and at different places in different frames of perception. In this case, the truly singular deity was the highest Power identified with Simon. Properly speaking, however, Simon was only the highest manifestation of this Power. The highest Power had three forms: Father, Son, and Spirit. The incarnation of the Father was Simon, while Jesus was the incarnation as Son. Both were thought to be the same being, evidently sharing the same message and power.

Such modalism helps to date this portion of Simonian theology. We know that Simonians were in Rome, and modalism debuted there not long before Irenaeus wrote. One of its theological architects was a man from Irenaeus's hometown, Noetus of Smyrna (flourished in the 160s CE). Noetus posited the ultimate unity of Father and Son, then sent his disciple Epigonus to Rome. There Epigonus taught a man called Cleomenes. Cleomenes, in turn, received the support of early catholic leaders, two of whom later became bishops (Zephyrinus and Callistus).[22] Irenaeus probably met several of these men in the 170s CE. It was likely during this time that Simonians developed their own version of modalism—with Simon at its center.[23]

Such modalism was a development in Simonian theology, though not a Christianization.[24] Simonians were already Christians, and the Christian roots of their theology can be traced as far back as the *Declaration*. The *Declaration* presents a single God in three phases: the one Who Stood, Stands, and Will Stand.[25] These three phases of the Godhead were not called Father, Son, and Spirit. By the 170s, however, the Infinite Power in three modes was called by the threefold name familiar in Christian baptismal formulas (Matt 28:19). The language of the gospel of Matthew was beginning to assert more influence.

In the *Declaration* "Simon" never identified himself with the One Who Stood, Stands, and Will Stand (despite the Refutator's claims). By the time we reach Irenaeus, however, Simon had become the triply powered Standing One. He had become the Father (the God who stood in eternity past), the Son (who took his stand in Judea as Christ), and the holy Spirit (who will stand eternally among the nations).

---

[21] *Ref.* 6.14.1.
[22] *Ref.* 9.7.1–2. See further Reinhard M. Hübner, *Der Paradox Eine: Antignostischer Monarchianismus im zweiten Jahrhundert* (Leiden: Brill, 1999); Litwa, *Found Christianities*, 202–10.
[23] Beyschlag, *Simon Magus*, 164–71.
[24] *Pace* Pearson, *Ancient Gnosticism*, 30. Pheme Perkins's opinion that second-century Simonians copied "a more successful Christian rival" portrays Simonians as secondary and reactionary (*Gnosticism and the New Testament* [Minneapolis: Fortress, 1993], 10). Mutual influence and innovation should at least be considered.
[25] *Ref.* 6.17.1.

Helen

Irenaeus devoted a large amount of space to Helen, indicating her importance among Roman Simonians.[26] In their minds, Helen was the creatrix (the "Mother of all"). She came to fill the role of the Seventh Power. Helen was also important for salvation. It is only those who believe in Simon *and Helen* who triumph over wicked powers.[27] The true Helen was not the sex worker redeemed in Tyre. She was, in her preincarnate state, the eternal Thought (*Ennoia*) of the eternal Mind, her Father—nothing less than the Logos in other Christian systems.[28]

The Simonian story of Helen is the story of creation. The creation is not the result of a fall, but of a determined divine plan. *Ennoia* herself did not slip. She quite naturally "leaped" away from her Father. The Father wanted through her to create the middle management level of the cosmos (angels or powers). These angels and powers did the dirty work of making objects in the material world. It is possible that Irenaeus distorted his data by saying that *angels*—not Wisdom herself—created. But even if his summary is correct, the angels were Wisdom's underlings. She retained her status as creatrix. The angels whom she bore were her instruments before they became her opponents.

The story of preincarnate Wisdom as creatrix could have derived from Proverbs, where Wisdom speaks: "the Lord founded me as the principle of his paths for his works ... I was with him causing harmony; I was the one in whom he rejoiced and daily I delighted before his face" (Prov 8:22, 30, LXX). The Simonian Wisdom did not sin by desire or unfaithfulness—or for any other reason. She was a tragic figure, detained by her own children. The powers imprisoned *Ennoia* and subjected her to every form of outrage. As a final insult, she was shut up within a human body and successively reincarnated into women known to be abused and exploited by men.

Before the Trojan War, *Ennoia* became incarnate in Helen of Troy. This connection with the Trojan Helen should not surprise, since the *Declaration* already reveals Simonian interest in Homer's epics. It quotes the *Odyssey* regarding the famous "holy moly."[29] For "Simon" in the *Declaration*, moly represents the bitter water turned sweet by Moses. By these waters, one escapes the fate of becoming a beast (a mere body plus irrational soul) and returns to the rational image of God.[30]

The Simonian view of Helen is infused with Pythagorean lore. Pythagoreans viewed Helen of Troy as a superhuman being who fell from the moon. After the counsels of her Father Zeus were accomplished, Helen was raptured back to her heavenly station.[31] The

---

[26] Lüdemann, *Untersuchungen*, 55–77; Beyschlag, *Simon Magus*, 135–41.
[27] Irenaeus, *Haer.* 1.23.3.
[28] Jackson Lashier, *Irenaeus and the Trinity*, VCSup 127 (Leiden: Brill, 2014), 92–148.
[29] *Ref.* 6.15.4, quoting [Homer,] *Od.* 10.304–6. See further Beyschlag, *Simon Magus*, 153–9.
[30] Heraclitus in *Homeric Problems*, 73 interpreted moly as wisdom which comes with difficulty but is sweet due to its benefits. (Konstan and Russel, *Heraclitus*, 119).
[31] Neocles of Croton in Athenaeus, *Learned Banqueters* 2.50 (57f); Eustathius, *Commentary on Homer's Odyssey* on *Od.* 4.122. Marcel Detienne shows that only the Pythagoreans considered the moon to be inhabited ("La légende pythagoricienne d'Hélène," *Revue de l'Histoire des Religions* 152 [1957]: 129–52). Pythagoras himself was a daimon from the moon (Iamblichus, *On the Pythagorean Way of Life*, ed. and trans. John Dillon and Jackson Hershbell [Atlanta: Scholars Press, 1991], 31, 144). See further Lowell Edmunds, *Stealing Helen: The Myth of the Abducted Wife in Comparative Perspective* (Princeton: Princeton University Press, 2016), 213–19; Karen ní Mheallaigh, *The*

Simonian story was more drawn out. *Ennoia* was reincarnated again and again until she finally ended up as a sex worker—also called Helen—forced to sell her body in a Phoenician brothel.[32]

The powers she bore are not said to be evil by nature. Nevertheless, they wanted to be viewed as ultimate, not born from anyone—an attitude indicating arrogance. Their pride had no place, however, and they were unaware of the highest Power. These lower powers lusted for lordship, causing them to clash and mismanage the cosmos.[33]

Excursus: The Exegesis of the Soul

On the topic of Wisdom's descent it is worth taking another brief detour to Nag Hammadi. The *Exegesis of the Soul* famously quotes Helen of Troy as she appears in Homer's *Odyssey*: "My heart turned from me. It is to my house that I want to return."[34] This Helen is allegorized as the wayward human soul, deceived by Aphrodite (sexual desire), but restored again to her "good, merciful, and handsome husband" (Christ).[35] The parallels with Simonian thought led one scholar to call the *Exegesis* Simonian.[36]

This conclusion goes too far. The *Exegesis* is not about Simon's Helen, but about the generalized soul. The Simonian Helen is the creatrix and she is never explicitly said to symbolize every soul. The story of *Ennoia* and the story of the soul are different in their details. Simon's Helen does not fall and thus has no need to repent. The soul in the *Exegesis* falls into flesh and becomes the object of abuse.[37] Simon's Helen is already abused as a heavenly being and then forced to incarnate. She returns to her Father (Simon), not to her "brother" as in the *Exegesis*.[38] According to Simonians, the Father himself redeems *Ennoia*, but in the *Exegesis* he sends the "bridegroom" (Jesus).[39]

Despite these differences, there may well be some Simonian influence on the *Exegesis*. Simonians were possibly the first to allegorize Homer's Helen. In certain respects, Simonians might also have acknowledged that the human soul, though distinct from Wisdom, relives, to some extent, her story. All souls may have been viewed as small-scale "Helens," micro-expressions of Wisdom, recapitulating part of *Ennoia*'s story.

The precise detail about Stesichorus probably goes back to Simonian tradition. Simonians invented the tradition, it seems, to illustrate the power of *Ennoia*-Helen.

Moon in the Greek and Roman Imagination: Myth, Literature, Science and Philosophy (Cambridge: Cambridge University Press, 2020), 127–8.

[32] Irenaeus, *Haer.* 1.23.2.
[33] Irenaeus, *Haer.* 1.23.2–3.
[34] *Exeg. Soul* (NHC II,6) 136.22–137.1, quoting *Od.* 4.260–1.
[35] *Exeg. Soul* (NHC II,6) 137.4–5.
[36] Sasagu Arai, "Simonianische Gnosis und die Exegese über die Seele," in *Gnosis and Gnosticism: Papers Read at the Seventh International Conference on Patristic Studies. Oxford, September 8th-13th 1975* (Leiden: Brill, 1977), 185–203 at 202. Arai was unable to find distinctive Simonian traditions in other Nag Hammadi texts ("'Simonianischen' in *AuthLog* und *Brontē*," in *Gnosis and Gnosticism: Papers Read at the Eight International Conference on Patristic Studies (Oxford, September 3rd-8th 1979)*, ed. Martin Krause [Leiden: Brill, 1981], 3–15).
[37] *Exeg. Soul* (NHC II,6) 127.25.
[38] *Exeg. Soul* (NHC II,6) 132.8.
[39] Rudolph, "Simon: Magus oder Gnosticus," 357.

Stesichorus, a sixth-century BCE lyric poet, thought he could revile Helen of Troy with impunity. But Helen was not a fictional character for the Greeks; she was a goddess.[40] In Greek lore, she was child of Zeus the high God and had at least two cult sites, in Sparta and in Rhodes.[41] In Stesichorus's time, the goddess unveiled her power—blinding the poet for his libel. The poet's penitence was to write his most famous work, the *Palinodes* (hymns of retraction). By her power and mercy, *Ennoia*-Helen restored the poet's sight.[42]

Reportedly, then, Simonians did not only accept the miracles in the gospels. Wisdom was active before Jesus, and worshiped as a Greek goddess. For Simonians, of course, Helen was more than your average goddess—she was the Mother of the universe. The *Declaration* calls her the Seventh Power, "generating all."[43] Though abused by men and passed around in bodies, she retained traces of her power.

According to Irenaeus, Simonians identified *Ennoia* who wandered in bodies as the lost sheep in the parable of the shepherd who searches out what was lost (Matt 18:12-14; Luke 15:1-7).[44] In other words, Jesus (aka Simon), who already spoke this parable, revealed the story of Helen. At the very least, the notice shows that Simonians read and cited the gospels (something known from the *Declaration*). They were not just readers, however, but allegorical interpreters. The savior/shepherd is, of course, Simon, who is simultaneously Jesus. There was no contradiction between creation and redemption. In Simonian Christianity, the one who willed creation to exist also came to redeem it.[45]

Salvation

Salvation begins with Helen. The highest Power descended to find and redeem his Thought. Wisdom restored could thus fulfill her creative role and renew the minds of all. Simon's redemption of Helen the enslaved sex worker was probably taken to be historical, but it also illustrates how far God would go to save human souls. Jesus supped with tax collectors and sinners, but he never entered a brothel to redeem a sex worker. When Simon came as Father in Samaria, presumably, he made the trip to Tyre

---

[40] Herodotus, *Hist.* 6.61; Pausanias, *Descr.* 3.15.3. See further Edmunds, *Stealing Helen*, 162–95.
[41] Timothy Gantz, *Early Greek Myth: A Guide to Literary and Artistic Sources*, 2 vols. (Baltimore: Johns Hopkins University Press, 1993), 1.318–23; 2.564–7, 571–6. Herodotus, *Hist.* 6.61.3; Isocrates, *Hel enc.* 10.63; Euripides, *Helen,* 1666–9. See further Jack Lindsay, *Helen of Troy: Woman and Goddess* (London: Constable, 1974); Ruby Blondell, *Helen of Troy: Beauty, Myth, Devastation* (New York: Oxford University Press, 2013), 43–7, 158–63, 219.
[42] Plato, *Phaedrus* 243a; cf. *Resp.* 9.586c; Isocrates, *Hel. enc.* 10.64; Pausanias, *Descr.* 3.19.11–3.20.1. See further C. M. Bowra, "Two Palinodes of Stesichorus," *Classical Review* 13 (1963): 245–52; D. Sider, "The Blinding of Stesichorus," *Zeitschrift für klassische Philologie* 117 (1989): 423–31; J. A. Davison, "Stesichorus and Helen," in *From Archilochus to Pindar: Papers on Greek Literature of the Archaic Period*, ed. J. A. Davison (London: St. Martin's Press, 1968), 196–225; Karen Bassi, "Helen and the Discourse of Denial in Stesichorus' Palinode," *Arethusa* 26, no. 1 (1993): 51–75; Blondell, *Helen*, 117–22.
[43] *Ref.* 6.18.3.
[44] Irenaeus, *Haer.* 1.23.2.
[45] Beyschlag, *Simon Magus*, 128–35.

to save his only daughter. Far from being locked in the "chain of injustice," Simon worked righteousness by freeing this woman from her chains.[46]

Simon was a descending and ascending God (compare John 3:13). When he descended, he assimilated himself to the intervening angelic powers until he took up Simon's flesh.[47] A similar story was told about Jesus in the *Ascension of Isaiah* (early second century CE). In this text, Jesus descends through all levels of heaven, taking the form of the angels in each heaven to pass by unnoticed.[48] If Simonians read this work, they probably assumed that the story of Christ was really the story of Simon. Simon (as a divine entity) was at one point manifest in Jesus, so it would not surprise if he descended in a similar way.

After redeeming Helen from slavery, Simon offered salvation to humans through his own knowledge (*epignōsis*).[49] That is to say, Simon saved people by offering his own wisdom.[50] A similar emphasis on saving knowledge can be found in John, where Jesus prays: "this is eternal life, that they know you, the only true God and Jesus Christ" (17:3). Despite the common script of "salvation by faith," knowledge is a stable and necessary component in most Christian theories of salvation (and faith assumes some modicum of knowledge). In Simonian lore, humans are saved by divine grace, not through works (Eph 2:8-9). Presumably the knowledge Simon bestowed was itself an act of grace.

Simonian salvation meant freedom from the angels and their laws. The careful reader will observe that *Mosaic* laws are not singled out for chastisement. Simonians, as we saw in the *Declaration*, valued the Pentateuch and allegorized it. The angels made by *Ennoia* ruled the nations and invented the laws and customs of countries in order to enslave human beings. Simonian salvation meant freedom from these national rules and conventions.[51]

Simonian ethics was, accordingly, anti-conventional. Yet Simonian liberation was not freedom to do anything. As in many Christian systems, human laws and conventions were replaced by what were thought to be divine regulations preserved in the gospels and Pauline writings. For all his accusations, Irenaeus never had a concrete case of Simonians acting immorally.

Our heresiologist claimed that Simonians rejected the Hebrew prophets. The author of *3 Corinthians* said the same. This claim can be fact-checked against the *Declaration*, where Isaiah is regularly quoted, and an image from Daniel appears.[52] Unless we view the rejection of the prophets as a development in Roman Simonian thought, we need not accept Irenaeus's claim.

Irenaeus noted that, in Simonian thought, the world would be destroyed, leading to the liberation of the redeemed. This sort of speculation is in line with the more pronounced apocalyptic views in *Great Power*: "When the fire burns up everything and

---

[46] Beyschlag, *Simon Magus*, 178–88.
[47] Beyschlag, *Simon Magus*, 171–8.
[48] *Asc. Isa.* 10.17–31. See further Jonathan Knight, "The Origin and Significance of the Angelomorphic Christology in *The Ascension of Isaiah*," *JTS* 63 (2012): 66–105 at 83–5.
[49] Irenaeus, *Haer.* 1.23.3.
[50] Lüdemann, *Untersuchungen*, 79–80.
[51] Beyschlag, *Simon Magus*, 193–203.
[52] *Ref.* 6.13.1; 6.14.7; 6.16.5.

has nothing more to burn, it will cease by itself.... At that time the children of matter will perish... Then the souls will be revealed as pure through the light of the Power."[53] Interestingly, Irenaeus never claimed that Simonians denied the resurrection or the resurrection of the flesh specifically.

Ritual

Irenaeus closed his report by describing Simonian ritual. Unfortunately, we hear little about who led their rites. The man of Lyon dubbed them "mystic priests" or "mystagogues." The name, even if sarcastic, suggests at least some level of organization in the Simonian group, with figures of greater wisdom guiding new initiates. Presumably these leaders performed the exorcisms which Irenaeus also mentioned. Such exorcisms were probably common among Christians in Rome at the time. The "spells" or "enchantments" Simonians supposedly used were possibly the hushed commands spoken in the act of exorcism.

Just as Irenaeus made Simon a magus, he made Simonians into magicians. We need accept neither claim. After all, Irenaeus flung the charge of magic against several of his Christian opponents.[54] Since some of these opponents were imagined to be Simon's disciples, the reputed sins of the sons could be attributed to the father.[55] The Simonian use of love charms is particularly dubious. Simonians were not ascetic, but they evidently did flee "evil lusts"—the same lusts that characterized the angels.[56] The use of demonic "familiars" also seems unlikely for a group said to exorcise demons.

Still, some of Irenaeus's remarks may find indirect and partial corroboration. We have an interesting passage, for instance, from the Coptic *Apocalypse of Peter* (probably late second or early third century CE). Here we find a group who "stands" by the power of wicked rulers. They are given the name of a man and a "naked woman," a woman who has many forms and who suffers in various ways.[57] Typically the multi-formed, much-suffering woman is identified with Helen. She is described as "naked" apparently because she was a former sex worker. We know that some Simonians (obviously named after Simon) were also called Helenians.[58] Simonians are thus the "standing" ones named after Simon and Helen.

If the reference in the *Apocalypse of Peter* is to Simonians, these same Simonians are portrayed as studying dreams. Apparently, they determined which dreams came from a daimon and which did not.[59] Unfortunately, that is the extent of the report in this *Apocalypse*. Irenaeus's account is only partially supported, since these Simonians are never depicted as *sending* dream attendants to cause dreams. They only tell their

---

[53] *Great Pow.* 46.29–47.11 See further Beyschlag, *Simon Magus*, 203–10.
[54] Irenaeus, *Haer.* 1.25.3, 5.
[55] Take the case of Menander in Irenaeus, *Haer* 1.23.5.
[56] *Great Pow.* 40.5–6.
[57] *Apoc. Pet.* (NHC VII,3) 74.28–34.
[58] Celsus in Origen, *Cels.* 5.62.
[59] *Apoc. Pet.* (NHC VII,3) 75.1–4.

clients which dreams come from daimones (and it is unclear whether they viewed these daimones as good or evil).

In Irenaeus's report, Simonians venerated statues representing Simon as Zeus and Helen as Athena. Assuming the accuracy of this data, one should probably clarify that Simonians did not worship Zeus and Athena as such. They worshipped the highest Power in the conventional form of the Greco-Roman high God, Zeus. Zeus was the "many-named" (*polyonomos*) deity, an epithet which might explain why Simonians called Simon, the ultimate manifestation of God on earth, by a variety of names.[60]

Athena, in turn, was an appropriate symbol of Simon's Thought, since she was born fully grown from her father's head.[61] Like other Christians, Simonians worshiped God in human form(s), but the worship was still directed toward God (the Highest Power and Wisdom). Zeus and Athena were but signs and symbols of *Ennoia* and the highest Power.[62]

It is worth pausing to reflect on the Simonian connection of Helen and Athena. Irenaeus is the first to mention it, though the tradition was probably early. In Greek lore, Helen and Athena were both daughters of Zeus. Yet Simonians needed something more to identify them. These goddesses, after all, were very different: Athena was the armored and immortal virgin, while Helen was a mortal abducted in the Trojan War. The key to their identification, I think, comes from the *Declaration*. Here, the Wisdom figure is called "the Seventh Power." The designation taps into Pythagorean lore. Pythagoreans called the number seven "Athena."[63] Simonians were at least familiar enough with Pythagorean lore to say that *Ennoia* transmigrated into different bodies. When Simonians identified the *Seventh* Power with Helen, they could in turn identify her with Athena, represented by the number seven. This was a specifically Simonian identification. Helen and Athena were not normally fused in Greco-Roman lore.

Conclusion

To sum up: between about 150 and 180 CE, Simonians lived in Rome alongside other Christian groups. During this time, Irenaeus presumably became familiar with them on his sojourns to Rome. On one of these visits, he obtained a revised version of Justin's *Syntagma*. Back in Lyon around 180 CE, Irenaeus wrote *Against Heresies* book 1 to undermine Valentinians in his and other regions. He did so by connecting them to a better known and already vilified Christian group, the Simonians. Despite Irenaeus's polemical ends, there seems to be no overriding reason to reject his report entirely. With care and critical sifting, parts of it can be used to gauge Simonian belief and practice in and around Rome in the mid to late second century CE.

---

[60] Beyschlag, *Simon Magus*, 160–4.
[61] Irenaeus, *Haer.* 1.23.4. Gantz, *Early Greek Myth*, 1.79–80, 83–7.
[62] Cf. *Ref.* 6.20.2.
[63] Philo, *Opif.* 100; *Leg. All.* 1.15.

Irenaeus claimed that all "heresies" have their origin from Simon.[64] He also said that the "crowd of gnostics" arose from Simonians.[65] The report is confusing, since Irenaeus also observed that Simonians got their starting points from "gnosis falsely-so-called" (1 Tim 6:20).[66] It seems like a case of circular reasoning, unless "false gnosis," which arose *before* Simon, is different than the "crowd of gnostics" which arose *after* him. All one can say is, given the early development of Simonian theology, it could well have influenced figures like Valentinus, Basilides, and Carpocrates. It would be better, however, not to lump these figures together into the diffuse category of "Gnosticism."[67]

The followers of Simon, said Irenaeus, called themselves "Simonians." But such a name was not meant to separate them from Christian identity. After all, self-designating "catholics" did not thereby exclude themselves from Christianity. Rather, they identified with a particular *type* of Christianity. By the same logic, Simonians were another sort of Christian group, the one founded by a Samarian, not a Judean, apostle.

A major problem for Irenaeus, it seems, was that Simonian Christianity looked rather like his own version of faith. It involved teaching about a high God with a subordinate creator figure said to represent God's mind. It included angels and archangels, some of whom became demonic and wreaked havoc on earth. It claimed that the redeemer descended to save his people. This redeemer was Jesus who died on a cross in Judea. Simonians preached a definitive end of the world. They performed exorcisms like many early catholics. They believed in salvation by grace, not through works (Eph 2:8-9). Simonians, like other Christians, appealed to the gospels and in particular to the parable of the lost sheep (Matt 18:12-14; Luke 15:1-7). They believed in a heavenly Savior. They upheld a trinitarian concept of God.

The Simonian focus on Simon, naturally, made all the difference. Simon evidently came to be viewed as the fullest manifestation of God ("the Father"). But insofar as the highest Power was also Jesus, the son of God, then Simonians also believed in Christ and had as much right to the name "Christian" as any other Jesus-believing group. We learn of no concrete case of Simonians rejecting the Hebrew prophets and they never attacked the Pentateuch or the gospels. As they read the gospels, they must have supposed that other Christians had yet to realize the higher truth: that Simon was Jesus in another—and higher—form. Accordingly, the truth of Jesus was the truth of Simon, and it was this insight, perhaps more than any other, that made Simonians Christians.

There are other differences distinguishing Simonian from early catholic Christianity. Simonians asserted a doctrine of transmigration. They applied it to Helen, but may have assumed that other souls transmigrated as well. Simonians comfortably redeployed stories and symbols from Greco-Roman lore, as we see in their use of Homer's epics and of Greco-Roman statuary. They worshiped God's Wisdom and claimed that she was incarnate in various women throughout history. This meant that there was some faint impress of truth even in Greco-Roman culture (Athena as her Father's Thought).

---

[64] Irenaeus, *Haer.* 1.23.2.
[65] Irenaeus, *Haer.* 1.29.1.
[66] White, "How to Read a Book," 125–49.
[67] Karen L. King, *What Is Gnosticism?* (Cambridge, MA: Belknap Press, 2003); Michael Williams, *Rethinking "Gnosticism": An Argument for Dismantling a Dubious Category* (Princeton: Princeton University Press, 1996), entire.

They had suspicions about human conventions as the legislation of wicked angels; though none of them was indicted for breaking state laws.

Some Simonians, at least, were highly educated. They were readers of Homer. They also apparently read the lesser known poet Stesichorus—or at least knew of him. They were familiar enough with Greco-Roman lore to see Athena, born from her Father's mind, as a symbol of Helen. Their identification probably assumes some knowledge of Pythagorean number theory (Athena as the virginal seven). They were also happy to see Zeus as a representation of Simon. They evidently knew about the latest theological developments among other Christians (Logos theology and modalism). They used allegory to interpret gospel parables. They also engaged in practices such as exorcism, led by "mystic priests."

Overall, apart from hackneyed rumors that Simonians performed "magic" and claims that they rejected the prophets—most traditions transmitted by Irenaeus seem at least partially reliable. In several ways, Irenaeus's report goes back to material Justin reported about 145 CE. Even so, one should reckon with significant changes in Simonian theology in the thirty-five years between 145 and 180 CE. Simonians changed with the times, adopting trinitarian modalism, for instance, and heightening their devotion to Simon. Other doctrines remained the same, such as the apocalyptic end of the world, and reference to God as the highest Power. Of all the surviving and substantive heresiological reports on Simon, Irenaeus's is the earliest and—despite its blending of previous reports and patent hostility—is probably the most dependable overall. It is this report, at any rate, that would be adopted, expanded, contracted, and distorted by the host of heresiologists to come.

6

Tertullian

Introduction

The talented writer and witty firebrand Tertullian (about 170–225 CE) was a man of Carthage in North Africa (modern Tunisia). Claims that he was trained as a lawyer and that his father was a soldier are based on unreliable biographical notices.[1] Virtually all we know of him comes from his writings. These documents show that he enjoyed an excellent education in literature and rhetoric. His knowledge of philosophy was considerable, though in this domain he may have been self-taught.

Tertullian composed most of his nearly three dozen works during the reign of the emperor Septimius Severus (193–211 CE). Toward the end of his life, he joined the New Prophecy, an originally Phrygian Christian movement featuring practices of fasting and ecstatic speech. Tertullian never formally left early catholic networks in Carthage, but he did begin referring to catholics as "soulish," as opposed to "spiritual."[2] In criticism of less rigorous Christians, he spoke out against the practice of remarriage, unveiled women in church, and the avoidance of persecution.[3]

By comparison with his attacks on Marcion, Apelles, and Valentinus, Tertullian wrote little against Simon and the Simonians. His knowledge of Simon depends almost entirely on Irenaeus's report. As a master of rhetoric, however, Tertullian reframed, rephrased, and rearranged this report, adding several polemical twists which give the illusion that he had special information. Only in a single case, it seems, did Tertullian have anything like independent data.

Attack on Simon

In his work *On the Soul* (203 CE), Tertullian attacked Simon in the course of a refutation of transmigration. The Simonian theory of transmigration highlighted Helen, but may

---

[1] Jerome, *Illustrious Men*, 53.
[2] Tertullian, *Praxeas* 1.7; *Modesty* 1.10; 21.16; *Resurrection* 22.1.
[3] See further Timothy Barnes, ed., *Tertullian: A Historical and Literary Study*, Revised ed. (Oxford: Clarendon, 2011); David Wright, "Tertullian," in *The Early Christian World*, ed. Philip F. Esler (London: Routledge, 2000), 2.1027–47; Geoffrey D. Dunn, *Tertullian* (London: Routledge, 2004); David E. Wilhite, *Tertullian the African: An Anthropological Reading of Tertullian's Contexts and Identities* (Berlin: de Gruyter, 2007), esp. 18–36.

have included other souls as well. As Tertullian observed, Simonians did not accept the view that human souls wandered in the bodies of beasts. Yet the North African still condemned "Simon" for asserting Helen's reincarnation:

> The insane opinion which reshapes human souls into bestial ones has not, so far, burst forth under the name of a heretic, but I necessarily attack and exclude the form of transmigration as consistent with those [Hellenic theories] above. By this means, Homer in the peacock will be refuted just as Euphorbus in Pythagoras. So too this version of soul travel or body shifting will be rebuffed and whatever aided the heretics cut down.
>
> For Simon, too, the purchaser of the holy Spirit in the Acts of the Apostles, later condemned to destruction by that very apostle—along with his money—wept in vain. As a solace for being punished, he turned to battle the truth, trusting in the power of his art. To accomplish the tricks of some power or other, he bought a certain Helen of Tyre from the public whorehouse with that very same money, a price he deemed worthy for the holy Spirit.
>
> He pretends he is the highest Father and that she is his first Thought by which he thought to produce angels and archangels. She, knowing his purpose, leapt forth from the Father and sunk down to the lower regions. Here, by her Father's predetermined plan, she bore angelic powers who were ignorant of the Father, the makers of this world. By these powers she was detained by a passion she did not requite. Lest, when she left, they be considered the progeny of another, she was abandoned to every outrage. In order that no one learn how to free her at reduced price, she succumbed to human form, imprisoned, as by chains, in flesh.
>
> Thus through many ages, rolled through all sorts of female forms, she became that Helen who was a massive fatality to Priam and, in time to come, to Stesichorus' eyes. She blinded him due to an insult in his poem, then bestowed his sight again when satisfied by his praise.
>
> In the same way, she migrated from body to body and finally—under a pet name of shame—prostituted herself as that cheaper Helen. She, then, was the lost sheep to whom the highest Father descended—Simon, of course. He first restored and let her ride him, whether on his shoulders or on his thighs, I don't know. At that point, he turned his attention to saving humans, as in a suit for damages, from those angelic powers. These powers were deceived as Simon changed his shape. He did the same with people, showing up as a sham person, first as Son in Judea and as Father in Samaria.
>
> O Helen! How you toil among poets and heretics. Once you were infamous for adultery, now for fornication. But wait—is not her deliverance from Troy more glorious than freedom from a brothel? You came from Troy at the price of a thousand ships, but not nearly a thousand bucks, I think, from that sex dungeon. For shame, Simon! You were slower in seeking her and more inconsistent in getting her back. Menelaus immediately pursued his lost wife; he immediately sought her who

had been abducted, and forced a decade-long war. He did not hide, use deceit, or jeering. I fear that he was more of a father to her since he labored more vigilantly to recover Helen, more daringly, and for a longer time. (Tertullian, *On the Soul* 34.1-5)[4]

In this *tour de force*, Tertullian did not quote Acts like Irenaeus. Instead, he summarized his own interpretation guided by the hand of his predecessor. The North African's interpretation was hostile and in many respects untamed by the text of Acts. For instance, Tertullian dubbed Simon "purchaser of the holy Spirit." But Simon in Acts did not wish to purchase the Spirit; he wanted training to transmit it (Acts 8:19). Simon was not "condemned to destruction" by Peter. Nor was he "cursed by the apostles" or "rejected from the faith."[5] In fact, Peter invited Simon to repent (Acts 8:22), and Simon begged for apostolic prayer and forgiveness (8:24).

The North African mentioned Simon's tears, which indicates he was reading what is sometimes called the "Western text" of Acts. Here Simon, after seeking Peter's prayers, "wept without ceasing" (8:24).[6] Tertullian chose to twist this rather patent sign of penitence, claiming that Simon wept "in vain." This interpretation is arbitrary, and determined by Irenaeus's view that Simon declared war on the apostles after renewing his magical training. Nothing of the sort is found in Acts.

In *On the Soul*, Tertullian omitted mentioning Simon's reputed statue in Rome. He did mention it, however, in his *Apologeticus* (13.9) when running through examples of Roman deification.[7] Simon, by virtue of receiving a statue, was deified by the Roman state. Tertullian never questioned this point or tried to verify the inscription supposedly dedicated to "a sacred god" (*sancti dei*). He sandwiched the deified Simon between "a common whore" (Larentina) and Antinous, boy-lover of Hadrian, made into a god. That Simon was a Roman state god was apparently no surprise to Tertullian.

When the heresiologist turned to Helen, he stretched his legs for several intuitive leaps. Simon "buys" Helen, as in Irenaeus, from the "brothel" (literally "the place of public lust"), but he does so, said Tertullian, with the very same money with which he tried to pay the apostles. This datum is unique. We need not imagine Tertullian had any other source for it beyond his own imagination. He melded together a tradition from Acts (Simon's offer of money) with a tradition stemming ultimately from Justin (the redemption of Helen). The pugilist made this arbitrary deduction, and on its fabricated foundation insulted Simon who supposedly rated Helen and the Spirit at equal price.

The assumption seems to be that Simon considered Helen to be the holy Spirit, for Tertullian omitted—I think deliberately—the tradition that Simon, as Father in Samaria and Son in Judea, was also *Spirit among the nations*. Simon, apparently, was not Spirit because Helen was. If Tertullian did understand the Simonian Helen this way, it touches on a point in the *Declaration* where the Seventh Power is the Spirit

---

[4] Text in Waszink, *De Anima*, 49–50.
[5] Tertullian, *Idol.* 9.6 (*maledictus ab apostolis de fide eiectus est*).
[6] See the apparatus in the *Novum Testamentum Graecum Editio Critica Maior III: Die Apostelgeschichte*, ed. Holger Strutwolf, Georg Gäbel, Annette Hüffmeier, Gerd Mink, and Klaus Wachtel. Part 1.1: Text (Stuttgart: Deutsche Bibelgesellschaft, 2017), 271.
[7] Gerald H. Rendall, trans., *Tertullian: Apology, De Spectaculis*, LCL (London: Heinemann, 1931), 72.

hovering over the waters (Gen 1:2).[8] Tertullian probably never read the *Declaration*, though its traditions may have floated independently.

According to Irenaeus, the angels detained *Ennoia* because they did not want to be considered another's offspring. Tertullian inserted the idea that they were *erotically* drawn to Helen (he never calls her *Ennoia*) and so imprisoned her. Here the North African may have imported an idea from the story of Helen of Troy, abducted due to the wiles of eros. This Helen consented to be loved by Paris, whereas Simon's Helen spurned the love of her angelic progeny. The fact that Helen's children wished to sexually abuse their Mother introduces an Oedipal element into the story.

One begins to detect some latent misogyny in several of Tertullian's remarks. He uniquely referred to Helen bought at "reduced price," giving the impression that she, in whatever form, was always up for sale. Simon's bid for Helen was less than a thousand dollars (in Latin, denarii), which Tertullian evidently considered a rock bottom price for a female sex slave. He insinuated Helen's selfish motives when she healed Stesichorus. He presented Helen as a disaster for men, including Priam, king of Troy, Stesichorus, and presumably Simon. (King Priam had allowed his son Paris to possess Helen as wife; at the end of the war, Priam was hacked to pieces as he clung pitifully to an altar.) Tertullian's Helen was not her real name, but a "pet name of shame" (used by ancient sex workers). She willingly prostituted herself (as opposed to being sold into sex slavery) and was thus guilty of "fornication" (*stuprum*). She was apparently easy prey for Simon, here portrayed with the same lust as the angels. Every bit of this "report" is little more than saber rattling, polemical window dressing based on earlier sources.

When it came to sexual imagery, Tertullian had few inhibitions. Simon as the good shepherd should have taken up Helen, the lost sheep, on his shoulders (as the Good Shepherd was commonly depicted in art).

Tertullian, however, suggested that one view Helen riding doggy style on Simon's "thighs." To put it crudely, Tertullian depicted Simon as a Casanova willing to pay for a permanent escort. The man of Carthage seems not to have realized how his own imagination—impure by his own standards—did violence to Simonian theology. As Tertullian well knew, Simonian's considered Simon to be the *Father* of Helen, not her lover. Nonetheless, Tertullian turned a story of redemption by grace into a soap opera of lust and incest.

The Carthaginian depicted Simon's salvific mission as something of an afterthought, but the redemption of Helen and of humanity were, for Simonians, organically related. The creatrix is redeemed first so that she can light the way of wisdom for all souls. Tertullian more or less repeated Irenaeus's charge that Simon, because he changed shape, was not really human. I doubt any Simonian would have agreed. Simon was as human as much as Jesus was, because Simon and Jesus were manifestations of the same being, the highest Power (see Chapter 5).

What is striking about Tertullian's report in *On the Soul* is its lack of interest in Simonians, as opposed to Simon. The North African omitted all the traditions reported by Irenaeus about Simonian ethics, freedom from conventions, salvation by grace, mystic priests, exorcism, as well as the idea that Simon became the father of all alternative Christian groups. In his *Prescription against Heresies*, however, Tertullian

---

[8] *Ref.* 6.14.4.

Figure 6.1 Christ the Good Shepherd, catacomb of San Callisto in Rome. Public domain, Wikimedia Commons.

referred in passing to the "discipline of Simonian magic"—no examples given.[9] In the same context, Tertullian accused Simonians of worshiping angels. This seems a baseless charge, since Simonians believed—and Tertullian reported—that they were *liberated* from angels and their powers. Presumably they would not worship their oppressors.

Later in *On the Soul*, Tertullian accused Simonians of solemnly promising to raise the departed souls of the prophets.[10] This is another extraordinary and unique tradition. Presumably, Tertullian had no reason to invent this one, since it contradicts Irenaeus's claim that Simonians rejected the prophets. Simonians could not have spurned the prophets if they went to the trouble of calling up their souls for information. What these Simonians inquired of the prophets is never told. It is unclear what Tertullian's source for this tradition was. Possibly it was tradition heard only in Africa.

Conclusion

If Tertullian could uniquely report a Simonian practice in North Africa he just might have encountered a Simonian group there. Based on such thin evidence, however, one

---

[9] Tertullian, *Praescr.* 33.12: *Simonianae autem magiae disciplina angelis serviens* ("The discipline of Simonian magic serves angels").
[10] Tertullian, *An.* 57.7.

can only speculate. There were strong networks between North Africa and Rome, and Christians participated in these networks as merchants, sailors, and literate experts. It would be no surprise if Simonians in Rome made it to the biggest city in North Africa of the time. But on this score, there is no solid evidence.

If we imagine Simonians in Carthage, we might envision them practicing distinctive rituals. One of these was a kind of séance in which they called up prophetic souls. The ritual might have been something like what we find in the famous passage about the medium at Endor (1 Sam 28:3-25).[11] The Israelite king Saul went to this female diviner and asked her to call up the soul of the prophet Samuel. She engaged in some sort of ritual invocation (the details are not supplied), and Samuel's ghost rose from the ground. Saul then inquired of the prophet. Samuel's answers, as it turned out, proved true—to Saul's chagrin. The truth of the prophecy vouches for the truth of the vision. Simonians, in their own minds, did not parley with demons; they spoke with the blessed dead.

The Simonian use of prophetic divination is a good example of how heresiologists can be used to check their colleagues. We already doubted the report (in Irenaeus and *3 Corinthians*) that Simonians rejected the prophets based on the use of Isaiah and Daniel in the *Declaration*. Tertullian supplies more evidence that Simonians respected the prophets by calling up their souls in search of knowledge. Presumably, Simonians would not have gone to such lengths if they did not consider the prophets reliable. If the prophets spoke truly after death, they spoke truth in life as well. This implies that Simonians considered their writings genuine, not inspired by wicked angels.

As noted in the introduction, Tertullian does not supply much more information about Simonians than Irenaeus. Accordingly, much of what we can deduce about Simonians from Irenaeus applies to Tertullian's report as well. Yet the North African included at least one other detail worth noting. He portrayed the Simonians as spiritual seekers, not knowers. In fact, they were apparently one of many alternative Christian groups who emphasized Jesus's saying, "seek and you shall find" (Matt 7:7).[12] According to Simonians, a person did not find the whole truth when they became a Christian. Becoming a Christian was only the beginning of a long journey toward spiritual understanding. The apostles themselves did not know the entire truth, and some of Jesus's teachings were secret as well. It took effort to find these secret truths which came only through restricted channels. In addition to discovering these private revelations, Simonians were open to new prophetic visions as well.

The report rings true. Everything we know about Simonians indicates an openness toward truth, a willingness to change and develop their thought over time in light of new understandings of truth. The diversity of Simonian lore is in part explained by this openness. They had a philosophical account of creation (the *Declaration*). They came to develop a theory of the Trinity. They drew from Homer as well as the

---

[11] Justin, *Dial.* 105.4. See further Rowan A. Greer and Margaret M. Mitchell, *The Belly-myther of Endor: Interpretations of 1 Kingdoms 28 in the Early Church* (Atlanta: SBL Press, 2007).

[12] Tertullian, *Praescr.* 8-10.

gospels. They accepted lore from prophets and the Pentateuch. Tertullian knew that his opponents—including the Simonians—had a basis for their beliefs in scripture, which is why he chose not to refute them on biblical grounds.[13] As in all cases, one must learn to distinguish Simonian belief from heresiological slander. Tertullian's report lilts toward libel, but, when sifted, some golden flecks appear, enriching our picture of the Simonians.

---

[13] Tertullian, *Praescr.* 15.4.

7

The Refutator

Introduction

The author of the *Refutation of All Heresies* (whom I will call the Refutator) has proven to be a puzzle. We do not even know his name. He depicted himself as a learned and hardworking scholar-bishop, a genuine intellectual in stark contrast to the putatively ignoramus bishop Zephyrinus and ex-slave banker Callistus. The Refutator strongly opposed Callistus, who claimed the laurels of leading the early catholic church in Rome (217–222 CE). The Refutator seems to have exercised episcopal—what he called "high-priestly"—authority over another Christian group in Rome, which, for him, represented the true church.[1]

Yet the church our author led looks more like a sect in sociological terms.[2] The Refutator enforced a strict morality and preserved social hierarchies. He was painfully conscious of living under the shadow of a dominant ecclesial "other." He took pride in the fact that he hounded Callistus for his "heresy" and opposed him in open debate.[3] If the author was not a "schismatic" (a pejorative term rooted in ecclesiastical politics), he was a minority Christian intellectual opposed to the most populous Roman church at the time, vying with its bishop for equal power and influence.[4]

Since the Refutator did not attack Callistus's successors, and spoke of few post-Callistan developments, his work was most likely published not long after Callistus died in 222 CE. The Refutator lived in Rome and perished under unknown circumstances some time before 250 CE. He cannot confidently be identified with an eastern writer or western martyr called "Hippolytus." The *Refutation* was not associated with the name "Hippolytus" until the late nineteenth century. Thus there is little reason to believe that he was martyred or that he reconciled with the early catholics in Rome.[5]

The Refutator based his report on Simon on a creative fusion of data from Justin and Irenaeus, combined with unique elements derived from his own research. As the fruits of his research, the Refutator paraphrased and quoted excerpts from the *Declaration*.

---

[1] *Ref.* 1, preface §6.
[2] Rodney Stark and William Sims Bainbridge, *The Future of Religion: Secularization, Revival and Cult Formation* (Berkeley: University of California Press, 1985), 24–6, 48–67, 99–125.
[3] *Ref.* 9.12.15.
[4] See further Allen Brent, *Hippolytus and the Roman Church in the Third Century: Communities in Tension before the Emergence of a Monarch-Bishop*, VCSup 32 (Leiden: Brill, 1995), esp. 415–17.
[5] *Ref.* 9.12.21. See further Litwa, *Refutation*, xl–xlii.

96 Simon of Samaria and the Simonians

The focus of this chapter, however, is not on the *Declaration* (Chapter 1), but on the report wrapped around it.

The Refutator's report against Simon opens *Refutation* book 6. It was preceded by the four "snake heresies" in book 5 (Naassenes, Peratai, Sethians, and Justin, author of *Baruch*), which the Refutator apparently thought came before Simon. After Simon, the Refutator treated Valentinus, since he connected Simonian and Valentinian lore. The Refutator's overall purpose was to prove that his enemies depended, not on biblical data, but on Greco-Roman philosophy, poetry, astrology, and mystery cult lore.[6] The report on Simon is no exception, though the Refutator never consistently linked Simon to any single philosopher or philosophical system.[7]

> It is fitting also to present the doctrines of Simon, from the town of Geittenos, a village in Samaria. I will show how those who followed him, too, after taking their starting points from him, ventured the same doctrines[8] in different terms. This Simon, as an expert in magic—by both toying with many people by the art of Thrasymedes . . . and by practicing mischief through demons—attempted to deify himself, though he was a mortal, a charlatan, and brimful of insanity. He it was whom the apostles refuted in Acts (8:20-23).

> Apsethos the Libyan, yearning to be considered a god in Libya, made a much wiser and more moderate attempt to deify himself. His story, not wholly incongruous with the desire of Simon—fool that he is—it seems right to relate, since it was worthy of Simon's attempt.

> Apsethos the Libyan set his heart on becoming a god. But when by meddling he totally failed to achieve his desire, he still wished to appear to have become one. Indeed, after some time, he truly seemed to have become a god. For the stupid Libyans made it their custom to sacrifice to him as to some divine power, supposing they were obeying a voice from heaven above.

> To explain: Apsethos, after gathering into one and the same cage a host of parrots, locked them up. (The province of Libya is full of parrots that clearly and closely imitate the human voice.) This fool raised the birds for a period of time, teaching them to say, "Apsethos is a god!" When the birds had practiced for a long time, and repeatedly squawked what Apsethos thought would make him be considered a god, he threw open the cage and released the parrots in all directions. When the birds flew, their squawk went out to all Libya, and their words spread as far as Greek territory.[9] This is how the Libyans, awestruck at the voice of the birds, and not understanding the trick performed by Apsethos, held him to be a god.

---

[6] *Ref.* 1, preface §8.
[7] The following translation of the Refutator's report is based on my 2016 edition of the *Refutation*, with small improvements based on a fresh reading of the sole surviving manuscript (Parasinus supplément grec 464).
[8] Δόγματα ("doctrines") is added by M. Marcovich, ed., *Hippolytus: Refutatio omnium haeresium*, PTS 25 (Berlin: de Gruyter, 1986), 212.
[9] Cf. Ps 18:5, LXX.

But one of the Greeks, when he accurately understood the artifice of the supposed god, not only refuted him through the same parrots, but also destroyed that boastful and vulgar man. This Greek, having confined many of the parrots, retaught them to say, "Apsethos, locking us up, forced us to say: 'Apsethos is a god!'" When the Libyans heard the parrots' palinode, they all came together with one intent and burnt Apsethos to the ground.[10]

So we must consider that Simon the magus conforms all the more to the Libyan who thus became a god insofar as he forms the exact image of Apsethos, and experienced a similar calamity.[11]

Let me attempt to "re-teach the parrots" of Simon to affirm that Simon "Who Stood, Stands, and Will Stand" was not the Christ. Instead, he was a mortal man, born from a woman's seed, from the mixing of blood lines and fleshly desire just like the rest of human beings. That this is actually the case, I will easily prove in my present report.

[The *Declaration* is here omitted. See Appendix 1] . . .

Simon . . . allegorizes the wooden horse, the figure of Helen with her torch, and a host of other things about which he, transferring to himself and his *Epinoia*, speaks volumes. She is the wandering sheep who, always taking up residence in women, disturbed the powers in the cosmos on account of her incomparable beauty. Thus the Trojan War happened because of her, since *Epinoia* dwelled in the woman who became the Helen of that time. In this way, when all the authorities claimed her, she stirred up faction and war among the nations in which she appeared. So also Stesichorus, when he reviled her in his verses, was struck blind. But when he repented, he wrote his "palinodes" in which he hymned her, and regained his sight.

She, after transmigrating under the control of angels and the lower authorities (who also, he says, made the world), later took her place at a brothel in Tyre, a city of Phoenicia. She it was whom Simon found when he descended. He claimed that he had come to search for his first . . .[12] to free her from her chains. After he redeemed her, he took her around with him, alleging that this was the lost sheep. Meanwhile, he called himself "the Power above all things."[13] But the liar was in love with this girl called Helen.[14] Accordingly, he bought and possessed her. Since he was ashamed before his disciples, he concocted this tale.

The Simonians, for their part, are imitators of Simon the deceiver and magician, and they perform the same works. They irrationally claim that it is necessary to

---

[10] For the theme of self-deification and its disastrous results, see Isa 14:12–14; Ezek 28; Dan 4; Acts 12:20–3; Philo, *Post.*, 114–15; Josephus, *Ant.* 4.2.4.
[11] The MS reading ἀπεικάζοντας, following ἡγητέον, is difficult. I read ἀπεικάζειν.
[12] The manuscript here is obscured. Marcovich reconstructs τα(ύ)τ(η)ς (*Hippolytus*, 226).
[13] Cf. Acts 8:10 (Samarians call Simon the great Power).
[14] Here ψυδρός ("liar") is an emendation of the MS reading ψυχρός ("cold-hearted," "heartless," "indifferent"). Other conjectures can be found in Marcovich, *Hippolytus*, 226.

have intercourse by virtue of their maxim: "all soil is soil, and it does not matter where one sows, just that one sows." In fact, they even congratulate themselves with regard to . . .[15] intercourse, calling it "perfect love." They use this slogan: "The holy joined to what is holy will be made holy." To be sure, they are not controlled by any supposed vice, since they have been redeemed!

Having redeemed Helen, Simon provided salvation to humans in the same manner: through his own knowledge. Since the angels mismanaged the world on account of their lust to rule, he said that he arrived for its rectification. He transformed and assimilated himself to the rulers, authorities, and angels. He appeared to be human but was not. He seemed to suffer in Judea, although he suffered nothing. But after appearing in Judea as Son, and in Samaria as Father, and among the rest of the nations as the holy Spirit, he allowed himself to be called by whatever name people wish to call him.

Now the prophets, inspired from the angels who made the world, spoke their prophecies. Accordingly, those loyal to Simon and Helen pay no attention to them up to the present time. They do whatever they want as free persons. They claim that they are saved by his grace, and that there is no cause of judgment if one acts evilly. This is because there is nothing evil by nature, but only by imposition. For the angels who made the world, he says, imposed whatever they wanted, aiming to enslave those who listen to their brand of teachings. But Simonians say that when their own people are redeemed, the world in turn will dissolve.

The disciples of this man perform feats of magic and use enchantments, philters, and love charms. Moreover, they send off the so-called "dream-sending demons" to disturb whoever they want. In fact, they employ, as a regular practice, so-called "assistants."

They possess a statue of Simon in the form of Zeus and Helen in the form of Athena. They worship these statues, calling the one "Lord," the other "Queen." If someone, catching sight of the statues of Simon or Helen, calls them "Simon and Helen," he is cast out as one ignorant of the mysteries.

This Simon, as he was deceiving many by his magic arts in Samaria, was refuted by the apostles. When he was laid under a curse, as it is written in Acts, he despaired and later attempted the same activities. Even at Rome, where he moved, he was at loggerheads with the apostles. Peter opposed him many times, since he was deceiving most people by magic arts.

In the end, this Simon went to Gitta, sat down under a plane tree, and taught. Finally, since he was close to being refuted due to the long delay of time, he said that if he was buried alive, he would rise on the third day. So, ordering a trench to be dug, he bid his disciples to bury him. They did what he commanded. There he remains till now—since he was not the Christ.

---

[15] The adjective here is obscured in the manuscript. If it is ξένῃ, as printed by Marcovich (*Hippolytus*, 227), it need mean no more than "foreign."

This is the man, and this is the myth of Simon! From it, Valentinus took his starting points, referring to it with different terminology. For by common consent, the aeons of Valentinus—namely, Mind, Truth, Word, Life, Human, and Church—are the six roots of Simon: Mind, Thought, Voice, Name, Reasoning, and Conception. (*Ref.* 6.7.1–9.2; 6.19.1–20.4)

Simon the Self-deifier

As with Justin, the Refutator underscored Simon's self-deification. Yet the Refutator took the accusation to a whole new level. He believed that Simon engineered the entire theology of the *Declaration* in order to make himself a god.[16] Like most Greco-Roman authors (including Christians), the Refutator considered self-deification to be utter madness and stupidity.[17]

To paint a picture of Simon's folly, the Refutator related the story of Apsethos. Here, as Edwards wryly observed, the Refutator "has the preacher's way of telling another man's story: his method is to ruin it by improving it, to edify without probity till he amuses without design."[18] Yet there is a barbed sort of design here. The implied reader is apparently meant to laugh at the dullness of Apsethos and to dismiss Simon as a "fool" even before his teaching is described.[19]

The Refutator did not invent Apsethos's story, though his tale does not match the plot of any other account.[20] There was, however, a core narrative on which those who wrote about him agreed: Apsethos obtained and trained a group of parrots to repeat the daring line, "Apsethos is a god." Now since birds were commonly thought to communicate the will of the gods (though usually through their flight), Apsethos wagered that those who independently heard the parrots, released far and wide, would take their mantra as a divine oracle.[21]

It is only when Apsethos frees the birds that the stories about him begin to diverge. In one account, the Libyans believe the birds and sacrifice to Apsethos as a god. In this tale, Apsethos was great a success. In another version, the birds forget their mantra and the plan is foiled.

The Refutator followed the first account. Yet unlike it, he added a macabre punishment. Tapping into common stereotypes of his day, he introduced a clever Greek to correct the "stupid" Libyans. This impressive Greek somehow recollected all the parrots (from Greece and Libya!) and taught them to say the impossibly long

---

[16] *Ref.* 6.14.1; 6.18.1.
[17] Litwa, *Desiring Divinity* 1–64.
[18] Edwards, "Bad Samaritan," 80.
[19] *Ref.* 6.7.2.
[20] In fact, no ancient writer agreed exactly on the Libyan's name. He is called Psapho (reminiscent of an Egyptian sage) in one author, Hanno (a Carthaginian name) in another, and Apsephas in a third. See Maximus of Tyre, *Or.* 29.4; Aelian, *Var. hist.* 14.30; and the scholium to Dio Chrysostom, *Orations* 1.14. These texts are printed and briefly commented on by Osborne, *Rethinking*, 70–3, 359–60.
[21] Edward Dixon, "Descending Spirit and Descending Gods: A 'Greek' Interpretation of the Spirit's 'Descent as a Dove' in Mark 1:10," *JBL* 128 (2009): 759–80.

sentence: "Apsethos, locking us up, forced us to say, 'Apsethos is a god.'"[22] When these brilliant birds managed to memorize their line, they were again sent to the winds. When the Libyans received the new message from the "gods," they flew into a frenzy and lynched Apsethos.

What is amusing about this tale is that—though the Refutator imagined himself as that clever Greek reteaching "Simon's parrots"—he himself was duped by the heresiological tradition.[23] The reader will recall that it is only with Justin (Chapter 4) that the tale of Simon's self-deification was first invented. The Refutator followed Justin's fictional framing of Simon without question, then mocked the Samarian as stupider than the Libyan. But the Refutator sparred with shadows. He attacked a man of straw.

The Refutator misleads in other ways as well. On the basis of the *Declaration*, he identified Simon with the one Who Stood, Stands, and Will Stand.[24] The assertion is arbitrary and shows that the Refutator contaminated his reading of the *Declaration* with the reports from Justin and Irenaeus. Nowhere in the *Declaration* does "Simon" refer to himself as the Standing One. The Standing designation refers to God (either as the Infinite or Seventh Power) in a triple phase of evolution.[25] The *Declaration* did propose a theory of deification, but in no way is it limited to Simon. The Simon of the *Declaration* was a revealer who opened up the path of deification to all. As the Refutator himself indicated, "There is, then, according to Simon, that blessed and incorruptible reality hidden *in every human being* . . . which is the One Who Stood, Stands, and Will Stand."[26]

There is, admittedly, a place in the *Declaration* that may have convinced the Refutator to find what he wished. It is the passage which solemnly relays, "I and you are one. What is before me is you. What is after you is I."[27] If the Refutator understood these lines as spoken by Simon, we can see how he might accuse Simon of self-deification. The context reveals, however, that the speaker of the phrase is the Seventh Power, said to "hover upon the waters" (Gen 1:2) in perfect assimilation to God (Gen 1:26). This singular Power is also called "Mother" and "Root of the universe."[28]

At some later stage, apparently, Simonians did identify Simon with the Infinite (or highest) Power. But the identification is never made in the *Declaration*. The Simon of the *Declaration* is not a self-deifier. To the contrary, deification was open to "*whoever attains the likeness.*"[29] Again, the witness of Clement is decisive: Simonians *as a group* assimilated to the Standing One, who was not identified as Simon.[30]

---

[22] On talking animals, see Janet E. Spittler, *Animals in the Apocryphal Acts of the Apostles: The Wild Kingdom of Early Christian Literature*, WUNT II/247 (Tübingen: Mohr Siebeck, 2008), 51–75.
[23] *Ref.* 6.9.1.
[24] *Ref.* 6.9.1.
[25] *Ref.* 6.12.2; 6.13.1; 6.18.4.
[26] *Ref.* 6.17.1, emphasis added.
[27] *Ref.* 6.17.2.
[28] *Ref.* 6.17.2–3.
[29] *Ref.* 6.12.3, emphasis added.
[30] Clement, *Strom.* 2.11.52.2.

Helen as Epinoia

Beginning in *Refutation* 6.19, the Refutator turned from Simon to Helen. Significantly, he used her divine name "*Epinoia*," as opposed to *Ennoia* (in Justin and Irenaeus), following the language of the *Declaration*. Although *Epinoia* does not refer to Helen in the *Declaration*, the Refutator, nodding to heresiological tradition, assumed that Helen of Tyre was a form of *Epinoia*.

Much of *Epinoia*'s story is rehash from Irenaeus. The Refutator began, however, with some new material. He claimed that Simonians allegorized the Trojan horse, the figure of Helen with her torch, "and a host of other things" applied to both Simon and *Epinoia*.[31] For this material, the Refutator evidently depended on another unknown source.

In Virgil's *Aeneid* (6.517-19) we learn that Helen, "pretending a dance, led around the Trojan women singing '*euhoe*' in Bacchic revels; she herself in their midst was holding a huge torch and was calling the Greeks from the top of the citadel."[32] It is a fascinating scene. The Trojan horse had already been hauled into the city, and the Trojans, deluded, were celebrating their victory over the Greeks. Helen knew the truth of the soldiers nestled in the horse's womb. She took the opportunity—in pretended festivity—to signal "attack" to the Greeks outside the city.

In the Simonian allegory, the Trojans were apparently understood as the wicked angels who abducted *Epinoia* from heaven and locked her up in their city (representing earth). Helen, whose very name (according to Hesychius) meant "torch," thus attempted to shine the light of her internal divinity signaling to her Father the path of rescue.[33] The Father, in this story, would be Simon, the divine warrior who tricked the Trojans by coming in secret. On the outside, that is, Simon looked like any other man after surreptitiously descending past the angelic guards of earth's walled "city." But he was the Father in flesh.

The Refutator related, like Irenaeus, how *Epinoia* was the lost sheep wandering in the wheel of transmigration. He added, however, a kind of flashback: *Epinoia* "disturbed the powers of the cosmos on account of her incomparable beauty."[34] Here, as we saw with Tertullian, an element from Helen of Troy's tale leaked into the account of *Epinoia*. Thus we have another motive for why the powers—*Epinoia*'s children—attacked her. It was not because they wanted to hide their origin (so Irenaeus), it was because they were sexually aroused. The Refutator's account of *Epinoia* is thus at once more bawdy and more Oedipal: the powers wanted to have sex with their Mother. (One wonders if the Refutator did not tell this version of the story to conform it to his account of Valentinian Wisdom, who caused "uproar" in the Fullness.[35])

Just as *Epinoia*'s beauty threw the powers into disarray, so did Helen of Troy. She was considered the cause of war when two political alliances—the city states of Greece

---

[31] *Ref.* 6.19.1.
[32] See further Meredith Prince, "Helen of Rome? Helen in Vergil's *Aeneid*," *Helios* 41, no. 2 (2014): 187–214.
[33] Hesychius, *Lexicon* E, #1995 (Latte and Cunningham, 2.81) ἑλένη = λαμπάς, δετή.
[34] *Ref.* 6.19.2.
[35] *Ref.* 6.31.1.

and Troy—came to blows. The Refutator's distinctive description of these details could have been pulled from a source. At the same time, they might be nothing more than imagined refurbishments taken from Homer. As below, so above. The beauty of *Epinoia* excited lust and war in both heaven and earth.

The fact that *Epinoia* was ransomed by Simon is known from Irenaeus. Yet again the Refutator provided his own twist, reminiscent of Tertullian: Simon was in love with Helen.[36] But the Refutator ran into the same logical problems. The whole point of Simonian salvation is that *Epinoia* is made free. Simon did not "buy" her for his own use. He freed her from her chains. The Oedipal implications are imported. Simon as the highest Power is, for Simonians, *Epinoia*'s Father, not her lover.

The Refutator then laid down the (already played) card, "like founder, like followers." Not only was Simon reportedly licentious, the Simonians were as well. This is another new charge unattested in Irenaeus. Yet like his precursor, the Refutator never presented any evidence. He could only report the putatively Simonian maxim, "all soil is soil and it does not matter where one sows, just that one sows."[37] Whether this saying is genuine or not and what it originally meant are unknown. Assuming its authenticity, it need have nothing to do with sex at all. If it did, it need mean no more than sex is necessary and natural; and one can choose one's mate from any gene pool. It does not imply that Simonians committed sexual crimes. According to the *Testimony of Truth* (late second century CE), Simonians legitimately took wives and produced children with no hint of decadence.[38]

Reportedly, Simonians preached "perfect love" in which "the holy joined to what is holy will be made holy."[39] The saying seems to rephrase something Paul said in 1 Corinthians: "The unbelieving husband is made holy by his wife and the unbelieving wife is made holy by her brother, thus your unclean children are now holy" (7:14). Apparently, however, Simonians were not worried about unbelieving spouses. Both spouses were considered holy and increased their holiness by (sexual) union. No "gnostic" body hatred here. The Refutator was irked at Simonians because they were *too* positive about sex.

In the next paragraphs of the report, the only modification of Irenaeus comes in the statement that Simonians see no reason for judgment even if one acts wrongly.[40] This remark replaces the point in Irenaeus that people are not saved by righteous works. It is not clear why the Refutator made this change; I doubt he had a source outside his own head. He himself would soon relate the Simonian point that liberated souls were eternally separated from the lost. Some sort of separation of sheep from goats seems to be implied.

There is another modification. According to the Simonians in Irenaeus, angels legislate to enslave humanity. In the report of the Refutator, however, these angels only enslaved those who *listened* to Simonian teachings.[41] Likely this tweak is again nothing

---

[36] *Ref.* 6.19.4.
[37] *Ref.* 6.19.5.
[38] *Test. Truth* (NHC IX,3) 58.2–4.
[39] *Ref.* 6.19.5.
[40] *Ref.* 6.19.7 (here reading, with the manuscript, μηδέν γὰρ εἶναι αἴτιον δίκης εἰ πράξει τις κακῶς).
[41] *Ref.* 6.19.8.

more than the Refutator's invention. It is the Refutator, moreover, who probably intuited that since angels made the laws, Simonians were relativists (believing that nothing is good or evil by nature). The inference seems wrongheaded, since Simonians did consider some activities good (like sex) and others evil (like the violence of angelic rape).

Next comes Simonian magical practice. The Refutator followed Irenaeus for the most part, but omitted the point that Simonians performed exorcisms. Apparently, for the Refutator, exorcisms were not magic, but miracle. Early catholics, after all, performed them.[42] Deleting Simonian exorcisms was thus another way to accentuate difference between Christian groups. What did count as magic were love charms and dream senders, though the Refutator clarified that these sandmen were sent to "disturb"—not to benefit—those who slept. He called them "demons," thus accenting their wickedness.

When it came to the worship of Simon and *Epinoia* under the forms of Zeus and Athena, the Refutator lavished more detail. Simonians called Simon "lord" or "master" and *Epinoia* "mistress" or "queen." They also expelled anyone who made the mistake of calling these statues "Simon and Helen." This is an important point, since heresiologists themselves often made this mistake. Simonians worshiped *Epinoia* and the highest Power—Simon and Helen were but manifestations of these divinities.

The Refutator twice noted that Simon was refuted by the apostles in Acts.[43] To be precise, he was reprimanded by Peter alone. The Refutator refrained from quoting Acts or introducing its author as "Luke," companion of the apostles (in contrast to Irenaeus). He did add, like Tertullian, that Peter "cursed" Simon. Yet the fact that Simon wailed in penitence when Peter urged it (Acts 8:23-24) hardly indicates damnation. Nothing in Acts, moreover, supports the Refutator's comment that Simon "despaired" and backslid into magic. The fact that Simon dueled with Peter in Rome is based on later tradition, some of which appears in the *Acts of Peter* (Chapter 11).

Although the Refutator acknowledged Simon's Roman debut, he mentioned nothing about his statue on Tiber Island. The omission is telling. One suspects that the Refutator—who lived in Rome—made further inquiries regarding Justin's statue report and found them wanting (Simon was not Semo). He therefore omitted the account. Later heresiologists (Epiphanius, Pseudo-Tertullian, and Filaster) would follow suit.

The Refutator tacked on a tradition about Simon's death—admittedly not as dramatic as Apsethos' end. Apparently it came from another (non-Irenaean) source (note the different spelling of Simon's village "Gitta," which appeared as "Geittenos" at the beginning of the report).[44] Simon apparently left Rome and returned to his hometown. There, sitting buddha-like under a plane tree, he instructed his disciples. He commanded that he be buried alive so as to rise on the third day. But the resurrection reputedly never happened.[45] It is surely a tale told by Simon's enemies. It resembles the report about Dositheus, who, too rigorous in his fasting, was found by his disciples

---

[42] Tertullian, *An.* 57.5.
[43] *Ref.* 6.7.1; 6.20.2.
[44] *Ref.* 6.7.1.
[45] *Ref.* 6.20.3.

covered in maggots and worms.[46] These reports have no basis in fact and contradict other accounts.

We know from Irenaeus that Simon appeared as the Son in Judea. But the report that Simon in his hometown claimed to be the messiah is unique to the Refutator. This is a point where the Refutator's loosely juxtaposed sources grind against each other. If Simon was the Father in flesh (as reported by Irenaeus and the Refutator), Simon would have no reason to claim the lesser status of the Jewish messiah. The assumption seems to have been that the false messiah would prophesy his own resurrection, but fail to achieve it. The true Christ died, was buried, and resurrected; the false one was buried alive, died, and decayed. There is nothing here but slander tied with the bright bow of fiction. This particular fiction, moreover, never surfaces again. There were, as we shall see, more violent and memorable ways of describing Simon's death (Chapter 11).

The Refutator's final point consists of a comparison of Valentinian aeons with Simonian "roots" (derived from the *Declaration*). Irenaeus had claimed that Valentinian doctrine went back to Simonian lore, but he never made direct comparisons. The Refutator tried to fill in the blank, though we cannot call his comparison careful. It is a one-off juxtaposition trying to convince the reader that the six roots found in the *Declaration* are actually the same as six aeons picked from Valentinian lore. To chart them:

Six Roots in the *Declaration*	Six Valentinian Aeons
1. Mind	1. Mind
2. Thought (*Epinoia*)	2. Truth
3. Voice	3. Word
4. Name	4. Life
5. Reasoning	5. Human
6. Conception	6. Church

The correlations are hardly exact. Only one of the roots corresponds in name with one of the aeons (Mind). The rest have different names and varied roles in the divine economy. The six roots are not called "aeons" in the *Declaration*. They represent the six days of creation or rather what is created on those days. Mind and Thought, for instance, are symbolized by heaven and earth; and Voice and Name are sun and moon, and so on.[47]

By contrast, the Valentinian aeons do not seem to have anything to do with creation. They are born prior to the generation of the physical world. There are not just six Valentinian aeons, moreover, but many (the canonical number was thirty and they were typically arranged in an 8-10-12 pattern).[48] The Refutator himself later listed them: "Deep and Mixture, Ageless and Union, Self-Grown and Pleasure, Unmoved and Blending, Only-born and Blessing." There are twelve more, in addition to the Father who bore them.[49]

---

[46] Epiphanius, *Pan.* 13.1.4.
[47] *Ref.* 6.13.1.
[48] *Ref.* 6.31.3.
[49] *Ref.* 6.30.4–5.

It was thus arbitrary for the Refutator to pick out six Valentinian aeons and say that they are—by common consent, no less—the "same" beings as the six roots of the *Declaration*. Although one can applaud him for trying to make some sort of connection between Simonian and Valentinian lore, the connection is weak and forced. Historically, Valentinians may well have adapted some elements of Simonian theology, but the Refutator failed to cogently show how. Suffice it to say that Valentinian theology did not derive from the *Declaration* in any straightforward way.

Conclusion

What can we learn about Simonians from the Refutator's report? Simonians upheld a story of creation and salvation, allegorized the Bible, and venerated statues of their saviors and teachers. They identified Jesus with Simon and theorized their own Trinity. Irenaeus knew of Simonians in late second-century Rome. The Refutator apparently assumed that Simonians were still in the city in the early third-century. He aimed to refute Simon's disciples. Evidently he considered these disciples to be real people. Their circle was probably not large. Yet their ideas were still dangerous enough to receive a lengthy and well-crafted attack.

The Refutator apparently had access to a few more Simonian texts and traditions than Irenaeus. Some of these traditions (such as Simon's death) seemed to have been invented by polemicists. Other traditions (that Simonians expelled those who did not understand what they worshiped) may well be accurate.

The Refutator voiced respect for Irenaeus, but wanted to go beyond him.[50] Accordingly, he sought new and more authentic material for his reports. On one of his hunts for new sources, the Refutator discovered the *Declaration*. The only other likely readers of this text were Simonians who viewed Simon as their founder. By the year 220 CE, the *Declaration* was possibly a century old. Its age indicates that Simonians preserved their sacred texts.

Simonians were apparently a living Christian community. The Refutator wrote that "until now" Simonians continue to take no concern about the creator angels.[51] They supported sex and "perfect love." They transformed Homer's poetical and miraculous fables into theological mysteries.[52] They rejected the book of Acts, presumably, and told counternarratives to refute it. They continued to believe that Simon had made it to Rome where he met with success, not failure. They lived as free people in an empire known for cruelty and with an economy built on slave labor. Whether they used love charms and "dream senders" is uncorroborated and may well be slander.

In short, the Refutator's report—despite its hostility and fictionalizing flair—indicates that Simonians were real people, a competing Christian group that still drew attention from early catholics in the third century CE. Though most of Simonian

---

[50] *Ref.* 6.42.1.
[51] *Ref.* 16.19.7 (ἕως νῦν).
[52] Heraclitus, *Homeric Problems*, 64 (Konstan and Russell).

history is lost, the group had not perished, but continued to be active in the eternal city. For them, Simon was Christ, to be sure, but much more; he was both Father (and Spirit) as well. *Epinoia* was just as important, moreover, and a faint memory of her survived in the epic literature regarding the fall of Troy. She still waved her allegorical torch, making sure there were signs and symbols of wisdom left in this world.

8

Origen of Alexandria

Introduction

Origen (185–about 253 CE) was a Christian ascetic theologian born in Alexandria, Egypt. First trained as a grammarian, he became well versed in philosophy.[1] Origen did not self-identify as a Platonist, but the influence of Platonism on his thought was considerable. In the midst of his studies, Origen secured a job teaching pre-baptized believers in a local church school. As he was teaching them to interpret scripture, Origen himself was refining the allegorical techniques that would soon make him (in-)famous.[2]

By common report, Origen literally enacted the saying of Jesus who said that some make themselves eunuchs for heaven's kingdom (Matt 19:12).[3] To modern ears, the idea that Origen had his testicles removed seems incredible.[4] Yet castration was widespread enough to be prohibited by Roman law.[5] And we know of at least one other Alexandrian Christian who, a generation before Origen, petitioned the governor to have his testicles cut off.[6]

---

[1] Porphyry in Eusebius, *Hist. eccl.* 6.19.5–6. Although I accept the view that Origen had the same teacher as Plotinus (Ammonius Saccas), I maintain that Origen the Christian theologian was different from Origen the writer of *On Daimones* (Porphyry, *Vita Plot.* 3, 14). For the debate, see Franz Heinrich Kettler, "Origenes, Ammonius Sakkas und Porphyrius," in *Kerygma und Logos*, ed. Adolf Martin Ritter (Göttingen: Vandenhoeck & Ruprecht, 1979), 322–8; F. M. Schroeder, "Ammonius Saccas," *ANRW* II.36.1, 493–526, esp. 494–509; Elizabeth DePalma Digeser, *A Threat to Public Piety* (Ithaca: Cornell University Press, 2012), 10, 18, 27, 30, 49, 64, 66, 75; Ilaria Ramelli, "Origen the Christian Middle/Neoplatonist: New Arguments for a Possible Identification," *Journal of Early Christian History* 1 (2011): 98–130; Mark Edwards, "One Origen or Two? The Status Quaestionis," *Symbolae Osloenses* 89, no. 1 (2015): 81–103.

[2] For the context of allegorical interpretation in Alexandria, see Robert Lamberton, *Homer the Theologian* (Berkeley: University of California Press, 1989), 1–133; David Dawson, *Allegorical Readers and Cultural Revision in Ancient Alexandria* (Berkeley: University of California Press, 1992).

[3] Eusebius, *Hist. eccl.* 6.8; cf. Jerome, *Epistle* 84.8.

[4] For discussion, see Peter Brown, *The Body and Society* (New York: Columbia University Press, 1988), 168–70; Daniel F. Caner, "The Practice and Prohibition of Self-castration in Early Christianity," *VC* 51 (1997): 396–415; Mathew Kuefler, *The Manly Eunuch* (Chicago: University of Chicago Press, 2001), 245–82; Christoph Markschies, "Kastration und Magenprobleme? Einige neue Blicke auf das asketische Leben des Origenes," in *Origenes und sein Erbe: Gesammelte Studien* (Berlin: de Gruyter, 2007), 15–34.

[5] Cassius Dio, *Roman History* 67.2.3 (LCL 176.318): Domitian "forbid anyone in the Roman Empire to be castrated anymore"; ibid., 68.2.4 (LCL 176.326); Nerva made becoming a eunuch illegal.

[6] Justin, *1 Apology* 29.1–2.

The early catholic bishop of Alexandria, Demetrius, initially lauded Origen's surgery. But when Theoctistus of Caesarea ordained Origen without Demetrius's approval, the latter raised a storm of protest. Demetrius claimed that a man with mutilated genitals could not become a priest and that Origen taught the salvation of the devil. This and other doctrinal issues (now muffled in the sources) led to Origen's excommunication by an Egyptian synod.[7] Origen became a priest and preacher after moving to Caesarea (232 CE).[8] Caesarea was the provincial capital on the coast of Palestine, just a few kilometers from the heartlands of Samaria.

Origen is not typically known as a heresiologist. Nevertheless, heresiology could be adapted to any genre, including commentary and sermon. We know from his surviving works that Origen frequently wrote against opposing groups, often mentioning an unholy trinity—Basilides, Valentinus, and Marcion.[9] Other groups, mostly mentioned in passing, included the Simonians. When dealing with Simonians, Origen chose not to develop the heresiological tradition launched by Justin and Irenaeus (Simon as father of heresies, worshiped in Rome, with a trinitarian theology).[10] Like he did for most of his opponents, Origen only provided a "deformed summary" of Simon "produced by tradition"—here mainly the tradition of Acts.[11] Most of Origen's detailed comments on the Simonians can be found in the work of his old age, an apologetic treatise called *Against Celsus*.[12]

Against Celsus

Celsus was a Middle Platonist (probably from Alexandria) who wrote an attack on Christianity called the *True Teaching* during the reign of Marcus Aurelius (161–180 CE).[13] Early in the course of his critique, Celsus put on the mask of a Jewish critic of Christianity.[14] In this capacity he attacked Jesus's virgin birth, his claim to divinity,

---

[7] Photius, *Bibliotheca* codex 118 at 93a (Henry): "a synod was convened against Origen . . . it was voted that he depart from Alexandria." For Origen's viewpoint, see his *Comm. Jo.* 6.1.8.
[8] John Anthony McGuckin, "Caesarea Maritima as Origen Knew It," in *Origeniana Quinta: Historia-Text and Method-Biblica-Philosophica-Theologica-Origenism and Later Developments*, ed. Robert J. Daly (Leuven: Peeters, 1992), 3–25.
[9] See the examples in Le Boulluec, *Notion of Heresy*, 464–579, 585.
[10] Le Boulluec, *Notion of Heresy*, 465.
[11] Le Boulluec, *Notion of Heresy*, 544. The paragraphs that follow adapt and develop my treatment of Origen in *Posthuman Transformation in Ancient Mediterranean Thought: Becoming Angels and Demons* (Cambridge: Cambridge University Press, 2021), 94–6.
[12] For Origen's life, see also Pierre Nautin, *Origène: sa vie et son oeuvre* (Paris: Beauchesne, 1977); Ronald E. Heine, *Origen: Scholarship in Service of the Church* (Oxford: Oxford University Press, 2011); Rebecca Lyman, "Origen of Alexandria," *ExpTim* 120, no. 9 (2009): 417–27; Arthur P. Urbano, "Difficulties in Writing the Life of Origen," in *The Oxford Handbook of Origen*, ed. Ronald E. Heine and Karen Jo Torjesen (Oxford: Oxford University Press, 2022), 118–35.
[13] On *Against Celsus* see Le Boulluec, *Notion of Heresy*, 468–85; Lona, *Die "wahre Lehre,"* 11–68. The text used here and below is M. Marcovich, ed., *Origenes Contra Celsum Libri VIII*, VCSup 54 (Leiden: Brill, 2001).
[14] In my view, Celsus did not replicate an authentic Jewish source (*pace* Maren Niehoff, "A Jewish Critique of Christianity from Second-Century Alexandria: Revisiting the Jew Mentioned in *Contra Celsum*," *JECS* 21, no. 2 [2013]: 151–75), but knew Jewish arguments of the time. See further Judith M. Lieu, "The Multiple Personalities of Celsus' Jew," in *Celsus in His World: Philosophy, Polemic,*

and the epiphany at his baptism.[15] Subsequently, Celsus' Jew raised questions about Jesus fulfilling prophecy, asking why Jesus should be the subject of the prophecies as opposed to "myriads of others," some of whom attained "ecstasy" and others who say that they are sons of God descended from heaven.[16] To quote some of his criticism: "if you (Jesus) say that every person born according to divine providence is God's son, how do you differ from another? . . . Myriads of people will refute Jesus, since they claim that the things prophesied about him were said about themselves."

In his reply, Origen acknowledged that Jesus had competitors who may have claimed to fulfill prophecies or to have been miraculously born. Nevertheless, he mentioned only the recent prophets "Theudas before the birth of Jesus," and Judas the Galilean, who was a "sage and introducer of new doctrines." After the time of Jesus, Origen claimed, Dositheus persuaded Samaritans that he was the messiah prophesied by Moses. At last came "Simon the Samarian magus,"

> who desired to hoodwink certain people. He deceived them at that time, but now one cannot find, I think, thirty Simonians total in the civilized world—and perhaps I speak of more than there are. In the region of Palestine they are very few, and in the rest of the world his name, by which he wanted to spread his glory, is absent. What is reported about them is from the Acts of the Apostles, and they are Christians who say these things about him. Yet clear perception testified that Simon was nothing divine. (*Cels.* 1.57)

Despite an appeal to "clear perception," Origen bypassed what Simonians themselves perceived about Simon's nature and impact. Origen admitted—though backhandedly—that the followers of Simon were Christians, since only Christians speak of him. In raising the examples of Theudas and Judas, Origen depended on Acts 5:36-37, where the character Gamaliel raised the same examples to illustrate men brought to nothing. Origen added the material about Dositheus, perhaps from the Pseudo-Clementine Basic Writing (see Chapter 12).[17] From this writing, Origen probably derived the artificial number of thirty Simonians.[18]

Overall, it seems that Origen was imprecise in his criteria for sources and uncareful in his use of them. He made explicit an error that was only implicit in Acts, that Theudas arose before Jesus's birth. In fact, as Josephus said, Theudas led a movement in the procuratorship of Fadus (44–46 CE)—about fifteen years after Jesus died.[19] Origen was also prepared to draw from an apparently novelistic source (the ancestor of the Clementine romances) and present it as historical data. It seems that Origen's only main source for Simon was the book of Acts, despite his proximity to Samaria and to Simonians there.

and Religion in the Second Century, ed. James Carleton Paget and Simon Gathercole (Cambridge: Cambridge University Press, 2021), 360–85.

[15] Origen, *Cels.* 1.28–49.
[16] Origen, *Cels.* 1.50.
[17] See further Edward C. Brooks, "Origen and the Clementine *Recognitions*," in *Origeniana Quinta*, 154–60.
[18] Ps.-Clement, *Hom.* 2.23.
[19] Josephus, *Ant.* 20.97–8.

Origen's critique also seems misdirected. Despite the fact that Celsus spoke of people claiming to be divine sons, none of Origen's four examples—Theudas, Judas, Dositheus, and Simon—ever claimed this according to surviving evidence. Simon reportedly said he was "somebody great" (Acts 8:9) and Theudas, according to Josephus, presented himself as a prophet.[20] Judas the Galilean claimed no higher identity than a "sage." Origen averred that Dositheus claimed to be the messiah prophesied by Moses in Deuteronomy 18:15. As Origen knew, however, this verse only speaks of a prophet like Moses, not the messiah specifically.[21]

Furthermore, Origen massaged the data to make it seem as if the groups formed by these persons quickly perished. The earliest example, Judas the Galilean, formed a loose-knit revolutionary network that lasted from at least 6 to 73 CE—some sixty-seven years.[22] Judas's sons, James and Simon, had continued this "philosophy" and were crucified in the late 40s CE.[23] One of Judas's descendants, Eleazar, was the leader of the Jews in the siege at Masada.[24] In brief, Judas did not spark a short-lived movement, and the revolutionary ideology he represented lasted perhaps until 135 CE, when Rome finally stamped out the embers of the Bar Kokhba revolt. Dositheus and Simon, both of the first century CE, formed groups that continued to survive into Origen's day (the mid-third century). Their movements were not as ephemeral as Origen wished his readers to believe.[25]

The next reference to Simonians comes from Celsus's own voice, in a passage displaying his knowledge of early Christian sects. In brief, Celsus knew of major divisions among early Christians—with some Christians agreeing they had the same God as the Jews and others calling the Judean Lord an opponent of the true God who sent Jesus.[26] Celsus also mentioned Valentinians, Gnostics, Christians who live by the Mosaic law, and some mysterious "Sybillists." Then come our Simonians:

> Celsus knew of Simonians who reverence as teacher Helena or Helenus and are called Helenians. But Celsus fails to notice that Simonians do not confess that Jesus is God's son at all, but maintain that Simon is a Power of God and relate some fantastical stories about him. For he thought that if he pretended to do miracles exactly like those which he thought Jesus pretended to do, he too would have as much power among people as Jesus had with the multitudes. (Origen, *Cels.* 5.62)

Celsus is the only ancient writer to notice that some Simonians were called "Helenians." He knew enough to infer that this name went back to a Simonian "teacher," but he did not know if this teacher was male or female (Helen or Helenus). Alain Le Boulluec

---

[20] Josephus, *Ant.* 20.97–8.
[21] In his *Commentary on Matthew Series* 33 (Heine, 589), Origen also mentioned Dositheus and Simon as men "who said they were Christs." In context, however, Simon is only "a Great power of God."
[22] Josephus, *Ant.* 18.4–9.
[23] Josephus, *Ant.* 20.102.
[24] Josephus, *J.W.* 7.253.
[25] See further Stanley Jerome Isser, *The Dositheans: A Samaritan Sect in Late Antiquity*, Studies in Judaism in Late Antiquity 17 (Leiden: Brill, 1976).
[26] Origen, *Cels.* 5.61.

thought that the confusion was part of Celsus's attempt to satirize Simonians, but on this score he may simply have been ignorant.[27] Helen was female, as the heresiologists knew. Presumably Origen did as well, despite the fact that he passed over her in silence. Since the days of Tertullian, Christian authors denigrated Helen as Simon's (secret) paramour. Despite the fact that, for Simonians, she represented Wisdom (*Ennoia* or *Epinoia*), heresiologists made no attempt to emphasize or even mention her teaching. Simonians did not view her as Simon's pet, but as an instructor in sacred lore. She was known for her intellectual talents. It was understandable that some Simonians were content to be called "Helenians," followers of Helen their teacher.[28]

Origen's claim that Simonians rejected Jesus's divine sonship is erroneous, in my view. From Irenaeus we gather that they did confess Jesus as God's son, but identified Simon and Jesus as modulated manifestations of the highest Power (Chapter 5).[29] The highest Power came as Jesus in Judea. There was a separate arrival of Simon and Jesus as divine son in Judea—but they were ontologically one. This means that the highest Power in Jesus, the same Power manifest in Simon, was both the Son in Judea and Father in Samaria.

Origen repeated Acts 8:10 (that Simonians proclaim Simon as the "Power of God"). He never cared to relate any of the "fantastical stories" Simonians told about Simon, yet some of them may have resembled those spoken about Jesus in the gospels. Simon and Jesus, said Origen, performed like wonders. Origen was not willing to place these wonderworkers on an even plane; he considered Simon a false imitator of Jesus. He also poisoned the well by demeaning Simon's motives. Simon worked Jesus-like wonders to gain Jesus-like control of the crowds.

After Celsus listed all the competing Christian sects, he accused them of daring to discuss "principles" (*archai*).[30] Simonians were evidently included in this critique. The attack shows that Simonians were not naïve worshipers of a Samarian. They pursued the pastime of philosophers. Regrettably, one gains no clear idea of what Simonian "principles" were from Celsus's—or Origen's—account. One can hypothesize, however, that the principles were similar to the "roots" we have already met in the *Declaration*: Mind and Thought, Voice and Name, Reasoning and Conception.[31] We know that Simonians were perfectly capable of philosophical reflection on cosmogony since we possess the *Declaration*—itself a philosophically informed commentary on the first three chapters of Genesis.

I turn to the third and final passage in *Against Celsus* that mentions Simon. Early in book 6, Celsus reportedly made an overall contrast between Christian and Platonic claims. Christians make arguments from authority and appeal to special revelation from a divine agent (Jesus). Platonists, by contrast, use human reason and the occasional spark of the imagination to ground their theology. The mere appeal to authority does

---

[27] Le Boulluec, *Notion of Heresy*, 479, n.61.
[28] The fact that "Helenians" honored Helen indicates that she was more than "an ancient Eliza Doolittle, testimony to male ego and female gullibility" (Nicola Denzey Lewis, "Women and Independent Religious Specialists in Second-Century Rome," in *Women and Knowledge*, 21–38 at 29).
[29] Irenaeus, *Haer.* 1.23.1.
[30] Origen, *Cels.* 5.65.
[31] *Ref.* 6.13.1.

not, Celsus observed, allow a person to distinguish between competing claims made by divine sons. If one "son of God" urges one thing, and another something else, how does one choose between them given that the criterion of knowledge is based only on their (claim to) authority? How does one ultimately know that information comes from God or not? God's many children sing out of tune.[32]

Origen met these observations with a reassertion of his own dogmatic claim: Jesus is "the only son of God" preached in the world—despite the fact that he now conceded that Dositheus was considered "son of God" as well:

> At present Jesus is preached in all the civilized world as the only son of God who visited the human race. For those who, like Celsus, supposed they could perform bogus miracles and for this reason planned likewise to do so in order that they too, in a similar manner, might gain control over people, were exposed as nonentities. I mean Simon the Samarian magus and Dositheus who chanced to be from the same region, since the first claimed that he was the so-called Great Power of God (Acts 8:10), and the second that he was the son of God. For there are no Simonians in the civilized world—even though Simon, to lead away more adherents, removed from his disciples any risk of death, which Christians have been taught to prefer, by teaching them to regard idolatry as a matter of indifference. In fact, from the beginning, Simonians were never conspired against. For the evil demon who conspired against the teaching of Jesus, knew that his plan regarding his own people would not be dissolved by Simon's teachings. Now the Dositheans did not flourish even in former days and now they have seriously dwindled, so that it is reported that their entire number does not reach thirty. And Judas the Galilean, as Luke wrote in the Acts of the Apostles, wanted to call himself somebody great, and before him Theudas. But because their teaching was not from God, they were executed, and all those who obeyed them were immediately scattered.

Here one must attempt to resolve Origen's own self-contradictions. Apparently the Alexandrian took the opportunity to correct his previous report about Dositheus. In this version, Dositheus did not claim to be messiah, as Origen earlier stated, but "son of God." (Apparently, even claiming to be "somebody great" amounted to a messianic claim for Origen.) Origen also adjusted his account about the number of Simonians. It was not Simonians who were thirty, but Dositheans. Simonians, Origen now claimed, had completely disappeared—a report which contradicts what he wrote before, namely that some Simonians (thirty, to be precise) remained in Palestine.[33]

Origen's failure to agree with himself highlights the carelessness and bias of his report. To make his argument work, Origen had to have Simonians uprooted from the world. Yet the rationale was evidently not based on observation.

---

[32] Origen, *Cels.* 6.11.
[33] Origen also presented Judas as calling himself "somebody great," whereas in fact this claim was only made by Theudas according to Acts 5:36.

There is also a potential logical fallacy. Essentially, we are to believe that because Origen's Jesus was still preached in the mid-third century, his movement must have been valid. Truth, from this point of view, is determined by success, and falsity by failure. But the logic does not follow. Truth is not true because it survives; it may well fail to convince—and in fact it often does. Besides, Simonian and Dosithean "truth" was still preached in the third century, as Origen elsewhere admitted.[34]

Origen claimed that Simon removed the fear of death by teaching his disciples to regard "idolatry" as a matter of indifference. But Simonians would not have accepted the label "idolatry" for their practices. Origen never even clarified what he considered Simonian "idolatry" to be. His was a common rhetorical strategy to associate heresy with "pagan" worship.[35]

Throughout this discussion, Origen assumed that Simonians were self-identifying Christians and he condemned them for not presenting the mark of the "true" Christian—martyrdom. Nonetheless, Origen's zeal for martyrdom was idiosyncratic even in his own day.[36] The actual Simonian teaching about what Christians should do in times of persecution is never clarified in the sources. One can, at any rate, take exception to Origen's general claim that Christians were taught to prefer death. Jesus reportedly said that, when his disciples were persecuted in one town, they should flee to the next (Matt 10:23). They were not to court death, as Origen knew, when they had a means to avoid it.[37]

It is to Origen's credit that he, at long last, made mention of Simon's "teachings," but, like most heresiologists, Origen never cared to explain these teachings fairly. In the end, we glean very little reliable information about Simonians from Origen's *Against Celsus*. And—despite the vastness of Origen's surviving works—his other notices on Simon are mostly brief rehashings of Acts 8, sometimes joined with Exodus 7:10-12 (Moses dueling with the Egyptian "magicians").

Other Works

In his *Commentary on John*, for instance, Origen observed, "Thus we know that Simon, who called himself the 'Power of God called Great' together with his money

---

[34] Origen, *Comm. Jo.* 13.27.162: "To this day there are Dositheans originating from him (Dositheus), possessing books of Dositheus and myths about him that he did not die but is still alive somewhere."
[35] Le Boulluec, *Notion of Heresy*, 480, 491.
[36] See *Origen: An Exhortation to Martyrdom, Prayer, First Principles Book IV, Prologue to the Commentary on the Song of Songs, Homily XXVII on Numbers*, trans. Rowan A. Greer (Mahwah: Paulist Press, 1979), 41–80. For further context, see Candida Moss, *Ancient Christian Martyrdom: Diverse Practices, Theologies, and Traditions* (New Haven: Yale University Press, 2012).
[37] Origen, *Cels.* 1.65; 8.44. See further Paul Hartog, "Patristic Departures from Matthew 10,23 with 'Flight' Connections in Origen," in *Origeniana Undecima: Origen and Origenism in the History of Western Thought. Papers of the 11th International Origen Congress, Aarhus University, 26–31 August 2013*, ed. Anders-Christian Jacobsen (Leuven: Petters, 2016), 831–42; Johan Leemans, "The Idea of 'Flight for Persecution' in the Alexandrian Tradition from Clement to Athanasius," in *Origeniana Octava: Origen and the Alexandrian Tradition. Papers of the 8th International Origen Congress, Pisa, 27–31 August* 2001, ed. L. Perrone (Leuven: Peeters, 2003), 901–11.

went off to destruction and annihilation."[38] This is no more than a hostile and selective reinscription of Acts 8 (specifically, vv. 10 and 20). Later in the same work, Origen wrote that "even the magus Simon was struck with wonder" when he saw people receive the Spirit from the apostles. He "wanted to receive this grace from Peter, desiring something most righteous through the mammon of unrighteousness."[39] Again, this is little more than a pejorative rephrasing of Acts 8:18-19, with a tag from Luke 16:9 (on "mammon" or wealth).

In his *Homilies on Jeremiah*, Origen drew a parallel between the reportedly false wonders of the Egyptians who opposed Moses and those of Simon: "What Christ Jesus used to do, these were signs of truth, and before him, what Moses was doing, was a power of truth; but the Egyptians were doing false signs and wonders (Exod 7:10-12). In the same way, after Jesus, what Simon Magus was doing so that the people of Samaria were deceived into supposing he was the 'Power of God'—these also were false signs and wonders."[40]

In this polemic, Simon is not given a fair chance. He is simply dismissed in light of a literary typology displaying, in binary fashion, supposedly true and false wonderworkers. It is a signal case of mythic thinking overwhelming historical description. According to Origen's myth, after God's true miracles appear, false "magicians" rise up in imitation. It happened in the days of Moses; so also in the days of Jesus (the new Moses). This homiletical aside is less about anything in the empirical world than it is about Origen's sense of what should happen in (salvation) history.

In the Catenae—strings of passages quoted from the church fathers—we find another gloss on Simon attributed to Origen. The first is a comment on Matthew 21:23, where the high priests and elders approach Jesus who was teaching in the temple. They ask: "By what authority do you do this? Who gave you this authority?" Origen observed:

> Some of them by other magical powers created an illusion and deceived many people. For consider with me what they said to the Savior: 'This one expels demons by Beelzebub, the ruler of demons' (Luke 11:15). From where could they say this if it did not happen by some among them? For contemplate with me Simon using the art of magic, deceiving many among the people. Again, they knew of the sorcerers who opposed Moses in Egypt with their works of magic by a foreign power. Consider with me God's authentic Power over other powers, which worked with Moses to overcome the Egyptian sorcerers, and the Power in the apostles opposing that of Simon.[41]

Here we find the same parallel between Simon and the Egyptian "sorcerers." Simon and these practitioners putatively worked their miracles through a "foreign" or "strange" power, a power that was overcome by the "authentic" force working in Moses and the

---

[38] Origen, *Comm. Jo.* 1.33.242.
[39] Origen, *Comm. Jo.* 6.33.167.
[40] Origen, *Hom. Jer.* 5.3.41.
[41] Origen, *Matthäuserklärung III. Fragmenta und Indices Erste Hälfte*, ed. Ernst Benz and Erich Klostermann, *Origenes Werke* 12, GCS 41.1 (Leipzig: Teubner, 1941), frag. 417.5, 10.

apostles. Again, this is Origen's imagined pattern of how history should work based on a typological reading of scriptural legend. As an illustrative polemical aside, it adds nothing to what we can know of Simon or Simonians.

According to another catena, Origen is said to have allegorically interpreted Deuteronomy 20:13. This verse presents a war directive given by Moses to the Israelites when they capture a city: "You will strike every male of the city with a murderous sword" (LXX). The literal interpretation speaks for itself—Israelites are to kill every captured male no matter what age or station, armed or unarmed. Origen tried to redeem the text by allegory: "Let the sword of the Spirit (Eph 6:17) be the Logos of God (Rev 19:12). And the sword of the Spirit, which is the Logos of God, is the one by which the wondrous disciples killed every male of the opposing power, like Simon and Elymas the magi, whose strong teachings the disciples destroyed."[42]

This time Simon is paired with the only explicit "magus" in Acts, Elymas (Acts 13:8-11). No new information is supplied, only the historical myth that the disciples of Jesus destroyed their "strong teachings." Once again we hear not a word about the content of these teachings, or why they were considered strong. (For Origen, it seems, they were "strong" only because they were scripturally coded as "male.") The question lingers: If the apostles managed to destroy Simonian teachings, why did they survive long enough for Origen to battle them? In the third century, Origen was still brandishing his sword against Simonians as if they were alive and well.

Conclusion

Most scholars agree that Origen was a profound theologian and a creative interpreter of scripture. When it comes to his information about Simon, however, he presented almost nothing reliable or credible. Only in his chief apologetic text, *Against Celsus*, did Origen provide anything that could be called distinctive. It is Christians who speak of Simon, since (Simonian) Christians cared about him. Despite Origen's attempt to bury these Christians, he revealed that they still existed in his own region (Palestine). He—perhaps wisely—related almost nothing substantive about their "strong teaching," apart from the fact that Simon was viewed as the Great Power (Acts 8:10) and that Simonians avoided martyrdom. Simon's miracles were strikingly and intentionally like those of Jesus (both men eventually "gained control" over the crowds)—but Origen refused an honest comparison. Some of what Origen said is inaccurate and slanderous from a Simonian point of view—for instance that Simonians taught "idolatry" and did not affirm that Jesus was God's son.

From Celsus we learn that some Simonians were called "Helenians," a fact which emphasizes the importance of Helen as a Simonian teacher. Simon's connection with Dositheus is rather vague. They are merely said to be from the same region (Samaria). When one compares the details, moreover, there is no great historical and theological similarity between Simon, Dositheus, Theudas, and Judas the Galilean. Despite

---

[42] Origen, *Adnotationes in Deuteronomium* (fragmenta e catenis) in *PG* 17.29, line 32.

Origen's regular attempt to group them as failed sons of God, only Dositheus, so Origen, claimed to be such, and his claim is contested.[43] (It is, frankly, obscure what Dositheus claimed about himself.)

It was perhaps inevitable that Simon be linked with the Egyptian ritual specialists from Exodus 7:10-12. In fact, by invoking these sages of old, Origen may have tapped into one of the tacit sources for the author of Acts. Simon, as a "magus" who opposed the true miracles of the apostles, was already in part conformed to the sorcerers known in Jewish scripture. At the same time, Origen gave no strictly logical or historical reason to think why Simon's miracles were false and imitative. He himself observed that Jesus was accused of doing his exorcisms by the power of Beelzebub.

Overall, Origen produced a profoundly apologetic portrait of Simon(ians) that does not go much beyond the classically pejorative reading of Acts 8 provided by other heresiologists. For more reliable and distinctive data, we must turn to one of Origen's greatest admirers in the ancient world, Eusebius of Caesarea.

---

[43] See Isser, *Dositheans*; Fossum, "Samaritan Sects," 290–333.

9

Eusebius of Caesarea

Eusebius (about 265–340 CE) lived in Caesarea, where Origen once taught. Although he is known for infusing a triumphalist tinge into Christian discourse, he mostly lived under the rule of non-Christian emperors—some of them Christianity's worst enemies. During his time, native Greek and Roman cults continued to dominate Caesarea's civic space. The city boasted of temples to Tyche (Fortune), Isis, Serapis, Demeter, and Apollo, as well as a Mithraic cave.[1] Perhaps the most famous cult site was the massive harbor temple to the divine Caesar Augustus.

The smoke of burning fat rose on the altars of these temples throughout Eusebius's lifetime. In fact, he lived through the decade of the harshest state persecution Christians had ever seen (from about 303 to 311 CE). The Christian emperor Constantine only gained power over the eastern empire well after Eusebius published the first seven books of his *Ecclesiastical History*. When exactly Eusebius published them is disputed, but it seems to have been around the time when he was appointed bishop of Caesarea (313–314 CE).[2] Eusebius wrote many works, but this one is the key source for Simon and thus the focus of this chapter.[3]

The *Ecclesiastical History* participated in a variety of genres including heresiology, apology, martyr drama, war history, national history, and intellectual history.[4] Ancient historians like Herodotus and Livy invented speeches which they considered plausible for the occasion. Eusebius avoided this practice; instead, he increased the reality effect

---

[1] Joseph Patrich, "Caesarea in the Time of Eusebius," in *Reconsidering Eusebius: Collected Papers on Literary, Historical, and Theological Issues*, VCSup 107 (Leiden: Brill, 2011), 1–24 at 9–10.

[2] I forgo discussion about multiple editions of *Hist. eccl.*, since this does not affect Eusebius's depiction of Simon in books 1–4. Those interested in this topic can see T. D. Barnes, "Some Inconsistencies in Eusebius," *JTS* 35 (1984): 470–5; A. Louth, "The Date of Eusebius' *Historia Ecclesiastica*," *JTS* 41 (1990): 111–23; R. Burgess, "The Dates and Editions of Eusebius *Chronici Canones* and *Historia Ecclesiastica*," *JTS* 48 (1997): 471–504.

[3] On Eusebius's life and other writings, see T. D. Barnes, "Eusebius of Caesarea," *ExpTim* 121, no. 1 (2009): 1–14; Marie Verdoner, *Narrated Reality: The Historia Ecclesiastica of Eusebius of Caesarea* (Frankfurt am Main: Peter Lang, 2011), 31–8; Aaron P. Johnson, *Eusebius* (London: I.B. Taurus, 2014), esp. 1–25, 85–112; Michael J. Hollerich, *Making Christian History: Eusebius of Caesarea and His Readers* (Berkeley: University of California Press, 2021), 1–46.

[4] David J. DeVore, "Genre and Eusebius' *Ecclesiastical History*: Towards a Focused Debate," in *Eusebius of Caesarea: Traditions and Innovations*, ed. Aaron Johnson and Jeremy Schott (Washington, DC: Center for Hellenic Studies, 2013), 19–50 at 44–5; Emanuela Prinzivalli, "La genre historiographique de l'*Histoire ecclésiastique*," in *Eusèbe de Césarée: Histoire Ecclésiastique commentaire, tome I*, ed. S. Morlet and L. Perrone (Paris: Cerf, 2012), 83–112.

of his history by quoting manifold documents—many of them selectively quoted and some even doctored.[5]

Most of the documents available to Eusebius were early Christian sources that had been collected by Origen as well as by Eusebius's mentor, Pamphilus. By the time Eusebius was put in charge of this collection, it was an impressive library.[6] Any library, however, is colored by the interests of its curators. Its contents still only covered a percentage of Christian literature as a whole. Eusebius had strongly opposing interests, for instance, to the Christians who collected the Nag Hammadi codices in the mid-fourth century. Although Eusebius's library contained many works—such as the *Acts of Peter*—he signaled their inauthenticity.[7]

Perhaps it is best to call the *Ecclesiastical History* an apologetic history. In it, Eusebius lauds and defends his particular network of Christians by looking back over the fields of textualized memory, plucking out those voices that seem to resonate with his fourth-century creed.[8] Alternative voices, in turn, are systematically denounced, and in some cases ignored.[9] In writing his history, Eusebius had many aims, one of which was to construct a genealogy of those whom he considered to be Christians—to relate their story, and to disqualify putative competitors as "savage wolves" (Acts 20:29).[10] Some writers in modern times have supposed that the purity of "the" church was corrupted in the reign of Constantine (died 337 CE).[11] Eusebius traced the corruption back to the rule of Hadrian (117–138 CE).[12] Yet he revealed that there were even earlier figures who—wrongly in his opinion—bore the Christian name. Menander of Antioch appeared about 80 CE. Cerinthus and the Nicolaitans lived in late-first-century Asia Minor. Still earlier was Simon of Samaria about 35 CE.[13]

In describing Simon, Eusebius rephrased and reinscribed the legends known from Acts, Justin, Irenaeus, and (probably) the *Acts of Peter*. In doing so, he elevated the style and register of the polemic. Heresy reports became historiography. But Eusebius's

---

[5] See, e.g., Ken Olson, "A Eusebian Reading of the *Testimonium Flavianum*," in *Traditions and Innovations*, 97–114; Meike Willing, *Euseb von Cäsarea als Häreseograph* (Berlin: de Gruyter, 2009), 422–5.

[6] Andrew James Carriker, *The Library of Eusebius of Caesarea*, VCSup 67 (Leiden: Brill, 2003); Anthony Grafton and Megan Williams, *Christianity and the Transformation of the Book: Origen, Eusebius, and the Library of Caesarea* (Cambridge, MA: Harvard University Press, 2006), 133–323.

[7] Eusebius, *Hist. eccl.* 3.25; cf. 3.3.2 on the *Acts of Peter* among other Petrine writings.

[8] Gregory Sterling, *Historiography and Self-definition. Josephus, Luke-Acts, and Apologetic Historiography* (Leiden: Brill, 1991); Arthur Droge, "The Apologetic Dimensions of the *Ecclesiastical History*," in *Eusebius, Christianity, and Judaism*, 492–509; Marie Verdoner, "Transgeneric Crosses. Apologetics in the Church History of Eusebius," in *Three Greek Apologists. Drei griechische Apologeten: Origen, Eusebius, and Athanasius*, ed. Anders-Christian Jacobsen and Jörg Ulrich (Frankfurt am Main: Peter Lang, 2007), 75–92.

[9] For instance, although Eusebius mentions Basilides, Valentinus, and Carpocrates, he failed to report their disciples, e.g., Isidore, Heracleon, Marcellina, and Epiphanes. See further Willing, *Euseb*, 396–401.

[10] Eusebius, *Hist. eccl.* 1.1.1.

[11] J. Z. Smith, *Drudgery Divine: On the Comparison of Early Christianities and the Religions of Late Antiquity* (Chicago: University of Chicago Press, 1990), 1–35.

[12] Eusebius, *Hist. eccl.* 4.7.1; cf. 3.32.7–8. See further Eusebius, *In Praise of Constantine: A Historical Study and New Translation of Eusebius' Tricenniel Orations*, H. A. Drake, ed. (Berkeley: University of California Press, 1978).

[13] Eusebius, *Hist. eccl.* 2.13; 3.26–9; 4.22.4–5.

notion of history was shaped by his theological myth. There was a battle between darkness and light, God and Satan, a battle reflected on earth as one between apostles and "heretics." This frame for seeing the world is not "in" the data, it is something Eusebius used to structure his narrative world. Eusebius was living at the culmination of his own conception of history, authorizing himself as the continuator of the good and contender against what is false and devilish.

Eusebius on Simon

In accordance with the canons of invective during his time, Eusebius burdened Simon with a heap of denigrations. Under the bishop's pen, Simon became Satan's envoy, a poison to the church, the great antagonist of the apostolic prince, archenemy of Christianity, father and founder of "heresy" with its myriad of twining branches.

For all of Eusebius's attempts to depreciate Simon, however, he was important to him.[14] In fact, Eusebius devoted more space to Simon than he did to any other perceived opponent, including Marcion. He mentioned Simon on numerous occasions in books 1–4 of the *Ecclesiastical History*. In book 2, Eusebius presented two main treatments of Simon. One of them (2.1.10-12) focuses on Simon in Acts (about 145 Greek words); the second treatment, twelve chapters later (2.13.1–2.15.1), addressed Simon in Justin and Irenaeus (about 590 Greek words). Books 3 and 4 deal with "successors" of Simon, including Menander, the Carpocratians, and Cerdo.[15] Later in book 4, Eusebius quoted the view of Hegesippus that Simon and the Simonians arose from the "seven sects among the people." "The people" here evidently refers to Jews, and the seven Jewish sects are listed as "Essenes, Galileans, Day Baptists, Masbotheans, Samaritans, Sadducees, and Pharisees."[16] One would think that, for Hegesippus—and by extension, Eusebius—Simon had something like a sectarian Jewish background, yet no precise intellectual pedigree is ever sketched. Eusebius was satisfied to trace Simon back to Satan who ever lurked behind the curtain of his history.[17]

Book 2 of the *Ecclesiastical History* rephrases and summarizes the initial chapters of Acts. Matthias is chosen as apostle to replace Judas (Acts 1:12-26); the seven deacons launch their ministry (Acts 6:5); James is introduced as the leader of the Jerusalem church (Acts 15); Stephen is killed and Christians disperse to Samaria, Phoenicia, Cyprus, and Antioch.

---

[14] For Eusebius on Simon, see Vincent Twomey, *Apostolikos Thronos: The Primacy of Rome as Reflected in the Church History of Eusebius and the Historico-apologetic Writings of Saint Athanasius the Great* (Münster: Aschendorff, 1982), 50–6; Willing, *Euseb*, 75–98. For Eusebius on "heresy," in general see Timothy D. Barnes, *Constantine and Eusebius* (Cambridge, MA: Harvard University Press, 1981), 133–5; Birger A. Pearson, "Eusebius and Gnosticism," in *Eusebius, Christianity, and Judaism*, ed. Harold W. Attridge and Gohei Hata (Leiden: Brill, 1992), 291–310; Doron Mendels, *The Media Revolution of Early Christianity: An Essay on Eusebius's Ecclesiastical History* (Grand Rapids: Eerdmans, 1999), 111–50.

[15] Eusebius, *Hist. eccl.* 3.26.1; 4.7.9; 4.11.2.

[16] Eusebius, *Hist. eccl.* 4.22.5–7.

[17] Willing, *Euseb*, 436–55; Hazel Johannessen, *The Demonic in the Political Thought of Eusebius of Caesarea* (Oxford: Oxford University Press, 2016).

Eusebius then turned to the mission of Philip. He paraphrased Acts 8:9-13, omitting discussion of Acts 8:14-24 (the main account of Simon's clash with Peter). Whatever the intent here, it has the effect of making the narrative neater. First, Eusebius discussed the ministry of Philip, then—twelve chapters later—he focused on Peter's activity. Philip, as related in Acts, enjoyed success in Samaria, which is how he encountered Simon. According to Eusebius:

> So much did divine grace cooperate with Philip that even Simon the magus, with many others, were drawn by his words. At the time, so great was Simon's popularity among the dupes he controlled by sorcery that he was considered the Great Power of God (Acts 8:10). On this occasion, even Simon was struck by the unexpected wonders accomplished by the divine power of Philip. He insinuated himself and played an act even as far as baptism into faith in Christ.
>
> What is really astounding is that this is done among those who still today continue from him this most defiled heresy. These people, following the method of their forefather, secretly slip into the church like a pestilential and scab-producing disease and do the greatest damage to as many as they can infect with their deadly and dire poison. At present, most of them, at least, have been driven out. They are caught when their depraved nature is exposed, as Simon himself was detected for what he was, and paid the fitting punishment. (Eusebius, *Ecclesiastical History* 2.1.10-12)

Eusebius replicated the same flashback we saw in Acts. He started with Philip, but then backtracked to explain how Simon was considered God's Great Power. Simon is initially demeaned by the fact that his former followers are called "dupes" (*ēpatēmenōn*). Together with these "dupes," Simon was drawn by the words of Philip. Acts says that Simon "believed" (evidently Philip's message) and was baptized, just like the others (Acts 8:12). Following Irenaeus, Eusebius affirmed that Simon only feigned faith, which meant that his baptism was a sham.[18] The ambiguity of Acts is thus dissolved and Simon is reduced to a man of deceit who practiced "sorcery" or "trickery" (*goēteia*)— an apparent redescription of Simon's practice as a "magus" (*mageuōn*, Acts 8:9). All this has a precedent in heresiology.

Yet then Eusebius said something new—something that surprised and astounded him. Simon's devotees still continue to baptize even up until his own time. This is indeed remarkable, since it indicates that Simonians continued to exist, apparently, up until the early fourth century CE, and that they continued to persist in their Christian identity, as indicated by their practice of that most Christian of all initiations, baptism. Eusebius's testimony thus contradicts Origen's when he reported that Simonians did not exist. (Though Origen, it will be remembered, contradicted himself on this point.[19])

What was Eusebius's source? No other surviving text suggests itself because no one else mentions baptizing Simonians. Was this simply a slip of the bishop's pen? Probably

---

[18] Irenaeus, *Haer.* 1.23.1 (*fidem simulavit*: "he faked faith").
[19] Origen, *Cels.* 6.11; cf. 1.57.

not, since it is precisely the kind of material Eusebius would have preferred to bury.[20] One should confront the idea, I propose, that Eusebius's source was his own eyes. The bishop could look around early-fourth-century Palestine and witness a living Simonian group continuing to practice baptism. What this means is that Eusebius, who refused to believe that Simon became a Christian, nonetheless revealed that Simonians were a baptizing—and evidently Christian—community, just as alive as they had been in the second century.

Eusebius added that Simonians, apparently in his day, enter "the" church—namely his ecclesial network. Of course Eusebius was displeased by this development, and claimed that most Simonians had been expelled. Yet he could not deny that they had an effect—which he pejoratively likened to poison and psoriasis (compare the *Epistle of the Apostles* 1.1). If Simonians did *not* present themselves as Christians—even in the fourth century—it is hard to see how they could have "slipped in" to the early catholic network, apparently to worship with those whom they considered their Christian siblings. We are not in a position to demean their intent in joining, or to ascribe to them a "depraved nature." Suffice it to say that Simonians considered their faith and Eusebius's to be compatible, or at least compatible with many persons in Eusebius's church.

We have to wait twelve chapters before we hear of Simon again. But when he returns, he comes in force, earning a full two chapters of discussion. The intervening material can be dealt with swiftly: after leaving Simon baptized in Samaria, Eusebius discussed the Ethiopian eunuch, a legend (from Tertullian) that Tiberius tried to deify Jesus by vote of the Roman senate, the career and embassy of Philo, the famine under Claudius, the martyrdom of James, the punishment of Agrippa I, the rebellion of Theudas, and the famine relief offered Judea by Helen, Queen of Adiabene. Only at this juncture did Eusebius finish his story of Simon:

> The enemy of human salvation, scheming to pillage the imperial city beforehand, leads the previously mentioned Simon there. So by the tricks and sorceries of this man, he is exalted and appropriates for his own deceit most of those living in Rome. Justin, not far from the apostles, one of our own people preeminent in reasoning, makes this clear.... He it is who writes in the first treatise to Antoninus in defense of our doctrine.... (Eusebius, *Ecclesiastical History* 2.13.1-2)

I omit Eusebius's quote from Justin's *First Apology* 26.3, since it repeats material treated in Chapter 4. Like Justin, Eusebius considered Simon to be a demonic agent. It was Satan who brought Simon to Rome (the "imperial city"). There Simon "appropriated" the majority of the Christian community by his "sorceries." If Eusebius had a written source for this story, it was not Justin, but perhaps some version of the *Acts of Peter*. These *Acts* relate that, when Simon came to Rome, all but seven Christians became his followers (Chapter 11).[21]

---

[20] Eusebius "works here like a reporter who quotes his sources but does not want to cite them in full because his audience will become impatient and perhaps learn some 'positive' lessons about the heresy, a prospect that he wishes to prevent" (Mendels, *Media Revolution*, 118, cf. 150).

[21] *Acts Pet.* 4.

After Eusebius quoted Justin, he invoked the next heresiologist:

> Irenaeus sings in tune with Justin in the first book of his *Against Heresies*. He writes both about Simon himself and about his unholy and defiled teaching. This material is at present superfluous to quote, since it is available to those who also want to know the leading heretics after Simon in order, as well as their principles, their lives, the main claims of their false teachings, and all their habits. (Eusebius, *Ecclesiastical History* 2.13.5)

Eusebius refrained from quoting Irenaeus's lengthy report on Simon, but paraphrased parts of it:

> We have transmitted that Simon was the first founder of heresy.[22] From him to the present time, those continuing his heresy pretend to live the sober and pure life of the Christian philosophy, so famous among all. They appear to abandon idol superstition but embrace it no less. Falling before paintings and images of Simon himself and his aforementioned companion Helen, they endeavor to worship them with offerings of incense, sacrifices and libations.

Eusebius indicates that up until his time, presumably, Simonians presented themselves as Christians. Yet not only that—they "pretended" to live according to the sober and pure Christian philosophy. This behavior would apparently mean that Simonians were making some sort of effort in order to appear morally upstanding in Roman society. On the outside, at least, they did not seem immoral, but ethically rigorous (as philosophers were generally considered to be).

Origen had presented Simonians as idolaters. Eusebius corrects him, though in an oblique way, by pointing out how Simonians resisted the ubiquitous worship of cult statues devoted to Augustus, Serapis, and so on. Yet Eusebius thought them inconsistent, since they venerated images of Simon and Helen. The mention of Helen picks up on her depiction in Justin, but Eusebius had no interest in revealing her larger significance to Simonians. The use of incense, sacrifices, and libations appears to be Eusebius's own addition to Irenaeus's report. These were standard ways to honor a god through an image in antiquity.[23] We do not actually know how Simonians venerated the statues of Simon and Helen. The idea that they prostrated themselves before them seems to be another hostile inference.

It is surprising how readily Eusebius omitted virtually all aspects of Simonian doctrine transmitted by Irenaeus. Eusebius viewed Simon as the founder of false gnosis, but he never revealed what this gnosis was. He was solely interested in Simonian liturgical and moral practice, yet spoke of these topics only in hit-and-run fashion. There are

---

[22] Irenaeus, *Haer.* 1.23.4; 1.29.1.
[23] Cf. Apuleius, *Apol.* 63.3.

things more unspeakable than these, which, they say, when one has first heard them, one will be stunned and—according to some written oracle of theirs—"will be awestruck." These are truly awe-inspiring, mind-blowing revelations, full of insanity. They are so bad that they cannot be transmitted in writing. In fact, this very thing is not spoken even by the lips of sober men on account of its excessive shamefulness and unspeakable vice. Whatever one might imagine as more defiled than any shame, their most defiled heresy overshot all this. They play sex games with wretched women, loaded with vices (2 Tim 3:6). The virtue-hating conspirator against human salvation and evil power first put forward Simon as the father and creator of such vices in those times, as it were a great antagonist of the great and inspired apostles of our Savior. (Eusebius, *Ecclesiastical History* 2.13.7–2.14.1)

Eusebius's reference to a "written oracle" (*logion eggraphon*) of the Simonians is noteworthy. No other source mentions it. We know that the *Declaration* presents itself as a kind of oracular speech. Were there more Simonian "oracles" that have been lost? Eusebius failed to mention the title of this oracle or how he came across it. We are left with hypotheses. It seems that Simonians offered incomers what they thought were awe-inspiring messages from God.

Eusebius—never loathe to recommend a book he approved—was not prepared to give any details about Simonian documents. When he heard the Simonian promise to inspire wonder, he thought of orgies. Once again, the bishop did not disclose his source for Simonian "shamefulness." It seems to have been little more than a pinch of Irenaeus, peppered with common rumors against all Christians, leavened with a dose of fancy. Irenaeus had written that the "mystic priests" of the Simonians "live lustfully" and that they use love charms.[24] This clipped and unevidenced remark, combined with Justin's insinuations of nightly orgies, may have been enough for Eusebius to conjure up the fire storm of "unspeakable vice."

History becomes fantasy when Simonians do works worse than can be imagined. In fact, Simonians are made to do what their forefather did—have sex with a reputedly dissolute woman. The aspersions originally cast against Simon and Helen are here turned against all Simonians (in the language of 2 Timothy). We have to turn to Epiphanius—whose lips were not so sober—to receive legends about Simonian semen collection.[25] Such reports cannot be taken as historical, especially from Eusebius who made clear that Simonians made a noticeable effort to live according to a sober, pure, and philosophic way of life.

Generally speaking, the bishop tried to maintain the argument that truth came prior to heresy; but with Simon, he stumbled. He had to admit that Simon appeared in what he called "apostolic times." (These times, for Eusebius, lasted until the very late first century when John reportedly died in Ephesus.[26]) Accordingly, "heresy" was not actually younger than the apostles. Eusebius never flagged this issue as a problem, but it throws a question mark against his usual assumption about the priority of his

---

[24] Irenaeus, *Haer.* 1.23.4.
[25] Epiphanius, *Pan.* 21.4.1.
[26] Eusebius, *Hist. eccl.* 3.31.3.

own doctrine. Simon was not someone who appeared after the apostles to distort their teaching. He was a man who lived and worked in their very midst.

Eusebius continued:

> Nevertheless, when the divine and superheavenly grace supported her servants, rising high through their manifestations and arrivals, the flame of the evil one was quickly extinguished. Through them, grace humbled and destroyed every lofty thing raised against the knowledge of God. Accordingly, there was founded no sort of organization either of Simon or of another of his offshoots during those apostolic times. For the light of truth over-conquered and overpowered everything, and the divine Logos himself, recently having shone on humans from God, reached his height on earth and lived his life among his own apostles. (Eusebius, *Ecclesiastical History* 2.14.2-3)

In response to the fact that Simon lived and practiced in apostolic times, Eusebius had to annul his effect somehow. He did so by concluding—on what grounds we do not know—that neither Simon nor his "offshoots" established any sort of "organization" (*sugkrotēma*) during the first century CE. In effect, Eusebius was willing to grant the presence of Simon among the apostles, but he erased the Simonians—or anything that looked like a different church in "apostolic times."

It is an odd remark, given that Eusebius mentioned Simon's disciples—the aforementioned Helen first, and later Menander. Menander (about 80 CE) is specifically said to have had disciples whom he baptized.[27] Eusebius also quoted Justin to the effect that "nearly all Samarians" follow Simon and they worshipped him in Rome by means of a statue set up in the reign of Claudius (37–54 CE).[28] All this data points to a group, and a group that had some level of organization with the ability to propagate itself. In saying that Simonians never organized in early times, Eusebius collided with his own evidence.

By "every lofty thing raised against the knowledge of God" (2 Cor 10:5), Eusebius alluded to the "gnosis falsely-so-called" (1 Tim 6:20)—in short, presumed gnostics—of whom Simon was the root. If these gnostic followers of Simon were not organized, it is hard to see why divine "grace" took the effort to knock them down. For Simonians, the recent advent of the Logos was no counter to Simon, since Simon himself was, in the report of Irenaeus, the son of God in Judea.[29]

The bishop wound up his report:

> So immediately the aforementioned sorcerer, struck in his mind's eye as by divine and overwhelming radiance, when at first he was caught by the apostle Peter in Judea among the people he harmed, departed on a great sea journey from east to west, and so took flight, supposing that only in this way could he live by his own views. When he disembarked at the city of Rome, the power lurking there

---

[27] Eusebius, *Hist. eccl.* 3.26.1-3.
[28] Eusebius, *Hist. eccl.* 2.13.3-4.
[29] Irenaeus, *Haer.* 1.23.1.

supported his great deeds so that in a little while he accomplished the goals of his endeavor, such that by the erection of a statue in the city he was honored as a god.

He did not, however, succeed in these matters for long. The all-good and most benevolent providence, during the reign of Claudius, led Peter to Rome, the persevering and great apostle, who for his virtue spoke before all the others, in order to face so great a corrupter of life. He, like a noble general of God, shielded by divine armor, shipping the precious merchandise of mental light from east to west—light itself and a saving reason for souls—preached the message of the heavenly kingdom. In this way, then, when the divine reason visited them, the power of Simon was extinguished immediately and undone—along with the man himself. (Eusebius, *Ecclesiastical History* 2.14.4–2.15.1)

This account reads like a plot summary from the *Acts of Peter*, stripped down to its core, and decorated with glowing epithets of Peter.[30] Simon and Peter sparring in Judea resemble *Acts of Peter* 5, his detection and exile from Judea may stem from *Acts of Peter* 17, his trip to Rome from *Acts of Peter* 4, his statue from *Acts of Peter* 10, and his death from chapter 32.[31] Naturally, as Eusebius brought these *Acts* into the orbit of history, he eliminated all of Peter and Simon's fantastical miracles (talking dogs, triple resurrections, heavenly ascents, and so on—see Chapter 11).[32]

The only correction Eusebius made (on the basis of Justin) was that the Roman clash between the apostle and his archenemy occurred in the reign of Claudius (not Nero). Simon's statue is narratively set up as the main signal of his success, though this time without any inscription (leaving the reader without any means of verifying the account). Everything smacking of a Simonian group is erased—the fact that nearly all Christians initially followed Simon is left out, not to mention his massive following among Samarians (reported by Justin). Yet—if we grant the literary account—Simon's statue must have been set up by someone; and it was only by a larger collective that Simon was presumably honored as a god. If it was only one person who did so, what threat did Simon pose?

Conclusion

If the goal of a historian is to tell the whole truth in all its relevant details, then Eusebius's occasional suppression of data and tendentious claims about Simon and his group make it difficult to call him a careful and meticulous historian.[33] He was, rather, an apologetic

---

[30] On Eusebius's use of negative epithets, see Mendels, *Media Revolution*, 145–7.
[31] Eusebius noted that Peter was crucified upside-down (*Hist. eccl.* 3.1), as in the *Acts Pet.*
[32] Twomey, *Apostolikos Thronos*, 52; cf. Willing, *Euseb*, 90–1.
[33] Eusebius's description of Simon "is almost impossible to get any 'objective' impression of Simon and his ideas. It is distorted in every conceivable way and resembles an article in a tabloid newspaper rather than the account of a serious historian" (Mendels, *Media Revolution*, 119). See further Robert Grant, "The Case Against Eusebius: Or, Did the Father of Church History Write History," *Studia Patristica* 12 (1971): 412–21; Thomas Heyne, "The Devious Eusebius? An Evaluation of the *Ecclesiastical History* and Its Critics," *Studia Patristica* 46 (2010): 325–31.

historian who omitted information for his own ends and reported slanderous rumors as facts.[34] Eusebius the historian was no less a heresiologist. Indeed, the bishop used the ancient genre of *historia* to do the work of heresiology. It was a brilliant way to coat certain fictions about Simon with the golden hue of facticity.

Eusebius did not make up information about the Simonians, but he did rearrange the false and negatively colored information of earlier reports. The idea that Simonians practiced orgies with wicked women can fairly easily be dismissed as libel. To ascribe "idolatry" to Simonians is a value judgment. They practiced a type of image veneration of entities representing God and divine Wisdom. (Such image veneration was not uncommon among Christians at the time.)

Although he aimed to shame and suppress the Simonians, Eusebius added some important information about them. Perhaps most importantly, Simonians continued to exist in Eusebius's day. This would mean that they had survived the ravages of the Great Persecution (303–311 CE). They continued to baptize new members like any other Christian group. They also persisted in presenting themselves as upstanding, sober, and moral citizens, followers of the Christian "philosophy."

Simonians were an early and long-lasting Christian group. There were Simonians in the first century (Helen and Menander), just as there were Simonians in the fourth. Simonians had continued to introduce themselves as Christians with the moral badges to prove it. Simonian virtue, whether seeming or true, had allowed them to escape detection by Roman authorities, to enjoy the great peace of the church in the late third century, and perhaps even to flourish as they worshiped in common with early catholics.

The early catholic church may well have excommunicated some Simonians in Eusebius's time, but it had not the power to root them out entirely. Eusebius's attempt to delegitimate and destroy Simonians, rhetorically speaking, ended up confirming that Simon and Simonians went back to the time of the apostles. In spite of the common thesis that "heresy" was late, derivative, and short-lived, Eusebius's story of Simon indicates that it was early, independent, and enduring. Simonians were around as early as the apostles and quickly became an international movement (in Palestine and Rome). They had written oracles with putatively awe-inspiring content, which remind one of the *Declaration*.

Simon was truly a worthy antagonist for the apostle Peter, not to mention Eusebius. He was the evil "other" and the great enemy of "the" church (meaning Eusebius's group). His influence was enduring and his memory alive. Though long dead, his legacy of founding virtually every other alternative Christian group was, surely, an accomplishment worthy of enshrinement in the library of Christian memory.[35]

---

[34] On Eusebius as historian, see Robert Grant, *Eusebius as Church Historian* (Oxford: Oxford University Press, 1980); Monika Gödecke, *Geschichte als Mythos. Eusebs "Kirchengeschichte"* (Frankfurt am Main: Peter Lang, 1987); Verdoner, *Narrated Reality*.

[35] Willing, *Euseb*, 460–4.

10

Epiphanius, Pseudo-Tertullian, and Filaster

Introduction

It is perhaps tempting to omit the later heresy reports on Simon. If our goal is to understand the historical Simon and the Simonians, what useful material can they offer beyond a conflated hodge-podge of previous reports, blended with novel fictions and fueled by hostile imaginations? By the late fourth century, we would not expect there to be new sources on the Simonians. At the same time, we are not at liberty to omit this material. When one cuts through this overgrown jungle, one can, on occasion, discover distinctive details and quotations from reliable sources which merit new analysis. It is in this sprit that I tackle the magnum opus of heresiology composed by Epiphanius of Salamis (about 377 CE).

As a young man, Epiphanius was trained in monastic disciplines in Egypt. About 335 CE, he returned to found his own monastery in the vicinity of his hometown in Palestine. In 367 CE, Epiphanius was made bishop of Salamis, then called Constantia, on Cyprus. Between 374 and 376 CE, he composed the—at that time—longest known heresy catalogue, comprising eighty different figures or groups. It was called the *Panarion*, or *Medicine Chest*. Into this catalogue, Epiphanius combined his knowledge of written sources, personal experience, and hearsay—which often results in the uneven quality of his reports.[1] Although Epiphanius's pen was dipped in bile (he openly apologized for his scurrilous language), he sometimes offers new information from sources long since lost.[2]

In the case of Simon, there is no strong reason to believe that Epiphanius employed Justin's *Syntagma*. It had long been replaced by Irenaeus's *Against Heresies*. Possibly Epiphanius knew the report on Simon in the *Refutation*. If he did, however, the bishop omitted key heresies (like Naassenes and Peratai), as well as any discussion of the distinctive elements in the Refutator's report on Simon (like Apsethos and the *Declaration*). Conversely, the Refutator and Epiphanius may have used the same source

---

[1] Epiphanius, *Pan.* proem. II, 2.4.
[2] Epiphanius, *Pan.* proem I, 2.3. On Epiphanius, see further Aline Pourkier, *L'hérésiologie chez Épiphane de Salamine* (Paris: Beauchesne, 1992), 29–52; Young Richard Kim, *Epiphanius of Cyprus: Imagining an Orthodox World* (Ann Arbor: University of Michigan, 2015), esp. 17–43; Andrew Jacobs, *Epiphanius of Cyprus: A Cultural Biography of Late Antiquity* (Berkeley: University of California Press, 2016); Todd S. Berzon, *Classifying Christians: Ethnography, Heresiology, and the Limits of Knowledge in Late Antiquity* (Berkeley: University of California Press, 2016).

for data about the Trojan horse and Helen with her torch, two Simonian allegories more fully reported in Epiphanius.[3]

Epiphanius is the only writer to quote from what appears to be a Simonian sayings source. According to this material, "Simon" related his own story in the first person. I will call it "the E source" and analyze its sayings in due course. Some have thought that the E source was the *Declaration*, in parts unquoted by the Refutator.[4] The theology of the E source differs, however, from the *Declaration* in several key points. For instance, it refers to "*Ennoia*" not "*Epinoia*," identifies *Ennoia* as Helen, and claims that the world was made by angels. All three ideas are foreign to the *Declaration*, which says that the world was made by the Seventh Power—not identified with Helen—without angelic aid.[5]

Below I translate Epiphanius's report on Simon, minus the bishop's attempted refutation.[6]

> The first heresy to begin in the time between Christ and the present belongs to Simon the magus. This heresy is composed of those who do not correctly and lawfully <believe> in the name of Christ, but in accordance with the corruption counterfeited among them, they perform shocking deeds.
>
> This Simon was a charlatan. He set out from Gitthon the city in Samaria (at present, a village). He produced illusions before the people of Samaria, deceiving and trapping them by his magic arts. He said that he was the great Power of God and that he descended from on high. He called himself the Father to the Samarians, but to the Jews he called himself Son. He suffered without undergoing suffering, in appearance only.
>
> This guy sweet-talked the apostles and was himself baptized by Philip, the same as the others, together with a large group. They welcomed, apart from Simon, the advent of the great apostles and through the application of their hands received holy Spirit. (Philip as a deacon did not have the authority of hand laying to give holy Spirit.)
>
> Simon did not have a correct disposition or way of thinking. He was addicted to shameful gain and the love of money and in no way strayed from his wretched line of work. He offered money to the apostle Peter so that he would give him authority to supply holy Spirit by hand laying. He reasoned that he would heap up a pile of money and make a profit by giving a little and receiving much in return by supplying Spirit to others.

---

[3] See further Andrew Jacobs, "Epiphanius's Library," in *From Roman to Early Christian Cyprus: Studies in Religion and Archaeology*, ed. Laura Nasrallah, AnneMarie Luijendijk, and Charlambos Bakirtzis (Tübingen: Mohr Siebeck, 2020), 133–52.
[4] Karl Holl, Marc Bergermann and Christian-Friedrich Collatz, ed., *Epiphanius I. Ancoratus and Panarion 1-33*, 2nd ed., GCS 10/1 (Berlin: de Gruyter, 2013), 240, apparatus.
[5] *Ref.* 6.13.1; cf. 6.14.4.
[6] In my translation I have been aided by the work of Frank Williams, *The Panarion of Epiphanius of Salamis: Book 1 (Sects 1-46)*, 2nd ed., Nag Hammadi and Manichean Studies 63 (Leiden: Brill, 2009), 61–7.

This man had an evil and delusional disposition from the demonic deceit endemic to magic. He was always ready, due to his own native evil, to show off the barbarous deeds of demons through his own juggleries.

He appeared in public and under the veil of Christ's name, like hellebore fused with honey, became a fatality to those caught by him. He inserted the dignity of Christ's name into his evilly devised deceit and infected his votaries with death.

Lecherous by nature, and stung by the shame of his own undertakings, this roving quack faked an insincere "deep" meaning for his dupes. For after finding a gypsy for himself named Helen from Tyre, he led her, not giving the slightest hint of hooking up with her. The charlatan had sex with this girly in secret shame and led his own disciples into imagining some mythical mirage. He called himself the great Power of God, of course, and he dared to call his whore-companion the holy Spirit, for whose sake, he claimed, he descended:

"In each heaven I was transformed, in accordance with the form of the beings in each heaven so I could avoid the notice of my angelic powers and come down to *Ennoia*"—also called Prunicus and the holy Spirit—"through whom I created the angels, who in turn created the world and human beings." Now this Helen is that one of old for whom Trojans and Greeks declared war. He was in the habit of telling a myth about these things, that the Power descended from above and transformed herself and that the poets allegorically spoke of this event. For on account of this power from above (which they call Prunicus, also known as Barbero or Barbelo in other heresies), displaying her beauty she drove them into a frenzy. She was sent to pillage the rulers who created this world.

These same angels made war because of her, though she suffered nothing. She set them up to produce their own mutual destruction through the lust she inspired in them for her. They restrained her so that she could not ascend and had sex with her, each one in each case with a female body in feminine adornment, since she was transferred from female bodies into different bodies of women. She came into beasts and other things, so that they could do their work through them. They killed and were killed, ensuring their own decrease through an effusion of blood. Afterward, she regathered her strength to be able to ascend back into heaven.

"She lived at that time among the Greeks and Trojans—indeed, long before the world began. After making the world, she created co-equal replicas through the invisible powers. She is the one who is now with me and the one for whom I came down. And she expected my advent, for she is *Ennoia*, the one Homer called Helen. And for this reason, Homer was compelled to write that she stood on a tower and secretly signaled to the Greeks through a torch the conspiracy against the Phrygians. Through the torch she displayed, as I said, the signal of the upper light."

And so the contested wooden horse in Homer, which the Greeks supposed came about through cunning, was in turn, as the charlatan continually said, the ignorance of the nations. Moreover, "just as the Phrygians ignorantly hauled it and drew within their own destruction, so also the nations, that is the people outside of my gnosis, through ignorance, haul destruction to themselves."

With regard to Athena, in turn, this deceiver said that with him she was called *Ennoia*. He used, you can be sure, statements of the holy apostle Paul, converting the truth to his own lie: "put on the breastplate of faith, the helmet and greaves of salvation, along with sword and shield." This fraud converted all these things into the mimicry of Philistion.[7] Words spoken by the apostle on account of steadfast reason, the fidelity of holy conduct, and the power of divine and heavenly speech, he converted to plain mockery—nothing more. "When then?" he asks, "All these things the armored one mystically portrays as the typical equipment of Athena."

Again, he kept calling that woman with him (the one taken from Tyre), as I said before, the same name as the ancient Helen with a secret indication. He calls her everything: *Ennoia*, Athena, Helen, among other things. "For her sake I have descended. This is the one written about in the gospel, the sheep that went astray."

Moreover, he delivered an image to his devotees—which of course represented him—and they worship it in the form of Zeus. Likewise he delivered to them another image, this one of Helen in the guise of Athena. His dupes worship these images.

He secretly established mysteries of shameful discharge from human bodies, to use polite language. I mean semen from men and the monthly menses of women. Men and women gather for mysteries with this most shameful collection. These indeed are the mysteries of life and gnosis of perfection! . . .

He himself privately supplies names to the rulers and authorities; and says that there are different heavens, and in each firmament and heaven he supposes there are powers and he gives them foreign-sounding names. One cannot be saved by any other means unless one learns this mystic lore with sacrifices of this kind to the Father of the universe as offered through these rulers and authorities.

This world, he says, was manufactured by evil rulers and authorities in deficiency. He taught that there is a corruption and destruction of the flesh; only souls are purified, and specifically those souls established in the mystic lore of his erroneous gnosis. Such was the beginning of the so-called gnostics.

He claimed that the law does not belong to God but to the left-hand power. The prophets do not exist from a good God, but from various kinds of powers. Each one determined rules as he wished. There is a law of one power, David has the law of another, Isaiah of another, Ezekiel of still another. He devotes each one of the prophets to one particular ruler. Yet all of them are from the left-hand power and outside the Pleroma. The one believing the old covenant in any respect acquires death. (Epiphanius, *Pan.* 21.1-5)

---

7. Philistion wrote mimes (farcical plays mocking scenes in mythology and from everyday life) and acted in them during the reign of Augustus. He is also mentioned in Epiphanius, *Pan.* 26.1.7; 33.8.2; 66.22.1.

We need not treat the material which overlaps with previous reports. Instead, we can focus on new information. By now, readers are familiar with the outrageous slings and arrows of heresiological invective; Epiphanius, for his part, made the bullets into cluster bombs. In addition to calling Simon by the (then standard) tag of "magus," the bishop named him "charlatan" (*goēs*), "fraud" (*apateōn*), "deceiver" (*planos*), and "roving quack" (*agurtēs*). In turn, he called Helen a "whore" (*pornas*), a "gypsy" (*rhembada*), in addition to "girly" (*gunaios*). Putting icing on the cake, Epiphanius (at the end of his report) likened Simon to "the snake-like filth hatched out of season from the infertile eggs of asps and other vipers."[8] We should not expect a fair treatment from the bishop of Salamis.

The bishop creatively blended his paraphrase of Acts 8 and Irenaeus's *Against Heresies*. He agreed with Irenaeus that Simon was not a Christian, at least not a true one. At the same time, he emphasized more than other heresiologists that Simon presented himself as a Christian. For Epiphanius, Simon's Christian identity was only a cover, but it was at least consistent.

Epiphanius added several details to Acts. Standard by now is the claim that Simon called *himself* the great Power, though it was actually others (Acts 8:10). Only from Epiphanius do we learn that Simon received baptism after "sweet talking" the apostles. Perhaps this is a colorful adaptation of Simon fawning on Philip (8:13). It was, at any rate, part of a consistent strategy to make Simon's conversion seem false. Another detail Epiphanius imported was Simon's refusal to welcome the "great" apostles (Peter and John). There is no need to posit a source for this material beyond the bishop's imagination.

As a bishop, Epiphanius felt the need to explain why Philip could not transmit Spirit through his hands. He could not do it, we are told, because he was only a "deacon"—a term Epiphanius understood in light of fourth-century church structures. The Spirit only came, Epiphanius claimed, when the right church officials were present—bishops like himself.

Epiphanius agreed with Irenaeus that Simon, even after baptism, never ceased being a magician. But he emphasized the profit motive and psychologized Simon even more. Simon reportedly offered Peter money as a kind of investment deal. In the future, he planned to charge for his Spirit-supplying services and believed he could secure great gains. There is nothing of the sort in Acts.

According to Epiphanius, Simon was in contact with demons. The Refutator accused Simonians of sending demons to inspire dreams. It was perhaps inevitable that demons be read back into Simon's own practice. Epiphanius never specified what exactly were the "barbarous deeds of demons" performed by Simon. In fact, he never mentioned any concrete "magical" practice at all, either for Simon or Simonians, with the exception of naming angels (distinctive to Epiphanius).

---

[8] Epiphanius, *Pan.* 21.7.2 (trans. Frank Williams). See further Ingvild Saelid Gilhus, "The Construction of Heresy and the Creation of Identity: Epiphanius of Salamis and His Medicine-chest against Heretics," *Numen* 62 (2015): 152–68; Joseph Verheyden, "Epiphanius of Salamis on Beasts and Heretics: Some Introductory Comments," *Journal of Eastern Christian Studies* 60 (2008): 143–73.

The tradition that Helen was the holy Spirit agrees with Tertullian's report, but it difficult to decide whether it is genuine Simonian lore. The reader will recall that, in Irenaeus's account, it is Simon who was believed to be "Spirit among the nations."[9] Epiphanius, like Tertullian, omitted this detail, presumably on purpose.

Only from the *Declaration* is it possible to understand *Ennoia* (there called *Epinoia* and the Seventh Power) as the Spirit hovering over the waters (Gen 1:2). It is not likely, however, that Epiphanius read the *Declaration*. Perhaps Epiphanius and Tertullian were dependent on a common—now unknown—source for Helen as holy Spirit.

Epiphanius himself added foreign names to his sources. In the first quote from the E source, he wrote in, I believe, two names for *Ennoia* that were not in his source. The first name was "Prunicus." Nowhere in any other Simonian source is *Ennoia* called "Prunicus," a name which appears in Epiphanius's Nicolaitan and Ophite reports.[10] Later Epiphanius referred to "Prunicus" and "Barbero" (aka "Barbelo"). The latter name is equally un-Simonian and appears in Epiphanius's Nicolaitan and "Gnostic" reports.[11] These names are not Simonian but helped Epiphanius to connect Simonians to other groups.

The bishop uniquely reported that the poets referred to *Ennoia*'s heavenly descent. How they did so we are never told. It is interesting that Epiphanius skipped over traditions of Wisdom's descent (Sirach 24; 1 Enoch 42), though he presumably knew them. Epiphanius, like most heresiologists, ignored *Ennoia*'s Jewish genealogy to emphasize her Homeric connections. Moreover, he conformed *Ennoia* to Barbelo and Prunicus, emanations said to have erotically excited the archons.[12] The effect of *Ennoia*'s beauty on the angels was already known to the Refutator and reflected in *Great Power*: "the powers lust to see my image."[13]

What is new is the Father's providential plan. It was *Ennoia*'s Father who deliberately sent her to the rulers in order to rob them of their power. This would indicate that, in the E source, *Ennoia*'s creation of the angels and her appearance before them were two separate events. First *Ennoia* created them, then she was sent to appear before them. In between these events, the angelic rulers somehow became wicked and the Father aimed to reduce their number. Ultimately, we are to understand, *Ennoia*'s fall and incarnations were part of an overarching divine plan.

Such a plan would explain why Ennoia "suffered nothing"—at least initially—from the angels who fought over her. In other reports, *Ennoia* seems harmed by these angelic attacks. Evidently, in Epiphanius's source(s), *Ennoia*'s Father protected her. In this way, the counsels of the Father were fulfilled.

Ennoia's troubles began when the angels detained her so that she could not ascend to her Father. It was at this point that they had sex with her—after forcing her to incarnate into various female bodies. So far Irenaeus. What is new is Epiphanius's claim that *Ennoia* also wandered into the bodies of beasts "and other things" (left undefined).

---

[9] Irenaeus, *Haer.* 1.23.1.
[10] Epiphanius, *Pan.* 25.3.2; 25.4.1; 37.3.2; 37.4.2. Cf. Irenaeus, *Haer.* 1.29.4.
[11] Epiphanius, *Pan.* 25.2.2, 4; 25.3.4; 26.1.9; 26.10.4; 26.10.10.
[12] Epiphanius, *Pan.* 25.2.4; cf. 26.1.9.
[13] *Great Pow.* 38.6–7.

The remark is idiosyncratic and irresponsible. It is doubly untrustworthy in light of Tertullian's note that Simonians never taught transmigration into animals.[14]

It is striking that *Ennoia* was able to gather strength to ascend back to heaven (from a beastly body, no less). Seemingly, this would make the descent of her Father superfluous. Nevertheless, the Father's descent was a key element in Simonian theology and is not absent from Epiphanius's report.

Ennoia's increased strength and independence is a theme in Epiphanius. She not only gathers strength to reascend, she makes "co-equal replicas"—apparently of herself—through invisible powers. To some extent, then, *Ennoia* was in control of her own incarnations, given the fact that she could recreate herself in multiple women called "Helen" through the course of time. *Ennoia* was, moreover, fully cognizant as she cycled through the bodies of women. She did not wallow in misery; she expected the advent of her Father.

Homer wrote of Helen because he was compelled—apparently by *Ennoia*—to compose her story. Put more positively, the blind bard was inspired by *Ennoia* (who plays the role of the Muses) to inscribe Helen's story with all its symbolic import. Thus Helen on the Trojan tower shows forth the light of heaven. The conspiracy of the Trojan horse was designed not so much against Phrygians, but against the rulers of this world. The horse represents the ignorance of the nations (or Gentiles) who—lacking Simon's gnosis—draw destruction to themselves. Simon's gnosis, we know from other reports, is the knowledge which frees people from angelic control.

Epiphanius distinctively indicated that Simonians used Pauline letters, and specifically the epistle to the Ephesians (6:14-17). This is not surprising, given the use of Paul (1 Cor 11:32) in the *Declaration*.[15] According to Epiphanius, Simonians allegorized the full armor of God as referring to Athena (that is, *Ennoia*'s) armor. *Ennoia* bore the image of a warrior goddess, outfitted with her famous helmet and shield. She was evidently well prepared to defend herself against angelic attack. For the Simonians known to Epiphanius, Helen was the armed Athena—a symbol of power and intelligence.

Because Epiphanius connected Simon with "Gnostics," he ascribed to Simonians the (in)famous rite of gathering semen and menses. Although Epiphanius never said that Simonians ate their collected discharge, this was probably the means by which Simonians were thought to offer "sacrifice." Here again we behold an irresponsible blending of reports. Epiphanius claimed that "Stratiotics" consumed their own semen and menses.[16] Stratiotics were a reputed sect of "Gnostics," whom Simon supposedly

---

[14] Tertullian, *An.* 34.1.
[15] *Ref.* 6.14.6 (1 Cor 11:32).
[16] Epiphanius, *Pan.* 26.4.3–8; 26.11.1. See further Roelof van den Broek, "Borborites," in *DGWE*, 194–6; Stephen Benko, "The Libertine Gnostic Sect of the Phibionites according to Epiphanius," *VC* 21 (1967): 103–19; Michel Tardieu, "Épiphane contre les Gnostiques," *Tel Quel* 88 (1981): 64–91; Stephen Gero, "With Walter Bauer on the Tigris: Encratite Orthodoxy and Libertine Heresy in Syro-Mesopotamian Christianity," in *Nag Hammadi Gnosticism and Early Christianity*, ed. C. W. Hedrick and R. Hodgson (Peabody: Hendrickson, 1986), 287–307; M. David Litwa, "The So-called Stratiotics and Phibionites: Three Notes on the 'Gnostics' of Epiphanius, Panarion 26," *VC* 76 (2022): 73–93.

Figure 10.1 The Varvakeion Athena, widely considered the most faithful and best preserved copy of the cult statue of the Athena Parthenos by Pheidias, which was erected in the Parthenon in 438 B.C. Courtesy National Archaeological Museum of Athens.

fathered. Evidently Epiphanius felt justified in imputing the claimed crimes of the children to their "father."

The bridge from Simonians to Stratiotics, however, is built on sand. Simonians offering semen and blood to the Father "through" rulers and authorities" does not cohere with any other testimony, including that provided by Epiphanius. Simonians never joined hands with wicked angels, and the perfect Father never required such sacrifices. Perhaps Epiphanius's imagination was sparked by the insinuation that Simonians enjoyed indiscriminate intercourse.[17] This was a standard—and stereotyped—charge, made against all varieties of Christians in antiquity.[18]

Also distinctive to Epiphanius is the report that Simon gave foreign-sounding (literally "barbaric") names to angelic rulers and authorities. It is true that we encounter demonic names in *Great Power* (namely, Sasabek and Berotth).[19] It is thus possible that Simonians knew such names. Nevertheless, naming demons is never mentioned in

---

[17] Justin, *1 Apol.* 26.7; *Ref.* 6.19.5; Clement of Alexandria, *Strom.* 7.17.108.2; cf. [Epiphanius,] *Anacephalaeosis* II, 21.2.

[18] See the sources cited in Chapter 4, n. 24 along with Thomas J. Whitley, "Poison in the *Panarion*: Beasts, Heretics, and Sexual Deviants," *VC* 70 (2016): 237–58, esp. 249–50.

[19] *Great Pow.* 41.29–30.

any other Simonian report, and it is likely another case of Epiphanian invention.[20] It was standard practice in magical papyri to refer to divine beings with foreign epithets, often Semitic in origin. If Simon was a "magus," Epiphanius may have inferred, he engaged in this practice as well.

The idea that angelic rulers made the world "in deficiency" need mean nothing more than that they created imperfectly. At the same time, the language is reminiscent of remarks Epiphanius made against Secundians and Ophites.[21] Valentinians are charged, more specifically, with upholding a defective creator.[22] The similar language hints that Epiphanius blended his reports.

Epiphanius conformed Simonians to Valentinians by asserting a Simonian "Pleroma" ("Fullness"). Yet Simonians did not have the concept of Pleroma, so it was impossible for anything to be inside or outside of it. Simonians also did not believe in anything called the "left-hand power." This power appears in a summary of the *Panarion*.[23] Possibly Epiphanius remembered it from his general reading and imputed it to Simonians.[24] By contrast, Simonians probably did believe that flesh was destroyed at the end of the world, but not because they considered it evil.

Epiphanius wrongly claimed that Simonians rejected the divine origin of the law (that is, the Pentateuch). The solemn use of the Pentateuch in the *Declaration* serves as a check on heresiology (Chapter 1). The mention of David, Isaiah, and Ezekiel need be nothing more than Epiphanius's imaginative expansion of Irenaeus. Irenaeus claimed that, for Simonians, the prophets were inspired by angels. Epiphanius "clarified" that each prophet lay under the charge of one particular power. The whole notion that Simonians rejected the prophets is contradicted by their use in the *Declaration*. The Simonian author of the *Declaration* quoted Isaiah several times, not as the mouthpiece of a wicked angel, but as the voice of the Seventh Power. Tertullian, for his part, claimed that Simonians invoked prophetic souls (Chapter 6).

The E Source

Having reviewed several examples of Epiphanian (mis)information, it is worthwhile attending to the sayings of the E source. There are five of these, and most appear in the first person. Simon reputedly said:

1. In each heaven I was transformed, in accordance with the form of the beings in each heaven so I could avoid the notice of my angelic powers and come down to

---

[20] Cf. Epiphanius, *Pan.* 25.3.5; 26.1.4; 31.3.3.
[21] Epiphanius, *Pan.*32.1.13; 37.1.10.
[22] Epiphanius, *Pan.* 36.5.6 (Heracleon).
[23] *Anacephalaeosis* (Holl, *Epiphanius* 2.4, line 1) describing Severus's view that women belong to the left-handed power. In the report on Severus, however, (*Pan.* 45), the left-handed power does not appear.
[24] Frank Williams (*Panarion*, 66, n. 37) cites several parallels, *Tri. Trac* 98.12–20; 104.9–11; 106.2–6, 18–21; *Gos. Phil.* 53.14–15; 60.26–8; *Nat. Rulers* 95.35–96.3; *Test. Truth* 43.10–12; *CH* 11.8.

Ennoia, through whom I created the angels, who in turn created the world and human beings.

2. She [*Ennoia*] lived at that time among the Greeks and Trojans—indeed, long before the world began. After making the world, she created co-equal replicas through the invisible powers. She is the one who is now with me and the one for whom I came down. And she expected my advent, for she is *Ennoia*, the one Homer called Helen. And for this reason Homer was compelled to write that she stood on a tower and secretly signaled to the Greeks through a torch the conspiracy against the Phrygians. Through the torch she displayed, as I said, the signal of the upper light.
3. Just as the Phrygians ignorantly hauled [the Trojan Horse] and drew within their own destruction, so also the nations, that is the people outside my gnosis, through ignorance haul destruction to themselves.
4. Put on the breastplate of faith, the helmet and greaves of salvation, along with sword and shield (Eph 6:14-17). . . . When then? All these things the armored one mystically portrays as the typical equipment of Athena.
5. For her [*Ennoia*'s] sake I have descended. This is the one written about in the gospel, the sheep that went astray.

The information in sayings 1 and 5 report data already known from Irenaeus (Simon's disguised descent from heaven and Helen as the lost sheep). If we only had these sayings, we might suppose that a person who knew Irenaeus's report recycled this material and put it in the mouth of Simon. Frank Williams thought that Epiphanius himself was the recycler, only pretending to have a source in which Simon spoke.[25]

Yet sayings 2–4 contain significantly new information. Some of this information was known to the Refutator, who reported the allegory of the Trojan horse and Helen with her torch (without, however, explaining them). Other data is unique, such as Helen on a tower, the identification of the torch with the upper light, the Trojan horse as ignorance, the notion that *Ennoia* created replicas of herself, that Homer was compelled to write of her, that people without gnosis invite their own destruction, and that the armor of God indicates the panoply of Athena (aka *Ennoia*).

This is material that Epiphanius, creative as he was, had no observable motive to make up. If Epiphanius invented something about Simonians, it was typically something pejorative (like orgies and demon invokation). He had no interest, it seems, in filling in any details of Simonian allegory. (The torch as the upper light, the armor of God as the armor of *Ennoia*, and so on). Accordingly, this material can tentatively be taken as Simonian lore from a (now lost) Simonian source (or possibly, sources) which used Simon as a mouthpiece.[26] This source was probably in existence by the early third century CE, since the Refutator had access to its traditions. It was a pseudepigraphical text attributed to Simon, just like the *Declaration*. This would mean that the Refutator was not the only heresiologist to discover a Simonian source written in Simon's own voice.

---

[25] Williams, *Panarion*, 62, n. 11.
[26] Beyschlag understood the E source to go back to the second century CE (*Simon Magus*, 37).

Pseudo-Tertullian

Before concluding this chapter, I add information from two other heresiologists because they used a source in common with Epiphanius. That source is called the *Syntagma Against 32 Heresies* (hereafter *Syntagma32*) authored by a shadowy writer usually called "Hippolytus." The text itself does not survive, but it was briefly summarized by Photius, a ninth-century Byzantine bishop.[27] Photius said that *Syntagma32* began with Dositheus and ended with Noetus. Epiphanius, along with two other heresiologists—Pseudo-Tertullian and Filaster—included these figures and preserved the same order for the roughly thirty heresies treated in between them. Since the late nineteenth century, it has been thought that all three heresiologists used *Syntagma32*, and I see no reason to disagree.[28]

Pseudo-Tertullian's name is a modern invention used to designate an otherwise unknown, Latin-speaking author probably working in the mid-third century CE. He epitomized and translated the *Syntagma32* into Latin. (Alternatively the epitome, made by someone else, preexisted Pseudo-Tertullian's translation.) The result was a "digest" heresiology called *Against All Heresies*. It may have originated or at least ended up in North Africa, since it was preserved as an appendix to Tertullian's *Prescription against Heresies*. Not much in this short report is unique, yet there are a couple of distinctive points:

> I turn myself to those who decided to be heretics on the basis of the gospel. The first of all these is Simon Magus, who in the Acts of the Apostles obtained a deserved and just judgment from the apostle. He dared to call himself the highest Power, that is, the highest God. He dared to say that the world was established by angels. He descended to seek his wandering daimon, who is Wisdom. As an apparition of God, he did not suffer among the Jews except in appearance. (Ps-Tertullian, *Against All Heresies* 1.1-2)

That Simon became a "heretic" on the basis of the gospel is a backhanded affirmation of his Christian identity, or at least his inspiration from Christian sources. Acts is read in typically heresiological fashion. A world made by angels probably comes from Irenaeus or *3 Corinthians*. What's new is Helen as "daimon" (or "demon") who is also called "Wisdom." We always knew that *Ennoia* was a Wisdom figure, but her identity as Wisdom is here made explicit for the first time.[29] Pseudo-Tertullian demonized Wisdom, of course, but this is little more than a value judgment. For Simonians she was a divine mediator and the creatrix. If the angels made the world, they did so through her.

---

[27] Photius, *Bibliotheca*, §121.
[28] See further Richard Adelbert Lipsius, *Zur Quellenkritik des Epiphanios* (Vienna: Braumüller, 1865); *Die Quellen der ältesten Ketzergeschichte neu untersucht* (Leipzig: Johann Ambrosius Barth, 1875); Pierre Nautin, *Hippolyte, Contre les hérésies* (Paris: Cerf, 1949); Pourkier, *L'hérésiologie*, 70–5.
[29] Later, in the Pseudo-Clementine *Recognitions* 10.33.2, Helen is called *sapientia* (wisdom).

Filaster

The other author who likely used *Syntagma32* was Filaster. Filaster, a contemporary of Epiphanius, lived in northern Italy and wrote in Latin. His early life is hidden in obscurity. He was said to have been a wandering preacher and ascetic. In the mid-fourth century, he opposed Auxentius, Arian bishop of Milan. Not long afterward, he was appointed bishop of Brescia in north Italy. In this role, he continued to oppose Arian theology along with a host of other perceived "heresies." In the early 380s CE, he composed his massive but somewhat slapdash *Diverse Heresies*, treating 28 heresies before Jesus and 128 after him. He died some time before 397. A laudatory sermon preached on his feast day (July 18) is now almost all that we have about his life.[30] Whether or not Filaster used Epiphanius's *Panarion* is still contested, since not all the heresies in the *Panarion* ended up in *Diverse Heresies* and overlapping material from Epiphanius could have been derived from an epitome or other sources.

This is what the bishop of Brescia had to say about Simon:

> After the suffering of Christ our Lord and his ascension into heaven, a certain Simon was a magus. He was Samarian by lineage, a Githean, from a well-known village in Samaria. He spent his time with magic arts, deceiving many people, calling himself a certain power above all other powers. The Samarians worship him as Father and praise him as the founder of his own dangerous heresy, and they strive to laud him with many praises. Although baptized by the blessed apostles, he backslid from their faith and sowed the seeds for a criminal and dangerous heresy.

> He said that he transformed himself in appearance, that is through a shadow, and in this way he suffered, although he did not, as he says, suffer. He dared to say that the world was made by angels and the angels were made by certain mental powers who preside over heaven.[31] He fooled <them when he descended from heaven, along with> the human race.

> He claimed there was another intellect who descended into the world for human salvation, namely the Helen in the Trojan War published and announced by worthless poets. The powers which made the world, he says, led by lust for this Helen, started a rebellion. For she produced lust, he says, in these powers, and when appearing in female form she was unable to ascend to heaven, since the powers which were in heaven did not allow her to ascend.

> She expected another power, namely the presence of Simon the magus himself, who saved her by his advent. The mechanism of the wooden horse, which the worthless poets say was in the Trojan war, he allegorizes as the ignorance of all irreligious nations. Now it should be agreed that this Helen who was with the magus was a prostitute from Tyre. She followed this same Simon magus, and with her Simon performed diverse magic tricks and diverse crimes.

---

[30] Gaudentius, "Sermo de vita et obitu beati Filastrii," in *S. Gaudentii episcopi brixiensis tractatus*, CSEL 68, ed. A. Glueck (Vindobonae: Hoelder-Pichler-Tempsky, 1936), 184–9.

[31] Here reading with the MSS *factos a quibusdam sensibus de caelo praeditis*.

Simon, when he fled the blessed apostle Peter from the city of Jerusalem, came to Rome. There he fought with the blessed apostle before the emperor Nero. He was beaten in every respect by the speech of the blessed apostles. Then, when struck by an angel, he deservedly perished, so that his magic was exposed and his lie manifest to all people. (Filaster, *Diverse Heresies* 29.1-9)

Again, we need not treat the material which overlaps with previous reports. Much of this report is hackneyed (Simon's self-deification, his backsliding, angelic lust, and so on) and inaccurate for reasons I have already discussed. We can focus on Filaster's distinctive contributions. The bishop of Brescia located the site of Peter and Simon's first confrontation in Jerusalem, not Samaria. Here he depended not on Acts, but evidently on some version of the *Acts of Peter* which also presented Nero—not Claudius—as the reigning emperor (Chapter 11).[32]

Filaster also used the *Acts of Peter* to the report Simon's death. Simon is struck by an angel—a highly ironic end, since Simonian gnosis promised freedom from angels.[33] Filaster seems to say that the angels were not immediately made by Wisdom, but by otherwise unidentified "mental powers" (*sensibus*). No other source mentions these beings, and we can probably discard them as needless duplications of Wisdom.

Filaster concurred with Epiphanius on two points. The first is that the incarnate *Ennoia* (here simply called Helen) expected her Father to save her and looked out for his advent. Second, Simonians allegorized Helen's torch and the Trojan horse. The latter point was also mentioned by the Refutator. That Filaster and Epiphanius depended on the *Refutation* is doubtful in my view. Neither of them mentions the *Declaration*, Apsethos, or any other distinctive element of the Refutator's account. When discussing Helen and her torch, all three heresiologists may have been dependent on a common source, likely *Syntagma32*, possibly the E source, or perhaps some other unknown document.

Conclusion

What, then, can we infer about Simonians from these late, accretive, and often inaccurate accounts? Perhaps it is best to say, first of all, what we should *not* infer. We should not infer that Simonians gathered their own semen and menses. They did not sacrifice to angels or through them. They did not reject the Pentateuch or the Prophets. They did not suppose that *Ennoia* appeared in the bodies of beasts. They also did not call *Ennoia* "Prunicus" or "Barbelo." All of this material was "fake news" written against Simonians, the result of heresiological blending.

---

[32] *Acts Pet.* 23.621–5.
[33] The angelic attack assumes a story like the one told in the *Passion and Acts of the Holy Apostles Peter and Paul* 56 (in David L. Eastman, *The Ancient Martyrdom Accounts of Peter and Paul*, WGRW 39 [Atlanta: SBL Press, 2015], 260–1). It is also reflected in the *Apostolic Constitutions* 6.9.4 (Metzger). Cyril of Jerusalem, *Catechetical Lectures* 6.15, where Peter and Paul join in prayer to bring Simon down from "a demon's chariot."

What we might reasonably infer, I believe, is as follows. Simonians continued to be a perceived problem in Palestine, North Africa, and Italy as far as late antiquity. Recall that Eusebius spoke of contemporaneous baptizing Simonians, evidently in Palestine.[34] According to Epiphanius's biography, moreover, Simonians survived on Cyprus.[35] Even if there were no Simonians on the island, however, Epiphanius still considered them a threat. Simon had fathered many Christian groups (such as the "Stratiotics") which continued to proliferate in Epiphanius's time. Simonian pseudepigrapha (the E source) continued to circulate, indicating that someone or some group was preserving and reading it. This source (or sources) indicates continued development of *Ennoia*'s story, with an added emphasis on her independence and power to defend herself. She did not suffer from initial angelic attacks; she expected her divine Father, and gained the power to ascend back to him on her own. There was also a new focus on the Father's providential plan. *Ennoia* did not fall into this world; she was sent to wreak havoc on the angels and rob them of their power. If these new developments represent Simonian modifications, it indicates that Simonians continued to survive and modify their portrait of *Ennoia* perhaps as late as the fourth century.

Simon's consistent use of Christ's name is not so much about Simon as it is about Simonians. It stands as evidence that Simonians continued to identify as Christians as far as the late fourth century. Since the days of Justin, indeed, they never ceased being Christians—a fact which explains why they continued to be hounded by heresiologists. Simonians not only used the gospels (the Lost Sheep parable), they used Pauline writings as well, as indicated by the quote from Ephesians. They treated Paul much like the other scriptures. They allegorized these writers so that they referred to figures in their own metanarrative (for instance, *Ennoia*, aka Athena, and Helen). Simonians may have allegorized the poets as well—apparently not just Homer—seeing in their works the symbols of *Ennoia*'s descent from heaven.

Although he never said so explicitly, Epiphanius imagined Simon as the father of all heresies. Practically, this meant that the bishop felt he was able to blend later heresies with Simonian thought. Sometimes the blending was probably unintentional. In the case of Simon, however, the bishop felt freer to mix a composite brew, since any heresy could stick to the "father of all heresies." Epiphanius considered Simon to be the progenitor of the "Gnostics" (aka "Borborites," "Coddians," "Stratiotics," and so on) who appear in *Panarion* 26.[36] Thus he attributed to Simonians the "Gnostic"—and specifically "Stratiotic"—practice of gathering semen and menses and made it seem as if "Prunicus" was another name for *Ennoia*.

Due in part to such blending, much material in later heresy reports—not just Epiphanius—proves unreliable. In this situation, careful sifting becomes even more important. Much of Epiphanius's unique data, for instance, seems to be based on nothing more than his own fictionalizing inferences. At the same time, some of his information—the quotes from the E source—promote a positive vision of *Ennoia* and Simon, and are probably trustworthy. Epiphanius did occasionally dramatize his sources,

---

[34] Eusebius, *Hist. eccl.* 2.1.12.
[35] Claudia Rapp, *The Vita of Epiphanius: An Historical and Literary Study*. 2 vols. (Dissertation. Oxford, 1991).
[36] Epiphanius, *Pan.* 26.1.1 and *Pan.* Proem I, 4.3.

leading his readers to believe he quoted first-hand accounts.[37] In my view, however, the bishop would not have invented large blocks of material that added essentially positive information about *Ennoia*'s hidden strength and the Father's mission. Thus we have no option but to keep doing what we have been doing throughout this volume: testing each tradition separately, not assuming its truth or falsity until we have checked it against different Simonian reports and already recognized Simonian lore.

---

[37] Epiphanius, *Pan.* 27.5.8.

11

The *Acts of Peter*

Introduction

In the *Acts of Peter* Simon seems to float, bobbing somewhere between myth and history. Generated by the story in Acts, but strangely uncontrolled by its details, the *Acts of Peter* return us to a Simon as a pure magus without theological depth. This Simon writes nothing and cherishes no scripture. His only resource is a bag of magic tricks, imitation miracles, a set of illusions which deceive people in the short run. This Simon was never a Christian, nor a Samaritan—not even a Samarian. He was, rather, a lawless Jew who existed solely for himself and only to destroy Christianity. Cursed and made into a reprobate, Simon fulfilled his predetermined role as antihero to Peter and dark mirror to Christ.

The *Acts of Peter* are typically dated to the later decades of the second century CE. They have to fit sometime before the monarchial episcopate at Rome yet after Christians began to conceive of senators joining their ranks. The place of origin is generally considered to be either Rome or Asia Minor. If the text did not originate in Rome, it probably used traditions developed in the eternal city, the site of the deepest cultural memory about Peter and Simon, and where Peter's martyrdom was much hallowed.[1]

For the purposes of this chapter, the *Acts of Peter* refers to a Latin text commonly called the *Actus Vercellenses* since it is housed in Vercelli (not far west of Milan), Italy.[2] The Latin translation derives from the later fourth century CE. Either the fourth-century

---

[1] See the history of research in Marietheres Döhler, *Acta Petri: Text Übersetzung und Kommentar zu den Actus Vercellenses*, TU 171 (Berlin: de Gruyter, 2018), 43–8. Döhler herself leans toward a Roman provenance. For an Asian provenance, see Christine M. Thomas, "The 'Prehistory' of the *Acts of Peter*," in *The Apocryphal Acts of the Apostles: Harvard Divinity School Studies*, ed. François Bovon, Ann Graham Brock and Christopher R. Matthews (Cambridge, MA: Harvard University Press, 1999), 39–62, and Jan Bremmer, "Aspects of the Acts of Peter: Women, Magic, Place and Date," in *The Apocryphal Acts of Peter: Magic, Miracles and Gnosticism*, ed. Jan Bremmer (Leuven: Peeters, 1998), 1–20. Matthew C. Baldwin argues that a written form of the *Acts of Peter* only appeared in the late third century CE (*Whose Acts of Peter? Text and Historical Context of the Actus Vercellenses*, WUNT II/196 [Tübingen: Mohr Siebeck, 2005], 3, 302). The late-fourth-century Latin translation in the *Actus Vercellenses* represents "an independent utterance" (300). But a papyrus fragment (P. Oxy 849) convinces other scholars that the original *Acts of Peter* dates to around 200 CE. For further discussion of the fragment and the broader argument, see Hans-Josef Klauck, *The Apocryphal Acts of the Apostles: An Introduction*, trans. Brian McNeil [Waco: Baylor University Press, 2008], 83–4; Döhler, *Acta Petri*, 37–41).

[2] A. Hilhorst, "The Text of the *Actus Vercellenses*," in *Apocryphal Acts of Peter*, 148–60.

translator—or more likely the seventh-century scribe—omitted several episodes from the original *Acts*. Possibly this was because it was thought that these episodes overlapped with the adventures of Peter in the Pseudo-Clementine *Recognitions*, a text which appears immediately before the *Acts of Peter* in the Vercelli manuscript. The *Acts of Peter* finishes the story, as it were, of Peter in the *Recognitions*, by telling the tale of the apostle's final showdown with Simon in Rome and how both men, in a violent and unusual manner, met their earthly ends.

In terms of genre, the *Acts of Peter* reads, to most modern readers, like a novel. For the ancient author, the work probably functioned more like a form of history, and specifically Roman church history. The author knew, by tradition, that Simon had come to Rome and met Peter; he then told their story as he thought it would have happened. The fantastical elements can be explained by the fact that, in apostolic times, miracles were rife. The author used sources, such as the book of Acts, to fire his imagination, but he felt free to omit and change its details, reusing and adapting its plots. In modern terminology, we might call the *Acts of Peter* a historical novella, much like what we find in the *Alexander Romance*.

The author's information about Simon seems to have been extrapolated from Acts 8 and 13 as well as from other traditions circulating about Simon.[3] Some of the oral traditions about Simon were perhaps loosely based on heresiological reports like Justin's *Syntagma*. At the same time, the writer had evidently never read a Simonian source (such as the *Declaration*) and was ignorant or uninterested in Simonian theology.[4]

Backdrop

I forgo summarizing the *Acts of Peter* in their entirety (a task already done).[5] My focus will be on Simon.[6] There are several parts of the narrative, however, that must be understood to grasp Simon in context. Some of these parts I rearrange to relate Simon's story more clearly.[7]

---

[3] David L. Eastman ("Simon the Composite Sorcerer," *NTS* 68 [2022] 407–417) argues that the figure of Simon the sorcerer in the Acts of Peter is a synthesis of Simon as he appears in Acts 8 and Elymas the magus in Acts 13. It is true that the Elymas episode explains some of the elements of Simon in the *Acts of Peter*, but not all (e.g. Simon claiming to be Christ, Simon able to fly, and Simon punished with death, not just blindness). Eastman admits that his inquiry by no means answers all our questions about the ubiquitous Simon.

[4] Below, the *Actus Vercellenses* will be quoted by chapter and line numbers in the edition of Döhler, *Acta Petri*, 49–144.

[5] Klauck, *Apocryphal Acts*, 84–101; Döhler, *Acta Petri*, 19–27.

[6] For Simon in the *Acts of Peter*, see G. P. Luttikhuizen, "Simon Magus as a Narrative Figure in the *Acts of Peter*," in *Apocryphal Acts of Peter*, 39–51; Alberto Ferreiro, *Simon Magus in Patristic, Medieval and Early Modern Traditions* (Leiden: Brill, 2005), 55–83, 147–200; Vidović, "Good Doggy," 58–72; Julia A. Snyder, "Simon, Agrippa, and Other Antagonists in the Vercelli *Acts of Peter*," in *Gegenspieler: Zur Auseinandersetzung mit dem Gegner in frühjüdischer und frühchristlicher Literatur*, ed. Michael Tilley and Ulrich Mell (Tübingen: Mohr Siebeck, 2019), 311–32.

[7] Some of the material herein revises and expands my treatment of Simon in Litwa, *Desiring Divinity*, 110–13.

The *Acts of Peter* roughly begins where the book of Acts left off. Paul is under arrest in Rome, but allowed to preach and make converts. He eventually converts his jailor, Quartus (Rom 16:23). Quartus urges Paul to leave prison and Rome itself (compare Acts 16:28-34). Paul only does so after receiving a vision. After a long and tearful departure with final instructions (compare Acts 20:17-38), Paul sets sail for Spain, leaving his tender flock vulnerable to the next charismatic wonderworker to appear on the scene.[8]

The curtain opens on Simon. He is called a "Jew" or "man from Judea" (*Iudaeum*) rather than a Samarian.[9] He had already gained fame as a miracle worker in Aricia, a few miles from Rome. He possessed a "teaching" (*doctrina*), but it is never explained.[10] Simon is never supplied with a lengthy speech. We only hear soundbites from his lips, lips sometimes forcefully sealed.

We first hear of Simon's self-conception via second-hand report. According to a group of anonymous Christians, Simon says "that he is the Great Power of God (*magnum virtutem dei*), and that without God he does nothing. Is he then himself the Christ (John 4:29)?" The Great Power, in the minds of this crowd, is distinguished from God, apart from whom Simon can do nothing (John 15:5).[11] Simon as "God's (Great) Power" is found twice more in the story—though all in second-hand reports.[12] By his own report—given much later in the story—Simon viewed himself as the Father's son.[13]

The "Great Power" title—with the added qualification "of God"— comes from Acts (8:10).[14] In Acts, however, the title was ambiguous. It could refer either to the highest God or to some subordinate power. The author of *Acts of Peter* understood it as a subordinate, and in so doing contradicted Irenaeus, wherein Simon is the *highest* Power above all others, the very Father in flesh who appears in Samaria.[15] The author never mentioned Samaria (Acts 8:4, 14), and depicted the confrontation between Simon and Peter (Acts 8:20-24) as occurring in Judea and Jerusalem specifically.[16] He had no independent tradition of these two in Judea, in my view; he simply moved the content of the original clash (Acts 8:20-24) to Jerusalem.

(Anti-)Christ

Acts and other biblical sources were launchpads for the author to reimagine Simon as a type of antichrist.[17] The antichrist, like Christ, views himself as the son of the

---

[8] For *Acts Pet.* 1-3 as added by a redactor, see Gérard Poupon, "Les 'Actes de Pierre' et leur remaniement," *ANRW* 2.25.6, ed. W. Haase (Berlin: de Gruyter, 1988), 4363-83.
[9] *Acts Pet.* 6.155.
[10] *Acts Pet.* 6.178.
[11] *Acts Pet.* 4.79-80.
[12] *Acts Pet.* 8.230; 10.300.
[13] *Acts Pet.* 31.816.
[14] Matthews, "The Acts of Peter," 211-12. See also Matthews, *Philip: Apostle and Evangelist: Configurations of a Tradition* (Leiden: Brill, 2002), 35-70.
[15] Irenaeus, *Haer.* 1.23.1; cf. Justin, *Dial.* 120.6.
[16] *Acts Pet.* 23.621-5. Cf. *Didascalia Apostolorum* 23.2 (Stewart-Sykes, *Didascalia*, 229).
[17] For this theme in later anti-Simon literature, see David L. Eastman, "Simon the Anti-Christ? The *Magos* as *Christos* in Early Christian Literature," *Journal of Early Christian History* 6, no. 1 (2016): 116-36.

Father. He proclaims himself to be god (2 Thess 2:4). By Satan's energy, he performs false signs and wonders to deceive people—even the elect (2 Thess 2:9; Matt 24:24).[18] Due to Simon's wonders, all but a handful of Christians in Rome become his followers.[19]

Simon as false Christ can appear in heresiology, but this was not the dominant heresiological model for understanding him.[20] In the *Declaration*, Simon is a prophet who announces that all people can become equal to the Infinite Power. According to Irenaeus, Simon is the highest Power.[21] As Father and the highest Power, Simon transcended any sort of messianic identity. One could infer, of course, that Simon as "Son in Judea," was actually Jesus, who was, in turn, the Christ. Simon, then, would also be Christ. Yet actual Simonians, it seems, never referred to Simon simply as "Christ."

In the *Acts of Peter*, by contrast, the crowds wonder if Simon is the Christ. As the narrative proceeds, however, Simon is portrayed as the great enemy of Christ (Jesus) and of the Christian message. He openly defames Jesus by calling him a craftsman's son and himself a craftsman.[22] Jesus was only a man, not an incarnate God, since a god is not born or crucified.[23] Simon arrives as an "angel—or messenger—of Satan" (2 Cor 12:7) to destroy Jesus's works.[24] None of this material is found in authentic Simonian lore.

In the *Acts of Peter*, Simon does not travel around with Helen. Helen is never mentioned and she plays no role in Simon's story. This is a significant departure from the heresiological tradition crafted by Justin and Irenaeus. Helen was so important to Simonians that some of them were called "Helenians."[25] Yet the author of *Acts of Peter* showed no interest in Helen or *Ennoia*, or anything resembling Simonian teaching.

Deification

In his opening debut in the *Acts of Peter*, Simon is portrayed (again second-hand), as a self-deifier; but—as in Acts—he is actually deified by others. Some Christians report the words of unidentified people who invite Simon to Rome as if he were emperor. They proclaim before him: "You are god in Italy, you are Savior of the Romans!"[26] Before this crowd, Simon makes a bold claim in a surprisingly "soft voice

---

[18] *Acts Pet.* 12.368.
[19] *Acts Pet.* 4.98.
[20] E.g., *Ref.* 6.9.1; 6.20.3.
[21] Irenaeus, *Haer.* 1.23.1.
[22] *Acts Pet.* 14.395; 23.629.
[23] *Acts Pet.* 23.631–2.
[24] *Acts Pet.* 4.95.
[25] Celsus in Origen, *Cels.* 5.62.
[26] *Acts Pet.* 4 (*tu es in Italia deus, tu Romanorum salvator*). See further Angelos Chaniotis, "Acclamations as a Form of Religious Communication," in *Die Religions des Imperium Romanum. Koine und Konfrontationen*, ed. Hubert Cancik and Jörg Rüpke (Tübingen: Mohr Siebeck, 2009), 199–218; Raban von Haehling, "Zwei Fremde in Rom: Das Wunderduell des Petrus mit Simon Magus in den acta Petri," *RQ* 98 (2003): 47–71 at 51–2.

(*voce gracili*)."²⁷ This "soft" or "thin" voice contrasts with Peter's normally stentorian tones²⁸ and would have been taken as a sign of weakness, servility, and effeminacy.²⁹

Yet if Simon speaks softly, he carries a big stick. He announces that tomorrow around one 'o'clock "you shall see me flying over the city gate" of Rome.³⁰ The next day, bystanders behold "in the distance a cloud of dust" in the sky, "like smoke with lightning bolts flashing from afar."³¹ The epiphany resembles the arrival of Yahweh as seen by Ezekiel. As the ancient prophet looked, "a stormy wind came out of the north: a great cloud with brightness around it and fire flashing forth continually" (Ezek 1:4, NRSV). In the cloud appeared a vast dome, and above it was a throne, "and seated above the likeness of the throne was something that seemed like a human form" (Ezek 1:26; cf. Exod 19:9).³² Perhaps we should imagine a parody because Simon comes, not in a cloud of light, but in a cloud of smoke and dust.

The cloud evaporates and Simon suddenly appears inside the gate, encircled by people, "with everyone worshiping him and recognizing that he was the one who was seen the day before."³³ Simon arrives in the manner of Yahweh (or Wisdom)—and virtually all Christians in Rome bow the knee. Simon is later said to bear "the name of the Lord"—a Lord who could technically be Jesus or the Judean god.³⁴ In light of his initial epiphany, however, Simon as Lord would be Simon as Yahweh.³⁵

Simon is welcomed into the home of a Christian senator by the name of Marcellus. (From a modern perspective, this is an openly non-historical element, since Christians in the mid-first-century did not attract Roman senators.)³⁶ It was Marcellus who was responsible for erecting the famous (though fictive) statue to Simon in Rome. Irenaeus reported the tradition that Simon "is said to have been honored with a statue due to his magic."³⁷ Justin was more specific. He said that the statue was on Tiber Island and inscribed: "To Simon, sacred god." Either the author of *Acts of Peter* did not read Justin or felt at liberty to recarve the epigraph: "To Simon, the young god."³⁸ The "young (*iuvenus*) god" is a rendition of the Greek adjective *neos* which could be translated "young" or "new." In Rome, for instance, both Gaius Caesar and Germanicus were called "young gods" (*neoi theoi*).³⁹ The author of the *Acts of Peter* evidently filled in details from his cultural knowledge.

---

²⁷ The softspoken Simon is later pilloried by a talking canine (*Acts Pet.* 12.354–5).
²⁸ *Acts Pet.* 7.199, 312.
²⁹ Callie Callon, *Reading Bodies: Physiognomy as a Strategy of Persuasion in Early Christian Discourse* (London: T&T Clark, 2019), 47–9.
³⁰ *Acts Pet.* 4.86.
³¹ *Acts Pet.* 4.90 (*tamquam fumus cum radiis eminus refulgens*).
³² The image also appears in Sirach 24:4, with Wisdom as the speaker: "my throne is in the pillar of cloud."
³³ *Acts Pet.* 4.90–2.
³⁴ *Acts Pet.* 17.432 (*nomen domini*).
³⁵ For Christ as bearing the name of Yahweh, compare Phil 2:10. See further Litwa, *Iesus Deus*, 181–214.
³⁶ T. D. Barnes, "Statistics and the Conversion of the Roman Aristocracy," *JRS* 85 (1995): 135–47.
³⁷ Irenaeus, *Haer.* 1.23.1 (*statua honoratus esse dicatur propter magiam*).
³⁸ *Acts Pet.* 10 (*Simoni iuveni deo*). See further Otto Zwierlein, *Petrus in Rom: Die literarischen Zeugnisse mit einer kritischen Edition der Martyrien des Petrus und Paulus auf neuer handschriftlicher Grundlage*, 2nd ed. (Berlin: de Gruyter, 2010), 129–33.
³⁹ As noted by Bremmer, "Aspects," 140.

In speaking of Simon's statue, the author(s) implicitly denigrated Simon. Justin and Irenaeus gave the impression that the statue was an official honor, given with the approval of the sacred senate and people of Rome. According to the *Acts of Peter*, however, the statue was set up by a single senator at Simon's own request. It represented, in other words, one of the many private deifications in Rome. It was not a public honor authorized by the august body of the senate. The private honor, moreover, was paid for by a man not in his right mind, but said to be deluded by Simon's magic.

Justin had written that nearly all Samarians worshiped Simon as the high God.[40] According to the *Acts of Peter*, virtually all Christians became Simonians—at least superficially—honoring Simon as the Christ. Ironically, the "real" Simon, in the *Acts of Peter*, was never a Christian, let alone a theologian; he was a magician ever motivated by greed and self-glorification.

Simon vs. Peter

Yet the spotlight on Simon was about to dim. Light had to oppose darkness as Horus battled Seth. God chose a worthy opponent for the magus: the very Peter who clashed with him in Acts. In fact, Peter is portrayed as recalling his encounter with Simon in Samaria—now said to be in Judea. In his reminiscence, the apostle fails to mention Simon's baptism and Christian faith, but remembers well how he rebuked him. Here, Peter's rebuke is not intended to save a wayward Christian soul; it is meant as a curse with no opportunity for repentance: "We cursed you (*malediximus te*) in your hearing: 'Do you want to tempt us with the possession of money?'"[41] Simon in Acts had no interest in tempting Peter. According to the *Acts of Peter*, Simon's motives were worthy. He offers money not to transmit Spirit, but to cure sick people.

Peter also relates that in Judea, Simon robbed a rich woman named Eubola with the help of accomplices. In fact, this was the cause for Simon's flight from Judea. Peter exposed the theft, and Simon reportedly slinked away.[42]

Hearing that Simon forestalled him in Rome, Peter set sail in the company of a friendly ship captain, Theon. Upon landing in Italy, Peter immediately sets out, without food or refreshment, on the stony path to Rome. His first stop, after a rendezvous with fellow Christians, was the house of Marcellus where Simon was staying. When the porter at Marcellus's house hesitates to announce Peter's presence, Peter sends in a large, talking dog to flush Simon out. The dog (who stands up on its hindlegs to deliver his message) is all it takes, it seems, for Marcellus to throw himself at Peter's feet in penitence.

After witnessing two more Petrine wonders, Marcellus orders Simon—somehow still conversing with the dog—out of his house. Pounded with a staff and slaps, rather

---

[40] Justin, *1 Apol.* 26.3.
[41] *Acts Pet.* 23.624–5.
[42] *Acts Pet.* 17.

like Jesus in the gospels, Simon is sent out of the house drenched with feces.[43] The slaves perform these deeds which doubly degrade Simon, formerly conceived of as an elite guest.[44]

When Simon later hurries to Peter's quarters for an audience, he invites him to debate: "Come down, Peter, and I will show you that you have trusted in a Jew and son of a carpenter." But unlike in the Pseudo-Clementines (Chapter 12), this Peter makes no time to debate. Instead, he sends a seven-month old baby to proclaim that Simon's father is the devil (John 8:44).[45] This speech, the longest tirade of the text, gives a taste for the anti-Simon vitriol throughout the book:

> You cause of horror to God and human beings, you outcast from truth and corruptor of all, most inferior seed, unfruitful fruit of nature! But for a little while and a brief time you appear, and after this, eternal punishment awaits you. Born from a shameful father, you who never send down roots to what is good, but into poison, you offspring of unbelief, destitute of all hope, not confounded when a dog exposes you, I—an infant—am forced by God to speak and still you don't blush.... Depart, therefore, from the gates in which the feet of the saints convene. For now, you will not corrupt innocent souls which have turned and mourn together in Christ. Your most perverted nature will be revealed and your elaborate con will fall to pieces. Now I speak to you my final word. Jesus Christ says to you, "Lose your voice, you who are forced by my name, and leave Rome until the coming Sabbath." (15.401-11)

Ironically the instant silencing of Simon seems very much like an act of magic. What is striking is how quickly Simon goes from deified to demonized man. Apart from this speech, he is directly called "that inconstant demon" and his regular titles are "son" and "angel" of Satan.[46]

A dream of Marcellus demonizes Simon all the more. In a vision of the night, the senator sees an Ethiopian woman dressed in filthy rags and dancing with a slave's collar around her neck. In the dream, Peter orders Marcellus to decapitate this woman, and Marcellus twice refuses. Then a man who looks like Peter—representing Christ—takes a sword and violently cuts up the woman's body.

It is a gruesome image. I refrain from discussing its racially sensitive implications and its potential to inspire religious violence. It is sufficient to point out that this woman is said to represent "all the power" of Simon and his "god" (Satan). Simon is the one who is depicted as black—a color associated with cowardice and cunning in antiquity.[47] He also dances, perhaps to indicate the cheap frivolity and distraction of

---

[43] *Acts Pet.* 14. Klauck observes how this story echoes the mocking of Jesus in the gospels (*Apocryphal Acts*, 92).

[44] Callie Callon, "Secondary Characters Furthering Characterization: The Depiction of Slaves in the *Acts of Peter*," *JBL* 131, no. 4 (2012): 797–818 at 801–2.

[45] *Acts Pet.* 15.403.

[46] *Acts Pet.* 17.455, 491, 838. A more intense demonization of Simon occurs in the *Didascalia* 23 (Stewart-Sykes, *Didascalia*, 229) and the *Apostolic Constitutions* 6.7.1 (Metzger) where Simon is an actual incarnation of Satan.

[47] Callon, *Reading Bodies*, 53.

his sorcery. The collar and chains probably reinforce Simon's servile status.[48] Simon as female emphasizes his weakness. Simon is the (wo)man whom Christ destroys. Peter is quite heartened by the vision.

Not long afterward, there is a great showdown between Simon and Peter in the Julian Forum. A carnivalesque feeling fills the air as the people of Rome, bored of their bread and circuses, gather to behold what seemed in their eyes the greatest contest of magic. The price of seating to the show is a piece of gold (and one wonders who is charging).[49]

Before the people, Peter recounts Simon's tawdry history, while Simon tries to engage in theological debate. "Men of Rome, is a god born? Is he crucified? He who has a master is no god!" Of course, for the Romans, many gods were born (Hermes, Dionysus, Heracles), and some of these same gods suffered. But Simon was evidently appealing to philosophical sensibilities: a man who is humiliated, who practices a degrading occupation, is no god. Scholars have heard echoes of Jewish criticisms against Simon, as well as the views of Christians who insisted on Jesus's humanity (the Theodotians).[50] Perhaps both are right. The point is, these are not *Simonian* criticisms, since Simonians (according to Irenaeus) had no problem with affirming the divinity of the Son in Judea.[51]

The spectacle quickly turns from word to deed. The crowd wants to see visible evidence of divine power. The prefect Agrippa rises as umpire. He generously offers one of his own slave boys to be killed for the purpose of resurrection—though there was already a corpse on hand. It was the body of a widow's son, whom Peter eventually raises after some narrative suspense. Growing impatient, Agrippa insists on the resurrection of his boy, a favorite of the emperor. Peter complies.

Then, almost circus-like, comes a third call for resurrection. A noblewoman's son, the young senator Nicostratus, is hauled in from his funeral. Peter allows Simon to take this one. Yet Peter wins the day, since Simon has only the power of a half-resurrection—making Nicostratus twitch, open his eyes, and bow in Simon's general direction.[52]

Ascent

But the climax is yet to come. Exposed by Peter time and time again, Simon applies to himself the type scene of injured Wisdom (1 En 42).[53] He declares,

> Men of Rome! Do you suppose that Peter has beat me, that he is stronger than me? You fawn on him as someone more powerful. He has seduced you. Tomorrow I will

---

[48] Callon, *Reading Bodies*, 52.
[49] *Acts Pet.* 23.608.
[50] Roman Hanig, "Simon Magus in den Petrusakten und die Theodotianer," *Studia Patristica* 31 (1997): 112–20; Snyder, "Simon, Agrippa," 324–6.
[51] Irenaeus, *Haer.* 1.23.1.
[52] *Acts Pet.* 28.725–7.
[53] Cf. the figure of Justice in Aratus, *Phaenomena: Introduction, Translation and Commentary*, ed. Douglas Kidd (Cambridge: Cambridge University Press, 1997), 96–136; Vergil, *Eclogues* 4.6; Ovid, *Met.* 1.149–50.

fly to the Lord whose power I know, because you injured me, and I will go to the Father of all, and say to him: your children did injury to me, so I return to you.[54]

The next day, the omnipresent crowd lines the Sacred Way to behold what they think is another marvel. Predictably, Peter arrives to oppose Simon. Looking down on Peter from a "high place," Simon declares that, "I, by ascending, will show to all this crowd what manner of being I am!" Quick as a flash, word becomes deed; Simon becomes airborne, zooming over Rome's temples and tombs.

Then Peter prays for his enemy: "Speed on your grace, Lord; and let him fall down from above and be crippled, though not die. Rather let him be disabled and break his leg in three places." Like a shot bird, Simon drops. After his predictable triple fracture, the Christian mob stones him like Stephen in Acts (Acts 7:59). As they do so, they sing a hymn.[55] One can surely see in Simon the fall of Lucifer (Luke 10:18) or of Icarus; but in his sufferings—and eventual death—one can also glimpse Christ mocked and Paul stoned all over again (Matt 23:37; John 8:59; Acts 14:20).

Other renditions of the story take additional delight in the death of Simon, and make Peter its more immediate cause. In the *Passion and Acts of the Holy Apostles Peter and Paul*, the chief apostle likewise prays for Simon's fall. When Simon hits the ground, his whole body splits into four pieces.[56] In the Vercelli *Acts*, at least, Simon still has a few faithful friends who drag him back to Aricia.[57] There he dies a few days later on the operating table.

Conclusion

Such is the man and such is the myth of Simon. If we read the *Acts of Peter* as a historical account, we would have to affirm that Simon was a Jewish, greedy, self-serving, self-exalting, demon-possessed enemy of Christianity who never quoted a word of scripture. He could not be a heretic because he was never a Christian, but an anti-Christian and an antichrist. Affirming any part of this portrait would, I believe, seriously misrepresent Simon and, by inference, later Simonians.

To be sure, no critical scholar accepts the polemical portrait of Simon in the *Acts of Peter*. At the same time, it is all too easy, in the manner of Eusebius, to whittle down some aspects of this portrait and present it in the form of historical data—for instance, that Simon was a magus who came to Rome, experienced success, and worked for money. None of these details can be verified even when they are shorn of their fantastical frills.

---

[54] *Acts Pet.* 31.813–17.
[55] *Acts Pet.* 7:54–60. The story is creatively retold in the *Apostolic Constitutions* 6.9.2–6 (Metzger). When the crowds acknowledge the flying Simon as a god, Peter brings him crashing down.
[56] Eastman, *Ancient Martyrdom Accounts*, 260–1. See further Zwierlein, *Petrus in Rom*, 59–74; Ferreiro, *Simon Magus*, 55–82, 133–46.
[57] The fact that Simon continued to have followers despite this disaster is also reported in the *Apostolic Constitutions* 6.9.5 (Metzger).

The anti-Simon polemic in the *Acts of Peter* is not well informed by authentic Simonian lore or even by heresiological reports. Heresiologists, for all their faults, were forced to keep at least one foot in reality. They wove in, to be sure, many fictional elements into their reports, but they did not write fiction as such. Admittedly, there was no firm line between fiction and history. They both bobbed and weaved on a sliding scale. Nevertheless, the *Acts of Peter* veers much more toward the fictional side of the scale. It never cites any sources, never offers anything more than a vague sense of time, and never stresses eyewitness observation.[58] Its author(s) and revisor(s) never even name themselves.

Of course, the author(s) tried to make these *Acts* look more like history. After all, we find the names of historical characters like Marcellus, which recalls the governor of Bithynia from 14 to 15 CE. In this case, however, there was little concern for precise chronology: how could this Marcellus, who attained his acme in 14 CE, still be active in the late 60s?[59] Similar chronological carelessness occurs in the Eubola flashback: here a road leads to Neapolis (in the mid-60s), though the city was not founded until 73 CE.

The *Acts of Peter* reveals its fictional nature by its use and development of characters. Nicostratus and Eubola are apparently made up. Agrippa invokes the name of two Jewish kings of the first century.[60] As a Roman prefect, however, his character is basically invented. The name "Quartus" is taken from Romans 16:23, but his role as a jailor (and liberator of Paul?) is fictional. Theon the ship captain also appears invented, though he may be loosely based on the centurion who transfers Paul to Rome in Acts 28. In sum, Theon, Agrippa, Nicostratus, and Eubola were almost certainly not real people with real histories.

Accordingly, the *Acts of Peter* is not controlled by anything one would call reliable historical memory. One can distinguish two kinds of memory, communicative and cultural. Communicative memory is the living, diffuse memory often passed on orally usually within a couple generations of an event. Cultural memory, by contrast, is the memory of deep time, preserved by institutions, embodied in rites, and inscribed in literature.[61] By the mid-second century CE, the communicative memory of Peter had largely shifted to cultural memory. This is the kind of memory that became important for identity construction in the *Acts of Peter*. Yet this kind of memory is not tied to the actual memories imprinted through direct observation.

It is worth considering how this "memory" arose. It seems that Acts 8 was generative for all later clashes depicting Simon and Peter.[62] At the same time, important details from Acts are left out—that Simon and Peter met in Samaria, that Simon offered money to transmit the Spirit, that Simon was offered a chance to repent. To be sure, the

---

[58] Christine M. Thomas, *The Acts of Peter, Gospel Literature and the Ancient Novel: Rewriting the Past* (Oxford: Oxford University Press, 2003), 3.
[59] Tacitus, *Annals* 1.74 with discussion in Thomas, *Acts of Peter*, 48–9.
[60] Thomas, *Acts of Peter*, 57–8; I. Karasszon, "Agrippa, King and Prefect," in *Apocryphal Acts of Peter*, 21–8.
[61] Dietrich Harth, "The Invention of Cultural Memory," in *A Companion to Cultural Memory Studies: An International and Interdisciplinary Handbook*, ed. Astrid Erll and Ansgar Nünnung (Berlin: de Gruyter, 2008), 85–96; Jan Assmann, "Communicative and Cultural Memory," in *A Companion to Cultural Memory Studies*, 109–18.
[62] Matthews, "Acts of Peter," 207–22.

author of *Acts of Peter* brought to the table an image of Simon ultimately dependent on Acts. But most of the other content of Simon's story seems invented: Simon coming to Rome in a stormy dust cloud, staying in the house of Marcellus, dueling with Peter in the forum, swindling Eubola, flying over Rome—there is no source for this material, it appears, other than second-century Christians' imagination.

In short, the Simon of the *Acts of Peter* does not indicate a real person, but a theological representation. The battle between Simon and Peter is not bound by time and space; it is an eternal battle between good and evil, apostle and anti-apostle, Christ and antichrist.[63] The Simon of this novella is a foil, an antihero necessarily opposed to the hero; an arbitrary caricature of an apparently real person who was—at least according to Acts—a baptized Christian (8:13).

To be sure, the *Acts of Peter* touches upon historical reality. This reality, however, is not that of Simon, but of (much) later writer(s) and editors. These writers were less concerned about the first-century Simon and later Simonians than they were about distinguishing Christ and antichrist, miracle from magic, and the "true" church from all other assemblies.[64] As a result, virtually nothing in the *Acts of Peter* can reliably be used as a source for understanding Simonians in Rome or elsewhere.

---

[63] Luttikhuizen, "Simon Magus," in *Apocryphal Acts of Peter*, 41; F. Lapham, *Peter: The Myth the Man and the Writings*, JSNTSup 239 (Sheffield: Sheffield Academic Press, 2003), 50.

[64] For social history on the basis of *Acts Pet.*, see, e.g., the work of Judith Perkins, *The Suffering Self: Pain and Narrative Representation in the Early Christian Era* (London: Routledge, 1995), 124–41; "Resurrection and Social Perspectives in the Apocryphal *Acts of Peter* and *Acts of John*," in *Ancient Fiction: The Matrix of Early Christian and Christian Narrative*, ed. Jo-Ann A. Brant, et al. (Atlanta: SBL Press, 2005), 217–37.

12

The Pseudo-Clementine *Homilies*

Introduction

Lively and memorable, the Pseudo-Clementines have the power to entice and bewitch readers into accepting their sketch of Simon as a crafty and murderous magician.[1] It is the fullest and most detailed depiction of Simon in any early account. As in the *Acts of Peter*, Simon appears as anti-apostle and occasionally as antichrist. Yet here Simon's priority is explained by the "doctrine of pairs." All reality, Peter claims, is made up of opposites wherein evil debuts before good, darkness before light, false before true.[2] Far from the common apologetic theory that heresy must come later, in this system, heresy proudly parades before its opponents. Simon is Peter's precursor in the mission to the Gentiles.[3] His miracles come before Peter, as does his teaching, his movement, and his success.[4]

The Pseudo-Clementine *Homilies* and *Recognitions* are two fourth-century CE Christian novels told by the man who supposedly became bishop of Rome.[5] Whether or not one grants the existence of a Clement (who seems to have been modeled on a Roman senator executed in the reign of Domitian), it is anachronistic to think that someone could become "bishop" of an entire city a generation or so after Jesus.[6] By the second century CE, the name "Clement" adorned two originally anonymous letters

---

[1] Some of the material herein revises and expands my treatment of Simon in Litwa, *Desiring Divinity*, 113-18.
[2] A problem here is that Adam the true prophet comes before Eve in the biblical account.
[3] *Hom.* 2.17. Simon is directly called Peter's precursor (προδρόμος) in *Hom.* 7.4.1.
[4] Further introductions to the Pseudo-Clementines can be found in Nicole Kelley, *Knowledge and Religious Authority in the Pseudo-Clementines: Situation the Recognitions in Fourth Century Syria*, WUNT II/213 (Tübingen: Mohr Siebeck, 2006), 1-35; Klauck, *Apocryphal Acts*, 193-216; Jan Bremmer, "Pseudo-Clementines: Texts, Dates, Places, Authors and Magic," in *The Pseudo-Clementines*, 1-24. For treatments of Simon specifically, see Dominique Côté, *Le thème de l'opposition entre Pierre et Simon dans les Pseudo-Clémentines* (Paris: Institute for Augustinian Studies, 2001), esp. 188-255; Päivi Vähäkangas, "Christian Identity and Intra-Christian Polemics in the Pseudo-Clementines," in *Others and the Construction of Early Christian Identities*, ed. Raimo Hakola, Nina Nikki and Ulla Tervahauta (Helsinki: Finnish Exegetical Society, 2013), 217-38 at 223-7; Annette Yoshiko Reed, *Jewish-Christianity and the History of Judaism*, TSAJ 171 (Tübingen: Mohr Siebeck, 2018), 148-52.
[5] Eusebius, *Hist. eccl.* 3.4.9; 3.4.15.
[6] Peter Lampe, *From Paul to Valentinus: Christians at Rome in the First Two Centuries*, ed. Marshall Johnson, trans. Michael Steinhauser (Minneapolis: Fortress, 2003); Bernard Pouderon, *La genèse du roman pseudo-Clémentin: Études littéraires et historiques* (Paris: Peeters, 2012), 49-72.

that survive today (1–2 Clement). It is perhaps no surprise that a novelist would try to discover—or, rather, invent—a backstory for this literary cipher.

It seems that an original novelist wrote a work called the *Circuits of Peter* (aka "the Basic Writing") about the second quarter of the third century. These *Circuits* were then adapted by the author of the *Homilies*—hereafter, the "Homilist"—and by an independent writer who wrote the *Recognitions*. The *Homilies* and *Recognitions* overlap and diverge at many points. Exactly how they relate to each other and to the Basic Writing has been explored by others.[7] My focus is on the *Homilies*, which seems to better preserve the Basic Writing than the later and more orthodox *Recognitions*. At the same time, much of what is said about Simon in the *Homilies* applies to the *Recognitions* as well.[8]

The *Homilies* have been called the first ancient Christian novel, and also the last.[9] Whatever we choose to call it, it is a heart-stirring tale: Clement, orphaned as a teenager in Rome, finds his long-lost mother and twin brothers—shipwrecked twenty years before—along with his father (who went in search of them) all tucked away in various spots along the Levantine coast within the space of a few days. This fable of a family re-found now frames and sweetens a series of doctrinal debates.

The work is fiction, but the Homilist coated it with a veneer of historicity. He prefaced the work with letters supposedly from Peter and Clement to James (Jesus's brother). He referred to historical places and sites. He used the names of those whom he thought were real people in the biblical universe. It seems he wanted to relate the "true history"—not just of Clement—but of Simon Peter and his archenemy—the other Simon. In so doing, he rewrote Peter's theology and view of scripture, creating a sort of counter Christianity with some distinctive features. A few of these features have been called "gnostic," and "Jewish-Christian," but when taken as a whole, they do not precisely fit any known system.

The sources for the *Homilies* include the Septuagint and the four Gospels—though the latter are represented as quoted from memory. Material used to construct Simon's character probably includes Justin's *1 Apology* (which reports Simon's hometown). The style and format of the *Acts of Peter* were also apparently in mind (though not its chronology).[10] Apart from the overall theme of Peter's clash with Simon, the Homilist did not use details from Acts 8.

---

[7] F. Stanley Jones, *Pseudoclementina Elchasaiticaque inter Judaeochristiana: Collected Stories* (Leuven: Peeters, 2012), 3–112; Frédéric Amsler, "État de la recherche récente sur le roman pseudo-clémentin," in *Nouvelles intrigues pseudo-clémentines. Plots in the Pseudo-Clementine Romance*, ed. Frédéric Amsler et al. (Prahins: Zèbre, 2008), 25–48. See also Jürgen Wehnert, *Pseudoklementinische Homilien: Einführung und Übersetzung* (Göttingen: Vandenhoeck & Ruprecht, 2010), 30–6. M. Vielberg, "Centre and Periphery in the Ancient and Christian Novel—A Comparison between the Pseudo-Clementine Homilies and Recognitions," in *The Pseudo-Clementines*, ed. Jan Bremmer (Leuven: Peeters, 2010), 255–84.

[8] In what follows, I use the critical edition of Bernard Rehm and Georg Strecker, ed., *Die Pseudoklementinen I: Homilien*, GCS 42, 3rd ed. (Berlin: Akademie, 1992).

[9] Jones, *Pseudoclementina*, 204. Contrast I. Czachesz, "The Clement Romance: Is it a Novel?" in *The Pseudo-Clementines*, 24–36.

[10] Other connections are covered by Matthew Baldwin ("The *Acts of Peter* and the *Pseudo-Clementines*. 'Connections Beyond Self-evidence,'" in *Nouvelles Intrigues*, 69–78), though he believes that the *Recognitions* may have influenced the *Acts of Peter*.

In the *Homilies* there is no sure sign of Simonian documents like the *Declaration*.[11] Yet there is one curious overlap: the *Declaration* refers to God as "the One who Stood, Stands, and Will Stand"; the *Homilies* speak of "the One who Stood, Will Stand, and who Opposes"—an intriguing parallel, but it is evidently tweaked and not enough to prove dependence.[12] In the *Homilies*, Simon calls himself "the Standing One," but this designation evidently comes from a separate tradition (more on this soon). Perhaps the most important source of all for the Homilist, it seems, was his own head. The author was deeply creative, and his inventiveness—the ability to combine details and create new ones—should not be underestimated.

Backstory

The reader will recall that of the *Acts of Peter* reduces Simon to a magician and a quack. The Homilist, however, combined the portraits of Simon the magus and Simon the theologian to create Simon the educated philosopher. To fill out his portrait, he added a host of invented details exposing Simon's former life: the name of his parents, his training in Egypt, his discipleship under John the "Day Baptist,"[13] his rise as John's successor, his skill as a dialectician and debater, not to mention his wild works of wonder.

What is important to keep in mind is that Simon's backstory is put in the mouths of two of his disaffected disciples, namely Nicetas and Aquila.[14] They are not, to say the least, neutral witnesses. Simon had reported his activities to them as a friend.[15] They betrayed his trust by revealing them to Simon's enemies (Peter and Clement). Thus everything they say must be taken not only with a grain of salt, but as data dyed in hostility.

> This Simon's father was Antony and his mother was Rachel. His nation was Samaria, from the village of Getthon, six schoeni distant from the city [Caesarea]. He came to Alexandria by Egypt and worked intensively on his Hellenic education. There he was considerably empowered by magic. Elated to the point of madness, he wanted to be considered the highest Power—higher even than the god who created the world. Sometimes he hints that he is Christ, and calls himself the "Standing One." He uses this address in the belief that he will stand forever and because his body cannot fall by reason of corruption. He says that the God who created the world is not the highest.

---

[11] *Pace* Lüdemann, *Untersuchungen*, 97; cf. Dominique Côté, "La fonction littéraire de Simon le Magicien dans les *Pseudo-Clémentines*," *Laval Théologique et Philosophique* 57, no. 3 (2001): 513–23 at 518.
[12] *Ref.* 6.17.1 (ἑστώς στάς στησόμενος); *Hom.* 18.12.1 (ὁ ἑστως στησόμενος ἀντικείμενος).
[13] *Hom.* 2.23.1.
[14] *Hom.* 2.25.4.
[15] *Hom.* 2.26.1.

He does not believe that corpses are raised. He denies Jerusalem, and substitutes it with Mt. Gerizim. Instead of our true Christ, he announces himself. Matters of law he allegorizes by his own whim. He says that a judgment is coming, but he does not expect it. He is convinced he will not be judged by God and dares to commit impiety as far as God himself. Accordingly, he secretly robs people of truth's possessions, from people ignorant that he uses godliness as a cover. They who believe him as someone trustworthy, in particular his version of pie-in-the-sky hope and the coming judgment, are in the process of being destroyed.

How he weaseled his way into the doctrine of godliness happened this way: There was a certain John the Day Baptist, forerunner of our Lord Jesus Christ according to the doctrine of pairs. Just as the Lord had twelve apostles bearing the same numbers as the twelve months of the sun, so John had thirty officials who filled out the number of the moon's cycle. In this number was a woman called Helen so that even this would not be poorly arranged. For the woman is half a man. Just as the course of the moon during the month does not make a complete cycle, Helen made the number thirty incomplete.

Of these thirty disciples, John's first and most esteemed was Simon. The reason he did not rule after John's death is as follows: he was on a journey to Egypt for the completion of his magical training when John was executed. A certain Dositheus, eager to rule, falsely announced that Simon had died and so Dositheus received the sect by succession.

Now Simon arrived not long after, fiercely laying claim to the position as his own. When he met Dositheus, however, he did not demand it, since he knew that the one who came first and beyond expectation to office is not removed. Accordingly, with feigned and short-lived friendship, he submitted to second place after Dositheus.

Subordinated not many days among the thirty co-disciples, Simon began secretly to slander Dositheus, accusing him of not accurately transmitting the teachings. He was alleging that Dositheus did this not as one jealously guarding the teachings, but as one ignorant of them. At some point, Dositheus, inwardly sensing that Simon's manufactured slander let loose against him sparked suspicion in many, arrived at the accustomed lecture hall in a rage, and, finding Simon, beat him with a rod. The rod, however, seemed to go through Simon's body as if it were smoke. Stunned at this, Dositheus said to him, "If *you* are the Standing One, then I will worship you." When Simon replied, "I AM!" Dositheus realized he was not the Standing One. He threw himself down, worshiped, and subordinated himself among the twenty-nine officials and set Simon in his own covertly coveted position. So it was that not many days later, while Simon stood, Dositheus fell down and died.

Now Simon, taking Helen with him, circles about disturbing the crowds to the present day, as you can see. He says that he brought down Helen herself from the highest heavens to this world, that she is a queen, the all-mother essence, and Wisdom. For her sake, he says, Greeks and Barbarians made war, producing a faded image of the truth, for at that time she actually abided with the most primal God.

Beside such things, he deceives many by convincingly allegorizing fictions with Greek myths, performing many terrifying wonders so that, if we did not know he did these through magic, we ourselves would have been deceived. (*Hom.* 2.22.2–2.25.3)

This account combines a host of details both new and old into a motley tapestry. The Homilist is the only author who explicitly indicates that Simon was a Samaritan—not just a Samarian—who preferred worship at Mt. Gerizim (compare John 4:20). Yet the portrait is inconsistent, since Samaritans worshiped the creator and abided by their own version of Mosaic law while the Pseudo-Clementine Simon spurned the creator and never obeyed Torah. Simon is never seen celebrating the Samaritan holidays or following their customs. We learn that he has a "sabbath" which he practices every eleven days—an unprecedented religious practice for either Jews or Samaritans.[16] Reportedly, Simon was not looking for the Samaritan messiah; he assumed that role for himself. It will not suffice to call Simon a marginal or renegade Samaritan. He is, rather, a unique combination of various and often incongruous traditions.

Simon, not Jesus, was recognized as John's most esteemed disciple.[17] John baptized people not once for repentance but every day—apparently as a rite of purification.[18] This "Day Baptist" evidently held the office of the Standing One which he passed on to his successors. This is the first time we ever hear of such an office. In the mid-third century, Origen paired Simon and Dositheus, but never said they were part of the same group.[19] In the *Homilies*, their fictional stories intertwine—they were old rivals as co-members of the same baptizing sect with which Jesus was associated (as known from the gospels). Apparently the leader of the sect inherited a rod like that of Moses—conveniently used to beat unruly members.[20] It was Simon who ultimately became John's successor. The gospels are thus transformed: Jesus did not assume John's mantle—Simon did. Oddly enough, as we read further into the *Homilies* Simon seems basically independent. His twenty-nine (and a half) co-officials are not developed as characters after this initial report.

Some of the other material is culled from heresiological reports—for instance, Simon's hometown, his journeys with Helen, his status a "magus," and so on. It is no surprise that Simon's statue goes unmentioned, since it had not been erected in the narrative time of the story (before Simon went to Rome). It is surprising, however, that none of the distinctive details from Irenaeus's report appear, apart from Simon the highest Power. Where, one can ask, is Simon the purchaser of the Spirit, Simon as Son in Judea and Father in Samaria, Simon as Father of *Ennoia*, as incarnate Savior of Helen who fooled the angels on his way down from the highest realm? Where is Simon's seeming suffering in Judea, his offer of salvation by grace, his veneration in the form

---

[16] *Hom.* 2.35.3.
[17] *Hom.* 2.23.4 (δοκιμώτατος).
[18] See further Claudio Gianotto, "Les baptêmes dans les *Pseudo-Clémentines*," in *Nouvelles intrigues*, 223–34.
[19] Origen, *Cels.* 1.57; 6.11.
[20] On the rod, see Stanley Isser, "Dositheus, Jesus, and a Moses Aretalogy," in *Christianity, Judaism and Other Greco-Roman Cults: Studies for Morton Smith at Sixty Part Four*, ed. Jacob Neusner (Leiden: Brill, 1975), 167–89 at 175–6; Fossum, *Name of God*, 117–20.

of Zeus, and so on?[21] This was juicy material to work with. Either the Homilist did not know Irenaeus's report or chose, largely, to ignore it.

Other material is apparently concocted, such as the name of Simon's parents (otherwise unknown), his relationship to John, and his education in Alexandria. The attention to Simon's Hellenic learning is distinctive, but unsurprising given the Homilist's distrust for Hellenic *paideia*. It is tempting to say that the Homilist had some sort of tradition about Simonians in Alexandria. But there is no certainty here, because in the ancient world, Alexandria—and Egypt more broadly—was widely coded as the place to learn magic.[22] According to the Homilist, Clement himself once planned to visit Egypt in order to practice necromancy.[23]

The Standing One

In the account of Nicetas and Aquila, Simon never calls himself Christ. When he self-identifies in the story, he claims to be the "Standing One."[24] We know from the *Declaration* that the Standing One could refer to the high God or to God's Image, the Seventh Power (Chapter 1). Simon as the Standing One is here evidently the high God above the creator. But Simonians did not believe in a demiurge other than Wisdom who used angels as her instruments.

To "stand" in this context probably has a Platonic sense: to be permanent, unchanging, and unmoving. Philo, Numenius, and Sethian literature all attribute the ability to stand to divine and angelic beings.[25] Philo made explicit that heroes like Moses were called to attain the stable tranquility of the Standing One, often by an ascent to heaven. Zostrianos in the work named after him stands on each level of heaven to

---

[21] Simon explicitly denies that he is (or was) God's son in *Hom.* 18.7.3.
[22] Origen, *Cels.* 1.28, 38, 46. See further D. Frankfurter, "Ritual Expertise in Roman Egypt and the Problem of the Category 'Magician,'" in *Envisioning Magic: A Princeton Seminar and Symposium*, ed. H. Kippenberg and Peter Schäfer (Leiden: Brill, 1997), 115-35 at 119-21; Dickie, *Magic and Magicians*, 205, 215-17, 229-31.
[23] On necromancy, see Dickie, *Magic and Magicians*, 237-9; Daniel Ogden, *Greek and Roman Necromancy* (Princeton: Princeton University Press, 2001); Jan Bremmer, *The Rise and Fall of the Afterlife* (London: Routledge, 2002), 71-86; Sarah Iles Johnston, *Ancient Greek Divination* (Malden: Wiley Blackwell, 2008), 171-5.
[24] For the Standing One title, see Ps.-Clem., *Hom* 2.22.7; 18.12.1; 2.24.6; *Rec.* 1.72.3; 2.7.1-3; 2.11.3; 3.47.3; See further Lüdemann, *Untersuchungen*, 97-101; Pieter F. Goedendorp, "If you are the Standing One, I also will worship you (Pseudo-Clementine Homilies II 24.6)," in *Proceedings of the First International Congress of the Société d'Études Samaritaines*, ed. Abraham Tal and Moshe Florentin (Tel Aviv: Chaim Rosenberg, 1991), 61-77, esp. 66-7; Jaan Lahe, *Gnosis und Judentum: Alttestamentliche und jüdische Motive in der gnostischen Literatur und das Ursprungsproblem der Gnosis*, Nag Hammadi and Manichean Studies 75 (Leiden: Brill, 2012), 136-7.
[25] Philo, *Post.* 27-8; *Conf.* 30; *Leg.* 3.9; *Somn.* 2.226; Numenius in Eusebius, *Prep. ev.* 11.20; *3 Steles Seth* (NHC VII 5), 119.4; 121.9-15. Cf. *Corp. herm.* 2.12; 10.14. See further Runia, "Witness or Participant?" 36-56 at 47-51; Michael A. Williams, *The Immovable Race: A Gnostic Designation and the Theme of Stability in Late Antiquity* (Leiden: Brill, 1985).

behold the realities that angelify him.[26] God as Standing One and Moses as standing with God is also a theme in the fourth-century Samaritan work *Memar Marqah*.[27]

If Simon as Standing One fits a Moses pattern, it is no sure inference that the Homilist tapped directly into Samaritan tradition or that he knew of a clear-cut role called "the Prophet like Moses."[28] The Samaritan evidence is in line with the more philosophical writers like Philo (a Jew from Alexandria) and Numenius (a Gentile in Syria).[29] The "Standing One" title has a Semitic flair, no doubt, but it was parallel to more abstract Hellenic terms such as "eternal" (*aiōnios*) and "immutable" (*atreptos*). Where the Simon of the *Homilies* departs from Platonism is his belief in *bodily* immutability. According to Nicetas and Aquila, Simon denied the immortality of the soul.[30] It was Simon's body that would never fall.

Simon's self-deification in the *Homilies* resonates with elements from the gospel of John. Jesus had reportedly used "I AM" as a claim to divinity (for instance, John 8:28, 58; 13:19, compare Exod 3:14; Isa 52:6). In John 19:5, Jesus's "I AM" brings people to the ground. In John, moreover, people once doubtful about Jesus are depicted as worshiping him (20:28). That Jesus is in himself invulnerable is revealed in his trial, wherein he says that only by his and the Father's will could injury come to him (John 18–19; cf. Matt 26:53). In short, the Simon of the *Homilies* is more like the Johannine Messiah than any comparable figure in fourth-century CE Samaritan thought.

As is often the case in the *Homilies*, there are kinks in the fabric of Simon's story. Nicetas and Aquila indicate that Simon considered himself to be the high God above the creator. Later, however, we learn that Simon believes in an unknown God who exists in "secret realms."[31] Never once does Simon identify this unknown God with himself. In fact, Simon seems to present himself as the messenger and interpreter of this God.[32] When Simon speaks for himself in the debates, he never calls himself the Standing One. It is Peter who mockingly denies Simon's right to the title, a title that Simon—at least in front of Peter—never assumes.[33]

From where did the Simonian use of the Standing One derive? It appears in the *Declaration*, but in a different form: "the One Who Stood, Stands, and Will Stand." In the *Declaration*, moreover, Simon never claims the title for himself. It is applied to God and the Seventh Power. We find the same usage in Clement of Alexandria, who relates that Simonians conform themselves to the Standing One—meaning God, not Simon.[34] This means that if the use of the Standing One title was recognized as Simonian in the second century, its *application to Simon* probably occurred later in the course of heresiological constructions of Simon's self-deification.

---

[26] Williams, *Immovable*, 73–4. For the Standing One in *Allogenes* (NHC XI 3), *Ap. John* (NHC II,1), and *Gos. Eg.* (NHC III,2; IV,2) see ibid., 52–7, 103–52.
[27] Beyschlag, *Simon Magus*, 45–7; Fossum, *Name of God*, 120–4; Haar, *Simon Magus*, 275–9.
[28] Pace Fossum, *Name of God*, 115 (for the "Moses pattern," see 124).
[29] Pace Fossum, *Name of God*, 120.
[30] *Hom.* 2.29.
[31] *Hom.* 3.2.2; 18.4.3; 18.4.5.
[32] *Hom.* 18.6.2; 18.9.3.
[33] E.g., *Hom.* 18.14.3.
[34] Clement, *Strom.* 2.11.52.2.

The earliest surviving evidence of the title's application to Simon seems to be the *Martyrdom of the Holy Apostle Peter* §2—an alternative ending to the *Acts of Peter*. Here Simon, immediately before his ascent to heaven, declares before the crowds: "I will fly up to God, whose power I am, though enfeebled. If then you have fallen, behold I am the Standing One (*ho Hestōs*)."[35] Ironically, the "Standing One" then moves speedily through the air.

The next time we hear of the title applied to Simon is in the *Homilies*, (which may here be dependent on the Basic Writing). It should be kept in mind, however, that the Homilist was a magpie who pulled from a variety of sources about Simon and wove together an assortment of claimed titles and backgrounds (magician, Christ, Samaritan, philosopher, Day Baptist, Standing One, etc.), some of which do not cohere with each other or even with Simon's own theology as it is presented later in the novel.

Helen

The Helen of the *Homilies* is similar to what we find in Justin Martyr—a subsidiary, voiceless tool of the roving Simon. That Simon brought her down from heaven contradicts the report of Irenaeus, where Simon zooms to rescue Helen who fell into flesh long ago. Simonians called her *Ennoia*—or *Epinoia* in the *Declaration*. According to Irenaeus, *Ennoia* made the world through angels.[36] The Homilist may not have known this story. Yet he rightly explained the identity of *Ennoia* as "Wisdom," the ultimate creatrix and all-mothering essence. Her title "queen" or "mistress" is known from the Refutator, but need not derive from the *Refutation* directly.[37]

What's new is Helen's association with the Greek Moon goddess, or Selene. (In fact, the *Recognitions* simply call Helen "Luna," the Latin word for moon.) Yet since Helen (*Helenē*) of Troy had long been linked to *Selenē*, the Moon, it was logical for the Homilist to make the connection from background cultural knowledge.[38]

Only hints that Simon's Helen was Helen of Troy remain for the Homilist. Simon is shamed as an allegorist of Greek myths, but he is never said to have allegorized Helen of Troy, her torch, or the wooden horse (as Irenaeus and the Refutator claimed). The Homilist either did not know these reports or misread them. After all, Helen was not "abiding by the primal God" during the Trojan War. In Irenaeus's report, she was the cause of the Trojan War when she, already incarnate, was abducted. The Homilist's account seems to have been influenced by the tradition that only Helen's phantom went to Troy; the real Helen remained in her heavenly fatherland.[39]

One final point about Helen: as we know from Celsus, Simonians had a high view of her such that some Simonians were named "Helenians."[40] It is perhaps needless to say, then, that the female Helen as "half a man" is misogyny stemming from the Homilist,

---

[35] *Mart. Pet.* 2 in Eastman, *Ancient Martyrdom Accounts*, 9.
[36] Irenaeus, *Haer.* 1.23.2; *Ref.* 6.18.3.
[37] *Ref.* 6.20.1.
[38] Eustathius, *Commentary on Homer's Od.* 4.122. See further Vincent, "Culte d'Hélène," 224.
[39] Cf. *Exeg. Soul* (NHC II,6). See further Norman Austin, *Helen and Her Shameless Phantom* (Ithaca: Cornell University Press, 2018).
[40] Origen, *Cels.* 5.62.

not the Simonians. When measured against other reports, the Homilist repeatedly misrepresented Simonian doctrine. His understanding of Helen is no exception.

Simon's Miracles

The miracles of Simon astound even Clement who is (perhaps too) eager to learn about them. He hears from Nicetas and Aquila that Simon makes statues walk, rolls himself on the fire without being burned, makes loaves out of stones (a Christ-like miracle from Matt 4:3 or Luke 4:3), becomes a serpent and a goat; makes himself two-faced, changes himself into gold; opens gates that are locked tight, and melts iron. At banquets, Simon produces images of every form and makes dishes invisibly move.[41] In the city of Tyre, Simon makes apparitions and illusions appear in the middle of the marketplace. Statues turn as he walks by and flitting shadows dance before him. People who try to convict Simon of sorcery all of the sudden become his friends.[42]

There are harmful miracles as well: Simon reportedly murders a young boy and then—in apparent competition with the creator—remakes his body using, not earth (Gen 2:7), but fiery air (*pneuma*).[43] It is a story both fascinating and odd. Young boys were used as mediums, and people who died violently were invoked by magicians as assistants.[44] Almost always, however, magicians called upon people who were already dead. They had no need to kill anyone, let alone a child, simply to gain an assistant.

In the Homilies, moreover, Simon had another reason not to kill. As he explains to Nicetas and Aquila, he does not even believe that the boy's soul is his assistant (since no soul survives death). When Nicetas and Aquila inquire who it is who assists Simon, he claims that a random daimon impersonates the boy's soul. But if all Simon needed was a daimon, killing the boy was a senseless waste of time.

According to the Homilist, Simon also inflicted diseases on his enemies. He did so by making them participate with daimones in dinner parties. This is black magic indeed. Yet such harmful wonders seem not far different from Peter who threatens to bring down a whole city by an earthquake.[45] If we widen the scope to other literature, Peter presided over the death of two donors in Acts 5 and Paul blinded Elymas in Acts 13. Yahweh manifested his power by plaguing Egypt and later killed thousands as a result of another man's sin (2 Sam. 24:15-16). Whether the wonders be helpful or harmful, they reveal sovereign power and glory.[46]

---

[41] *Hom.* 2.32.2.
[42] *Hom.* 4.4.2-3.
[43] The source for Simon killing a young boy may have been *Acts Pet.* 25.653. See further Tobias Nicklas, "Simon Magos: Erschaffung eines Luftmenschen (pseudo-Clemens Hom II,26; Rec II,15)," in *Nouvelles intrigues*, 409-24.
[44] Boys as mediums: Origen, *Princ.* 3.3.3; *PGM* 1.86-7, 2.56, 3.710, 4.89; Apuleius, *Apol.* 42-4. See further T. Hopfner, "Die Kindermedien in den griechisch-ägyptischen Zauberpapyri," in *Recueil d'études dédiées à la mémoire de N. P. Kondakov* (Prague: Kondakov Seminar, 1926), 65-74. For assistants, see Scibilia, "Supernatural Assistance," 71-86.
[45] *Hom.* 7.9.5.
[46] See further Tuzlak, "The Magician and the Heretic," 422; Giovanni Battista Bazzana, "'Magic' in the *Klementia*: Reflections on an Episode of Transformation," in *In Search of Truth in the Pseudo-Clementine Homilies: New Approaches to a Philosophical and Rhetorical Novel of Late Antiquity*, ed. Benjamin M. J. De Vos and Danny Praet, WUNT 496 (Tübingen: Mohr Siebeck, 2022), 395-411.

The Gospel Spreads

In the *Homilies*, Simon spreads his gospel throughout Syria. All up the Levantine coast, from Caesarea to Laodicea to Antioch, Peter is Simon's hound closely nipping at his heels, affording him no rest.[47] The apostle even sends spies into Simon's camp to reconnoiter what Simon will say in the scheduled debates.[48] Simon often runs to avoid Peter, but there are two great encounters that occur in Caesarea and Laodicea.[49]

In these encounters, Simon is made a mouthpiece for everything the author of the *Homilies* fears: Hellenic education, allegorizing, Marcionite theology, bits of Ophite exegesis, varieties of polytheism, and, not least of all—Paulinism.[50] Simon is still, for the homilist, the father of all heresies, thus every accusation against later heresies stuck to him.[51] Simon is so covered by the barnacles of later accusations that he is barely visible. The Homilist was not interested in making Simon represent distinctively Simonian lore. Even the idea of God as Standing One is not distinctly Simonian; nor is the idea that Simon alone was the Standing One. According to both Clement of Alexandria and the *Declaration*, all Simonians tried to conform themselves to the Standing One (God).

Although none of Simon's speeches can be taken as distinctly Simonian, it is intriguing to see how biblically informed they are. The basis of Simon's arguments are verses from the Septuagint and sayings from Jesus. Simon can spin a web of scripture off the tip of his tongue. In one debate, Simon rattles off eleven passages from various biblical books (Genesis Exodus, Deuteronomy, Joshua, Jeremiah, and the Psalms) to show that there are many gods, not one.[52] Peter admits that the "law" frequently speaks of gods in the plural, but he prioritizes passages—all from Deuteronomy and Isaiah— which say that God is one.[53]

Repeatedly, Peter meets Simon's biblical arguments with dialectical maneuvers,[54] inquiries about Simon's sincerity,[55] along with *ad hominem* attacks. When Simon asks Peter to explain the origin of the devil, Peter accuses him of being more evil than the

---

[47] *Hom.* 7.12.3.
[48] *Hom.* 3.2.1; 3.73.2–3.
[49] Caesarea: *Hom.* 3.29–58; Laodicea: *Hom.* 16–19.
[50] See further A. Salles, "Simon le magicien ou Marcion?" VC 12 (1958): 197–224; H. J. W. Drijvers, "Adam and the True Prophet," in *History and Religion in Late Antique Syria* (Aldershot: Brookfield, 1994), 314–23; F. Stanley Jones, "Marcionism in the *Pseudo-Clementines*," in *Pseudoclementina*, 152–71; Pierluigi Piovanelli, "'Le ennemi est parmi nous.' Présences rhétoriques et narratives de Paul dan les *Pseudo-clémentines* et autres écrits apparentés," in *Nouvelles intrigues*, 241–8; Jürgen Wehnert, "Antipaulinismus in den Pseudoklementinen," in *Ancient Perspectives on Paul*, ed. Tobias Nicklas, Andreas Merkt and Joseph Verheyden (Göttingen: Vandenhoeck & Ruprecht, 2013), 170–90; Côté, "La fonction littéraire," 513–23.
[51] *Hom.* 16.21.
[52] *Hom.* 16.5.3–16.6.12.
[53] *Hom.* 16.7.
[54] E.g., *Hom.* 3.40; 18.8–9.1; 16.10. Simon himself points out to Peter: "It's clear you flee from the scriptures" (πρόδηλος εἶ φεύγων ἀπὸ τῶν γραφῶν) (3.41.1). Peter retorts that Simon departs from the "order of inquiry" (τάξιν ζητήσεως) (3.41.2; cf. 15.10.5; 16.2.1).
[55] *Hom.* 18.5.1.

author of evil himself.[56] Peter also calls Simon a snake sent as the ally of Evil.[57] The taunts are out of character for a man who preached love for enemies in imitation of God.[58]

Peter secretly acknowledges before his disciples that the Bible has false passages mixed in, though he generally conceals this belief from the crowds.[59] At one point, however, Simon's argument forces Peter to admit publicly that scriptural texts that speak ill of God and do not agree with creation are "false" (*pseudeis*).[60] Yet Simon fails to press home his advantage. The fact that Peter takes a scissors to the scriptures never fazes the crowds.

Intriguingly, there are structural resemblances shared by the theologies of Simon and Peter. According to Peter, there is one supreme God, and two lower powers—evil and good—who control the present and coming age, respectively.[61] In Simon's view, there is one supreme unutterable God and two lower powers, one who creates the world and another who lays down laws.[62] The main difference is that Peter's supreme God is the creator, and Simon's supreme God is a being above the creator. Yet the pattern of high God plus two powers (one harsh, the other beneficent) is consistent and ancient. It can be found as far back as Philo.[63]

The Curtain Closes

After days of wrangling at Laodicea, Simon refuses to debate with a man who will not change his mind about the creator's oneness and goodness. At this remark, Peter digs in his heels, adding that even if the creator is incomparably wicked—more wicked

---

[56] *Hom.* 19.6.3–5. See further J. Verheyden, "The Demonization of the Opponent in Early Christian Literature. The Case of the Pseudo-Clementines," in *Religious Polemics in Context*, ed. T. L. Hettema and A. van der Kooij (Leiden: Brill, 2005), 330–59.

[57] *Hom.* 2.33.4–5.

[58] *Hom.* 12.26.

[59] *Hom.* 2.37–52.

[60] *Hom.* 19.1.2; 3.42.3; 18.9.1–3. Specifically, Peter remarks that the passage declaring that Yahweh repented after creating humanity (Gen 6:6) is "false" (ψεῦδός) as well as the text saying that Yahweh tempted (ἐπείραζεν) Abraham (Gen 22:1 LXX) (*Hom.* 3.43.2). Peter appeals to an oral tradition informing Scripture, but does not clarify how that tradition was passed on from Moses to Jesus. In the end, whatever Peter deems true appears to be ascribed to "the True Prophet" (Jesus). See further Karl Shuve, "The Doctrine of the False Pericopes and the other Late Antique Approaches to the Problem of Scripture's Unity," in *Nouvelles intrigues*, 437–45; Kelley Coblentz Bautch, "Obscured by the Scriptures, Revealed by the Prophets: God in the Pseudo-Clementine *Homilies*," in *Histories of the Hidden God: Concealment and Revelation in Western Gnostic, Esoteric, and Mystical Traditions*, ed. April D. DeConick and Grant Adamson (Abingdon: Oxon, 2014), 120–36; Donald H. Carlson, *Jewish-Christian Interpretation of the Pentateuch in the Pseudo-Clementine Homilies* (Minneapolis: Fortress Press, 2013), 51–76.

[61] *Hom.* 20.2–3. See further Patricia Duncan, *Novel Hermeneutics in the Greek Pseudo-Clementine Romance*, WUNT 395 (Tübingen: Mohr Siebeck, 2017), 52–6.

[62] *Hom.* 18.4.5; 18.11.3; 18.12.1. The latter passage is Peter's rendition of Simon's theology. Its accuracy is indicated by Simon's insulted reaction: Peter reveals the mysteries to the profane.

[63] Philo, *Abr.* 119–22; *Mut.* 28–9; *Conf.* 137; *Mos.* 2.99; *Somn.* 1.162–3.

than the scriptures or any person can conceive him—still Peter would not give up worshiping him.[64]

The crowds applaud Peter's arguments. Implied readers are encouraged to do the same. Still, even opponents of Simon can admit that some of his points are sound, the product of legitimate curiosity. Simon himself relates that, "I stretch out so eagerly for the truth that for its sake I do not hesitate to put myself at risk."[65] Despite the insults heaped upon Simon, one can at least admire his stamina. Although Peter's friend Faustus declares Peter the winner in the final debate, Simon refuses to surrender.[66]

Ultimately Peter depends not on reasoned debate to rid himself of Simon; he calls upon imperial might. Simon blackens Peter's reputation by calling him the same thing Peter called Simon—a magus, sorcerer, and a murderer.[67] It seems the apostle's reputation is ruined until a team of Peter's spies convince Simon that an agent of the emperor—the centurion Cornelius from Acts 10!—is seeking to arrest him. Simon craftily changes Faustus's appearance to look like his own.[68] Faustus's family—including Clement—is horrified. Yet Peter has a sort of X-ray vision that can see through the trick. For tactical purposes, Peter impels Faustus to retain Simon's visage so that Faustus can impersonate Simon, and incriminate "himself" with lying and sorcery.[69] But the actual Simon is tireless. At the end of the novel, he is back in Judea, making plans—we can only imagine—to set sail for Rome.

Conclusion

It should be clear by now why I have placed Simon's novelistic portraits last in my history. Although the *Homilies* and the *Acts of Peter* provide the most enticing of tales, they are the least historically reliable sources for reconstructing Simon and the Simonians.[70] Like the *Acts of Peter*, the *Homilies* mostly reveal the conflicts of its own time and place (fourth-century Syria).[71] It is an immensely important document for thinking about the later Christian reception of Simon as antichrist, anti-Christian, mad scientist, Faustian son of the devil who sold his soul to sin, and so on.[72] But for understanding anything like the historical Simon and Simonians in Syria and elsewhere, it must be bracketed, used with caution, and only after other sources have been squeezed of every drop of historical sap they contain.

Perhaps most readers take this as obvious: Simon in the Pseudo-Clementines is a fiction based on fourth-century facts. Occasionally, however, scholars still vouch for

---

[64] *Hom.* 18.22.3.
[65] *Hom.* 19.7.4.
[66] *Hom.* 19.24.2, 6.
[67] *Hom.* 9.13.1–2.
[68] *Hom.* 20.12.
[69] See further Côté, *Le theme de l'opposition*, 56; Étienne Barilier, "La revanche de Simon le Magicien," in *Nouvelles intrigues*, 9–22 at 14–15.
[70] Beyschlag, *Simon Magus*, 48–67; Lüdemann, *Untersuchungen*, 91–6.
[71] Kelley, *Knowledge*, 179–212.
[72] See further Ferreiro, *Simon Magus*; Bernard Pouderon, *Métamorphoses de Simon le magicien: Des Actes des apôtres au Faustbuch* (Paris: Beauchesne, 2019).

historical elements in the novels. Kurt Rudolph, for instance, wrote that the "disputations of the pseudo-Clementine writings possibly contain reminiscences of the doctrines put forward by Simon, or handed down by his school, as for instance the doctrine of the 'supreme, incomprehensible power,' of the lowly creator of the world and of the captivity of the soul."[73] The comment is misleading, in my view, since the supreme Power as incomprehensible is not specifically Simonian. Simonians, furthermore, never believed in a lower creator (like the Sethian "Yaldabaoth") apart from Wisdom. Finally, the soul's "captivity" is not a theme Simon underscores in the *Homilies* (it seems to be a fairly generalized "gnostic" trait).

Even graver problems arise when scholars allow data from the Pseudo-Clementines to frame their entire approach. In her presumably historical description of Simon, for instance, April DeConick relates that Simon belonged to "a Samaritan Baptist group, practicing water initiation and ritual bathing."[74] After being educated in Alexandria, Simon went back home to Samaria, joined Dositheus's group and fell in love with "Luna." All this material manifestly comes from the Pseudo-Clementines, though none of it can stand historical scrutiny.

If the *Acts of Peter* cannot be used as a historical source for reconstructing Simon and the Simonians, much less can the Pseudo-Clementines. From beginning to end, these accounts are fiction—creative, thought-provoking, engaging—but fiction nonetheless. The Homilist was not interested in constructing a faithful portrait of Simon or the Simonians. He selectively conflated a whole series of sources to create a many-headed monster that never before existed—Simon as Paul, as Marcionite, as Hellenic intellectual, as Samaritan, as dialectician, and so on.

Evidently, the Homilist had many Christian opponents in fourth-century Syria. By using the character of Simon, he rolled them up and reduced them all to one. As a result, Simon's character does not always cohere. Perhaps it is unsurprising that Simon, who made himself two-faced, should have so many facets. But should not the Standing One have more stability? This is the irony of the novel. Simon the Standing One is in fact a changeling and a shifty opportunist. The only constant for Simon is that he plays the villain, the polar opposite to Peter, the apostle's evil twin. But this is a dualism rooted in the Homilist's theology, not in historical data.

According to the Homilist, Simon was never a Christian. Indeed, Simon was anything but Christian. He was a "Day Baptist," a Samaritan, a philosopher, a magus, and a necromancer—all things to all people, in order to damn some. As a result of this portrait, Simon's Christianity and the Christian identity of his movement are erased. At best, real Simonians are replaced by a small group of twenty-nine (and a half) sectarians who appear in a flashback, then suddenly vanish.

So what, in the end, can we glean from the Homilist's deeply revisionary depiction of Simon? Could we hypothesize that there really were Simonians in fourth-century Syria? Perhaps there were. It would be hazardous, however, to use the Pseudo-Clementines as evidence for this. What we may infer is that the *memory* of Simon was strong enough in Syria to create new fictional accounts of Christianity's supposed

---

[73] Rudolph, *Gnosis*, 297.
[74] DeConick, *Gnostic New Age*, 99.

archenemy. At the same time, it would be imprudent to begin any historical search for Simon with the Pseudo-Clementines. In my view, almost nothing in these novels goes back to the second century, let alone the first. After all, the Homilist basically bypassed our three most important second-century sources for understanding Simon: Irenaeus, the book of Acts, and the *Declaration*.

Truth be told, the *Homilist* lived nearly three centuries after Simon and probably had no better sources for understanding him than we do. He was never interested in uncovering the historical Simon or real Simonians. He desired, rather, to create his own many-headed hydra to defeat his own enemies in his own time. Like the producers of the *Acts of Peter*, he mixed together source material with information invented out of his own head. What he created was an entertaining and engaging tale. For those interested in the historical Simon(ians), however, it is better to begin with the Simonian primary sources and then the heresy reports. If we incautiously employ elements from the Pseudo-Clementine novels to derive Simon's "true history," we step into a Charybdis of untruths from which no parallel, distant or close, can save us.

Conclusion

This book has been a great experiment: instead of allowing the heresiological reports to control the data on Simon, we have let the *Declaration* stand as the first foundation of Simonian wisdom. Upon this foundation, we have laid stones from other sources, properly sifted from the dust and dirt of slander and fiction. The building stands incomplete, a shell of what it once was, since the fragmentary and paraphrased sources never give a full picture. In shape, the building is better described as a great tree with multiple branches representing Simonianism in different areas, chiefly Rome, Samaria, and Alexandria.

Simonian Christianity developed in different ways in different regions and times. The *Declaration* is probably an Alexandrian document written between 120 and 150 CE. It was composed by an independent Simonian who never claimed to lead a community. Its oracular tone might gesture toward inspiration, but the book never became canonical for Simonian Christians. As such, it did not control what Simonians in Rome could say at the end of the second century or in Palestine in the beginning of the fourth. In many cases, however, the *Declaration* can be used as a touchstone to check the heresiologists—such as when they say that Simonians as a whole rejected the Hebrew prophets.

Fortunately, there are other ways of fact-checking hostile reporters. Some of them contradict each other, indicating that at least one of them errs. All of them distort information in a similar way using the rhetorical tools of invective. We can see the distortions since we have the document that was decisive for all of them, Acts 8. A patient analysis of what this chapter does and does not say has exposed the main trends of heresiological hermeneutics. According to Acts, Simon was a baptized Christian who prayed for repentance after offering money to transmit the Spirit. Heresiologists, however, twisted the text such that Simon feigned faith, never lost his magical mentality, and turned in rage against the apostles. The Simon who did the deeds of a magus (Acts 8:9) earned "Magus" as his epithet. Yet none of Simon's "magical" deeds are ever described until we come to the (late second century CE) *Acts of Peter*.

Of course, heresiologists did more than create the stereotypical picture of Simon. Just as they depicted Simon as non-Christian, they presented Simonians in the same way. They demonized Simon and his group, attributed to them licentious acts and rites they did not perform. They denounced Simonian allegory and engagement with the broader Hellenic—and specifically poetic—culture. They made all Simonians into magicians, portrayed them as idolaters, and reported nasty rumors about their ethical and ritual behaviors.

As time moved forward, heresy reports became further mixed and degraded. Irenaeus sketched late-second-century Simonian theology as it had developed in

Rome by about 175 CE. Bits and pieces of his rearranged report were reinscribed and subtly distorted by Tertullian, the Refutator, Eusebius, Epiphanius, and Filaster. The distortions mostly center on Helen, who goes from redeemed sex slave to Simon's pet, hooked to the leash of his lust, and—as Tertullian quipped—accustomed to "riding his thighs." Most of these heresiologists tend to distort any hint of Helen's historical and theological importance for Simonians—that she was a teacher, an avatar of Wisdom, an incarnation of the creatrix, and so on. Only from Celsus, critic of Christianity, do we learn that some Simonians were called "Helenians" after their venerated teacher.[1]

Simon and Helen

Wading through this morass, what can we reliably say about the historical Simon and his companion Helen? Not very much, unfortunately. Simon probably lived and worked in Samaria. He may well not have been Samarian by birth. He shows no strong signs of having been a Samaritan (worshiping at Mt. Gerizim, obeying the regulations of the Samaritan Pentateuch, celebrating Samaritan holidays). Only a generation or two after his death was Simon depicted as a magus. His actual self-description is unknown. His journey to Egypt, discipleship under John the "Day Baptist," and takeover of John's community are all third or fourth-century fictions.[2]

In my view, Simon was neither a magus nor a gnostic. He was a religious leader in Samaria who became a Christian sometime in the mid-30s CE. We can extrapolate that he used his leadership skills to manage a Christian group in Samaria by the late 30s or early 40s. Perhaps he performed wonders before or after his conversion, or both. Like Paul and several other early Christian leaders, Simon possibly came to Rome in the 40s or 50s. It is not certain that he established a movement which survived him. How he died is unknown. Stories of him being buried alive or shot down by apostolic prayer are polemical legends first appearing in the late second century.

Virtually nothing else about Simon can be claimed. We do not know how he described himself. We do not know if he was educated, interpreted scripture, or read philosophy. We cannot trace any firm elements of his thought. All we can intuit is that second-century Christian movements in Samaria, Rome, and Alexandria looked back to Simon as their founder and that the leaders of these movements were informed by an eclectic mix of Pythagorean, Stoic, and Platonic thought.

Regrettably, even less can be known about the historical Helen. The story of her as a redeemed sex worker might be slander, with no more historical backing than the legend of Mary Magdalene as it came to be imagined in late antiquity. It would, at any rate, be incongruous with Helen's identification with Wisdom if the historical Helen had no intellectual talents of her own. She was Simon's companion and not necessarily

---

[1] Origen, *Cels.* 5.62.
[2] To my knowledge, only Morton Smith ever accepted the idea that Simon was a follower of John the (Day) Baptist ("The Account of Simon Magus in Acts 8," in *Studies in the Cult of Yahweh: New Testament, Early Christianity, and Magic*, vol. 2, ed. Shaye J. D. Cohen, 2 vols. [Leiden: Brill, 1996], 140-51 at 144).

his paramour. The notion that they were lovers clashes with the theology in which they are portrayed as Father (Mind) and daughter (Thought). Even if Simon and Helen were in a sexual relationship, there seems nothing sordid about it. Simonians accepted sex and reportedly preached "perfect love."

Precisely how Simon and Helen (both of whom likely died in the 60s or 70s CE) were connected to later Simonians (who begin to appear about 120) is a mystery. There is nothing but an ugly ditch with no secure data—only inferences and hypotheses sometimes masquerading as historical facts. Frankly, Simon and Helen may have been of no great importance for Simonians until about 140 CE, when they were identified with established figures in Simonian theology, namely Mind and Thought. In turn, Simon's identification with the Standing One seems to have been made in the early third century.

Primarily, then, my history is about Simonians. It begins, not in the mid-first century, but in the early second. For the purposes of reconstruction, I have considered relatively late novelistic writings like the *Acts of Peter* and the Pseudo-Clementines unreliable, at least for establishing the framework for historical analysis. Instead, I have gleaned the remnants of Simonian thought and practice from the *Declaration*, which I consider to be our earliest—and our only—genuinely Simonian document. I have also employed the *Great Power*, an apocalypse employing Simonian terms and traditions. Only after studying these sources have I turned to heresy reports. These reports include fictional elements, omit important information, and pejoratively interpret their data. At the same time, the heresiologists were not outright liars. Some of their evidence is trustworthy, though it must be judged for consistency and congruency with the other reports, not to mention Simonian sources like the *Declaration* (Chapter 1) and the E source (Chapter 10).

The Simonians: A Profile

What follows is my synthetic sketch of Simonian Christianity from the second to the fourth century CE, based on the findings in the preceding chapters. We begin, not in Samaria, but in Alexandria, with the author of the *Declaration* (or Declarator). In my view, this author was a learned Simonian, with interests in cosmogony and embryology, who wove together an eclectic philosophy to explain the first six days of creation. This Simonian pulled his or her lore from an allegorical reading of the Pentateuch, the Hebrew prophets, the book of Wisdom, the gospel of Matthew (and possibly Luke), with tags from a Pauline epistle (1 Corinthians). His call for *all* people to assimilate to the (triple-phased) Standing One is echoed later in the second century by Clement of Alexandria.

If the Declarator wrote in Simon's own voice, he did not say that Simon alone was the Standing One or the Infinite Power. Rather, identification with the Infinite Power, through conformation to the Seventh Power, was a destiny open to all. This author was already allegorizing Homer (e.g., the famous "holy moly" in the *Odyssey*), but he never mentioned Helen (of either Tyre or Troy) and never identified her as an avatar of

Epinoia. In terms of the content of Simonian theology, the figures of Simon and Helen were not of detectable importance.

There is no strong evidence that the Declarator was a Samaritan or that he came from a Samaritan background. He may well have been of a Jewish background, but Jews in Alexandria after 117 CE had become sparse after a massive pogrom.[3] What we can reasonably say is that the Declarator was philosophically informed. More than likely, he was a type of Christian, despite the fact that Jesus does not appear in what survives of the *Declaration*. The Refutator, at any rate, assumed that the Declarator was a Christian—otherwise he would not have bothered to excerpt his work in a catalogue of Christian "heresies."

Around the same time the Declarator wrote, his fellow countryman composed an apocalypse called the *Great Power*. There is not enough evidence to say that he was a Simonian. At the same time, he or she was familiar with Simonian terms and traditions. This author worshiped the Great Power and saw the human soul as in some sense its image. Instead of being a subordinate figure, however, the Great Power now appears as the high God. Jesus's defeat of demons in the underworld is highlighted, though he is again never named. The Simonian interest in cosmogony is continued, but this time a single, lower creator appears, and there is much more of a focus on the apocalyptic end of the world (a common—though not a distinctive—Simonian belief).

If we were to follow the heresiologists, we would think that Simon and Helen were always the focus of Simonian theology. In early-second-century CE Alexandria, at least, they were not. The picture changes, however, when we shift to Rome in the mid-second century. Here it is assumed that Simon himself was the Great Power and that this meant, moreover, that he was the high (or "primal") God, not a subordinate figure. Roman Simonians identified Simon's Helen with God's Thought (*Ennoia*) and told the story of how she created the world, was abused, and later redeemed by God in the person of Simon. The author of Acts assumed this theological shift, I believe, when he connected Simon to the Great Power (Acts 8:10)—though he never presented Simon himself as claiming this epithet.

The author of Acts undercut the Simonians, presumably in Samaria, by undermining their founder. For the first time, Simon did the deeds of a "magus" and was deified by supposed dupes who later became Philip's converts. Simon's own conversion was never denied, even if he was never allowed to become a Christian leader and aspersions were cast upon his character. The strategy of Acts was not to deny Simon's Christian identity, but to deprive him of any legitimate authority and power to convey Spirit. In this way, Simonian Christianity could be dismissed as aberrant, illegitimate, and destined to be replaced by the author's own "apostolic" brand.

Justin Martyr testified that a significant contingent of Samarian Simonians came to Rome, perhaps in the aftermath of the Bar Kokhba revolt (132–135 CE). He said that virtually all of them—together with some from other ethnicities—worshiped Simon in the form of a god called Semo(n) Sanctus on Tiber Island. He raised suspicions

---

[3] Eusebius, *Hist. eccl.* 4.2-3; Dio Cassius, *Roman History*, 68.32; 69.8. See further Miriam Pucci Ben Zeev, *Diaspora Judaism in Turmoil 116-117 CE: Ancient Sources and Modern Insights* (Leuven: Peeters. 2005); William Horbury, *The Jewish War Under Trajan and Hadrian* (Cambridge: Cambridge University Press, 2014).

about their supposed orgies and invited Roman officials to open an investigation. He taunted Simonian theology, according to which Simon became "the primal God," and he associated the historical Simon with Helen, a redeemed sex worker. Justin could not hide, however, the fact that Simonians were commonly recognized as Christians and that they confessed the crucified Christ.[4]

Irenaeus clarified Simonian traditions, in part because he had a revised copy of Justin's (now lost) *Syntagma*. Simon the "primal God" was actually Simon the Father in Samaria, who also appeared as Son in Judea. Simon's double appearance explains how Simonians could confess the stories of Jesus and Simon at the same time. Simon and Jesus were avatars of the same being, the highest Power, although Simon, as Father, provided the higher revelation. Simon was also present in his community as the Spirit among the nations. By Irenaeus's time, the followers of Simon were called "Simonians"—with some of them named "Helenians" as well.[5] Their Christian identity, however, is underscored by their belief in Christ and in a Trinitarian theology. These elements of their thought cannot be thrown out as late accretions. The whole reason Justin and Irenaeus mentioned Simonians is that they appeared as Christians to virtually everyone.

Simonians in Rome proposed a related but distinct theology than that developed in Alexandria in the early second century. Simon was identified with the Highest Power. As such, he mediated salvation to Simonians via his peculiar knowledge, a gnosis he revealed by grace to those who believed in him. Helen, Simon's companion, was an incarnation of the abused *Ennoia*, who still possessed remnants of her creative powers (healing the blindness of Stesichorus, for instance). She was the creatrix, but long ago she had delegated her powers to angelic children who then turned on her in their desire to be worshiped as primary gods. These false gods, in turn, legislated the laws of different countries. The redemption of *Ennoia* was the beginning of salvation for all fallen souls. Simon came to redeem Helen as her Father, not her lover.

Simonians sojourned in Rome side by side with other Christians from at least 150 to 220 CE, as testified by the Refutator. This author published a lengthy attack on the Simonians shortly after 222 CE. He uniquely included paraphrased excerpts from a Simonian text that had travelled from Alexandria to Rome, the *Declaration*. Simonians may even have spread to North Africa, given Tertullian's evident concern about what might be described as their séances. Tertullian uniquely testified that Simonians, apparently in his vicinity, called up the souls of the prophets in a rite of divination.

According to Irenaeus, Simonians also practiced exorcism and image veneration, worshiping the Highest Power and *Ennoia* via statues of Zeus and Athena. They allegorized Homer (Helen with her torch and the Trojan horse), and perhaps other poets like Stesichorus. If the Simonians were moderately ascetic (Eusebius commented on their "philosophic" way of life), they had no problem with sex, and supported "perfect love" between couples in their community. Although they traced human laws and conventions to arrogant angels, they were not lawless and, despite Justin's pleas, never drew attention from the Roman government at any point in their history.

---

[4] Justin, *1 Apol.* 35.2.
[5] Celsus in Origen, *Cels.* 5.62.

Origen revealed that not all Simonians had moved to Rome. A few had remained behind in Palestine and were still there in the mid-third century CE. Eusebius confirmed that, apparently in his region (Palestine), Simonians continued to baptize their disciples and even to join in worship with early catholics. The bishop of Caesarea added that Simonians presented themselves as upstanding, sober, and moral citizens. They had awe-inspiring written oracles, perhaps akin to the *Declaration*.

At the end of the fourth century CE, Epiphanius employed a source in which Simon spoke in the first person (the E source). Although some think that Epiphanius or one of his colleagues made up the quotations, this is unlikely. It contains too much distinctive information that presents Simon and *Ennoia* in a positive light. The E source portrays a stronger *Ennoia*, who did not suffer at the hands of her angelic children and who could gather her strength to ascend back to her Father. Such developments might indicate that Simonians were revising their theology as late as the fourth century.

In terms of scripture, Simonians not only used Christian gospels (the Lost Sheep parable), they employed Pauline writings as well, as indicated by the use of 1 Corinthians 11:32 in the *Declaration* and the allegory of Ephesians 6:12-18 (to refer to Athena-*Ennoia*) as reported by Epiphanius. The *Declaration* itself is never cited as a scriptural work. According to Irenaeus, Simonians rejected the Hebrew prophets as inspired by malign angels. Nevertheless, Isaiah and Daniel are quoted in the *Declaration*, and Tertullian says that Simonians divined by invoking prophetic souls.

Simonians confessed a doctrine of transmigration. They applied it to Helen, but may have assumed that other souls were reborn as well. They worshiped God's Wisdom and claimed that she was incarnate in various women throughout history. This meant that there was some faint impress of truth even in Greco-Roman lore and poetry. The acceptance of transmigration and an emphasis on the power of the number seven indicates at least some interaction with Pythagorean teaching as well.

Some Simonians were highly educated and most seem to have been worldly. They were readers of Homer. The Declarator, at least, knew elements of Stoic, Empedoclean, and Aristotelian thought. There seems to be a bit of Virgil, or Virgilian tradition assumed in the allegory of Helen and her torch. Simonians knew enough of Greco-Roman lore to see Athena, born fully armed from her Father's head, as a symbol of Helen. They were happy to see the "many-named" Zeus as a representation of Simon the Highest Power.

Simon cannot be credited with spawning every alternative Christian group in antiquity. At the same time, Simonian theology may well have informed other early Christian theologies, such as Valentinian, Carpocratian, Basilidean, and even early catholic varieties. Some early catholics of the late second and early third centuries were modalists—at least according to the Refutator. A Simonian wrote the first known Christian *hexaemeron*, and several early catholic theologians, in the centuries to come, followed suit.[6] The Simonians' eclectic adaptation of Greek philosophy and poetry foreshadowed later developments in Christian theology as well.

Between the mid-second and the late fourth centuries CE, at least, Simonians self-identified as Christians. It is only the heresiologists who tried to deprive them of

---

[6] See, e.g., the works of Basil the Great and Ambrose under the title *Hexaemeron*.

that identity. We do well in not following them. At the same time, it is true that the Simonians created a distinctive brand of Christianity. With Homer in one hand and the Gospels in the other, they forged their own identity, created their own practices, developed their own theology, and dodged internecine attacks. Despite being under near constant fire, we have no Simonian treatise attacking their opponents, though some later Simonian theology (Simon as Spirit) seems to respond to heresiological invective in Acts 8 (Simon could not give Spirit). Far from being late and derivative, the Simonians were a relatively early Christian group. Their continuous survival, from at least the early second to the late fourth century, indicates the robustness and perceived cogency of their doctrines among some as well as their ability to "stand" or perdure through time.

Simon of Samaria was considered to be the Christ, inasmuch as he was God's son in Judea. To Simonians, however, he was much more. He was the Father in flesh who offered a higher revelation to his initiates—his own distinctive knowledge. Much of this knowledge is still a mystery to us, and presenting it in anything like a plausible form is a chore due to heresiological mudslinging. Battered and beaten throughout time, the ever-standing Simon became like Christ in a deeper sense. Though killed and continuously buried in the retellings of Christian myth, Simon refused to die. He kept rising, as it were, from the grave of Christian memory.

To some, Simon comes as a ghost to haunt them; to others, he is a Christian "father" worth resurrecting. Suffice it to say, the Great Power has not grown weak. Make of him what you will. My purpose in this book was never to rein in anyone's imagination, but to focus it with a basically sympathetic and historical portrait of Simon and the Simonian movement(s), based on reliable sources. I have sifted every known major tradition from the second to the fourth centuries CE, trying my best to check individual doctrinal elements and practices against the most reliable Simonian sources. The case is cumulative, and it is certain that other scholars will disagree with the details of my reconstruction.

The point is to keep going, sharpening our tools and our methods as we go forward. I have intentionally sought to weaken confidence in many heresiological sources (in particular, the novelistic ones), but no discouragement is intended. As has happened throughout time, readers will discover the Simon that they want—and need. In this study, I may have stripped Simon of his title "(first) gnostic," but he remains a true knower of some wild and worthwhile lore. I may also have deprived him of his epithet "Magus," but every bit of his magic remains. And so this volume comes to a close, but the end is only the beginning. The great wheel of scholarship grinds on. A new wave of Simonian studies is ready to rise, and with the aid of divine and creative Thought, the project has only begun.

Appendix 1

Reconstruction of *The Great Declaration*

Note: The following reconstruction and translation of the *Declaration* updates the translation in my edition of the *Refutation of All Heresies* (SBL Press, 2016). It is based on a fresh reading of the single manuscript in which it is preserved (Parasinus supplément grec 464). I have removed most instances of "he says" (φησίν) and "they say" (φάσι), as well as the comments and introductions of the Refutator. The numeration (e.g., 6.9.4) refers to the book, chapter, and verse in the *Refutation*. I make one transposition by inserting 6.18.2-7 between 6.12 and 6.13 to restore what I believe is the original order. I also include verses from Genesis (LXX) in bold type and additions to the text in curly brackets. Words in angled brackets represent emendations.

The Great Declaration

6.9.4. This is the letter of declaration, of voice, and of name from the Thought (*Epinoia*) of the Great and Infinite Power. Thus it will be sealed, hidden, veiled, and stored in the dwelling in which the root of the universe is established, {the root of aeons, powers, and thoughts; the root of gods, angels, and spirits sent forth; the root of things that are and of things that are not, of things born and unborn, of things comprehensible and incomprehensible; the root of years, months, days, hours—an indivisible point from which the smallest being begins and grows by degrees. Although it is nothing, and is composed of nothing, it will generate by its own thought an incomprehensible magnitude.}[1] 6.9.5. The dwelling is that human born from bloodlines in whom dwells the infinite Power, the root of the universe.

Now the infinite Power is fire, for "God is a flaming and devouring fire" (Deut 4:23-24; Heb 12:29) The fire is not simple, as most people claim, supposing that the four elements and fire are simple bodies. Rather, the nature of the fire is double, with something hidden and also something revealed. 6.9.6. The hidden things are hidden in the manifest things of the fire, and the manifest things of the fire come about due to the hidden things. 6.9.7. And the manifest of the fire contains all in itself—whatever one can conceive or not among visible things—whereas the hidden aspect contains everything intelligible and removed from sense perception that one may or may not think.

6.9.8. In general, one can say that the supercelestial fire is the treasury of all existing things, perceptible and intelligible, hidden and manifest. It is like the massive tree

---

[1] The information in curly brackets is taken from what I understand to be a longer quotation of this passage in the *Declaration* found in the Naassene report (*Ref.* 5.9.5).

seen by Nebuchadnezzar in a dream, "a tree that nourishes all flesh" (Dan 4:10-12). 6.9.9. The visible aspect of the fire consists of the trunk, branches, leaves, and the bark surrounding them. All these manifest parts of the massive tree are destroyed by the all-consuming flame of fire.

6.9.10. But the fruit of the tree, if it is fully shaped according to its model and receives its own form, is set in the storehouse, not into the fire. For fruit grows to be set in the storehouse; but the chaff—that is, the trunk—is meant to be thrown in the fire, since it came about not for itself but for the sake of the fruit.

6.10.1. This is what is written in scripture, "The vineyard of the Lord Sabaoth is the house of Israel, and a person of Judah is a beloved new shoot" (Isa 5:7 LXX). If a person of Judah is a beloved new shoot, it is proved that the tree is nothing other than a human being.

6.10.2. Now concerning distinction and separation, scripture has adequately pronounced. Those fully made in the image are sufficiently instructed by what is said: "All flesh is grass, and all the glory of flesh like a flower of grass. The grass is dried up, and its flower falls, but the speech of the Lord remains forever" (Isa 40:6-7 LXX). Now the speech is speech and word born in the mouth of the Lord, and there is no other place of birth.

6.11.1. This is the nature of the fire. All existing things—whether visible or invisible, soundable or sounding, numerable or numbers—are perfect intelligibles. Each of its infinitely many <parts> is conceived of as able to speak, think, and be active, exactly as Empedocles says:

> For we behold earth from earth, water by water,
> Aether by <gleaming> aether, fire by annihilating fire,
> <Affection> by affection, <and> strife by baneful strife.

6.12.1. For all the invisible parts of the fire "have intelligence and <a share in thought>."
And so the world that was born arose from unborn fire. It began to exist in the following way.

From the principle of that fire, the born world took six primal roots of the principle of generation. 6.12.2. These roots arose from the fire in pairs:

> Mind – Thought (*Epinoia*)
> Voice – Name
> Reasoning – Conception (*Enthumēsis*)

In these six roots is the entire infinite Power—in potentiality, not in actuality. The infinite Power is the One who Stood and Will Stand.
6.12.3. Whoever attains the likeness (while being in the six powers) will be in substance, in potential, in magnitude, in finished perfection one and the same as the Unborn and

Infinite Power. This one will be in no way at all inferior to that Unborn, Unchanging, and Infinite Power. 6.12.4. But whoever remains in potential only in the six powers, and is not fully formed according to the model, vanishes away and is destroyed. It works just as the human mind's potential to learn grammar or geometry. If a potentiality acquires a technical skill, it becomes a light for generated beings; but if it does not acquire it, it is left as darkness without a skill, and perishes—as if it did not exist—when the person dies.

[In a principle, God made the heaven and the earth (Gen 1:1)]

6.18.2. To you, then, I speak what I speak and write what I write—this very writing. There are two offshoots of all the aeons, having neither beginning nor end. They are from a single root or power, namely invisible and incomprehensible Silence.

6.18.3. One of these appears above: a Great Power, Mind of the universe, pervading all things, and male. The other is below: Thought (*Epinoia*), who is magnificent, female, and generates all things. Hence they correspond to each other and form a pair. In the intervening space is an immeasurable expanse of air, which has neither beginning nor end.

6.18.4. In this air, the Father upholds all things and nourishes those beings that have beginning and end. He is the One Who Stood, Who Stands, Who Will Stand. This one is an androgynous power as is right for the infinite preexisting Power, having neither beginning nor end, and existing in unity.

From this Power, the Thought (*Epinoia*) in the unity came forth and became two. 6.18.5. (Now the Father was one, for having her in himself, he was alone. Although he preexisted, he is still not "first." He became a second deity when he appeared to himself from himself. Neither was he called "Father" before she called him "Father.") 6.18.6. Since, then, he himself, having advanced from himself, manifested to himself his own Thought, so also the Thought who appeared did not make him. But when she saw him, she hid the Father in herself—that is, his power—an androgynous power and Thought. Thus they correspond to each other. This is because power does not at all differ from thought; they are one. Power is discovered from things above, while Thought is discovered from things below. 6.18.7. It works the same way with what is manifested from them. Though one, they are discovered to be two. The androgynous contains the female in himself. So also there is Mind in Thought (*Epinoia*). They are inseparable. Although one, they are discovered to be two.

6.13.1. Mind and Thought, the first pair of six powers (with the seventh following) are "Heaven and Earth." Now the male Mind above watches over and cares for his partner, while Earth below receives the fruits akin to her as they rain down from heaven. For this reason, the Logos—often having in view the offspring of Mind and Thought (that is, Heaven and Earth)—says:

> Listen, Heaven, and hear, Earth, because the Lord has spoken!
> Children I fathered and exalted, but they set me aside (Isa 1:2 LXX).

The one who speaks these words is the Seventh Power, the One Who Stood, Who Stands, Who Will Stand. For he is the cause of these goods which Moses praised and called "very good" (Gen 1:31).

["God made the two great illuminators, the great illuminator for the principles of the day and the lesser illuminator for the principles of the night" (Gen 1:16).]

"Voice and Name" are sun and moon.

["God said 'Let there be a hard plate in the middle of the water and let it separate between water and water'" (Gen 1:6).]

"Reasoning and Conception" are air and water.

In all these the Great Power is mixed and blended. He is the Infinite Power, the Standing One.

6.14.1. Moses said: "in six days God made the heaven and the earth, and on the seventh day, he rested from all his works" (Gen 2:2). 6.14.2. When they [the scriptures] say that there are three days before sun and moon (Gen 1:3-13), they hint at Mind and Thought (*Epinoia*) (that is, Heaven and Earth) plus the Seventh Power, the Infinite. These are the three powers that arose before all the others.

6.14.3. When (the scriptures) say, "Before all the aeons you fathered me" (Prov. 8:23) such things are said concerning the Seventh Power. The Seventh Power is herself a power that existed in the Infinite Power, which arose before all the aeons.

6.14.4. She is the Seventh Power about whom Moses speaks: "and divine Spirit hovered above the waters" (Gen 1:2). This is the Spirit. It contains everything in itself, as an image of the Infinite Power. It is "an image from an incorruptible form, alone ordering everything" (Wisd 7:27; 8:1). 6.14.5. For she is the power that hovered above the waters. She was born from the incorruptible form and alone orders everything.

When some such creation occurred, "God formed the human being by taking dust from the earth" (Gen 2:7). He formed the human being not simply, but in a two-fold manner: "according to the image and according to the likeness" (Gen 1:28). 6.14.6. The "image" is the Spirit hovering above the water. If it is not made in the likeness, it will be destroyed with the world. It remains only in potentiality, not in actuality. This is what the verse means: "so that we might not be condemned with the world" (1 Cor 11:32).

Yet if it is made in the likeness and comes to be from an undivided point, the small will become great, and the great will attain the infinite and unchanging eternity, no longer as something born.

["And Lord God planted a paradise in Eden, in the eastern regions, and put the human there" (Gen 2:8).]

6.14.7. How, then, and in what way does God form the human being? In paradise, for thus it seemed right to him. Paradise stands for the womb. Scripture teaches that this is true when it says, "I am the one forming you in the womb" of your mother. Moses figuratively called the womb "paradise," if it is right to believe the Logos.

Appendix 1

["A river proceeds out of Eden to water the paradise. From there it is split into four principles" (Gen 2:10).]

6.14.8. "But if God forms the human in the womb of a mother, that is, as I said, in paradise, let the womb signify paradise, "Eden" the placenta, and let "the river flowing out of Eden to water paradise" signify the umbilical cord. This umbilical cord, "splits into four branches." For on each side of the umbilical cord there are two arteries extended that serve as channels of breath, and two veins that serve as channels of blood.

6.14.9. Now when the umbilical cord flows from Eden (the placenta), it is organically joined with the fetus at the epigastrium (or the "navel" in common speech). Secondly, the two veins coursing along what are called the "gates of the liver" nourish the fetus as conveyers of blood brought from Eden (the placenta). 6.14.10. At the same time, the arteries (which we said were channels of breath) that surround the bladder on both sides along the broad bone join the great artery—the one along the spine called the "aorta." Consequently, the breath produces movement in the embryo as it flows into the heart through its side entries.

6.14.11. Accordingly, the fetus formed in paradise neither receives food through the mouth nor breathes in through the nostrils. It exists in fluids. If it breathed, death would immediately ensue, for the fetus would suck in from the fluids and perish. In point of fact, the fetus is entirely bundled in what is called the "amniotic membrane," and is nourished through the umbilical cord. It receives the substance of breath through the aorta running along the spine.

6.15.1. Now the river flowing out of Eden is divided into four branches or channels. These refer to the four sense faculties of the fetus: vision, hearing, smell, and taste. The child possesses only these senses while it is being formed in "paradise." This represents the Law that Moses laid down. In accord with this very Law were written each of the books, as the titles reveal.

6.15.2. The first book is *Genesis*. The title of the book sufficed for the knowledge of the universe. For this "genesis" signifies vision, into which one branch of the river is divided. This is because the world was seen by vision.

6.15.3. The title of the second book is *Exodus*, for it was necessary for the child, when born, to cross the Red Sea (Red refers to the blood), then come to the desert, and taste bitter water. The water beyond the Red Sea is bitter. This water signifies the road of knowledge during this life, since it travels through bitter toils. 6.15.4. But that bitter water is "converted" by Moses—that is, the Logos—to become sweet (Exod 15:22-25).

These points apply in general for all people, as can be heard from those who quote the poets:

Twas black in root, but its flower like unto milk.
The gods call it *mōly*. 'Tis hard to dig up
For men who are mortal. Yet gods can do all things. ([Homer,] *Odyssey* 10.304-6)

6.16.1. This passage spoken by the Gentiles suffices for those with an obedient ear to gain knowledge of the universe. Only the one who tasted this fruit was not made a beast by Circe. What is more, he used the power of this special fruit to mold, stamp, and return to their own former shape those who had already been transformed into beasts. 6.16.2. For through that milky and divine fruit, a man is found to be trustworthy and loved by that witch.

Similarly, *Leviticus* (the third book) refers to the sense of smell and respiration. This is because that whole book concerns sacrifices and offerings. Wherever there is a sacrifice, a pleasant odor from the sacrifice arises from the incense offerings. The sense of smell is the judge of this pleasant odor.

6.16.3. *Numbers* is the fourth book. It means taste, wherever the spoken word is active. It is called this because we speak everything in numerical order.

Deuteronomy was written for the fully formed child's sense of touch. 6.16.4. Just as the sense of touch, by handling what is seen by the other senses, sums them up and confirms them—judging whether something is hard, hot, or sticky—so also the fifth book of the law is the summation of the four written before it.

6.16.5. Therefore, all the unborn realities are in us in potentiality, not in actuality, like the skill of grammar or geometry. So if one encounters apt speech and instruction, the bitter will turn sweet—that is, "the spears will turn to sickles and the swords into plows." There will not be chaff and wood (things born for fire), but fruit mature and formed according to the model, as I said—equal and like unto the unborn and infinite Power.

6.16.6. But if it remains a tree only, not producing fully formed fruit, it is done away with. "For the axe is near to the roots of the tree. Every tree, not producing good fruit is cut down and thrown into the fire" (Matt 3:10; Lk 3:9).

6.17.1. There is, then, that blessed and incorruptible reality hidden in every human being—in potentiality, not in actuality—which is the One Who Stood, Stands, and Will Stand. He stood above in the Unborn Power. He stands below in the flow of waters, born in an image. He will stand above alongside the blessed infinite Power, if made in the likeness. 6.17.2. Accordingly, there are three standing aeons, and apart from these three, the Unborn One is not ordered. He is the one hovering upon the waters, and formed according to the likeness. He is perfect, heavenly, and inferior to the Unborn Power in no conceivable way.

> I and you are one.
> What is before me is you.
> What is after you is I.

6.17.3. This is the single power, divided above and below, giving birth to herself, increasing herself, seeking herself, finding herself, being mother of herself, father of herself, sister of herself, partner of herself, daughter of herself, son of herself, mother and father, yet one—the root of the universe.

6.17.4. Moreover, the source of generation for those who are born is from fire. For all those to whom generation is allotted, the source of the desire for generation comes from fire. Accordingly, the desire for changeable generation is called "burning."

6.17.5. Although it is one, the fire has two modes of conversion. In the male, the blood is turned into semen (characterized, like fire, by heat and a whitish color). In the woman, however, the same blood is turned into milk. Accordingly, the "turning" in the male becomes generation, whereas the "turning" in the female becomes nourishment for the offspring. This is the meaning of "the flaming sword that *turns* to guard the way of the tree of life" (Gen 3:24). 6.17.6. The blood turns to semen and milk, and this power itself becomes father and mother, the sowing of what is generated and growth for what is nourished. It needs nothing, and is self-sufficient.

The tree of life is guarded by the flaming sword that turns, as I mentioned. This flaming sword is the Seventh Power, self-derived, containing everything, and situated within the six powers. 6.17.7. If the flaming sword is not turned, that good tree will be corrupted and destroyed. But if the fire turns into semen and milk, the one situated in these potentially, when he encounters apt speech and the place of the Lord in which speech is born, will be vastly enlarged and grow. Though beginning as from the tiniest spark, he will become an infinite and unchanging power in an unchanging eternity, no longer born in the finite world.

6.18.1. One is born and able to suffer when in potentiality, but passionless from birth when formed according to the likeness (Gen 1:28). Thus becoming perfect, one moves out from the first two powers (namely, Heaven and Earth).

Appendix 2

Translation of *The Concept of Our Great Power*

Note: What follows is my translation of *Great Power*, following the text printed by Frederik Wisse.[1] In making my translation, I have profited from the translations and notes printed by Francis E. Williams (2001), Hans-Martin Schenke (2001), and Marvin Meyer (2007).[2] Words in parenthesis are my additions to the text to aid the reader. Words in square brackets represent deletions. Words in angled brackets represent emendations. All subtitles in italics are mine. I have made one transposition, setting 43.3-11 before 39.16, which seems to better accord with the text's logic.

The Perception of Thinking
The Understanding of the Great Power

Introduction: Salvation for Those Who Know the Great Power (36.1-27)

Now, the one who will know our Great Power will become invisible. No fire will burn this one. This one will be purified, and will destroy all your chains. For every person in whom my form will be revealed within will be saved, from seven days until 120 years. These are the ones under constraint to gather the end of everything, to gather the writings of our Great Power, so that she writes your name in our great light and fulfills their thoughts and their works so that they will be purified and triumph completely. Then they come to an end and are gathered in the place of the blind. But you will see me and prepare your dwellings in our Great Power.

Exhortation: Know the One who Came (36.28-37.5)

Know he that came and how he came (Noah/Christ) so that you will know what is being revealed. Know how it knows itself, to what extent it is one or what kind of thing it is, or how it came into being. Why don't you (pl.) seek how you will become it, how you have become it?

---

[1] Frederik Wisse and Francis E. Williams, "The Concept of Our Great Power," in *Nag Hammadi Codices V,2-5 and VI with Papyrus Berolinensis 8502, 1 and 4*, ed. Douglas M. Parrot, NHS 11 (Leiden: Brill, 1979), 299–324.
[2] Williams, *Mental Perception*, 1-22; Schenke, "Das Verständnis," in *Nag Hammadi Deutsch*, 2.483-93; Meyer, *Nag Hammadi Scriptures*, 391–402.

The Original Abyss (37.6-12)

Contemplate the vast quantity of the water. It is infinite and inexhaustible (Gen 1:2). Its beginning and end support the earth from below. It breathes in the air. Gods and angels are in it.

Lord of the Abyss (37.12-23)

The one exalted over all these contains both fear and light (Gen 1:1, 3). My writings are revealed by him. I established the administration of fleshly creations, for no one had power to stand apart from that one, nor did the living age have power apart from this one. He owns its contents. He thinks purely.

The Spirit (37.23-29)

Then look upon the Spirit and know where it is (Gen 1:2). It gave it to people to receive life from itself every day. It has life in itself (John 5:26). It gave it to all of them.

The Rest of Creation (37.29–38.5)

Then the darkness with Hades ignited the fire. The one who belongs to me will destroy it from within. His eye could not tolerate my light. The spirits with the waters were set in motion. Then the rest (of creation) appeared. And the whole age of creation with their powers of the fire emerged from the water.

The Birth of the Human Soul (38.5-12)

The Power (of the creator) arose in the midst of the powers. And the powers lust to see my image. And the soul arose as the impression of my image (Gen 1:26). This is the sort of deed that happened. See what it is like, for before it happened, the age of the flesh had no (spiritual) sight.

The Flood Story (38.13–39.15)

The fleshly age emerged with the bodies of giants. They were allotted many days in the creation. For when they defiled them, they went into the flesh. The father of the flesh [the water] himself executed judgment. For when he found Noah, pious and worthy, the father of the flesh subjected the angels. And he (Noah) preached piety for 120 years. But no one listened to him. He made an ark of wood. And the one whom (God) found entered it.

Then the flood came.

In this way, Noah was saved with his children, since if the ark was not made for people to enter, the waters of the flood would not have come. Thus he considered and took thought for the safety of gods, angels, and the powers of the Great One—all of them [...] along with their luxurious behavior. He removed them from the age and nourished them in resting places. So the judgment of the flesh attained resolution. The deed of the single Power stood firm.

Intervening Exhortation (43.3-11)

Observe how the ages that were have passed. Observe how vast was his water in that age which melted away, ages of such vastness! Observe how people should prepare and stand and become an unceasing eternity.

The Animate Age (39.16–33)

Now in turn comes the age of soul. It is small and mixed with body. It is spawned from a defiled soul, since the first defilement of the creation found strength. It produced every deed: many deeds of wrath, rage, jealousy, envy, hatred, slander, contempt, war, lying, conspiracy, bouts of pain and pleasure, humiliation, pollutions, acts of duplicity, illnesses, and violent judgments arbitrarily decreed.

Intervening Exhortation (39.33–40.9)

Are you still sleeping? Are you experiencing a dream? Wake up and shake yourselves. Then taste and eat true food. Dispense the Logos and the water of life. Cease from evil lusts and desires and what is unlike (your nature), and from wicked opinions which have no foundation.

The Mother of Flame (40.9–23)

The mother of the flame did not prevail. She brought fire into the soul and the earth. And she sent fire upon all those within her. Her fuel came to an end; she did not find a (place) to burn. She will dissolve by herself. It (the world) will become bodiless. Material things burn until everything is purified, with all evil. For when it finds nothing to burn, it will save itself alone until it comes to an end.

The Story of Christ's Triumph (40.24–42.23)

Then in this age, namely the one of soul, the human who knows the Great Power will come. He will receive and know me. He will drink in truth from the milk of his mother. He will speak in parables. He preaches the age to come, just as Noah preached in the first age of the flesh. Regarding his words he speaks, he spoke to all in 72 tongues. By his message, he opened the gateway of the heavens. And he shamed the master of Hades. He raised dead persons. He destroyed his (Hades's) lordship.

Then a great disturbance arose. The rulers of rage rose against him. They wanted to hand him over to the master of Hades. Then they got to know one of his followers. They lit fire to his soul. He handed him over. No one knew (Jesus's) his identity. They proceeded to arrest him. They only brought themselves to judgment.

They handed him over to the master of Hades. They handed him through Sasabek and Berotth. He (had) prepared himself to go down and refute them. Then the master of Hades took him. He had no way of seizing the mode of his flesh to show him to the rulers. Rather, he was saying, "Who is this? What is this? His message destroyed the law of the age! He is from the Logos of the power of life." He (Jesus) was strong enough to command the rulers. And no one could do anything to dominate him. The rulers sought him who came. They did not know that this one is the sign of their destruction and the shifting of the age.

The sun set in the daytime. The day became dark. The demons shuddered. After these things, he will be revealed ascending above. Then there will be revealed the sign of the coming age. And the (past) ages will melt away.

The Mission after Jesus's Death (42.22–43.2)

Those who understand these things I discuss will be blessed, and they will be revealed and blessed since they will understand the truth, since you rest in the heavens. Then many will follow. And they will be active in the region of their birth. They will travel. They will publish (*or:* abandon) his word according to their desire.

Flashback: Jesus in the First Age (43.11–29)

At the beginning, after his preaching, he preached the second age, that the first must perish in time. He lived the first age, traveling within it until it perished. He preached 120 years. This is the perfect number, highly exalted. He wasted the borderland of the west and destroyed the east. Then his seed <was saved>, along with those who want to walk on the side of the great Logos and his preaching.

The Rulers Strike Back (43.29–44.10)

Then the rage of the rulers ignited. They were ashamed about their destruction; they fumed and raged against the Life (John 14:6). Cities shuddered. Mountains collapsed. The ruler comes up with the rulers of the western lands as far as the east, namely the place where the Logos first appeared. Then the earth shook, and the city trembled. Then the birds ate and were gorged on the corpses. The earth mourned along with the inhabited world. They became a wasteland.

The Ruler of the West (44.10–31)

Then, when the times are fulfilled, then evil rises high as far as the final end of the Logos. Then the ruler of the west arose. And from the east he will perform a work. He will teach people in his wickedness. He wishes to destroy every teaching of the message (*logos*) of true wisdom. He loves the lying wisdom. For he engaged what is ancient. He wished to introduce evil though he clothed himself in dignity. He could not, since great was the defilement of his clothes. Then he raged; he appeared; he wanted to go up and cross over to that place. Then the season comes. He complied, and changes the edicts.

The Counterfeit and the Antichrist (44.31–45.24)

Then the time came when the small child grew up. When he reached his peak, then the rulers send the counterfeit to that person—so they will know our Great Power.

They were expecting him to perform for them a sign and he bore great signs. He became king over the whole earth and of those under heaven. He set his throne over the end of the earth since he I will make god of the world. He will perform signs and wonders (2 Thess 2:9). Then they will turn aside and go astray. Then people at that time will follow him. They will introduce circumcision. And he will judge the uncircumcised, the people. Indeed, he sent many heralds at first to preach about him.

The Final Conflagration (45.24–47.8)

When the time prepared for the earthly empire is fulfilled, then the purification of souls will come, since evil has surpassed them. All the powers of the sea will shake and dry up. The firmament did not pour down dew; springs will cease, rivers will not flow into springs, and the waters of the springs of the earth will cease. Then the abysses will be obliterated and open, the stars will grow large, and the sun will perish.

I will withdraw with everyone who knows me, and they will go into the immeasurable light. Nothing of the flesh seized them, neither will fiery delight. They will become weightless and holy. Nothing will drag them down. I watch over them under my hand. They possess a holy garment. The fire has no power to burn them.

Then there is darkness, a gale, and just enough time to shut one's eyes when it comes and destroys them all. They will be punished until their purification. Then their time is appointed for them to gain possession and be reckoned up: 1468 years.

When the fire burns up everything and has nothing more to burn, it will cease by itself. Then will be fulfilled the [second] power, the mercy to come [. . .] through Wisdom [. . .] Then the firmament will fall down into the abyss. At that time the children of matter will perish. They will not exist from then on.

Description of Final Salvation (47.9–48.15)

Then the souls will be revealed as pure through the light of the power. This Power is exalted over all powers, measureless, and universal—I along with all those who know me. And they will be in the beautiful age, the age of the bridal chamber prepared by Wisdom. They give glory before the single one, who is unattainable. They will behold him because he loves them. They all will become images in his light. They will beam with light all around. They have rested in his rest.

The souls that were punished he will release. They come into purity and see the holy things. They will cry aloud: 'Have mercy on us, you Power above all powers!' Since . . . and in the tree of violence that exists in . . . they don't see him since they don't seek him, nor did they believe us. But they acted according to the creation of the rulers with other rulers. We too acted according to the birth of the flesh of creation set down by the law-giving ruler. Yet we have come to be in the unchanging eternity.

The Understanding of Our Great Power

Bibliography

Primary

Adler, Ada, ed. *Suidae Lexicon*. 5 vols. Stuttgart: Teubner, 1984–1989.
Aelian. *Historical Miscellany*. Edited by N. G. Wilson. LCL. Cambridge, MA: Harvard University Press, 1997.
Apuleius. *Opera quae supersunt*. Edited by C. Moreschini. 3 vols. Stuttgart: Teubner, 1991.
Aratus. *Phaenomena: Introduction, Translation and Commentary*. Edited by Douglas Kidd. Cambridge: Cambridge University Press, 1997.
Aristotle. Translated by H. Rackham, et al. 23 vols. LCL. Cambridge, MA: Harvard University Press, 1926–2011.
Athenaeus. *Learned Banqueters I-III.106e*. Translated by S. Douglas Olson. LCL 204. Cambridge, MA: Harvard University Press, 2006.
Augustine. *Concerning the City of God against the Pagans*. Translated by Henry Bettenson. London: Penguin, 1972.
Chariton. *Callirhoe*. Translated by G. P. Goold. LCL. Cambridge, MA: Harvard University Press, 1995.
Charlesworth, James H. ed. *The Old Testament Pseudepigrapha*. 2 vols. New York: Doubleday, 1983.
Clement of Alexandria. *Extraits de Théodote*. Edited by François Sagnard. SC 23. Paris: Cerf, 1970.
Clement of Alexandria. *Paedagogus*. Edited by Miroslav Marcovich. VCSup 61. Leiden: Brill, 2002.
Clement of Alexandria. *Stromata, Quis dives salvetur*. Edited by Otto Stählin, Ludwig Früchtel, and Ursula Treu. GCS 15, 17. 4th ed. Berlin: Akademie, 1970–1985.
Corpus Inscriptionum Latinarum VI. Inscriptiones urbis Romae Latinae, Eugenius Bormann and Guilemus Henzen. vol. 6, Part 1. Berlin: Georg Reimerus, 1876.
Cyril of Jerusalem. *Procatachesis and Catecheses 1–12*. Translated by Leo McCauley and Anthony Stephenson. Fathers of the Church. Washington, DC: CUA Press, 2005.
des Places, Édouard, ed. *Numénius: Fragments*. Paris: Belles Lettres, 2003.
Dillon, John M. *Alcinous: The Handbook of Platonism*. Oxford: Clarendon, 1995.
Dio Chrysostom. Translated by J. W. Cohoon. 5 vols. LCL. Cambridge, MA: Harvard University Press, 1932–1951.
Diogenes Laertius. *Vitae philosophorum*. Edited by Miroslav Marcovich. Stuttgart: Teubner, 1999.
Dionysius of Halicarnassus. *The Roman Antiquities Books III-IV*. Translated by Ernest Cary. LCL 347. Cambridge, MA: Harvard University Press, 1939.
Döhler, Marietheres. *Acta Petri: Text Übersetzung und Kommentar zu den Actus Vercellenses*. TU 171. Berlin: de Gruyter, 2018.
Eastman, David L. *The Ancient Martyrdom Accounts of Peter and Paul*. WGRW 39. Atlanta: SBL Press, 2015.

Elliott, J. K. *The Apocryphal New Testament: A Collection of Apocryphal Christian Literature in an English Translation*. Oxford: Clarendon, 1993.

Epiphanius. *Ancoratus und Panarion haer. 1–33*. Edited by Karl Holl, Marc Bergermann, and Christian-Friedrich Collatz. 2nd ed. GCS NF 10/1. Berlin: de Gruyter, 2013.

Euripides. Translated by David Kovacs, et al. 8 vols. LCL. Cambridge, MA: Harvard University Press, 1994–2009.

Eusebius. *Die Theophanie. Die griechischen Bruchstücke und Übersetzung der syrischen Überlieferung*. Edited by Hugo Gressman and Adolf Lamniski. 2nd ed. Berlin: Akademie, 1992.

Eusebius. *Histoire ecclésiastique*. Edited by Gustav Bardy. 4 vols. SC. Paris: Cerf, 1952–1960.

Eusebius. *In Praise of Constantine: A Historical Study and New Translation of Eusebius' Tricenniel Orations*. Edited by H. A. Drake. Berkeley: University of California Press, 1978.

Eustathius. *Commentarii ad Homeri Odysseam*. Edited by J. G. Stallbaum. vol. 1 Cambridge: Cambridge University Press, 2010.

Galen. *De foetuum formatione*. Edited by Diethard Nickel. Corpus Medicorum Graecorum V 3,3. Berlin: Akademie, 2001.

Galen. *Über die Anatomie der Gebärmutter*. Edited by Diethard Nickel. Corpus Medicorum Graecorum V 2,1. Berlin: Akademie, 1971.

Gaudentius. *S. Gaudentii episcopi brixiensis tractatus*. Edited by A. Glueck. CSEL 68. Vindobonae: Hoelder-Pichler-Tempsky, 1936.

Greer, Rowan A. and Margaret M. Mitchell, ed. *The Belly-myther of Endor: Interpretations of 1 Kingdoms 28 in the Early Church*. Atlanta: SBL Press, 2007.

Heine, Ronald E. *The Commentary of Origen on the Gospel of St Matthew*. 2 vols. Oxford: Oxford University Press, 2018.

Heraclitus. *Homeric Problems*. Edited by Donald A. Russell and David Konstan. Atlanta: SBL Press, 2005.

Herodotus. *The Landmark Herodotus: The Histories*. Edited by Robert B. Strassler. Translated by Andrea L. Purvis. New York: Anchor Books, 2007.

Hippocrates. *The Hippocratic Treatises on Generation, On the Nature of the Child, Diseases IV*. Edited by Iain M. Lonie. Ars Medica 7. Berlin: de Gruyter, 1981.

Hippocrates. *Oeuvres completes Tome XI*. Edited by Robert Joly. Paris: Belles Lettres, 2003.

Homer. Translated by A. T. Murray. 4 vols. LCL. Cambridge, MA: Harvard University Press, 1919–1925.

Iamblichus. *On the Pythagorean Way of Life*. Edited and translated by John Dillon and Jackson Hershbell. Atlanta: Scholars Press, 1991.

Irenaeus of Lyon. *Contre les hérésies livres I-V*. Edited by Adelin Rousseau and Louis Doutreleau. SC 100, 153, 211, 263-64, 294. Paris: Cerf, 1965–82.

Isocrates. Translated by Larue van Hook. vol. 3. LCL 373. Cambridge, MA: Harvard University Press, 1945.

Jerome. *De Viris Illustribus*. Edited by W. Herding. Leipzig: Teubner, 1879.

Josephus, *Opera*. Edited by Benedict Niese. 7 vols. Berlin: Weidmann, 1887–1889.

Justin. *Philosopher and Martyr, Apologies*. Edited by Denis Minns and Paul Parvis. Oxford: Oxford University Press, 2009.

Kühn, Karl Gottlob. *Galeni opera omnia*. 20 vols. rpt. Hildesheim: Olms, 1965–1967.

Latte, Kurt and Ian C. Cunningham. *Hesychii Alexandrini Lexicon*. 3 vols. Berlin: de Gruyter, 2020.

Litwa, M. David, ed. *Refutation of All Heresies*. WGRW 40. Atlanta: SBL Press, 2016.

Lucian. *Oeuvres*. Edited by Jacques Bompaire. 4 vols. Budé. Paris: Belles Lettres, 1993–2008.
Marcovich. ed. *Hippolytus: Refutatio omnium haeresium*. PTS 25. Berlin: de Gruyter 1986.
Maximus of Tyre. *The Philosophical Orations*. Edited and translated by M. B. Trapp. Oxford: Oxford University Press, 1997.
Metzger, Marcel. *Les Constitutions Apostoliques*. SC 329. 3 vols. Paris: Cerf, 1986.
Meyer, Marvin, ed. *The Nag Hammadi Scriptures: The International Edition*. New York: HarperOne, 2007.
Migne, J.-P. *Patrologiae cursus completus series Graeca*. vol. 60. Paris: Migne, 1857–1866.
Nock, A. D. and A.-J. Festugière. *Hermès Trismégiste. Corpus Hermeticum Tome I*. 13th printing of the 2nd ed. Paris: Belles Lettres, 2018.
Novum Testamentum Graecum Editio Critica Maior III: Die Apostelgeschichte. Edited by Holger Strutwolf, Georg Gäbel, Annette Hüffmeier, Gerd Mink, and Klaus Wachtel. Part 1.1. Stuttgart: Deutsche Bibelgesellschaft, 2017.
Origen. *An Exhortation to Martyrdom, Prayer, First Principles Book IV, Prologue to the Commentary on the Song of Songs, Homily XXVII on Numbers*. Translated by Rowan A. Greer. Mahwah: Paulist Press, 1979.
Origen. *Commentaire sur Saint Jean*. Edited by Cécile Blanc. 5 vols. Paris: Cerf. 1966–1992.
Origen. *Die Kommentierung des Buches Genesis*. Edited by Karin Metzler. Berlin: de Gruyter, 2010.
Origen. *Matthäuserklärung III. Fragmenta und Indices Erste Hälfte*. Edited by Ernst Benz and Erich Klostermann. Origenes Werke 12. GCS 41.1. Leipzig: Teubner, 1941.
Origen. *Origène. Homélies sur Jérémie*. Edited by P. Nautin. vol. 1. SC 232. Paris: Cerf, 1976.
Origen. *Origenes Contra Celsum Libri VIII*. Edited by Marcovich. VCSup 54. Leiden: Brill, 2001.
Ovid. *Les Fastes*. Edited by Robert Schilling. 2 vols. Budé. Paris: Belles Lettres, 1992–93.
Ovid. *Métamorphoses*. Edited by Georges LaFaye. 3 vols. Budé. Paris: Belles Lettres, 1965–1969.
Philo. *Opera*. Edited by Leopold Cohn and Paul Wendland. 7 vols. Berlin: de Gruyter, 1962–1963.
Photius. *Bibliothèque. Tome II: Codices 84–185*. Edited by René Henry. Paris: Belles Lettres. 2003.
Plato. *Complete Works*. Edited by John M. Cooper. Indianapolis: Hackett, 1997.
Plutarch. Translated by Frank Cole Babbit, Harold Cherniss, et al. 28 vols. LCL. Cambridge, MA: Harvard University Press, 1914–2004.
Porphyry. *Fragmenta*. Edited by Andrew Smith. Leipzig: Teubner, 1993.
Porphyry. *On Plotinus, Ennead 1*. Translated by A. H. Armstrong. LCL 440. Cambridge, MA: Harvard University Press, 1966.
Preisendanz, Karl and Albert Henrichs, ed. *Papyri Graecae magicae: Die griechischen Zauberpapyri*. 2 vols. Berlin: de Gruyter, 1973–74.
Rahlfs, Alfred and Robert Hanhart. *Septuaginta id est Vetus Testamentum graece iuxta LXX interpretes*. 2nd ed. Stuttgart: Deutsche Bibelgesellschaft, 2006.
Rehm, Bernard and Georg Strecker, ed. *Die Pseudoklementinen I: Homilien*. GCS 42. 3rd ed. Berlin: Akademie, 1992.
Rehm, Bernard and Georg Strecker. ed. *Die Pseudoklementinen II. Rekognitionen in Rufins Übersetzung*. 2nd ed. Berlin: Akademie, 1994.

Roberts, Alexander and James Donaldson, ed. *Ante-Nicene Fathers*. vol. 8. Peabody: Hendrickson, 1995.
Robinson, James, ed. *The Coptic Gnostic Library: A Complete Edition of the Nag Hammadi Codices*. 5 vols. Leiden: Brill, 2000.
Rufus of Ephesus. *Oeuvres de Rufus d'Éphèse*. Edited by C. Daremberg and C. É. Ruelle. Paris: Imprimerie Nationale, 1879.
Simplicius. *In Aristotelis physicorum libros commentaria*. Edited by Hermann Diels. Berlin: Reimer, 1892.
Soranus. *Maladies des femmes, Tome 1 Livre 1*. Edited by P. Burguière, Danielle Gourevitch, and Yves Malinas. Paris: Belles Lettres, 2003.
Stewart-Sykes, Alistair. *The Didascalia Apostolorum: An English Version with Introduction and Annotation*. Turnhout: Brepols, 2009.
Strabo. *Geography*. Translated by Horace Leonard Jones. 8 vols. LCL. Cambridge, MA: Harvard University Press, 1917.
Suetonius. *Lives of the Caesars*. Edited by J. C. Rolfe. 2 vols. LCL. Cambridge, MA: Harvard University Press, 1913-14.
Tacitus. *The Annals*. Translated by John Jackson. LCL 312. Cambridge: Cambridge University Press, 1937.
Tatian. *Gegen falsche Götter und falsche Bildung: Tatian, Rede an die Griechen*. Edited by Heinz-Günther Nesselrath. SAPERE 28. Tübingen: Mohr Siebeck, 2016.
Tertullian. *Opera*. Edited by E. Dekkers, A. Gerlo, and A. Kroymann. 2 vols. CCSL 1.1-2. Turnholt: Brepols, 1954.
Tertullian. *Traité de la prescription contre les hérétiques*. Edited by R. F. Refoulé and P. de Labriolle. SC 134. Paris: Cerf, 2017.
Theodoret. *Unterscheidung von Lüge und Wahrheit*. Edited by Benjamin Gleede. GCS NF 26. Berlin: de Gruyter, 2020.
Varro. *On the Latin Language*. Translated by Roland G. Kent. LCL 333. Cambridge, MA: Harvard University Press, 1938.
Vergil. *Énéide Livres I-IV*. Edited by J. Perret. Budé. Paris: Belles Lettres, 1977.
Waszink, J. H., ed. *Quinti Septimi Florentis Tertulliani: De Anima*. VCSup 100. Leiden: Brill: 2010.
Watson, Francis, ed. *An Apostolic Gospel: The 'Epistula Apostolorum' in Literary Context*. Cambridge: Cambridge University Press, 2020.
Wehnert, Jürgen. *Pseudoklementinische Homilien: Einführung und Übersetzung* Göttingen: Vandenhoeck & Ruprecht, 2010.
Williams, Frank. *The Panarion of Epiphanius of Salamis: Book 1 Sects 1-46*. 2nd ed. Nag Hammadi and Manichean Studies 63. Leiden: Brill, 2009.

Secondary

Ackermann, Hans Christoph and Jean-Robert Gisler, ed. *Lexicon Iconographicum Mythologiae Classicae (LIMC)*. Zurich und Munich: Artemis, 1981–.
Adamik T. "The Image of Simon Magus in the Christian Tradition." Pages 52–64 in *The Apocryphal Acts of Peter: Magic, Miracles and Gnosticism*. Edited by Jan Bremmer. Leuven: Peeters, 1998.
Aejmelaeus, Lars. *Die Rezeption der Paulusbriefe in der Miletrede Apg. 20:18–35*. Helsinki: Suomalainen Tiedeakatemia, 1987.

Aland, Barbara. *Was ist Gnosis? Studien zum frühen Christentum, zu Marcion und zur kaiserzeitlichen Philosophie*. Tübingen: Mohr Siebeck, 2009.
Allen, J. P. *Genesis in Egypt: The Philosophy of Ancient Egyptian Creation Accounts*. New Haven: Egyptological Seminar, 1988.
Amsler, Frédéric, ed. *Nouvelles intrigues pseudo-clémentines. Plots in the Pseudo-Clementine Romance*. Prahins: Zèbre, 2008.
Arai, Sasagu. "Simonianische Gnosis und die *Exegese über die Seele*." Pages 185–203 in *Gnosis and Gnosticism: Papers Read at the Seventh International Conference on Patristic Studies. Oxford, September 8th–13th 1975*. Leiden: Brill, 1977.
Arai, Sasagu. "'Simonianischen' in *AuthLog* und *Bronté*." Pages 3–15 in *Gnosis and Gnosticism: Papers Read at the Eight International Conference on Patristic Studies Oxford, September 3rd–8th 1979*. Edited by Martin Krause. Leiden: Brill, 1981.
Armstrong, Karl L. *Dating Acts in its Jewish and Greco-Roman. Contexts*. London: Bloomsbury, 2021.
Assmann, Jan. "Communicative and Cultural Memory." Pages 109–18 in *A Companion to Cultural Memory Studies: An International and Interdisciplinary Handbook*. Edited by Astrid Erll and Ansgar Nünnung. Berlin: de Gruyter, 2008.
Aubin, Melissa. "Beobachtungen zur Magie im Neuen Testament." *Zeitschrift für Neues Testament* 7 (2001): 16–24.
Austin, Norman. *Helen and Her Shameless Phantom*. Ithaca: Cornell University Press, 2018.
Baldwin, Matthew C. *Whose Acts of Peter? Text and Historical Context of the Actus Vercellenses*. WUNT II/196. Tübingen: Mohr Siebeck, 2005.
Barnes, T. D. *Constantine and Eusebius*. Cambridge, MA: Harvard University Press, 1981.
Barnes, T. D. "The Date of Ignatius." *ExpTim* 120 (2008): 119–30.
Barnes, T. D. "Eusebius of Caesarea." *ExpTim* 121, no. 1 (2009): 1–14.
Barnes, T. D. "Some Inconsistences in Eusebius." *JTS* 35 (1984): 470–5.
Barnes, T. D. "Statistics and the Conversion of the Roman Aristocracy." *JRS* 85 (1995): 135–47.
Barnes, T. D. *Tertullian: A Historical and Literary Study*. Revised ed. Oxford: Clarendon, 2011.
Barrett, C. K. "Light on the Holy Spirit from Simon Magus." Pages 281–95 in *Les Actes des Apôtres: Traditions, redaction, théologie*. Edited by J. Kremer Leuven: Leuven University Press, 1979.
Bassi, Karen. "Helen and the Discourse of Denial in Stesichorus' Palinode." *Arethusa* 26, no. 1 (1993): 51–75.
Bautch, Kelley Coblentz. "Obscured by the Scriptures, Revealed by the Prophets: God in the Pseudo-Clementine *Homilies*." Pages 120–36 in *Histories of the Hidden God: Concealment and Revelation in Western Gnostic, Esoteric, and Mystical Traditions*. Edited by April D. DeConick and Grant Adamson. Abingdon: Oxon, 2014.
Bazzana, Giovanni Battista. "'Magic' in the *Klementia*: Reflections on an Episode of Transformation." Pages 395–411 in *In Search of Truth in the Pseudo-Clementine Homilies: New Approaches to a Philosophical and Rhetorical Novel of Late Antiquity*. Edited by Benjamin M. J. De Vos and Danny Praet. WUNT 496. Tübingen: Mohr Siebeck, 2022.
Behr, John. *Irenaeus of Lyon: Identifying Christianity*. Oxford: Oxford University Press, 2013.
Benko, Stephen. "Pagan Criticism of Christianity During the First Two Centuries." Pages 1055–118 in *ANRW* 2.23.2. Edited by Wolfgang Haase. Berlin: de Gruyter, 1980.

Benko, Stephen. "The Libertine Gnostic Sect of the Phibionites According to Epiphanius." *VC* 21 (1967): 103–19.
Ben Zeev, Miriam Pucci. *Diaspora Judaism in Turmoil 116–117 CE: Ancient Sources and Modern Insights*. Leuven: Peeters, 2005.
Berger, Klaus. "Propaganda und Gegenpropaganda im frühem Christentum: Simon Magus als Gestalt des samaritanischen Christentums." Pages 313–17 in *Religious Propaganda and Missionary Competition in the New Testament World: Essays Honoring Dieter Georgi*. Edited by Lukas Bormann, Kelly del Tredici, and Angela Standhartinger. Leiden: Brill, 1994.
Bergmeier, Roland. "Die Gestalt des Simon Magus in Act 8 und in der simonianischen Gnosis—Aporien einer Gesamtdeutung." *ZNW* 77 (1986): 267–75.
Berzon, Todd S. *Classifying Christians: Ethnography, Heresiology, and the Limits of Knowledge in Late Antiquity*. Berkeley: University of California Press, 2016.
Beyschlag, Karlmann. *Simon Magus und die christliche Gnosis*. WUNT 16. Tübingen: Mohr Siebeck, 1974.
Bianchi, Ugo, ed. *Le origini dello Gnosticismo: Colloquio di Messina 13–18 Aprile 1966*. Leiden: Brill, 1967.
Bird, Michael F. *Jesus Among the Gods: Early Christology in the Greco-Roman World*. Waco: Baylor University Press, 2022.
Blondell, Ruby. *Helen of Troy: Beauty, Myth, Devastation*. New York: Oxford University Press, 2013.
Böhm, Martina. *Samarien und die Samaritai bei Lukas: Eine Studie zum religionshistorischen und traditionsgeschichtlichen Hintergrund der lukanischen Samarientexte und zu deren topographischer Verhaftung*. WUNT II/111. Tübingen: Mohr Siebeck, 1999.
Bonazzi, Mauro. "Eudorus of Alexandria and the 'Pythagorean' Pseudepigrapha." Pages 385–404 in *On Pythagoreanism* Edited by Gabriele Cornelli, Richard McKirahan, and Constantinos Macris. Berlin: de Gruyter, 2013.
Bowra, C. M. "Two Palinodes of Stesichorus." *Classical Review* 13 (1963): 245–52.
Brakke, David. "The Seed of Seth at the Flood: Biblical Interpretation and Gnostic Theological Reflection." Pages 41–62 in *Reading in Christian Communities: Essays on Interpretation in the Early Church*. Edited by Charles Bobertz and David Brakke. Notre Dame: University of Notre Dame Press, 2002.
Bremmer, Jan N. "Aspects of the Acts of Peter: Women, Magic, Place and Date." Pages 1–20 in *The Apocryphal Acts of Peter: Magic, Miracles and Gnosticism*. Edited by Jan Bremmer. Leuven: Peeters, 1998.
Bremmer, Jan N. *The Pseudo-Clementines*. Edited by Jan N. Bremmer. Leuven: Peeters, 2010.
Bremmer, Jan N. *The Rise and Fall of the Afterlife*. London: Routledge, 2002.
Bremmer, Jan N. "Simon Magus: The Invention and Reception of a Magician in a Christian Context." *Religion in the Roman Empire* 5 (2019): 246–70.
Brent, Allen. *Hippolytus and the Roman Church in the Third Century; Communities in Tension before the Emergence of a Monarch-Bishop*. VCSup 32. Leiden: Brill, 1995.
Brent, Allen. "Ignatius of Antioch in Second Century Asia Minor." Pages 62–86 in *Intertextuality in the Second Century*. Edited by D. J. Bingham and C. N. Jefford. Leiden: Brill, 2016.
Brooks, Edward C. "Origen and the Clementine *Recognitions*." Pages 154–60 in *Origeniana Quinta: Historia-Text and Method-Biblica-Philosophica-Theologica-Origenism and Later Developments*. Edited by Robert J. Daly. Leuven: Peeters, 1992.

Brown, Peter. *The Body and Society*. New York: Columbia University Press, 1988.
Buck, P. Lorraine. "Justin Martyr's *Apologies*: Their Number, Destination, and Form." *JTS* 54 (2003): 45–59.
Burgess, R. "The Dates and Editions of Eusebius *Chronici Canones* and *Historia Ecclesiastica*." *JTS* 48 (1997): 471–504.
Burrus, Virginia. "The Heretical Woman as Symbol in Alexander, Athanasius, Epiphanius, and Jerome." *HTR* 84, no. 3 (1991): 229–48.
Callon, Callie. *Reading Bodies: Physiognomy as a Strategy of Persuasion in Early Christian Discourse*. London: T&T Clark, 2019.
Callon, Callie. "Secondary Characters Furthering Characterization: The Depiction of Slaves in the *Acts of Peter*." *JBL* 131, no. 4 (2012): 797–818.
Caner, Daniel F. "The Practice and Prohibition of Self-castration in Early Christianity." *VC* 51 (1997): 396–415.
Carbonaro, Paul. "Simone le magicien et la Bible grecque." *RB* 121–123 (2014): 414–26.
Carlson, Donald H. *Jewish-Christian Interpretation of the Pentateuch in the Pseudo-Clementine Homilies*. Minneapolis: Fortress Press, 2013.
Carriker, Andrew James. *The Library of Eusebius of Caesarea*. VCSup 67. Leiden: Brill, 2003.
Castelli, Emanuele. "Saggio introduttivo: L'*Elenchos*, ovvero una 'biblioteca' contro le eresie." Pages 21–56 in *'Ippolito.' Confutazione di tutte le eresie*. Edited by Aldo Magris. Brescia: Morcelliana, 2012.
Chaniotis, Angelos. "Acclamations as a Form of Religious Communication." Pages 199–218 in *Die Religions des Imperium Romanum. Koine und Konfrontationen*. Edited by Hubert Cancik and Jörg Rüpke. Tübingen: Mohr Siebeck, 2009.
Cherix, Pierre. *Le concept de notre grande puissance*. Göttingen: Vandenhoeck & Ruprecht, 1982.
Chiapparini, Giuliano. "Irenaeus and the Gnostic Valentinus: Orthodoxy and Heresy in the Church of Rome Around the Middle of the Second Century." *ZAC* 18, no. 1 (2013): 95–119.
Colpe, Carsten. *Einleitung in die Schriften aus Nag Hammadi*. Münster: Aschendorff, 2011.
Colpe, Carsten. "Heidnische, jüdische und christliche Überlieferung in den Schriften aus Nag Hammadi I." *JAC* 15 (1972): 5–18.
Congourdeau, Marie-Hélène. "L'embryologie dans le Corpus hippocratique." Pages 19–30 in *Sur la manière don't l'embryon reçoit l'âme*. Edited by Luc Brisson. Paris: J. Vrin, 2012.
Conzelmann, Hans. *A Commentary on the Acts of the Apostles*. Translated by James Limburg et al. Hermeneia. Philadelphia: Fortress, 1987.
Cook, Arthur Bernard. *Zeus: A Study in Ancient Religion*. vol. II, Part 1. Cambridge: Cambridge University Press, 1925.
Costantini, Leonard. "Dynamics of Laughter: The Costumes of Menippus and Mithrobarzanes in Lucian's *Necyomantia*." *American Journal of Philology* 140, no. 1 (2019): 101–22.
Côté, Dominique. "La fonction littéraire de Simon le Magicien dans les *Pseudo-Clémentines*." *Laval Théologique et Philosophique* 57, no. 3 (2001): 513–23.
Côté, Dominique. *Le thème de l'opposition entre Pierre et Simon dans les Pseudo-Clémentines*. Paris: Institute for Augustinian Studies, 2001.
Crowfoot, J. W. *The Buildings at Samaria Samaria-Sebaste I*. London: Palestine Exploration Fund, 1942.

Dalgaard, Kaspar. "Peter and Simon in the Acts of Peter: Between Magic and Miracles." Pages 169–80 in *Studies on Magic and Divination in the Biblical World*. Edited by Helen R. Jacobus, et al. Piscataway: Gorgias Press, 2019.

Davison, J. A. "Stesichorus and Helen." Pages 196–225 in *From Archilochus to Pindar: Papers on Greek Literature of the Archaic Period*. Edited by J. A. Davison. London: St. Martin's Press, 1968.

Dawson, David. *Allegorical Readers and Cultural Revision in Ancient Alexandria*. Berkeley: University of California Press, 1992.

DeConick, April D. *The Gnostic New Age: How a Countercultural Spirituality Revolutionized Religion from Antiquity to Today*. New York: Columbia University Press, 2016.

de Jáuregui, Miguel Herrero. "Ancient Conversion between Philosophy and Religion: Conversion and Its Literature." Pages 135–50 in *Anthropology in the New Testament and its Ancient Context. Papers from the EABS Meeting in Piliscsaba/Budapest*. Edited by Michael Labahn and Outi Lehtipuu. Leuven: Peeters, 2010.

De Jonge, Albert. *Traditions of the Magi: Zoroastrianism in Greek and Latin Literature*. Leiden: Brill, 1997.

den Dulk, Matthijs. *Between Jews and Heretics: Refiguring Justin Martyr's Dialogue with Trypho*. London: Routledge, 2018.

den Dulk, Matthijs. "Justin Martyr and the Authorship of the Earliest Anti-Heretical Treatise." *VC* 72 (2018): 471–83.

Derrett, J. Duncan. "Simon Magus Acts 8 9–24" *ZNW* 73 (1982): 52–68.

Detienne, Marcel. "La légende pythagoricienne d'Hélène." *Revue de l'Histoire des Religions* 152 (1957): 129–52.

DeVore, David J. "Genre and Eusebius' *Ecclesiastical History*: Towards a Focused Debate." Pages 19–50 in *Eusebius of Caesarea: Traditions and Innovations*. Edited by Aaron Johnson and Jeremy Schott. Washington, DC: Center for Hellenic Studies, 2013.

De Vos, C. "Popular Graeco-Roman Responses to Christianity." Pages 869–89 in *The Early Christian World*. Edited by P. F. Esler. London: Routledge, 2000.

Dickie, Matthew W. *Magic and Magicians in the Greco-Roman World*. London: Routledge, 2001.

Digeser, Elizabeth DePalma. *A Threat to Public Piety*. Ithaca: Cornell University Press, 2012.

Dillon, John. *The Middle Platonists: 80 BC to AD 220*. 2nd ed. Ithaca: Cornell University Press, 1996.

Dillon, John. "Xenocrates' Metaphysics: Fr. 15 Heinze R3-examined." *Ancient Philosophy* 5 (1986): 47–52.

Dixon, Edward. "Descending Spirit and Descending Gods: A 'Greek' Interpretation of the Spirit's 'Descent as a Dove' in Mark 1:10." *JBL* 128 (2009): 759–80.

Drijvers, H. J. W. "Adam and the True Prophet." Pages 314–23 in *History and Religion in Late Antique Syria*. Aldershot: Brookfield, 1994.

Droge, Arthur. "The Apologetic Dimensions of the *Ecclesiastical History*." Pages 492–509 in *Eusebius, Christianity, and Judaism*. Edited by Harold W. Attridge and Gohei Hata. Leiden: Brill, 1992.

Duncan, Patricia. *Novel Hermeneutics in the Greek Pseudo-Clementine Romance*. WUNT 395. Tübingen: Mohr Siebeck, 2017.

Dunn, Geoffrey D. *Tertullian*. London: Routledge, 2004.

Dunn, J. D. G. *The Acts of the Apostles*. Valley Forge: Trinity Press, 1996.

Eastman, David L. "Simon the Anti-Christ? The *Magos* as *Christos* in Early Christian Literature." *Journal of Early Christian History* 6, no. 1 (2016): 116–36.
Eastman, David L. "Simon the Composite Sorcerer," *NTS* 68 (2002): 407–17.
Edmonds, Radcliffe. *Drawing Down the Moon: Magic in the Ancient Greco-Roman World*. Princeton: Princeton University Press, 2019.
Edmunds, Lowell. *Stealing Helen: The Myth of the Abducted Wife in Comparative Perspective*. Princeton: Princeton University Press, 2016.
Edwards, Mark J. "One Origen or Two? The *Status Quaestionis*." *Symbolae Osloenses* 89, no. 1 (2015): 81–103.
Edwards, Mark J. "On the Platonic Schooling of Justin Martyr." *JTS* 42 (1991): 17–34.
Edwards, Mark J. "Simon Magus." In *The Oxford Dictionary of the Christian Church*. Edited by Andrew Louth, 4th ed. Oxford: Oxford University Press, 2022. Accessed April 7, 2023. https://www.oxfordreference.com/view/10.1093/acref/9780199642465.001.0001/acref-9780199642465-e-6651.
Edwards, Mark J. "Simon Magus, the Bad Samaritan." Pages 69–91 in *Portraits: Biographical Representations in the Greek and Latin Literature of the Roman Empire*. Edited by Mark Edwards and Simon Swain. Oxford: Clarendon, 1997.
Edwards, Mark J. "Some Early Christian Immoralities." *Ancient Society* 23 (1992): 71–82.
Elmer, Ian J. "The Pauline Letters as Community Documents." Pages 37–53 in *Collecting Early Christian Letters*. Edited by Bronwen Neil and Pauline Allen. Cambridge: Cambridge University Press, 2015.
Engberg-Pedersen, Troels. *Cosmology and Self in the Apostle Paul: The Material Spirit*. Oxford: Oxford University Press, 2010.
Erbes, Carl. "Petrus nicht in Rom sondern in Jerusalem gestorben." *Zeitschrift für Kirchengeschichte* 22 (1901): 1–47.
Fabien, Patrick. "La conversion de Simon le magician Ac 8,4–25." *Bib* 91 (2010): 210–40.
Faivre, Alexandre and Cécile Faivre. "Rhétorique, histoire et débats théologiques: A propos d'un ouvrage sur Simon 'le magicien.'" *Revue des Sciences Religieuses* 73, no. 3 (1999): 293–313.
Fears, J. R. "Jupiter and Roman Imperial Ideology." Pages 3–141 in *ANRW* I.17.1. Edited by Wolfgang Haase. Berlin: de Gruyter, 1981.
Ferreiro, Alberto. *Simon Magus in Patristic, Medieval and Early Modern Traditions*. Leiden: Brill, 2005.
Fitzmyer, Joseph. *The Acts of the Apostles: A New Translation with Introduction and Commentary*. AB 31. New York: Doubleday, 1998.
Flusser, D. "The Great Goddess of Samaria." *Israel Exploration Journal* 25, no. 1 (1975): 13–20.
Foerster, Werner. *Gnosis: A Selection of Gnostic Texts*. Edited by R. McL. Wilson. 2 vols. Oxford: Clarendon, 1972.
Fossum, Jarl. *The Name of God and the Angel of the Lord: Samaritan and Jewish Concepts of Intermediation and the Origin of Gnosticism*. WUNT 36. Tübingen: Mohr Siebeck, 1985.
Fossum, Jarl. "Samaritan Sects and Movements." Pages 293–389 in *The Samaritans*. Edited by Alan D. Crown. Tübingen: Mohr Siebeck, 1989.
Fossum, Jarl. "The Simonian Sophia Myth." *Studi e Materiali di Storia delle Religioni* 53 (1987): 185–97.
Foster, Paul and Sara Parvis, ed. *Irenaeus: Life, Scripture, and Legacy*. Minneapolis: Fortress, 2012.
Frankfurter, David. "Ancient Magic in a New Key: Refining an Exotic Discipline in the History of Religions." Pages 3–20 in *Guide to the Study of Ancient Magic*. Edited by David Frankfurter. Leiden: Brill, 2019.

Frankfurter, David. "Ritual Expertise in Roman Egypt and the Problem of the Category 'Magician.'" Pages 115–35 in *Envisioning Magic: A Princeton Seminar and Symposium*. Edited by H. Kippenberg and Peter Schäfer. Leiden: Brill, 1997.

Frenschkowski, Marco. *Magie im antiken Christentum: Eine Studie zur Alten Kirche und ihrem Umfeld*. Stuttgart: Anton Hiersemann, 2016.

Frickel, Josef. *Die "Apophasis Megale" in Hippolyts Refutatio VI 9–18: Eine Paraphrase zur Apophasis Simons*. Rome: Pontifical Institute of Oriental Studies, 1968.

Frickel, Josef. *Hellenistische Erlösung in christlicher Deutung. Die gnostische Naassenerschrift: Quellenkritische Studien, Strukturanalyse, Schichtenscheidung, Rekonstruktion der Anthropos-Lehrschrift*. Leiden: Brill, 1984.

Frickel, Josef. "Hippolyt von Rom: Refutation, Buch X." Pages 217–44 in *Überlieferungsgeschichtliche Untersuchungen*. Edited by Franz Paschke. Berlin: Akademie, 1981.

Gamble, Harry Y. *Books and Readers: A History of Early Christian Texts*. New Haven: Yale University Press, 1995.

Gantz, Timothy. *Early Greek Myth: A Guide to Literary and Artistic Sources*. 2 vols. Baltimore: Johns Hopkins University Press, 1993.

Garrett, Susan. *The Demise of the Devil: Magic and the Demonic in Luke's Writings*. Minneapolis: Fortress, 1989.

Georges, Tobias. "Justin's School in Rome—Reflections on Early Christian 'Schools.'" *ZAC* 16 (2012): 75–87.

Gero, Stephen. "With Walter Bauer on the Tigris: Encratite Orthodoxy and Libertine Heresy in Syro-Mesopotamian Christianity." Pages 287–307 in *Nag Hammadi Gnosticism and Early Christianity*. Edited by C. W. Hedrick and R. Hodgson. Peabody: Hendrickson, 1986.

Gilhus, Ingvild Saelid. "The Construction of Heresy and the Creation of Identity: Epiphanius of Salamis and His Medicine-chest against Heretics." *Numen* 62 (2015): 152–68.

Gödecke, Monika. *Geschichte als Mythos. Eusebs "Kirchengeschichte"*. Frankfurt am Main: Peter Lang, 1987.

Goedendorp, Pieter F. "If you are the Standing One, I also will Worship you Pseudo-Clementine Homilies II 24.6." Pages 61–77 in *Proceedings of the First International Congress of the Société d'Études Samaritaines*. Edited by Abraham Tal and Moshe Florentin. Tel Aviv: Chaim Rosenberg, 1991.

Graf, Fritz. *Magic in the Ancient World*. Translated by Franklin Philip. Cambridge, MA: Harvard University Press, 1997.

Grafton, Anthony and Megan Williams. *Christianity and the Transformation of the Book: Origen, Eusebius, and the Library of Caesarea*. Cambridge, MA: Harvard University Press, 2006.

Grant, Michael. *Greek and Roman Historians: Information and Misinformation* London: Routledge, 1995.

Grant, Robert. "The Case Against Eusebius: Or, Did the Father of Church History Write History." *Studia Patristica* 12 (1971): 412–21.

Grant, Robert. *Eusebius as Church Historian*. Oxford: Oxford University Press, 1980.

Grau, Sergi. "Conversion to Philosophy in Diogenes Laertius: Forms and Functions." Pages 219–37 in *Religious and Philosophical Conversion in Ancient Mediterranean Traditions*. Edited by Athanasios Despotis and Hermut Löhr. Leiden: Brill, 2022.

Gregory, Andrew. "Among the Apologists? Reading Acts with Justin Martyr." Pages 169–86 in *Engaging Early Christian History: Reading Acts in the Second Century*. Edited by Rubén R. Dupertuis and Todd Penner. Durham: Acumen, 2013.

Gregory, Andrew. *The Reception of Luke and Acts in the Period before Irenaeus: Looking for Luke in the Second Century*. WUNT II/169. Tübingen: Mohr Siebeck, 2003.
Haar, Stephen. *Simon Magus: The First Gnostic?* BZNW 119. Berlin: Walter de Gruyter, 2003.
Haenchen, Ernst. *The Acts of the Apostles: A Commentary*. Oxford: Blackwell, 1971.
Haenchen, Ernst. "Gab es eine vorchristliche Gnosis?" *ZTK* 49 (1952): 316–49.
Haenchen, Ernst. "Simon Magus in der Apostelgeschichte." Pages 267–80 in *Gnosis und Neues Testament: Studien aus Religionswissenschaft und Theologie*. Edited by Karl-Wolfgang Tröger. Berlin: Gütersloh, 1973.
Hall, Bruce W. *Samaritan Religion from John Hyrcanus to Baba Rabba*. Sydney: Mandelbaum Trust, 1987.
Hanegraaff, Wouter, ed. *Dictionary of Gnosis and Western Esotericism*. Leiden: Brill, 2006.
Hanig, Roman. "Simon Magus in den Petrusakten und die Theodotianer." *Studia Patristica* 31 (1997): 112–20.
Hanson, Ann Ellis and Monica H. Green. "Soranus of Ephesus: *Methodicorum princeps*." Pages 969–1073 in *ANRW* II.37.1. Edited by Wolfgang Haase. Berlin: de Gruyter, 1996.
Hanstein, Sebastian. *Studien zur Redaktionellen Gestaltung des Sonderguts in der Schrift, "Widerlegung aller Häresien" unter besonderer Berücksichtigung der Darstellung der sog. Peraten*. Rheinischen Friedrich-Wilhelms-Universität Bonn, 2020.
Harrill, J. Albert. *The Manumission of Slaves in Early Christianity*. Tübingen: Mohr Siebeck, 1995.
Harth, Dietrich. "The Invention of Cultural Memory." Pages 85–96 in *A Companion to Cultural Memory Studies: An International and Interdisciplinary Handbook*. Edited by Astrid Erll and Ansgar Nünnung. Berlin: de Gruyter, 2008.
Hartog, Paul. "Patristic Departures from Matthew 10,23 with 'Flight' Connections in Origen." Pages 831–42 in *Origeniana Undecima: Origen and Origenism in the History of Western Thought. Papers of the 11th International Origen Congress, Aarhus University, 26-31 August 2013*. Edited by Anders-Christian Jacobsen. Leuven: Petters, 2016.
Heine, Ronald E. *Origen: Scholarship in Service of the Church*. Oxford: Oxford University Press, 2011.
Heintz, Florent. *Simon "Le magicien": Actes 8, 5–25 et l'accusation de magie contre les prophètes thaumaturges dans l'antiquité*. Paris: Gabalda, 1997.
Heyne, Thomas. "The Devious Eusebius? An Evaluation of the *Ecclesiastical History* and Its Critics." *Studia Patristica* 46 (2010): 325–31.
Hill, Charles E. "The *Epistula Apostolorum*: An Asian Tract from the Time of Polycarp." *JECS* 7, no. 1 (1999): 1–53.
Hill, Charles E. *The Johannine Corpus in the Early Church*. Oxford: Oxford University Press, 2004.
Hjelm, Ingrid. "Simon Magus in Patristic and Samaritan Sources: The Growth of a Tradition." Pages 263–84 in *Die Samaritaner und die Bibel / Samaritans and the Bible: Historische und literarische Wechselwirkungen zwischen biblischen und samaritanischen Traditionen*. Edited by Jörg Frey, Ursula Schattner-Rieser, and Konrad Schmid. Berlin: de Gruyter, 2012.
Hollerich, Michael J. *Making Christian History: Eusebius of Caesarea and His Readers*. Berkeley: University of California Press, 2021.
Hopfner, T. "Die Kindermedien in den griechisch-ägyptischen Zauberpapyri." Pages 65–74 in *Recueil d'études dédiées à la mémoire de N. P. Kondakov*. Prague: Kondakov Seminar, 1926.

Horbury, William. *The Jewish War Under Trajan and Hadrian*. Cambridge: Cambridge University Press, 2014.

Horsley, G. H. R. *New Documents Illustrating Early Christianity*. North Ryde: Macquarie University, 1983.

Horsley, G. H. R. *New Documents Illustrating Early Christianity: A Review of the Greek Inscriptions and Papyri Published in 1976*. Sydney: Macquarie University, 1981.

Hovhanessian, Vahan. *Third Corinthians: Reclaiming Paul for Christian Orthodoxy*. Frankfurt am Main: Peter Lang, 2000.

Hübner, Reinhard M. *Der Paradox Eine: Antignostischer Monarchianismus im zweiten Jahrhundert*. Leiden: Brill, 1999.

Hughes, Bettany. *Helen of Troy: Goddess, Princess, Whore*. London: Pimlico, 2005.

Hurtado, Larry. *How on Earth did Jesus Become a God?: Historical Questions about Earliest Devotion to Jesus*. Grand Rapids: Eerdmans, 2005.

Isser, Stanley. *The Dositheans: A Samaritan Sect in Late Antiquity*. Studies in Judaism in Late Antiquity 17. Leiden: Brill, 1976.

Isser, Stanley. "Dositheus, Jesus, and a Moses Aretalogy." Pages 167–89 in *Christianity, Judaism and Other Greco-Roman Cults: Studies for Morton Smith at Sixty Part Four*. Edited by Jacob Neusner. Leiden: Brill, 1975.

Jacobs, Andrew. "Epiphanius's Library." Pages 133–52 in *From Roman to Early Christian Cyprus: Studies in Religion and Archaeology*. Edited by Laura Nasrallah, AnneMarie Luijendijk, and Charlambos Bakirtzis. Tübingen: Mohr Siebeck, 2020.

Jacobs, Andrew. *Epiphanius of Cyprus: A Cultural Biography of Late Antiquity*. Berkeley: University of California Press, 2016.

Johannessen, Hazel. *The Demonic in the Political Thought of Eusebius of Caesarea*. Oxford: Oxford University Press, 2016.

Johnson, Aaron P. *Eusebius*. London: I.B. Taurus, 2014.

Johnson, Steven R. "Hippolytus's *Refutatio* and the *Gospel of Thomas*." *JECS* 18, no. 2 (2010): 305–26.

Johnston, Sarah Iles. *Ancient Greek Divination*. Malden: Wiley Blackwell, 2008.

Johnston, Steve. "La Correspondance apocryphe entre Paul et les Corinthiens: Problèmes relies à l'identification des adversaires." Pages 187–230 in *Colloque international. "L'évangile selon Thomas et les textes de Nag Hammadi." Québec, 29–31 mai 2003*. Edited by Louis Painchaud and Paul-Hubert Poirier. Bibliothèque Copte de Nag Hammadi: Études 8. Québec: Presses de l'Université Laval, 2007.

Jonas, Hans. *The Gnostic Religion: The Message of the Alien God and the Beginnings of Christianity*. Boston: Beacon, 1958.

Jones, F. Stanley. *Pseudoclementina Elchasaiticaque inter Judaeochristiana: Collected Stories*. Leuven: Peeters, 2012.

Kahn, Charles H. *Pythagoras and the Pythagoreans: A Brief History*. Indianapolis: Hackett, 2001.

Kalvesmaki, Joel. *The Theology of Arithmetic: Number Symbolism in Platonism and Early Christianity*. Washington, DC: Center for Hellenic Studies, 2013.

Kapparis, Konstantinos K. "The Terminology of Prostitution in the Ancient Greek World." Pages 222–55 in *Greek Prostitution in the Ancient Mediterranean 800 BCE-200 CE*. Edited by Allison Glazebrook and Madeleine Mary Henry. Madison: University of Wisconsin Press, 2011.

Keener, Craig. *Acts: An Exegetical Commentary*. 4 vols. Grand Rapids: Baker Academic, 2013.

Kelley, Nicole. *Knowledge and Religious Authority in the Pseudo-Clementines: Situation the Recognitions in Fourth Century Syria*. WUNT II/213. Tübingen: Mohr Siebeck, 2006.
Kemboly, Mpay. *The Question of Evil in Ancient Egypt*. London: Golden House, 2010.
Kettler, Franz Heinrich. "Origenes, Ammonius Sakkas und Porphyrius." Pages 322–8 in *Kerygma und Logos*. Edited by Adolf Martin Ritter. Göttingen: Vandenhoeck & Ruprecht, 1979.
Kim, Young Richard. *Epiphanius of Cyprus: Imagining an Orthodox World*. Ann Arbor: University of Michigan, 2015.
King, Karen L. "Social and Theological Effects of Heresiological Discourse." Pages 28–49 in *Heresy and Identity in Late Antiquity*. Edited by Eduard Iricinschi and Holger M. Zellentin. Tübingen: Mohr Siebeck, 2008.
King, Karen L. *What is Gnosticism?* Cambridge, MA: Belknap Press, 2003.
Kippenberg, Hans G. *Garizim und Synagoge: Traditionsgeschichtliche Untersuchungen zur Samaritanischen Religion der aramäischen Periode*. Berlin: de Gruyter, 1971.
Klauck, Hans-Josef. *The Apocryphal Acts of the Apostles: An Introduction*. Translated by Brian McNeil. Waco: Baylor University Press, 2008.
Klauck, Hans-Josef. *Magic and Paganism in Early Christianity: The World of the Acts of the Apostles*. Translated by Brian McNeil. Minneapolis: Fortress, 2003.
Klijn, A. F. J. "The Apocryphal Correspondence Between Paul and the Corinthians." *VC* 17 (1963): 2–23.
Klinghardt, Matthias. *The Oldest Gospel and the Formation of the Canonical Gospels*. 2 vols. Leuven: Peeters, 2021.
Knight, Jonathan. "The Origin and Significance of the Angelomorphic Christology in *The Ascension of Isaiah*." *JTS* 63 (2012): 66–105.
Knoppers Gary, N. *Jews and Samaritans: The Origins and History of Their Early Relations*. Oxford: Oxford University Press, 2013.
Knust, Jennifer. *Abandoned to Lust: The Politics of Sexual Slander in Early Christian Discourse*. New York: Columbia University Press, 2006.
Kuefler, Mathew. *The Manly Eunuch*. Chicago: University of Chicago Press, 2001.
Lahe, Jaan. *Gnosis und Judentum: Alttestamentliche und jüdische Motive in der gnostischen Literatur und das Ursprungsproblem der Gnosis*. Nag Hammadi and Manichean Studies 75. Leiden: Brill, 2012.
Lamberton, Robert. *Homer the Theologian*. Berkeley: University of California Press, 1989.
Lampe, Peter. *From Paul to Valentinus: Christians at Rome in the First Two Centuries*. Edited by Marshall Johnson. Translated by Michael Steinhauser. Minneapolis: Fortress, 2003.
Lancellotti, Maria Grazia. *The Naassenes: A Gnostic Identity among Judaism, Christianity, Classical and Ancient Near Eastern Traditions*. Münster: Ugarit-Verlag, 2000.
Lapham, F. *Peter: The Myth the Man and the Writings*. JSNTSup 239. Sheffield: Sheffield Academic Press, 2003.
Lashier, Jackson. *Irenaeus and the Trinity*. VCSup 127. Leiden: Brill, 2014.
Le Boulluec, Alain. *La notion d'hérésie dans la littérature grecque II-II siècles*. 2 vols. Paris: Augustinian Studies, 1985.
Le Boulluec, Alain. *The Notion of Heresy in Greek Literature in the Second and Third Centuries*. Edited by David Lincicum and Nicholas Moore. Translated by A. K. M. Adam et al. Oxford: Oxford University Press, 2022.
Leemans, Johan. "The Idea of 'Flight for Persecution' in the Alexandrian Tradition from Clement to Athanasius." Pages 901–11 in *Origeniana Octava: Origen and the*

Alexandrian Tradition. Papers of the 8th International Origen Congress, Pisa, 27-31 August 2001. Edited by L. Perrone. Leuven: Peeters, 2003.

Lewis, Nicola Denzey. "Women and Independent Religious Specialists in Second-Century Rome." Pages 21–38 in *Women and Knowledge in Early Christianity*. Edited by Ulla Tervahauta, et al. Leiden: Brill, 2017.

Lieu, Judith M. "The Multiple Personalities of Celsus' Jew." Pages 360–85 in *Celsus in His World: Philosophy, Polemic, and Religion in the Second Century*. Edited by James Carleton Paget and Simon Gathercole. Cambridge: Cambridge University Press, 2021.

Lindsay, Jack. *Helen of Troy: Woman and Goddess*. London: Constable, 1974.

Lipsius, Richard Adelbert. *Die Quellen der ältesten Ketzergeschichte neu untersucht*. Leipzig: Johann Ambrosius Barth, 1875.

Lipsius, Richard Adelbert. *Zur Quellenkritik des Epiphanios*. Vienna: Braumüller, 1865.

Litwa, M. David. *Becoming Divine: An Introduction to Deification in Western Culture*. Eugene: Cascade, 2013.

Litwa, M. David. *Carpocrates, Marcellina, and Epiphanes: Three Early Christian Teachers of Alexandria and Rome*. London: Routledge, 2022.

Litwa, M. David. *Desiring Divinity: Self-deification in Ancient Jewish and Christian Mythmaking*. Oxford: Oxford University Press, 2016.

Litwa, M. David. *Earliest Christianity in Alexandria*. Cambridge: Cambridge University Press, 2024.

Litwa, M. David. *Found Christianities: Remaking the World of the Second Century CE*. London: T&T Clark, 2022.

Litwa, M. David. "Gnostic Self-deification: The Case of Simon of Samaria." *Gnosis* 1 (2016): 157–76.

Litwa, M. David. *How the Gospels Became History: Jesus and Mediterranean Myths*. New Haven: Yale University Press, 2019.

Litwa, M. David. *Iesus Deus: The Early Christian Depiction of Jesus as a Mediterranean God*. Minneapolis: Fortress, 2014.

Litwa, M. David. "Literary Eyewitnesses: The Appeal to an Eyewitness in John and Contemporaneous Literature." *NTS* 64, no. 3 (2018): 343–61.

Litwa, M. David. *The Naassenes: Exploring an Early Christian Identity*. London: Routledge, 2023.

Litwa, M. David. *Posthuman Transformation in Ancient Mediterranean Thought: Becoming Angels and Demons*. Cambridge: Cambridge University Press, 2021.

Litwa, M. David. "The So-called Stratiotics and Phibionites: Three Notes on the 'Gnostics' of Epiphanius, *Panarion* 26." *VC* 76 (2022): 73–93.

Litwa, M. David. *We Are Being Transformed: Deification in Paul's Soteriology*. Berlin: de Gruyter, 2012.

Logan, Alastair H. B. "Magi and Visionaries in Gnosticism." Pages 27–44 in *Portraits of Spiritual Authority: Religious Power in Early Christianity, Byzantium and the Christian Orient*. Edited by Jan Willem Drijvers and John W. Watt. Leiden: Brill, 1999.

Löhr, Winrich Alfried. *Basilides und seine Schule: Eine Studie zur Theologie- und Kirchengeschichte des zweiten Jahrhunderts*. WUNT 83. Tübingen: Mohr Siebeck, 1996.

Lona, Horatio. *Die 'Wahre Lehre' des Kelsos übersetzt und erklärt*. Freiburg: Herder, 2005.

Lookadoo, Jonathan. "The Date and Authenticity of the Ignatian Letters: An Outline of Recent Discussions." *Currents in Biblical Research* 19, no. 1 (2020): 88–114.

Louth, A. "The Date of Eusebius' *Historia Ecclesiastica*." *JTS* 41 (1990): 111–23.

Lüdemann, Gerd. "The Acts of the Apostles and the Beginnings of Simonian Gnosis." *NTS* 33 (1987): 420–6.

Lüdemann, Gerd. *The Acts of the Apostles: What Really Happened in the Earliest Days of the Church*. Amherst: Prometheus, 2005.

Lüdemann, Gerd. "Die Apostelgeschichte und die Anfänge der simonianischen Gnosis." Pages 7–20 in *Studien zur Gnosis*. Edited by Gerd Lüdemann. Frankfurt am Main: Peter Lang, 1999.

Lüdemann, Gerd. *Early Christianity According to the Traditions in Acts: A Commentary*. Translated by John Bowden. London: SCM Press, 1989.

Lüdemann, Gerd. *Untersuchungen zur simonianischen Gnosis*. Göttingen: Vandenhoeck & Ruprecht, 1975.

Luttikhuizen, Gerard. "The Apocryphal Correspondence with the Corinthians and the Acts of Paul." Pages 75–91 in *The Apocryphal Acts of Paul*. Edited by Jan Bremmer. Kampen: Kok Pharos, 1996.

Lyman, Rebecca. "Origen of Alexandria." *ExpTim* 120, no. 9 (2009): 417–27.

Lyman, Rebecca. "The Politics of Passing: Justin Martyr's Conversion as a Problem of 'Hellenization.'" Pages 34–54 in *Conversion in Late Antiquity and the Early Middle Ages: Seeing and Believing*. Edited by K. Mills and A. Grafton. Rochester: University of Rochester Press, 2003.

Macrae, Duncan E. "Simon the God: Imagining the Other in Second-century Christianity." Pages 64–86 in *Geneses: A Comparative Study of the Historiographies of the Rise of Christianity, Rabbinic Judaism, and Islam*. Edited by John Tolan. Abingdon: Routledge, 2019.

Magen, Yitzhak. *Flavia Neapolis Shechem in the Roman Period*. 2 vols. Jerusalem: Israel Antiquities Authority, 2009.

Magness, Jodi. "The Cults of Isis and Kore at Samaria-Sebaste in the Hellenistic and Roman Periods," *HTR* 94, no. 2 (2001): 157–77.

Malina, Bruce and John Pilch. *Social-Science Commentary on the Book of Acts*. Minneapolis: Fortress, 2008.

Männlein-Robert, Irmgard. "Eudoros von Alexandrien." Pages 555–62 in *Die Philosophie der Antike Band 5/1. Philosophie der Kaiserzeit und der Spätantike*. Edited by Christoph Riedweg, Christoph Horn, and Dietmar Wyrwa. Basel: Schwabe, 2018.

Mansfeld, Jaap. *Heresiography in Context: Hippolytus's Elenchus as a Source for Greek Philosophy*. Leiden: Brill, 1992.

Mansfeld, Jaap and David Runia, eds. *Aëtiana V: An Edition of the Reconstructed Text of the Placita with a Commentary and a Collection of Related Texts. Part 4: English Translation, Bibliography, Indices*. Leiden: Brill, 2020.

Marguerat, D. "Magic and Miracle in the Acts of the Apostles." Pages 100–24 in *Magic in the Biblical World: From the Rod of Aaron to the Ring of Solomon*. Edited by T. Klutz. London: Bloomsbury, 2003.

Markschies, Christoph. *Christian Theology and its Institutions in the Early Roman Empire: Prolegomena to a History of Early Christian Theology*. Waco: Baylor University Press, 2015.

Markschies, Christoph. "Genesis 1 and the Beginnings of Gnosticism." *ZAC* 26, no. 1 (2022): 25–44.

Markschies, Christoph. *Gnosis: An Introduction*. Translated by John Bowden. London: T&T Clark, 2003.

Markschies, Christoph. "Kastration und Magenprobleme? Einige neue Blicke auf das asketische Leben des Origenes." Pages 15–34 in *Origenes und sein Erbe: Gesammelte Studien*. Berlin: de Gruyter, 2007.

Mason, Anita. *The Illusionist*. Abacus: Sphere Books, 1983.

Mason, Steve. *Josephus and the New Testament*. 2nd ed. Peabody: Hendrickson, 2003.
Mason, Steve. "Was Josephus a Source for Luke-Acts?" Pages 199–246 in *On Using Sources in Graeco-Roman, Jewish and Early Christian Literature in Honor of Joseph Verheyden*. Edited by John S. Kloppenborg, Geert Roskam, and Stefan Schorn. Leuven: Peeters, 2022.
Matthews, C. R. "The Acts of Peter and Luke's Intertextual Heritage." *Semeia* 80 (1997): 207–22.
Matthews, C. R. *Philip: Apostle and Evangelist: Configurations of a Tradition*. Leiden: Brill, 2002.
McGuckin, John Anthony. "Caesarea Maritima as Origen Knew It." Pages 3–25 in *Origeniana Quinta: Historia-Text and Method-Biblica-Philosophica-Theologica-Origenism and Later Developments*. Edited by Robert J. Daly. Leuven: Peeters, 1992.
Meeks, Wayne. "The Divine Agent and his Counterfeit in Philo and the Fourth Gospel." Pages 43–67 in *Aspects of Religious Propaganda in Judaism and Early Christianity*. Edited by Elisabeth Schüssler Fiorenza. Notre Dame: University of Notre Dame Press, 1976.
Meeks, Wayne. "Simon Magus in Recent Research." *Religious Studies Review* 3 (1977): 137–42.
Mendels, Doron. *The Media Revolution of Early Christianity: An Essay on Eusebius's Ecclesiastical History*. Grand Rapids: Eerdmans, 1999.
Mheallaigh, Karen ní. *The Moon in the Greek and Roman Imagination: Myth, Literature, Science and Philosophy*. Cambridge: Cambridge University Press, 2020.
Minov, Sergey. "Noah and the Flood in Gnosticism." Pages 215–36 in *Noah and His Books*. Edited by Michael E. Stone. Atlanta: SBL Press, 2009.
Montserrat Torrents, Josef. "El Pensamiento de Nuestro Gran Poder VI 36,1–48.15." Pages 113–28 in *Textos gnósticos: Biblioteca de Nag Hammadi. III Apocalipsis y otros escritos*. Madrid: Trotta, 2000.
Montserrat Torrents, Josef. *Los Gnósticos: Introducciones, tradución y notas*. Madrid: Gredos, 1983.
Moreland, Milton. "Jerusalem Destroyed: The Setting of Acts." Pages 17–44 in *Engaging Early Christian History: Reading Acts in the Second Century*. Edited by Rubén R. Dupertuis and Todd Penner. Durham: Acumen, 2013.
Moss, Candida. *Ancient Christian Martyrdom: Diverse Practices, Theologies, and Traditions*. New Haven: Yale University Press, 2012.
Müller, Detlef G. "Die Epistula Apostolorum." Pages 1062–92 in *Antike christliche Apokryphen in deutscher Übersetzung I. Band Evangelien und Verwandtes. Teilband 2*. Edited by Christoph Markschies and Jens Schröter. Tübingen: Mohr Siebeck, 2012.
Nautin, Pierre. *Hippolyte, Contre les hérésies*. Paris: Cerf, 1949.
Nautin, Pierre. *Origène: Sa vie et son oeuvre*. Paris: Beauchesne, 1977.
Niehoff, Maren. "A Jewish Critique of Christianity from Second-Century Alexandria: Revisiting the Jew Mentioned in *Contra Celsum*." *JECS* 21, no. 2 (2013): 151–75.
Nutton, Vivian. *Ancient Medicine*. 2nd ed. London: Routledge, 2013.
Ogden, Daniel. *Greek and Roman Necromancy*. Princeton: Princeton University Press, 2001.
Olson, Ken. "A Eusebian Reading of the *Testimonium Flavianum*." Pages 97–114 in *Traditions and Innovations*. Edited by Aaron Johnson and Jeremy Schott. Washington, DC: Center for Hellenic Studies, 2013.
Osborne, Catherine. *Rethinking Early Greek Philosophy: Hippolytus of Rome and the Presocratics*. London: Duckworth, 1987.

Patrich, Joseph. "Caesarea in the Time of Eusebius." Pages 1–24 in *Reconsidering Eusebius: Collected Papers on Literary, Historical, and Theological Issues*. VCSup 107. Leiden: Brill, 2011.

Pearson, Birger A. *Ancient Gnosticism: Traditions and Literature*. Minneapolis: Fortress, 2007.

Pearson, Birger A. "Eusebius and Gnosticism." Pages 291–310 in *Eusebius, Christianity, and Judaism*. Edited by Harold W. Attridge and Gohei Hata. Leiden: Brill, 1992.

Penner, Todd. *In Praise of Christian Origins: Stephen and the Hellenists in Lukan Apologetic Historiography*. Emory Studies in Early Christianity. London: T&T Clark, 2004.

Perkins, Judith. "Resurrection and Social Perspectives in the Apocryphal Acts of Peter and Acts of John." Pages 217–37 in *Ancient Fiction: The Matrix of Early Christian and Christian Narrative*. Edited by Jo-Ann A. Brant, et al. Atlanta: SBL Press, 2005.

Perkins, Judith. *The Suffering Self: Pain and Narrative Representation in the Early Christian Era*. London: Routledge, 1995.

Perkins, Pheme. *Gnosticism and the New Testament*. Minneapolis: Fortress, 1993.

Pervo, Richard. *Acts: A Commentary*. Hermeneia Minneapolis: Fortress, 2009.

Pervo, Richard. "Acts in the Suburbs of the Apologists." Pages 29–46 in *Contemporary Studies in Acts*. Edited by Thomas E. Phillips. Macon: Mercer University Press, 2009.

Pervo, Richard. *The Acts of Paul: A New Translation with Introduction and Commentary*. Cambridge: James Clarke & Co., 2014.

Pervo, Richard. *Dating Acts between the Evangelists and the Apologists*. Sonoma: Polebridge, 2006.

Pétrement, Simone. *A Separate God: The Christian Origins of Gnosticism*. New York: Harper & Row, 1990.

Phelan, James. *Experiencing Fiction: Judgments, Progressions, and the Rhetorical Theory of Narrative*. Columbus: The Ohio State University Press, 2007.

Pinch, Geraldine. *Egyptian Mythology: A Very Short Introduction*. Oxford: Oxford University Press, 2004.

Poucet, Jacques. "'Semo Sancus Dius Fidius.' Une première mise au point." Pages 53–68 in *Recherches de philologie et de linguistique*. Edited by M. Hofinger. Leuven: Leuven University Library, 1972.

Pouderon, Bernard. *La genèse du roman pseudo-Clémentin: Études littéraires et historiques*. Paris: Peeters, 2012.

Pouderon, Bernard. "La notice d'Hippolyte sur Simon: Cosmologie, anthropolgie et embryologie." Pages 49–72 in *Les Pères de l'église face à la science médicale de leur temps*. Edited by Véronique Boudon-Millot and Bernard Pouderon. Paris: Beauchesne, 2005.

Pouderon, Bernard. *Métamorphoses de Simon le magicien: Des Actes des apôtres au Faustbuch*. Paris: Beauchesne, 2019.

Poupon, Gérard. "Les 'Actes de Pierre' et leur remaniement." Pages 4363–83 in *ANRW* 2.25.6. Edited by W. Haase. Berlin: de Gruyter, 1988.

Pourkier, Aline. *L'hérésiologie chez Épiphane de Salamine*. Paris: Beauchesne, 1992.

Prince, Meredith. "Helen of Rome? Helen in Vergil's *Aeneid*." *Helios* 41, no. 2 (2014): 187–214.

Prinzivalli, Emanuela. "La genre historiographique de l'Histoire *ecclésiastique*." Pages 83–112 in *Eusèbe de Césarée: Histoire Ecclésiastique commentaire, tome I*. Edited by S. Morlet and L. Perrone. Paris: Cerf, 2012.

Pummer, Reinhard. *Early Christian Authors on Samaritans and Samaritanism: Texts, Translations and Commentary*. TSAJ 92. Tübingen: Mohr Siebeck, 2002.

Pummer, Reinhard. *Samaritans in Flavius Josephus.* Tübingen: Mohr Siebeck, 2009.
Quispel, Gilles. *Gnosis als Weltreligion.* Zürich: Origo, 1951.
Rahner, Hugo. *Greek Myths and Christian Mystery.* Translated by E. O. James. London: Burnes & Oates, 1963.
Ramelli, Ilaria. "Origen the Christian Middle/Neoplatonist: New Arguments for a Possible Identification." *Journal of Early Christian History* 1 (2011): 98–130.
Rapp, Claudia. *The Vita of Epiphanius: An Historical and Literary Study.* 2 vols. Dissertation. Oxford, 1991.
Rasimus, Tuomas. "Jezebel in Jewish and Christian Tradition." Pages 109–32 in *Women and Knowledge in Early Christianity.* Edited by Ulla Tervahauta, et al. Leiden: Brill, 2017.
Reed, Annette Yoshiko. *Jewish-Christianity and the History of Judaism.* TSAJ 171. Tübingen: Mohr Siebeck, 2018.
Remus, Harold. "Magic, Method, Madness." *MTSR* 11 (1999): 258–98.
Rius-Camps, Joseph and Jenny Read-Heimerdinger. *The Message of Acts in Codex Bezae: A Comparison with the Alexandrian Tradition.* 3 vols. Library of New Testament Studies 302. New York: T&T Clark, 2006.
Rosenberg, M. ed. *City Coins of Palestine: The Rosenberger Israel Collection.* Jerusalem: Rosenberg, 1977.
Rudolph, Kurt. *Gnosis: The Nature & History of Gnosticism.* Translated by Robert McLachlan Wilson. Edinburgh: T&T Clark, 1984.
Rudolph, Kurt. "Simon: Magus oder Gnosticus? Zum Stand der Debatte." *Theologische Rundschau* 42, no. 4 (1977): 279–359.
Runia, David T. *On the Creation of the Cosmos according to Moses: Introduction, Translation, and Commentary.* PACS 1. Leiden: Brill, 2001.
Runia, David T. "Witness or Participant? Philo and the Neoplatonic Tradition." Pages 36–56 in *The Neoplatonic Tradition: Jewish, Christian and Islamic Themes.* Edited by A. J. Vanderjagt and D. Pätzold. Cologne: Dinter, 1991.
Salles, A. "Simon le magician ou Marcion?" *VC* 12 (1958): 197–224.
Salles-Dabadie, J .M. A. *Recherches sur Simon le Mage: L'"Apophasis megalè.'* Paris: Gabalda, 1969.
Sandmel, Samuel. "Parallelomania." *JBL* 81 (1962): 1–13.
Sanzo, Joseph E. "Early Christianity." Pages 198–239 in *Guide to the Study of Ancient Magic.* Edited by David Frankfurter. Leiden: Brill, 2019.
Schenke, H.-M. "Das Verständnis unserer grossen Kraft, NHC VI,4." vol. 2, pages 483–93 in *Nag Hammadi Deutsch.* Edited by Hans-Martin Schenke, Hans-Gebhard Bethge, and Ursula Ulrike Kaiser. 2 vols. Berlin: de Gruyter, 2001.
Schenke, H.-M. "Die Bedeutung der Texte von Nag Hammadi für die moderne Gnosisforschung." Pages 13–76 in *Gnosis und Neues Testament: Studien aus Religionswissenschaft und Theologie.* Edited by K.-W. Tröger. Berlin: de Gruyter, 1973.
Schenke, H.-M. "Hauptprobleme der Gnosis: Gesichtpunkte zur einer neue Darstellung des Gesamtphänomens." Pages 160–73 in *Der Same Seths: Hans-Martin Schenkes Kleine Schriften zu Gnosis, Koptologie und Neuem Testament.* Edited by Gesine Schenke Robinson, Gesa Schenke, and Uwe-Karsten Plische. Leiden: Brill, 2012.
Schmithals, Walther. *The Office of Apostle in the Early Church.* Translated by John E. Steely. Nashville: Abingdon, 1969.
Scholten, Clemens. "Zum Herkunftsort des Simon Magus." *VC* 69 (2015): 534–41.
Schroeder, F. M. "Ammonius Saccas." Pages 493–526 in *ANRW* II.36.1. Edited by Wolfgang Haase. Berlin: de Gruyter, 1987.

Scibilia, Anna. "Supernatural Assistance in the Greek Magical Papyri: The Figure of the Parhedros." Pages 71–86 in *The Metamorphoses of Magic*. Edited by Jan N. Bremmer and Jan R. Veenstra. Leuven: Petters, 2003.

Secord, Jared. *Christian Intellectuals and the Roman Empire: From Justin Martyr to Origin*. University Park: Pennsylvania State University Press, 2020.

Segal, Arthur. *Temples and Sanctuaries in the Roman East: Religious Architecture in Syria, Iudaea/Palaestina and Provincia Arabia*. Oxford: Oxbow, 2013.

Sider, D. "The Blinding of Stesichorus." *Zeitschrift für klassischen Philologie* 117 (1989): 423–31.

Smith, Geoffrey S. *Guilt by Association: Heresy Catalogues in Early Christianity*. Oxford: Oxford University Press, 2014.

Smith, J. Z. *Drudgery Divine: On the Comparison of Early Christianities and the Religions of Late Antiquity*. Chicago: University of Chicago Press, 1990.

Smith, J. Z. "Trading Places." Pages 13–27 in *Ancient Magic and Ritual Power*. Edited by Marvin Meyer and Paul Mirecki. Religions in the Greco-Roman World 129. Leiden: Brill, 1995.

Smith, Morton. The Account of Simon Magus in Acts 8." vol. 2, pages 140–51 in *Studies in the Cult of Yahweh. New Testament, Early Christianity, and Magic*, Edited by Shaye J. D. Cohen. 2 vols. Leiden: Brill, 1996.

Smith, Morton. *Jesus the Magician*. New York: Harper & Row, 1978.

Snyder, H. Gregory. "Above the Baths of Myrtinus: Justin Martyr's 'School' in the City of Rome." *HTR* 100, no. 3 (2007): 335–62.

Snyder, Julia A. "Simon, Agrippa, and Other Antagonists in the Vercelli *Acts of Peter*." Pages 311–32 in *Gegenspieler: Zur Auseinandersetzung mit dem Gegner in frühjüdischer und frühchristlicher Literatur*. Edited by Michael Tilley and Ulrich Mell. Tübingen: Mohr Siebeck, 2019.

Spittler, Janet E. *Animals in the Apocryphal Acts of the Apostles: The Wild Kingdom of Early Christian Literature*. WUNT II/247. Tübingen: Mohr Siebeck, 2008.

Stark, Rodney and William Sims Bainbridge. *The Future of Religion: Secularization, Revival and Cult Formation*. Berkeley: University of California Press, 1985.

Sterling, Gregory. *Historiography and Self-definition. Josephus, Luke-Acts, and Apologetic Historiography*. Leiden: Brill, 1991.

Stratton, Kimberly B. "The Rhetoric of 'Magic' in Early Christian Discourse: Gender, Power and the Construction of 'Heresy.'" Pages 89–114 in *Mapping Gender in Ancient Religious Discourses*. Edited by Todd Penner and Caroline Vander Stichele. Leiden: Brill, 2007.

Strelan, Rick. *Strange Acts: Studies in the Cultural World of the Acts of the Apostles*. BZNW 126. Berlin: de Gruyter, 2004.

Talbert, Richard J. A. *Barrington Atlas of the Greek and Roman World*. Princeton: Princeton University Press, 2000.

Tardieu, Michel. "Épiphane contre les Gnostiques." *Tel Quel* 88 (1981): 64–91.

Temkin, Owsei. *Hippocrates in a World of Pagans and Christians*. Baltimore: Johns Hopkins University Press, 1991.

Theissen, Gerd. "Simon Magus—Die Entwicklung seines Bildes vom Charismatiker zum gnostischen Erlöser." Pages 407–32 in *Religionsgeschichte des neuen Testaments: Festschrift für Klaus Berger*. Edited by Axel von Dobbeler, Kurt Erlemann, and Roman Heiligenthal. Tübingen: A. Francke, 2000.

Thomas, Christine M. *The Acts of Peter, Gospel Literature and the Ancient Novel: Rewriting the Past*. Oxford: Oxford University Press, 2003.

Thomas, Christine M. "The 'Prehistory' of the *Acts of Peter*." Pages 39–62 in *The Apocryphal Acts of the Apostles: Harvard Divinity School Studies*. Edited by François Bovon, Ann Graham Brock, and Christopher R. Matthews. Cambridge, MA: Harvard University Press, 1999.

Thorsteinsson, Runar M. "By Philosophy Alone: Reassessing Justin's Christianity and His Turn from Platonism." *Early Christianity* 3 (2012): 492–517.

Townsend, John T. "The Date of Luke-Acts." Pages 47–62 in *Luke-Acts: New Perspectives from the Society of Biblical Literature Seminar*. Edited by Charles H. Talbert. New York: Crossroad, 1984.

Trapp, Michael. "Neopythagoreans." Pages 347–64 in *Greek and Roman Philosophy 100BC–200AD, Volume II*. Edited by Robert W. Sharples and Richard Sorabji. London: Institute of Classical Studies, 2007.

Tuzlak, Ayse. "The Magician and the Heretic." Pages 416–26 in *Magic and Ritual in the Ancient World*. Edited by Paul Mirecki and Marvin Meyer. Leiden: Brill, 2002.

Twelftree, G. H. "Jesus and Magic in Luke-Acts." Pages 46–58 in *Jesus and Paul: Global Perspectives in Honor of James D. G. Dunn. A Festschrift for his 70th Birthday*. Edited by B. J. Oropeza, D. K. Roberson, and D. C. Mohrmann. London: T&T Clark, 2009.

Twomey, Vincent. *Apostolikos Thronos: The Primacy of Rome as Reflected in the Church History of Eusebius and the Historico-apologetic Writings of Saint Athanasius the Great*. Münster: Aschendorff, 1982.

Tyson, Joseph B. *Marcion and Luke-Acts: A Defining Struggle*. Columbia: University of South Carolina Press, 2006.

Ulrich, Jörg. "Justin Martyr." Pages 51–66 in *In Defence of Christianity: Early Christian Apologists*. Edited by Jakob Engberg, et al. Frankfurt am Main: Peter Lang, 2014.

Ulrich, Jörg. "What Do We Know about Justin's 'School' in Rome?" *ZAC* 16 (2012): 62–74.

Urbano, Arthur P. "Difficulties in Writing the Life of Origen." Pages 118–35 in *The Oxford Handbook of Origen*. Edited by Ronald E. Heine and Karen Jo Torjesen. Oxford: Oxford University Press, 2022.

Vähäkangas, Päivi. "Christian Identity and Intra-Christian Polemics in the Pseudo-Clementines." Pages 217–38 in *Others and the Construction of Early Christian Identities*. Edited by Raimo Hakola, Nina Nikki, and Ulla Tervahauta. Helsinki: Finnish Exegetical Society, 2013.

Vähäkangas, Päivi. "'That Ill-formed Little Fox': Valentinians as the Enemy in Irenaeus's *Against Heresies*." Pages 83–104 in *The Faces of the Other: Religious Rivalry and Ethnic Encounters in the Later Roman World*. Edited by Maijastina Kahlos. Turnhout: Brepols, 2011.

Van den Broek, Roelof. "Simon Magus." Pages 1069–73 in *DGWE*. Edited by Wouter Hanegraaff. Leiden: Brill, 2007.

van der Horst, Pieter W. *Hellenism-Judaism-Christianity: Essays on Their Interaction*. Kampen: Kok Pharos, 1994.

van der Horst, Pieter W. *Japhet in the Tents of Shem: Studies on Jewish Hellenism in Antiquity*. Leuven: Peeters, 2002.

van Winden, J. C. M. *An Early Christian Philosopher: Justin Martyr's Dialogue with Trypho Chapters One to Nine: Introduction, Text, and Commentary*. Leiden: Brill, 1971.

Verdoner, Marie. *Narrated Reality: The Historia Ecclesiastica of Eusebius of Caesarea*. Frankfurt am Main: Peter Lang, 2011.

Verdoner, Marie. "Transgeneric Crosses. Apologetics in the Church History of Eusebius." Pages 75–92 in *Three Greek Apologists. Drei griechische Apologeten: Origen, Eusebius, and Athanasius*. Edited by Anders-Christian Jacobsen and Jörg Ulrich. Frankfurt am Main: Peter Lang, 2007.

Verheyden, Joseph. "The Demonization of the Opponent in Early Christian Literature. The Case of the Pseudo-Clementines." Pages 330–59 in *Religious Polemics in Context*. Edited by T. L. Hettema and A. van der Kooij. Leiden: Brill, 2005.

Verheyden, Joseph. "Epiphanius of Salamis on Beasts and Heretics: Some Introductory Comments." *Journal of Eastern Christian Studies* 60 (2008): 143–73.

Vidović, Goran. "Good Doggy, Bad Dog: Rivalry between Peter and Simon Magus in Early Christian Apocryphal Literature." *Philotheos* 16 (2016): 58–72.

Vincent, L.-H. "Le culte de Helene à Samarie." *RB* 45, no. 2 (1936): 221–32.

Visotzky, Burton L. "Overturning the Lamp." *Journal of Jewish Studies* 38, no. 1 (1987): 72–80.

von Haehling, Raban. "Zwei Fremde in Rom: Das Wunderduell des Petrus mit Simon Magus in den acta Petri." *RQ* 98 (2003): 47–71.

von Staden, Heinrich. *Herophilus: The Art of Medicine in Early Alexandria*. Cambridge: Cambridge University Press, 1989.

Wagemakers, Bart. "Incest, Infanticide and Cannibalism: Anti-Christian Imputations in the Roman Empire." *Greece & Rome* 57, no. 2 (2010): 337–54.

Walker, William O. "The Portrayal of Aquila and Priscilla in Acts: The Question of Sources." *NTS* 54 (2008): 479–95.

Walton, Steve. *Leadership and Lifestyle: The Portrait of Paul in the Miletus Speech and 1 Thessalonians*. SNTSMS 108. Cambridge: Cambridge University Press, 2004.

Wehnert, Jürgen. "Antipaulinismus in den Pseudoklementinen." Pages 170–90 in *Ancient Perspectives on Paul*. Edited by Tobias Nicklas, Andreas Merkt, and Joseph Verheyden. Göttingen: Vandenhoeck & Ruprecht, 2013.

Weiss, Hans Friedrich. *Frühes Christentum und Gnosis: Eine rezeptionsgeschichtliche Studie*. Tübingen: Mohr Siebeck, 2008.

White, Benjamin L. "How to Read a Book: Irenaeus and the Pastoral Epistles Reconsidered." *VC* 65 (2011): 125–49.

White, Benjamin L. *Remembering Paul: Ancient and Modern Contests Over the Image of the Apostle*. Oxford: Oxford University Press, 2014.

White, Hayden. "The Question of Narrative in Contemporary Historical Theory." *History and Theory* 23, no. 1 (1984): 1–33.

Whitley, Thomas J. "Poison in the *Panarion*: Beasts, Heretics, and Sexual Deviants." *VC* 70 (2016): 237–58.

Wilhite, David E. *Tertullian the African: An Anthropological Reading of Tertullian's Contexts and Identities*. Berlin: de Gruyter, 2007.

Williams, Francis E. *Mental Perception: A Commentary on NHC VI,4, The Concept of Our Great Power*. Nag Hammadi and Manichean Studies 51. Leiden: Brill, 2001.

Williams, Michael A. *The Immovable Race: A Gnostic Designation and the Theme of Stability in Late Antiquity*. Leiden: Brill, 1985.

Williams, Michael A. *Rethinking "Gnosticism": An Argument for Dismantling a Dubious Category*. Princeton: Princeton University Press, 1996.

Willing, Meike. *Eusebius von Cäsarea als Häreseograph*. Berlin: de Gruyter, 2008.

Wilson, Robert McL. "Simon and Gnostic Origins." Pages 485–91 in *Les Actes des Apôtres: Traditions, Redaction, théologie*. Edited by J. Kremer. Leuven: Leuven University Press, 1979.

Winston, David and J. Dillon, ed. *Two Treatises of Philo of Alexandria: A Commentary on De Gigantibus and Quod Deus Sit Immutabilis*. Chico: Scholars Press, 1983.

Wiseman, T. P. *Clio's Cosmetics: Three Studies in Greco-Roman Literature*. Totowa: Rowman and Littlefield, 1979.

Wiseman, T. P. "Lying Historians: Seven Types of Mendacity." Pages 122–46 in *Lies and Fiction in the Ancient World*. Edited by Christopher Gill and T. P. Wiseman. Exeter: University of Exeter Press, 1993.

Woodman, A. J. *Rhetoric in Classical Historiography: Four Studies*. London: Croom Helm, 1988.

Wright, David. "Tertullian." vol. 2, pages 1027–47 in *The Early Christian World*. Edited by Philip F. Esler. London: Routledge, 2000.

Yamauchi, Edwin. *Pre-Christian Gnosticism: A Survey of the Proposed Evidence*. London: Tyndale Press, 1973.

Yli-Karjanmaa, Sami. "Clement of Alexandria's Position on the Doctrine of Reincarnation and Some Comparisons with Philo." *Studia Patristica* 110 (2021): 75–90.

Yli-Karjanmaa, Sami. *Reincarnation in Philo of Alexandria*. Studia Philonica Monographs 7. Atlanta: SBL Press, 2015.

Zangenberg, Jürgen. "Δύναμις τοῦ θεοῦ. Das religionsgeschichtliche Profil des Simon Magus." Pages 519–40 in *Religionsgeschichte des neuen Testaments: Festschrift für Klaus Berger*. Edited by Axel von Dobbeler, Kurt Erlemann, and Roman Heiligenthal. Tübingen: A. Francke, 2000.

Zangenberg, Jürgen. *Frühes Christentum in Samarien: Topographische und traditionsgeschichtliche Studien zu den Samarientexten im Johannesevangelium*. Tübingen: Francke, 1998.

Zecchi, Marco. *Sobek of Shedet: The Crocodile God in the Fayyum in the Dynastic Period*. Perugia: Tau, 2010.

Zhmud, Leonid. "Pythagorean Number Doctrine in the Academy." Pages 323–44 in *On Pythagoreanism*. Edited by Gabriele Cornelli, Richard McKirahan, and Constantinos Macris. Berlin: de Gruyter, 2013.

Zwierlein, Otto. *Petrus in Rom: Die literarischen Zeugnisse mit einer kritischen Edition der Martyrien des Petrus und Paulus auf neuer handschriftlicher Grundlage*. 2nd ed. Berlin: de Gruyter, 2010.

Index

Acts of Peter   1–2, 7, 10, 21, 67, 103, 118, 121, 125, 139, 142–55, 160, 165–7, 169
Alexandria   21–6, 70–1, 107–8, 155, 158–9, 162, 165–71
angels   9, 17–18, 25, 35–6, 57, 75, 80, 83–4, 86, 89, 91–3, 97–8, 101–3, 105, 128–9, 131–40, 145, 148, 157–60, 171–2, 175, 183
antichrist   1, 29, 30, 34, 35, 144, 150, 152–3, 164, 185
Apocalypse of Peter (Coptic)   84
Apsethos   96–7, 99, 100, 103, 127, 139
Aristotle   15
Armstrong, K. L.   39–41
ascent/flight of Simon over Rome   10, 149–50, 160
Athena   5, 25, 68, 75, 85–7, 98, 103, 130, 133–4, 136, 140, 171–2

baptism   43, 48–9, 52, 54, 76, 79, 107, 109, 120–1, 124, 126, 128, 131, 138, 140, 147, 152, 157, 167, 172
Barbelo   129, 132, 139
Basilides and Basilideans   27, 37, 62, 86, 108, 172
Beyschlag, K.   5–7
Bremmer, J.   10

Callistus of Rome   75, 95
Carpocrates and Carpocratians   27, 86, 119, 172
Celsus   3, 23, 45–6, 70, 108–13, 160, 168
Cerinthus   55–6, 118
Christ, Simon as   3, 63, 79, 86, 97–8, 104, 106, 142, 144–6, 152, 155–6, 158, 160–1, 171, 173
Claudius   9, 63, 64, 67, 76, 121, 124–5, 139
Clement of Alexandria   23, 26, 29, 65, 100, 159, 162, 169
Clement of Rome   153–5, 158, 161, 164

Cleobius   56
curse   3, 98, 147

daimon/demon   47, 76, 84–5, 137, 161
death of Simon   15, 103–5, 125, 139, 150
Declaration   2, 6–7, 9, 11–31, 33–8, 43, 45, 52–4, 57, 58, 68, 71, 78–9, 82–3, 85, 90–3, 95–7, 99–101, 104–5, 111, 123, 126–8, 132–3, 135–6, 139, 143, 145, 155, 158–60, 162, 166–7, 169–72, 175–81
DeConick, A. D.   9, 48, 165
deification   10, 26, 45–6, 53, 71, 90, 100, 145–7
Dositheus   103, 109–10, 112–13, 115–16, 137, 156–7, 165
dreams   64, 75, 84, 85, 98, 103, 105, 131, 148, 176, 184

Edwards, M. J.   7, 99
Egypt   17, 23–4, 30–2, 36–8, 41, 54–5, 78, 107–8, 113–14, 116, 127, 155–6, 158, 161, 168, *see also* Alexandria
Elymas   47, 115, 143 n.3, 161
Empedocles   15, 26, 176
Ennoia   18, 53, 63, 68, 71, 75, 80–3, 85, 91, 101, 111, 128–30, 132–3, 136–7, 139–41, 145, 157, 160, 170–2
Epinoia   18, 25, 45, 53, 57, 68, 97, 101–4, 106, 111, 128, 132, 160, 170, 175–8
Epiphanius   4, 6, 9, 10, 49, 103, 123, 127–41, 168, 172
Epistle of the Apostles   55–6, 58–9, 76, 121
E source   128, 132, 135–6, 139–40, 169, 172
Ethiopian woman   1, 148
Eubola   147, 151–2

Eudorus of Alexandria 22–3, 26
Eusebius of Caesarea 10, 54, 67, 116–26, 140, 150, 168, 170–2
Exegesis of the Soul 81–2

faith 1, 6, 37, 48, 50–1, 74, 76, 83, 85–6, 90, 120–1, 131, 136, 138, 147, 150, 167, 170–1
fiction 1, 4, 7, 10, 39, 41, 52, 60, 82, 100, 104–5, 126–7, 140, 151, 154, 157, 164–5, 167–9
Filaster 6, 10, 103, 138–40, 168
Fossum, J. 6–7, 48
Frickel, J. 13–14

Gerizim 4–5, 52, 60–1, 156–7, 168
Gitta 4, 98, 103
gnosis 76, 86, 122, 124, 130, 133, 136, 139, 171
gnostic 1, 5–9, 11, 24, 86, 102, 110, 124, 130, 132–3, 140, 154, 165, 168, 173
Great Declaration, see Declaration
Great Power 5–8, 12, 16, 18–19, 22, 24–5, 28–30, 34, 35, 37, 38, 43–6, 52–4, 63, 78, 112, 115, 120, 128–9, 131–2, 134, 144, 170, 173, 177, 178, 184–6

Haar, S. 2, 8, 48, 51
Hadrian, emperor 21, 32, 34, 90, 118
Heintz, F. 8
Helen (of Troy and Tyre) 5, 7, 9–10, 15, 18–19, 23–4, 33–4, 37, 63, 67–70, 75, 80–91, 97–8, 101–3, 110–11, 115, 121–2, 124, 126, 128–33, 136–9, 145, 156–7, 160–1, 168–72
Helenians 23, 70, 84, 110–11, 115, 145, 160, 168, 171
Herophilus 20–1, 23, 26
holy Spirit 43, 74, 78–9, 89–90, 98, 128–9, 132
Homer and Homeric poetry 26, 80, 81, 86–7, 89, 93, 102, 105, 107, 129, 132–3, 136, 140, 169, 171–3, 179

Ignatius 42, 57–8

Infinite Power 14, 16, 19, 26, 79, 145, 169, 175–8, 180
Irenaeus 3, 6, 10, 13, 15, 18–19, 35, 42–3, 49, 53, 57, 67, 70, 73–88, 90–3, 95, 100–5, 108, 111, 118–20, 122–4, 127, 131–2, 135–7, 144–5, 147, 149, 157–8, 160, 166–7, 171–2
Isaiah 26, 58, 83, 93, 130, 135, 162, 172

Jesus 3, 21, 27, 30, 32–3, 37, 42–3, 48, 51, 55–7, 64, 70, 71, 74, 77–9, 81–3, 86, 91, 93, 105, 107–16, 121, 138, 145–6, 148–9, 153–4, 156–7, 159, 162, 170, 171, 184–5
Jews 6–8, 27, 32, 40, 62, 71, 74, 77, 104, 108–10, 116, 119, 128, 132, 137, 142, 144, 148–51, 154, 157, 159
John the "Day Baptist" 119, 155–7, 160, 165, 168
Judas the Galilean 41, 109–10, 112, 115
Julian, emperor 32
Jupiter, *see* Zeus
Justin Martyr 3, 6, 10, 13, 18–19, 24, 33, 37, 54, 59–74, 76–8, 85, 87, 90, 95–6, 99–101, 103, 108, 118–19, 121–5, 127, 140, 143, 145–7, 154, 160, 170–1

Kore, *see* Persephone

law of Moses 9, 33, 83, 110, 130, 135, 156–7, 162–3, 179, 180, 185–6
Logos 18, 30–1, 35, 64, 67–8, 71, 77, 80, 87, 115, 124, 177–9, 184–5
Lost Sheep parable 75, 80, 82, 86, 89, 91, 97, 101, 136, 140, 172
Lüdemann, G. 5–7, 48, 53
Luna 160, 165

Macrae, D. 10
magician 3, 5, 10, 47, 49, 52, 64, 76, 84, 97, 113–14, 131, 147, 153, 155, 160–1, 167
magus 2–9, 11, 43, 46–7, 53, 63–5, 74, 84, 97, 109, 112, 114–16, 120, 128, 131, 135–8, 142, 147, 150, 155, 157, 164–5, 167–8, 170, 173
Marcellus 146–8, 151–2

Marcion(ites) 48, 58, 62, 88, 108, 119, 162, 165
memory 16, 39, 106, 118, 126, 142, 151, 154, 165, 173
Menander 62, 118–19, 124, 126
Meyer, M. 32–3, 182
Mind 5, 15, 18, 22–3, 25–6, 29–30, 45, 68, 71, 75, 80, 86–7, 99, 104, 111, 169, 176–8
miracle/wonder 8, 11, 43, 46–7, 50–1, 63–5, 67, 71, 76, 82, 103, 110–12, 114–16, 120, 123, 125, 142–5, 147, 149, 152–3, 155, 157, 161, 168, 186
monad 22–3, 43
money 43, 49–50, 74, 89–90, 113, 128, 131, 147, 150–1, 167
Moses 6, 8, 18, 30, 80, 109–10, 113–15, 157–9, 177–9

Naassene Preacher 16–17, 21–2, 96, 127
Nero 40, 125, 139
Noah 30–5, 37, 182–4
Numenius 23, 158–9

Ophite 17, 132, 135, 162
oracle/oracular speech 30, 99, 123, 126, 167, 172
Origen 10, 37, 107–18, 120, 122, 157, 172

Paul, apostle 21, 27, 30, 38–42, 46, 49–50, 52, 56–8, 76, 83, 102, 130, 133, 140, 144, 150–1, 161–2, 165, 168–9, 172
Pearson, B. 8–9
Peratai 96, 127
perfect love 98, 102, 105, 169, 171
Persephone 44, 68
Peter, apostle 1, 4, 8, 21, 43, 48–52, 74–6, 84, 90, 98, 103, 114, 120, 124–5, 128, 131, 139, 142–53, 161–7, 169
Philo of Alexandria 25–6, 121, 158–9, 163
Platonism 9, 24, 61, 67, 107, 159
Polycarp 58, 73
Power 58, 73, *see* Great Power; Infinite Power

prophet like Moses 6, 8, 110, 159
prophets 4, 8, 30, 46, 52, 57–8, 61, 75, 83, 86–7, 92–4, 98, 109, 130, 135, 139, 167, 169, 171–2
Prunicus 129, 132, 139–40
Pseudo-Clementines 2, 4, 7, 9–10, 24, 109, 143, 148, 153–66, 169
Pseudo-Tertullian 6, 10, 103, 137–9
Pythagorean 22, 25, 60, 80, 85, 87, 168, 172

Quartus 144, 151

Refutator 2, 9, 12–19, 21, 27, 37, 79, 95–106, 127, 128, 131–2, 136, 139, 160, 168, 170–2, 175
ritual 3, 9–10, 36, 84–5, 93, 116, 165, 167, *see also* baptism
Rome 5, 9–10, 21, 31–2, 34, 37, 40, 52–5, 59, 62–5, 67, 71–4, 77, 79, 84–5, 90, 93, 95, 98, 101–3, 105, 108, 110, 121, 124–6, 139, 142–54, 157, 164, 167–8, 170–2
Rudolph, K. 5, 165

salvation 5, 26, 28–30, 35, 38, 75, 80, 82–3, 86, 91, 98, 102, 105, 108, 114, 121, 123, 130, 136, 138, 157, 171, 182
Samaritan(s) 1, 3–4, 6–9, 52, 60, 142, 157, 159–60, 165, 168, 170
Schenke, H.-M. 33, 182
Sebaste 4, 7, 44, 46, 68–9
self-deification 1, 99–100, 139, 159
Semo Sancus 10, 65–7, 72, 103, 170
Sethian(s) 158, 165
Seventh Power 15, 18, 25, 30, 37, 68, 78, 80, 82, 85, 90, 100, 128, 132, 135, 158–9, 169, 177–8, 181
sex 8, 18, 36, 65, 70, 80–2, 84, 89, 91, 101–3, 105, 123, 129, 132, 168–9, 171
Silence 22–4, 177
Soranus 19–21, 23, 26
spirit 9, 18, 24–5, 29, 34, 38, 42–3, 47–53, 57, 74, 76, 78–9, 89–90, 98, 106, 114–15, 128–9, 131–2, 147, 151, 157, 167, 170–3, 179, 183, *see also* holy Spirit

Standing One   7–8, 23, 25, 30, 79, 100, 155–60, 162, 165, 169, 178
Stesichorus   75, 81–2, 87, 89, 91, 97, 171
Stoic(ism)   60, 168, 172
Stratiotics   133–4, 140
Syntagma Against 32 Heresies   137–9
Syntagma Against All Heresies   6, 62–3, 73–4, 85, 127, 143, 171

Tertullian of Carthage   10, 58, 67, 88–94, 101–3, 111, 121, 132, 135, 168, 171–2
Testimony of Truth   102
Theissen, G.   7
Theon   147, 151
Theudas   41, 44, 109–10, 112, 115, 121
Third Corinthians   56–9, 73–4, 76–7, 83, 93, 137
Thought, *see Epinoia*; *Ennoia*
Tiber island   5, 63, 65–7, 72, 103, 146, 170
torch   68–9, 97, 101, 106, 128–9, 136, 139, 160, 171–2
Trajan, emperor   21, 32

transmigration   37, 86, 88–9, 101, 133, 172
Trinity   79, 86–7, 93, 105, 108, 171
Trojan (wooden) horse   97, 101, 128–9, 133, 136, 138–9, 160, 171

Valentinus and Valentinians   5–7, 17, 27, 33, 46, 57–8, 73–4, 85–6, 88, 96, 99, 101, 104–5, 108, 110, 135, 172
Virgil   101, 172

Williams, F.   29, 31–2, 34, 36, 136, 182
wisdom   5, 15, 24–6, 30, 32–4, 37, 57, 68, 72, 78, 80–6, 91, 101, 106, 111, 126, 132, 137, 139, 146, 149, 156, 158, 160, 165, 167–9, 172, 185–6

Zangenberg, J.   7
Zephyrinus   79, 95
Zeus   5, 25, 46, 60–1, 66–8, 71, 75, 80, 82, 85, 87, 98, 103, 130, 158, 171–2

www.ingramcontent.com/pod-product-compliance
Lightning Source LLC
Chambersburg PA
CBHW051522230426
43668CB00012B/1703